A History of Jazz
in America

Da Capo Press Music Reprint Series
GENERAL EDITOR
FREDERICK FREEDMAN
VASSAR COLLEGE

A History of Jazz in America

BY BARRY ULANOV

DA CAPO PRESS • NEW YORK • 1972

in Publication Data

(Da Capo Press music reprint series)
1. Jazz music. 2. Music—U.S.—History and
criticism. I. Title.
ML3561.J3U5   1972   785.4'2'0973   74-37324
ISBN 0-306-70427-7

This Da Capo Press edition of *A History of Jazz in America*
is an unabridged republication of the first edition published
in New York in 1952. It is reprinted by special arrangement
with The Viking Press.

A HISTORY OF JAZZ IN AMERICA

Also by Barry Ulanov

THE INCREDIBLE CROSBY
DUKE ELLINGTON

A History of
JAZZ
in America

BARRY ULANOV

THE VIKING PRESS · NEW YORK · 1952

Parts of this book appeared
in abbreviated form in *Metronome*.

For Joan

CONTENTS

viii CONTENTS

CONTENTS

CONTENTS

 **PREFACE**

The opening words of chapter one of this book describe the American scene as Henry James saw it from the vantage-point of Europe. That point must also be acknowledged as the source of perspective for American jazz: it was from there that our music was first seen in its vastness and energy as a cultural contribution of a major order.

Anybody writing about jazz in the United States must be appreciative of the early efforts of the Europeans, the documentary labors of its first chroniclers, Hugues Panassié and Robert Goffin, and the creative enthusiasm of its first serious audiences in England and France and elsewhere on the Continent. I am especially aware of my own indebtedness to Messrs. Panassié and Goffin, whose books showed me, when I was a college freshman, that there was order and meaning in the colorful confusion of jazz, and to the European devotees, who latterly demonstrated to me that the abandon of the jazz audience could also be creative and discerning. Finally it remained for some Roman musicians in the summer of 1950 to pose some of the questions and in the following summer for some bebop artists on the island of Mallorca to answer others which—both questions and answers—have informed much of the structure of this book.

I do not mean in any of this to diminish the contributions to jazz of the American critics and the audiences at home, but simply to indicate an order of precedence, both general and personal. Elsewhere in these pages I have attempted some recognition of the special importance of John Hammond and George Simon to jazz in the United States, without indicating, as I should like to do, the instrumental part those generous men played in my career. In the same way, as friend and as colleague, I shall always be deeply obliged to Helen Oakley, Bob Bach, Barbara Hodgkins, and Leonard Feather. Finally, many of the insights which may be present here were gained under the tutelary guidance of jazz musicians themselves, among whom I am especially grateful to the following: Duke Ellington, Billy Strayhorn, Toby Hardwick, the late Chick Webb, Red Norvo, Woody Herman, Lennie Tristano, Mildred Bailey, Stan Kenton, Roy Eldridge, and John LaPorta.

BARRY ULANOV

A HISTORY OF JAZZ IN AMERICA

Chapter 1

WHAT IS JAZZ?

In *The American Scene*, Henry James said of American cities, "So there it all is; arrange it as you can. Poor dear bad bold beauty; there must indeed be something about her . . . !" The same can be said of American jazz.

On the surface there is disorder and conflict in jazz. No common definition of this music has been reached. It resists dictionary definition, and its musicians splutter nervously and take refuge in the colorful ambiguities of its argot. Nonetheless, its beauty can be probed; its badness can be separated from its boldness. The process is a difficult one, as it is in any art, and in jazz two arts, the composing and the performing arts, are joined together. But if one goes beneath the surface and does not allow the contradictions and the confusions of appearances to put one off, much becomes clear, and the mystery at the center is seen to be the central mystery of all the arts.

The cortex of jazz consists of several layers, alternately hard and soft, complex in structure, and hard to take apart. It is compounded of the history of the music and of the many styles of jazz. At first the history seems disjointed and the styles contradictory. One marks a confounding series of shifts in place and person and style. One finds a music dominated by Negroes in New Orleans, by white musicians in Chicago, by important but apparently unrelated figures in New York. One discovers a disastrous split in jazz inaugurated by the swing era and intensified during the days of bebop and so-called progressive jazz. But then one looks and listens more closely, and order and continuity appear.

Americans have long been wedded to the boom-and-bust cycle, and their culture reflects that dizzying course. Jazz is not like that; it has no cycles; it doesn't spiral. Whether you adopt the approach of the economic historian, the cultural anthropologist, or the aesthetic

3

philosopher, you will not find an easy reflection of a theory in jazz. While much of America—crises and ecstasies and even a moment or two of exaltation—has found its way into jazz, the history of jazz is a curiously even one, chaotic at any instant, but always moving ahead in what is for an art form almost a straight line.

For most of its history, jazz, rejected in its homeland, has had consciously to seek survival, conscientiously to explain and defend its existence. From its early homes, the Ozark hills, the Louisiana bayous, the Carolina cotton fields, the Virginia plantations, through the New Orleans bordellos and barrelhouses to its latter-day efflorescence it has been alternately condemned and misunderstood. Variously banned and bullied and sometimes cheered beyond its merits, jazz has led a lonely life but a full one. It is still with us and looks to be around for quite a while.

No matter what the fortunes of jazz, its nucleus has remained constant, little touched by extravagances of opinion, sympathetic or unsympathetic. The nucleus of jazz—as differentiated from its cortex—contains its nerve center, its source of life, and here are its mystery and meaning. The nucleus of jazz is made up of melody, harmony, and rhythm, the triune qualities of the art of music which, as everybody knows, can be fairly simply defined. In bare definition, melody is any succession of notes, harmony any simultaneity of tones, rhythm the arithmetic measure of notes or tones. In closer examination, melody appears as a vast variety of things, ranging from so simple a tune as "Yankee Doodle" to the complexity of one of Arnold Schoenberg's constructions. In more detailed analysis, harmony shows up as a vertical ordering of a Bach fugue, or a tight structuring based entirely on whole tones in the impressionism of Debussy. But bewildering as the complications of melody and harmony can be, they are easier to analyze and verbalize than rhythm or any of its parts, and rhythm is the most important of the three in jazz.

Before attempting a synoptic definition of jazz as a noun (or discussing the misuse of "jazz" as a verb and "jazzy" as an adjective), and of the various corollary terms that explain the meaning of this music, it might be instructive to examine definitions by musicians themselves. The following definitions were made by jazz musicians in 1935, when their music was undergoing a revival as a result of the then current vogue for the jazz that went by the new name of swing. Benny Goodman was a great success, and jam sessions had become public again. Musicians themselves found it difficult to define "swing," by which of course they merely meant the 1935 version of jazz, which wasn't very different from the 1930 or 1925 music. Let us examine the definitions.

⁎Wingy Manone: "Feeling an increase in tempo though you're still playing at the same tempo."

Marshall Stearns and John Hammond (jazz authorities) and Benny Goodman: "A band swings when its collective improvisation is rhythmically integrated."

Gene Krupa: "Complete and inspired freedom of rhythmic interpretation."

Jess Stacy: "Syncopated syncopation."

Morton Kahn and Payson Re: "Feeling a multitude of subdivisions in each beat and playing or implying the accents that you feel; that is, if the tune is played at the proper tempo, so that when you're playing it, you'll feel it inside."

Glenn Miller: "Something that you have to feel; a sensation that can be conveyed to others."

Frankie Froeba: "A steady tempo, causing lightness and relaxation and a feeling of floating."

Terry Shand: "A synthetic cooperation of two or more instruments helping along or giving feeling to the soloist performing."

Ozzie Nelson: "A vague something that you seem to feel pulsating from a danceable orchestra. To me it is a solidity and compactness of attack by which the rhythm instruments combine with the others to create within the listeners the desire to dance."

Chick Webb: "It's like lovin' a gal, and havin' a fight, and then seein' her again."

Louis Armstrong: "My idea of how a tune should go."

Ella Fitzgerald: "Why, er—swing is—well, you sort of feel—uh—uh—I don't know—you just swing!"

These musicians were looking for a new set of terms that would catch the beat so basic to jazz; they were stumped for the words to describe the kind of improvisation necessary to jazz.

In the simple, compressed, sometimes too elliptic vocabulary of the jazz musician, one learns a great deal about the music he plays. One learns that "jazz" is a noun, that it is not American popular music (as it has often been thought to be), that the jazz musician is most interested in the rhythmic connotation of the word and in little else. If you tell him that some say the term comes from the phonetic spelling of the abbreviation of a jazz musician named Charles (Charles, Chas., Jass, Jazz), he is not in the least interested. If you tell him that there is a great deal of substance to the claim that the word comes from the French word *jaser*—to pep up, to exhilarate—he may nod his head with a degree of interest but ask you, "What about the beat?" You will learn from the jazz musician that "swing" is no longer a noun, in spite of the fact that it was first so used in the title of a Duke Ellington recording in 1931, "It Don't Mean a Thing if It Ain't Got That Swing," which gives it a kind of ex cathedra endorsement. You will learn that "swing" is a verb, that it is a way of describing the beat, even as Ellington's title for another tune, "Bouncing Buoyancy," is a description of the same beat, even as the term "jump" is, even as "leaps" is, even as the description of jazz as "music that goes" is, even as in the thirties the compliment of "solid" to performer or performance was like "gone," "crazy," "craziest," "the end," and "cool" today. They are descriptions of the beat.

From an examination of jazz musicians' own words, it is possible to glean the subtle, unruly, and almost mystical concept of the jazz spirit, or feeling, or thinking—it is all these things and is so understood by the jazz musician himself. The jazzman has his own way of getting at the center of his music, and thus he formulates his own musical language. Also he converts the musical language into a verbal dialect of his own. In his own set of terms, musical and verbal, he thinks, he feels; he rehearses, he performs; he scores, he improvises; he gets a beat.

To get that elusive beat, a jazzman will do anything. Without it, he cannot do anything. With it, he is playing jazz, and that is a large and satisfying enough accomplishment. When a jazzman picks up a familiar tune, banal or too well-known through much repetition, and alters its rhythmic pattern in favor of a steady if sometimes monotonous beat, and varies its melodies and maybe even changes its chords, he is working freely, easily, and with as much spontaneity as he can bring to his music. That freedom, ease, and spontaneity brought him to jazz; within those determining limits he will find a place for himself or get out, or join one of the bands whose frightening parodies of jazz are so often more popular than the real thing. It is by his formal understanding of certain definite values that the jazz musician has conceived, organized, and developed his art. It has been hot; it has become cool. It has jumped and swung; it has sauntered.

It has borrowed; it has originated. It has effected a change, a literal transformation; inherited conventions have gradually been restated, reorganized, and ultimately restructured as a new expression. It may be that jazz musicians have simply rediscovered a controlling factor in music, the improvising performer. Without any awareness of what he has done, the jazzman may have gone back to some of the beginnings of music, tapping once more the creative roots which nourished ancient Greek music, the plain chant, the musical baroque and its immediate successors and predecessors. We know that seventeenth- and eighteenth-century composers were improvisers and that when they brought their scores to other musicians they left the interpretation of parts to the discretion of the performers, even as an arranger for a jazz band does today.

But the jazz musician has brought more than procedures, composing conceptions, and improvisation to his music. Techniques have been developed that have broadened the resources and intensified the disciplines of certain instruments far beyond their use in other music. Colors have been added to solo instruments and to various combinations and numbers of instruments that are utterly unlike any others in music. New textures have emerged from a conception of tonality and of pitch that is not original but is entirely fresh in its application. The improvising jazz musician has a different and more responsible and rewarding position from that of his counterparts in earlier art and folk music. The rhythmic base of music has been reinterpreted, making the central pulse at once more primitive than it has been before in Western music, and more sophisticated in its variety.

This, then, is how one might define jazz: it is a new music of a certain distinct rhythmic and melodic character, one that constantly involves improvisation—of a minor sort in adjusting accents and phrases of the tune at hand, of a major sort in creating music extemporaneously, on the spot. In the course of creating jazz, a melody or its underlying chords may be altered. The rhythmic valuations of notes may be lengthened or shortened according to a regular scheme, syncopated or not, or there may be no consistent pattern of rhythmic variations so long as a steady beat remains implicit or explicit. The beat is usually four quarter-notes to the bar, serving as a solid rhythmic base for the improvisation of soloists or groups playing eight or twelve measures, or some multiple or dividend thereof.

These things are the means. The ends are the ends of all art, the

8　　A HISTORY OF JAZZ IN AMERICA

expression of the universal and the particular, the specific and the indirect and the intangible. In its short history, jazz has generally been restricted to short forms and it has often been directed toward the ephemeral and the trivial, but so too has it looked toward the lasting perception and the meaningful conclusion. Much of the time jazz musicians have sought and obtained an unashamed aphrodisiac effect; they have also worshiped in their music, variously devout before the one God and the unnamed gods. Like poets and painters, they are of all faiths, their doctrines are many; but they are united in one conviction, that they have found a creative form for themselves, for their time, for their place.

At the opening of the *Gradus ad Parnassum*, the dialogue offered as a study of counterpoint by Johann Josef Fux in 1725, the music master Aloysius warns the student Josef: "You must try to remember whether or not you felt a strong natural inclination to this art even in childhood." The student answers: "Yes, most deeply. Even before I could reason, I was overcome by the force of this strange enthusiasm and I turned all my thoughts and feelings to music. And now the burning desire to understand it possesses me, drives me almost against my will, and day and night lovely melodies seem to sound around me. Therefore I think I no longer have reason to doubt my inclination. Nor do the difficulties of the work discourage me, and I hope that with the help of good health I shall be able to master it." Several jazz musicians have read Fux, even as Haydn and Beethoven did, though perhaps with less immediate application. They have, however, echoed the pupil's "strange enthusiasm"; that, these jazz-men said, was their experience, their "burning desire." Following the "inclination," jazz musicians have not had much of the help of good health; some of them have flaunted their doggedly unreasonable living habits and suffered the personal and public consequences of the habits and of the flaunting. All this their music has reflected, and sometimes it is noisy and grotesque as a result. More often it has a fullness and richness of expression. Slowly, clearly, the music is maturing, and, for it and with it and by it, so are the musicians.

$\mathcal{C}hapter\ 2$

ANCESTORS

According to legend, the beat which is at the center of jazz, as well as a fringe of decorative melody, came over to the Americas from West Africa in the slave ships. This tradition holds that the American Negro shaped jazz by imposing a heavy layer of his native jungle chants and rhythms upon the European materials he found in the land of his enforced adoption. For some years now a crew of industrious anthropologists and social scientists has been hard at work trying to make this story stick. It is a seemingly impressive story, buttressed with footnotes, interlarded with quotations from German authorities, generously sprinkled with the commonplaces of academic pretension; it confirms the average man's impression of the Negro as a jungle-formed primitive whose basic expression is inevitably savage; it sits well with the editors and readers of the country's chi-chi magazines, where this conception of jazz finds high favor. From the point of view of jazz musicians themselves, however, the theory distorts the facts out of all resemblance to the true history of the music that has been played as jazz, by jazzmen, since the end of the nineteenth century. Whatever its merits as myth, it doesn't fit with the facts of the music itself. It won't do.

The impetus for this interpretation, it seems to me, lies within the musical tastes of the men who make it. In the case of some writers, a devotion to the music of Jelly Roll Morton, Baby Dodds, Jimmy Yancey, George Lewis, and their singing and playing contemporaries, clearly informs the detailing of jazz history. But is this kind of writing purely informative, or is it prejudiced, based on personal taste? In the case of anthropologists like Melville J. Herskovits, the highly placed and indefatigable chief spokesman for this line of inquiry, a professional interest in Negro culture governs the approach to jazz. In addition, that taste for and appreciation of the *recherché*, the re-

9

mote, which is the inevitable development of a specialized knowledge
—in this instance, the specialized knowledge of African music—has
been the spur to some questionable activity in the field of jazz history,
and to some curious, unmusical identifications in jazz performances.
It is vital in understanding the issue to realize the large part that the
cultural anthropologist plays in our academic life. Coupling his resources with the genuine discoveries of the clinical psychiatrist and
the less certain speculations of the amateur psychoanalyst, the cultural
anthropologist has made vast attacks upon his own world as well
as on the surviving remnants of antecedent societies. One of the results is the concept of an African music lodged in the *unconscious*
of American Negroes. "It must be emphasized," Rudi Blesh writes in
Shining Trumpets, "that Dodds has no first-hand knowledge of African drumming and music. He thinks of himself, on the contrary, as
a 'modern' jazz-drummer and evolves all of his effects directly from
the unconscious." Much of Herskovits's argument in his book, *The
Myth of the Negro Past*, offers eloquent testimony to the stubborn
strength and beautiful variety of African culture (however consciously or unconsciously induced), of which the Negro anywhere,
as direct inheritor, and the rest of us, as subsidiary heirs, may very
well be proud.

Certainly the African background of the first jazz musicians played
some part in their music. But one must remember that they were at
a considerable remove from "the Dark Continent." The music they
fashioned in New Orleans, where jazz began, was an elaborate compound of many folk strains, few of them bearing more than an echo,
a distant one, of Africa. In André Gide's 1927 and 1928 journals,
Travels in the Congo, one may find a very exciting and surely reliable
description of African music as it sounds to the Western ear—in this
case an unusually sensitive ear, one trained to a point of high amateur
proficiency in music. The jazz Africanists offer him as an exhibit; I
should like to do so also.

Gide describes a dance performed by the race of the Massas. He
is very impressed by the natives of this country. He finds them
"robust, agile, and slender." Watching them dance, he finds that
they have nothing in common "with the slow, gloomy circling in
which certain colonials pretend to see an imitation of sexual acts, and
which, according to them, always ends in an orgy." Nonetheless, the
dance, as he describes it, ends in a kind of intensely animated trance:

In the moonlight it ceased to be lyrical, and became frenzied—demoniac. Some of the women looked possessed. One old woman executed a solo in a corner by herself. She went on like a lunatic, waving her arms and legs in time to the tom-tom, joined the circle for a moment, and then, suddenly giving way to frenzy, went off again to a solitary place, fell down, and went on dancing on her knees. A very young girl almost at the same moment left the circle, like a stone shot from a sling, made three leaps backwards, and rolled in the dust like a sack. I expected spasms and hysterics; but no, she lay a lifeless mass, over which I bent, wondering whether her heart was still beating, for she gave not a sign of breath. A little circle formed around her; two old men bent down and made passes over her, shouting out I know not what strange appeals—to which she made no answer. But the tom-tom seemed to wake her; she dragged herself along, forced herself to dance, and fell down again for the last time on her side, her arms stretched out, her legs half bent, in an exquisite pose— and nothing succeeded in stirring her from it.

This is not the kind of dancing that is done to jazz; whatever frenzy has been present in jazz dancing is much closer to sexual orgy than the African trance. Likewise, the music that Gide describes is vaguely related to jazz, but is by no means the same thing; it has only a general resemblance to many different kinds of primitive music, European as well as American. So, too, the intensity that leads to trance resembles a whole variety of frenzied folk dancing in Western culture—the Italian tarantella, flamenco dances in Spain, the czardas in Hungary, and a whole set of Russian peasant and Cossack dances. Africans have no monopoly on religious ecstasy or secular joy manifested rhythmically. This is not to deny the vitality and beauty of their culture, but rather to give it its own place in the pantheon of Western culture.

Gide attempted to transcribe some of the music of the Massas; the next day, reflecting on his transcription, he had doubts and summed up one of his impressions of African music:

In thinking it over last night, it seems to me that I transcribed yesterday's tune wrongly and that the intervals are greater than our tones, so that between C and the dominant below there is only one note. It may seem monstrous that I should not be certain of it. But imagine this tune yelled by a hundred persons, not one of whom sings the exact note. It is like trying to distinguish the main line among quantities of little strokes. The effect is prodigious and gives a polyphone impression of harmonic richness. The same need makes them put beads on the wires of their little "pianos"—a horror of the clean sound—a need to confuse and drown its contours.

Superficially, this might appear to be consonant with descriptions of jazz and the experience of listening to it. But there is never anything in jazz, not even at its most primitive, that suggests a tune yelled by a hundred persons; whatever delicacies of pitch and liberties of intonation, there is never a chaotic cacophony such as Gide describes, in which not one of the hundred or so persons sings an exact note. In the same way, the description of beaded piano-wires suggests jazz honky-tonk piano; but the honky-tonk piano was the result of the poor equipment of brothels and barrelhouses, not of a "need to confuse and drown . . . contours."

A comparative analysis of African and American music does not yield clear parallels. For one thing, jazz is a measured music, the structure of which depends upon fixed beats, occurring in rhythmic patterns as unmistakable and immediately identifiable as the pulse of a metronome. African drumming, submitted to the most painstaking of auditions, simply does not break down into a structured rhythmic music; there are shifts of time and points and counterpoints of rhythm that make accurate notation impossible. As for the melodic qualities and quantities of African music, these too are shaped by a tonal and rhythmic conception entirely outside the Western diatonic tradition. To speak of the blue notes—the flattened third and seventh— as they are inflected against their natural position within a fixed key, or the alterations of pitch of jazz singers or instrumentalists, or their swooping glissandos, as American developments of African music is to talk unlettered nonsense. The basic chordal and melodic and rhythmic structure of the blues and of the jazz that has developed out of the blues is firmly within the orbit of Western folk music. There is far more of the sound of jazz in Middle-European gypsy fiddling than there is in a corps of African drummers.

One cannot and one should not, in the heat of a forensic rage, dismiss the real contribution of African Negroes to jazz. Without looking to the mysterious reaches of the unconscious, one can find a considerable administration of rhythmic discipline imposed by Southern Negroes, whether of the first or third or fifth American generation, upon the music they found around them. One must understand, however, using one's own tutored listening, that the music they found was basic to the music they made. One must know something of the

music of the English and Scottish settlers in the Atlantic states in
the seventeenth and eighteenth centuries, of the Irish and German in
the nineteenth, of the French who preceded the Negroes to the Louisiana Territory. All this music, some of it stately and consciously
composed according to the dancing customs of the aristocracy, some
of it expressing acceptance of class position and some expressing protest, was compounded of a mixture of cultures.

A detailed summary of sources indicates again and again the
breadth, the depth, and the grandeur of the ancestry of jazz. One
can no more neglect the Protestant hymn tune than the Morris dance,
no more underestimate the effect of the spiritual on dozens of vaudeville circuits around the United States than the vestiges of African
ceremonial in Congo Square, New Orleans. These evidences, gleaned
from listening to the music, make clear that New Orleans was the ineluctable starting-point for a story that is orderly for all its academic
confusion, American because of its polyglot origins and development—a tapestry of impressions and expressions that becomes the
richly textured history of jazz.

The long reach in time and space of the African slave trade was
the first factor in that history. It started in 1442, as best we can assign
a date, when the Portuguese voyager Antam Gonsalvez brought ten
Africans to Lisbon to save their souls. The trade was reinforced by
Columbus a half-century later when he dispatched five hundred Indians from Central America to Spain, suggesting they be sold in the
markets of Seville. Voyagers, travelers, admirals, and pirates all supported the trade, helped it expand, made it a vital part of European
social and industrial life for three and a half centuries. Both Queen
Elizabeth and her Spanish opponent, Philip II, invested in it; the Holy
Roman Emperor, Charles V, and Bonnie Prince Charlie added to their
riches by means of it. Sir Francis Drake and John Paul Jones, the
naval vessels of England, France, Spain, Portugal, Sweden, Denmark,
and Holland carried cargoes of tightly packed black men, women,
and children to be sold as slaves. In 1807 the slave trade was legally
prohibited in England and the United States. The Danes had outlawed
it in 1802; the Swedes followed suit in 1813, the Dutch in 1814, France
under Napoleon in 1815, the Spanish in 1820. But an outlaw trade
replaced officially sanctioned commerce in Negroes: Western seas
still were the graves of hundreds of slaves who died en route to
the Americas; high prices were still being paid for able hands—$1100

in New Orleans markets, $350 in Cuba, where smugglers had made them plentiful, $25 to $50 worth of rum or gunpowder or cloth on the Guinea coast.

The slaves brought their African melodies and tom-tom beats on the bottoms of tubs and tin kettles. The Puritans brought their emasculated versions of the Italian, Dutch, and English madrigals. During the Civil War in England the Puritans had destroyed organs, in order to remove these Romish traces from the churches and yet prevent taverns from using them for profane purposes. But concerts remained popular under the aegis of Oliver Cromwell himself, and psalm-singing was indulged in with an intensity that approached indecency. In the New England towns of the Puritans church organs were again banned; they were "the devil's bag-pipes." In Plymouth congregations were without musical instruments save the deacon's pitch-pipe, and psalms were sung from memory. Children's noisy contributions to psalmody were silenced with birch rods, but neither statute, religious proscription, nor physical punishment could cramp the creative musical spirit. And other assaults on the ascetic service were forthcoming: trumpets and drums were introduced into churches to serve the function of bells, and the jew's-harp was a popular instrument even in church.

In eighteenth-century Boston and Salem, and in similar cities and settlements, the minuet was the music of dancing assemblies and festooned balls. Cotillions were danced to English country tunes. Lower down in the class structure, fancy and fatiguing fiddling accompanied dancing at weddings and in taverns. There were jigs from Ireland and reels from Scotland and a merriness that often went the whole night through. In New York there were long rows of houses of entertainment of all kinds on the Bowery, and an ease of musical conscience too, since Dutch Calvinism had made its peace with the things of this world. In Philadelphia the worldly found their weal in the suburbs, where Quaker restrictions did not hold so strongly. In Charleston the Huguenots enacted strict Sunday blue laws, but dancing and singing remained integral parts of daily life in town and country, at private balls and public taverns, as they also did in Maryland and Virginia and Georgia.

The organ was brought back into church in 1700 in Port Royal, Virginia, and at about that time at the Swedish Gloria Dei Church in Philadelphia; in 1713 an organ was installed in the Anglican King's

Chapel in Boston. There were able and successful choirs in the mid-eighteenth century in New York (Trinity) and in the Moravian settlement at Bethlehem, Pennsylvania (the College of Music). In Charleston too there was a St. Cecilia Society after 1762, which organized an orchestra and sponsored indoor and open-air concerts, and Carolinians saw the first opera performed in the colonies, the English poet laureate Colley Cibber's *Flora, or Hob-in-the-Well.* In Philadelphia Francis Hopkinson, who signed the Declaration of Independence, represented New Jersey in the Continental Congress, and as chairman of the Navy Board probably designed the American flag, became the first known native American composer. His lovely song, "My Days Have Been so Wondrous Free," was a hit in 1759. And two years later Newark-born James Lyon collected psalm tunes for the Presbyterian church of which he was a clergyman, and added some of his own composition. That collection, named *Urania* after the heavenly Venus and muse of astronomy, established Lyon as the second American composer. In all the thirteen colonies part-singing and harpsichord playing were growing in popularity.

A secular spirit joined to patriotism emerged in the new music. "Yankee Doodle," originally a French-and-Indian-War song probably designed as a British gibe at the shabby American soldier, underwent countless variations after it was proudly appropriated by the Revolutionists. In 1778 Francis Hopkinson wrote "The Battle of the Kegs," a satirical song based on an incident in Philadelphia during the Revolution, and there were innumerable songs dealing with the more serious battles, the Boston Tea Party, and the Revolutionary heroes. After the war patriotic songs signalized the emotional and intellectual realization of sovereignty. "Hail, Columbia," by Francis Hopkinson's son Joseph, was written in 1798 to appease both political factions in the first presidential administration ("Firm united let us be, Rallying around our Liberty"). "The Star-Spangled Banner," written during the War of 1812 by Francis Scott Key while he was detained on a British frigate during the night bombardment of Baltimore's Fort McHenry, was inspired by the resistance of the American garrison and the sight of the flag still unfurled and waving at dawn. "America" ("My Country, 'Tis of Thee") was written in 1831 by Samuel Francis Smith to a tune he had found in a German music book—he was unaware that the British had used it for "God Save the King."

While many art songs have exactly the same characteristics and similar word-of-mouth histories, it is chiefly the popular song, almost by definition, which endures through its quick adoption by the musically illiterate who form the bulk of singing populations. The English ballads were quickly naturalized in Virginia and neighboring states. Moving through the Southern mountains, retaining an energetic rhythmic motion, a touching variety of emotion, and sprightly Elizabethan diction, the ballads became other things—the blues, spirituals, hillbilly songs. The ballads "Barbara Allen" and "Chevy Chase" were variously adopted and adapted, changed, chastened, or made ribald, as basic strains in a folk tradition must be. In the same way, "Oh, Dear, What Can the Matter Be?" moved into the colonies and stayed with us until it received ultimate canonization as a jazz song, a base for improvisation.

"Malbrouk s'en va-t-en guerre" is an example of export and import trade in music: the tale of this French nursery-song hero goes back to the Middle Ages, can be found in the *chansons de geste*, the verse romances based on the deeds of Charlemagne and his paladins, composed from the eleventh to the thirteenth centuries and sung in cloisters, châteaux, and marketplaces. In England, Malbrouk's tune, which also has medieval antecedents, was coupled with such familiar sets of lyrics as "For he's a jolly good fellow" and "We won't go home until morning," which in turn became attractive to Americans. In the United States one of the best known of many, many versions is that hurled about by the voices of Rotary and Kiwanis members, "The bear went over the mountain"—and needless to say the tune also filtered through a generation or more of jazz.

In American cities of the early nineteenth century the songs were chiefly those fashioned abroad. Dr. Thomas Arne, from whose masque *Alfred* comes the melody of "Rule, Britannia," wrote many songs, some operas and oratorios (his famous patriotic song made him the butt of Richard Wagner's comment that the whole English character can be expressed in eight notes). In America, as in England, his songs were among the most popular in the decades immediately following his death in 1778—both his most pallid ballads and his attractive settings of Shakespeare lyrics ("Under the greenwood tree," "Blow, blow, thou winter wind," etc.). "Auld Lang Syne" was one of many Scottish songs to become popular, along with "The Bluebells of Scotland," from which hundreds of piano and violin students suffered. From Ireland came Thomas Moore's "The Last Rose of Summer"—which has been fading annually since 1813, but not in popularity—and also his "The Minstrel Boy" and "The Harp That Once Thro' Tara's Halls," another student "piece" of invidious association. "Silent Night," written for Christmas Eve, 1818, in the Austrian village of Arnsdorf by Franz Gruber and Joseph Mohr, was a great seasonal favorite. The American John Howard Payne's words and the Englishman Sir Henry Bishop's music made "Home, Sweet Home" an immediate hit, and it, like many another popular song in this period, was interpolated in operas, such as *The Barber of Seville*, where it was sung in the lesson scene. Carl Maria von Weber's "Invitation to the Dance" was a great favorite in the 1820s and survived long enough in popular affection to appear as Benny Goodman's theme song, "Let's Dance," in 1935. "The Old Oaken Bucket," written by an American poet and set to a Scottish tune, and "John Peel" ("D'ye ken John Peel?"), over from England, moved from the family parlor to the glee club, where both have long remained.

In the hills and mountains, down on the farm and up on the river, another transformation was taking place, an unconscious naturalization of the European musical inheritance that led to the blues and jazz. In the Southern Appalachians they were singing:

> Blow your horn and call your dog,
> Blow your horn and call your dog,
> We'll go to the back woods and catch a ground hog.
> Rang tang fiddle de day.

In the Southern Highlands they were singing "Frankie and Albert" ("She killed her man, who wouldn't treat her right"); this was to become "Frankie and Johnnie," and later one of Duke Ellington's most persuasive sets of variations on the blues. In Mississippi they were singing a song of hard times:

> Come listen a while, I'll sing you a song
> Concerning the times—it will not be long—
> When everybody is striving to buy
> And cheating each other, I cannot tell why.
> And it's hard, hard times.

There were tales of God and tales of man, tales of lovers who were knotted and more who were not. The themes were clear, the music was all around, to be imitated and absorbed and changed by a new poet, a new singer, the American Negro.

Chapter 3

THE NEGRO SYNTHESIS

Whether slave or free man, the Negro in the nineteenth century was thought of as a child, happy on his feet, facing misery with a joyful chant, a Little Black Sambo whose major interest was in pancakes, not panaceas. But the Negro back in the hills and on the plantations was fleshing his music with his own aches and pains, his own unhappiness and his few moments of jubilation, compounded of sensual ecstasy and occasional religious exaltation. First came the work song—not the spiritual, not the joyous song.

The Negro didn't respond to the backbreaking labor of slavery with a jubilant shout. Such music as he created in the cotton fields and in the warehouses and on the levees was at the command of his masters. As Duke Ellington put it, in looking back over the history of the music of which he is such a distinguished representative, "At this point we encounter a myth which must be exploded. Fearful of the silence of these groups of blacks, their masters commanded them to raise their voices in song, so that all opportunity for discontented reflection or plans for retaliation and salvation would be eliminated." The best surviving examples of the work song are not from the plantations but from railroad workers and men in the levee camps and, most pitiful of all, the chain gangs. There are hollers of the kind that Huddie Ledbetter (Leadbelly) brought into the night club and the concert hall, such as the "Steel Laying Holler"—"Aw right, aw right. Ev'rybody get ready. Come on down here, come on boys. Bow down. Aw right, up high, aw right. Thow'ay." There are chants of tie-shuffling and tie-tamping; there are brief epics of wrecks, and of enormous distances encompassed by railroads taking the workers far from home.

From the levee camps came the shack bully holler and the holler of the levee camp—"Cap'n, cap'n, you mus' be cross; six 'clock in hell

18

THE NEGRO SYNTHESIS 19

'fo' you knock off." In the levee camp too there was talk of getting into town, where a measure of barroom joy and main-street hell-raising was afforded the emancipated Negro after the Civil War. Many of the songs of the seventies and eighties celebrated the good times in town. On the plantation, lyric characterization was given the plant enemy, the boll weevil—"The boll weevil is a little bug f'um Mexico, dey say; he come to try dis Texas soil and thought he'd better stay, a-lookin' for a home, just a-lookin' for a home." Later there were songs about the prodigious exploits of Negroes, some of which became the legend of John Henry. There were plaints about the difficulties of Negro life. There were celebrations of animals like the groundhog and the horse; there were celebrations of drinking exploits, of sexual conquests, and of the interrelation of the two when love came to be like whisky. Simile and metaphor were drawn from the things the Negro saw and heard. All these in later evolutions became the natural material of blues lyrics.

Along with the secular songs grew the Negro spirituals. The more kindly slave masters and overseers, feeling perhaps in some way responsible for the plight of their black charges, and themselves of a religious nature, taught the Bible to the oldest and wisest of their slaves. As they had done with the facts of plantation and levee and chain-gang life, these slaves, as Duke Ellington says, "studied the Book of Wisdom and set to music words of comfort and hope, which year after year were handed down to their colored brethren." But the setting to music of the Word of God, however fresh the setting may have been to the Negro doing it, was not always to tunes of his own devising. The long line of music which had developed in America from the days of the Puritans was the Negro's inheritance; he reached unconsciously into the treasure of the white man's music. And while the Negro was building his religious music, so was the white man. A comparison of the so-called white spirituals and the so-called Negro spirituals shows enormous exchanges of melody, rhythm, and lyric. Early in the twentieth century Cecil Sharp, in his collection of some five hundred songs of the Southern Appalachians, demonstrated the broad content of American folk songs and the depth of their British ancestry. But later G. P. Jackson in three books, *White Spirituals in the Southern Uplands* (1933), *Spiritual Folksongs of Early America* (1937), and *White and Negro Spirituals* (1943), showed the equally large part played by America's own makers—Negro and white—

poets, musicians, protesters, accepters, singers of life. In Jackson's books the borrowings of the Negro are made clear; but so too is the extent of his transformation of white materials, and of his own distinctive creations. Especially during and after the Civil War did the Negro fashion a music of his own. Pressed into Southern armies, Negroes had much to worry and complain about and to narrate in their songs. The triangle, famous in the drama and the novel, became a dominant concern: like his master, the Negro often left a wife or a sweetheart at home; like his master, the Negro often lost his wife or sweetheart to another man—here was the material of song. And then there was coming home, a feeling as full, as plagued by doubts, alternately as joyous and grievous as all the other homecomings stretching back to Ulysses.

While the Negro was fashioning his own music, the white man was looking on; and as the Negro had borrowed from him, he borrowed in turn from the Negro. Our first record of the white man's awareness of the Negro's music appears late in the eighteenth century. Letters describe Negroes playing their fiddles in Maryland taverns or strumming their banjos, made of flat gourds and strung with horsehair, before their cabins. The homemade instruments of the Negro are described in some detail, the tambo, bones, quills, fife, triangle; and so are the Negro rowing songs, among them the few real African strains found in America, most of them transformed into the dialect and diction of Creole, the French-Spanish patois to which Louisiana Negroes added some African inflections. In 1795 a young man named Gottlieb Graupner came to America. He arrived in Charleston from Hanover, Germany, listened to banjo music and Negro songs, and learned. In 1799, donning blackface, he introduced himself as "The Gay Negro Boy" in an interlude between acts at the Federal Street Theatre in Boston. This was the beginning of Negro minstrels and minstrelsy. Though Graupner left his burnt cork behind in 1810 when he organized the Boston Philharmonic Society as a kind of reaction against the "fuguing" tunes of William Billings, which suggested jazz syncopation more than they did classical music, minstrelsy had made a beginning and it was here to stay for quite a while.

Thomas "Jim Crow" Rice, a white man with a sensitive ear, heard an old Negro hostler singing one of the horse songs of his people in a stableyard one day in the early 1830s. From this Negro's repeated refrain, Rice's nickname and a whole tradition arose:

> Wheel about, turn about,
> Do jis' so,
> An' ebery time I wheel about,
> I jump Jim Crow.

Rice used the song and its refrain as a kind of interlude in *The Rifle*, a play about backwoodsmen. It was immediately successful and was changed from interlude to afterpiece, and other Negro melodies and dances were threaded through the play. In blackface, Rice made popular "The Long-Tailed Blue," a ballad narrating the story of the wearer of the coat, a story of trials and tribulations. Later he added happier variations on the coat theme. To the hostler's song, with all its lyric embroidery, and "The Long-Tailed Blue," Rice added studies of a variety of Negroes—the dandy, the plantation worker, the flat-boat man, and the singer. He took his program to London, where he was a huge success. In 1842 the development of the Negro character was still further expanded when Dan Emmett, an Irish backwoodsman with a face that was almost a caricature of the stock Yankee, gathered three other Yankees to play the fiddle, the tambo, the bones, and the banjo, made end men and interlocutors of them and dressed them all up in that long-tailed blue. The full-sized minstrel show was born. To group singing was added a walk-around by the chorus—the minstrel-show equivalent of the Greek choral ode—and some of the rhythms of the Negro spiritual and, later, of the blues began to make their ways into minstrelsy.

Daniel Decatur Emmett, who was the subject of *Dixie*, an engaging Bing Crosby motion picture, was the author of "Dixie's Land," best known as "Dixie," "Written and Composed Expressly for Bryant's Minstrels by Dan D. Emmett, Arranged for the Piano Forte by W. L. Hobbes." The song was first sung in public in 1859. Emmett was a Northerner and didn't intend to write a war anthem. For the South the song became a tearful reminder of the Confederate Army; for the North it evoked distant times and places, the longest trip away from home that many had ever made. "Dixie's Land" was the name originally invented by some Negro slaves sent to Charleston by Johaan Dixie, to describe their original owner's farm on Manhattan Island.

"Dixey Land" was an alternate name for Dixie's Line, the Mason and Dixon Line established in 1769 on the basis of the surveying by two English astronomers, Charles Mason and Jeremiah Dixon, separating Pennsylvania from Maryland and Virginia. Before the Civil War Dixon's Line came to mean the line that separated the slave states from the free states. But Dixie was also an Americanization of the French word for ten, *dix*, which was printed on New Orleans ten-dollar bills. All these meanings and overtones of meanings became a part of the single word Dixieland, which from before 1917 to the present has designated a music essentially New Orleans in character.

Before Dan Emmett, and until some years after his death in 1904, minstrelsy was a major form of American entertainment. There were the Virginia Minstrels and the Kentucky Minstrels, the Congo Melodists who became Buckley's New Orleans Serenaders, the Ethiopian Serenaders, the Sable Harmonizers, the Nightingale Serenaders, and the great names that linger on for the quality of their music and their performances, MacIntyre and Heath, Lew Dockstader, and Dan Bryant. Popular among the minstrel singers was a tune that originated in the work of one of the first of the black-faced impressionists, Bob Farrell, although the claim is sometimes made that another early blackface minstrel, George Washington Dixon, composed it. The tune is "Zip Coon," now better known as "Turkey in the Straw." Nobody now alive remembers when "Zip Coon" or "Turkey in the Straw" was not the musical symbol of life on the farm, of the country hick, of animal noises, of everything rural in America. But popular as this and other "coon songs" were and are, much more successful in the nineteenth century were the songs written for E. P. Christie and others by Stephen Collins Foster.

Stephen Foster, born in Pennsylvania, little-traveled in the South, shows the distance a composer of "Negro songs" could get from the Negro. Almost all of Foster's lovely melody seems to be based on the music of minstrelsy. So thoroughly had the antecedents of white and Negro music in America been absorbed by the minstrel composer, so effectively had the Negro's own music been imitated by white composers for blackface singers, that, although most of the music written for minstrel shows seems weak and ineffective beside the Negro's own music, minstrelsy provided an abundant source for the songs of Stephen Foster. Whatever their remove from the Negro himself,

Foster's songs do approach the simple beauty and rhythmic vitality of the Negro's music.

Like W. C. Handy, who sold his "Memphis Blues" outright soon after it was composed, Stephen Foster disposed unprofitably of most of his early songs. "Oh! Susanna" was in effect donated to the Cincinnati publisher W. C. Peters. "Old Folks at Home" went to the minstrel E. P. Christie for fifteen dollars, for which sum Christie also bought the right to claim the writing and composing of the song, although Foster did receive royalties and credit for it before he died. The tragedy of Stephen Foster's life—and there is sufficient nobility in his music to grant his failure such stature—is not entirely due to his early unforeseeing disposal of his songs. Some years before his death he was earning a sizable income for a composer in the middle of the nineteenth century. When he died in New York in 1864 he had been long separated from his wife and family, his habits were dissolute, he was without food or funds and had been perilously ill for quite a while. He died after suffering a cut in his throat when he fainted across the washbasin of his room in the American Hotel on the Bowery. When he died he was six months short of thirty-eight. He had thirty-eight cents in his purse, and a small piece of paper on which he had written the possible title or opening line of a song, "Dear Friends and Gentle Hearts."

For considerably less than the emolument of a Jerome Kern, Irving Berlin, or George Gershwin, he left an edifice of song which only such later popular composers could challenge, and even their impressive efforts don't achieve the nearly uniform quality of his almost two hundred songs. Through almost all those songs run the melodic line and rhythmic accent of the American Negro, from whom Kern, Berlin, and Gershwin and all their contemporaries, successors, followers, and imitators borrowed copiously. "Oh! Susanna," "De Camp Town Races," and "Away Down Souf" suggest the lilt and beat of ragtime and much other early jazz. The enduring "Old Folks at Home" and "My Old Kentucky Home" and "Old Black Joe" have a plaintiveness, within an infectiously accented rhythmic frame, which suggests the blues. The ease with which "Old Folks at Home," under its later and more familiar name, "Swanee River," fits the ensemble and solo needs of the Jimmie Lunceford and Tommy Dorsey jazz bands in arrangements by Sy Oliver is not happenstance. The cheer with which arrangers greeted "Jeannie with the Light Brown Hair," when that song written by Foster to his wife was available to them during the absence of ASCAP music from the air, indicates some of its relationship to jazz.

Before, during, and after the Civil War there were more songs like those Stephen Foster wrote, but without the quality of his work; however, they do have the warmth of melody and tricks of rhythmic accent that suggest nothing so much as jazz. "The Arkansas Traveler" and "Listen to the Mocking Bird" have been taken up by jazz bands. Septimus Winner, who wrote "Listen to the Mocking Bird," also did "Ten Little Injuns," which later became known as "Ten Little Niggers," to the discomfort of Negroes and many white men. He was one of the many who created new words for "Dixie," beginning with the line, "I'm captain of a darkie band." His long life stretched from 1827 to 1902, and his contributions, published under the pseudonym of Alice Hawthorne, range from "Listen to the Mocking Bird," which was published as a "Sentimental Ethiopian Ballad," to the more exaggerated sentimentality of "Whispering Hope" and "What Is Home Without a Mother?" But only his Bird is fit to rank with such masterpieces of the fifties as "Jingle Bells," "Pop Goes the Weasel," and "Skip to My Lou."

The Civil War produced "Maryland, My Maryland" and two versions of the tune earlier known as "Glory Hallelujah"—"John Brown's Body" and Julia Ward Howe's "The Battle Hymn of the Republic." But nothing out of the war, with the possible exception of the partisan version of "Dixie," approached the song by the Irish bandmaster Patrick Gilmore, "When Johnny Comes Marching Home." To those whose first inkling of the driving quality of the marching Johnny was Glenn Miller's recorded performance of it, it may come as a great surprise to learn that the song was written in 1863. And although most people who heard Benny Goodman's record of "When You and I Were Young, Maggie" realized that that song was not contemporary with the swing era, few realized that it went back to 1866; its form follows so exactly that of the popular song of the twentieth century that it is hard to place it much before World War I.

The spiritual really came alive in the decade from 1870 to 1880. In 1871 the Fisk Jubilee Singers, out of Nashville's Fisk University, one of the first and still one of the best institutions of higher learning for Negroes, made their first concert tour. Thereafter in their jaunts around America and in the concert tours of other Negro institutions like the Hampton Institute, such songs as "Deep River," "Go Down, Moses," "Heaven," "Little David, Play on Your Harp," "Swing Low, Sweet Chariot," and "Sometimes I Feel like a Motherless Child" were standard parts of a growing repertory. These began to appear in popular song collections, to be sung in parlors, on the concert stage, and in cabarets. The Negro had found a voice all his own; his music challenged in popularity Sir Arthur Sullivan's "The Lost Chord," which first reached the United States in 1877, and the enormously successful songs from *H.M.S. Pinafore* and *The Mikado*. The Negro spiritual was accepted along with Johann Strauss's waltzes. By the end of the nineteenth century it was even admitted that Negroes sang their own songs as well as or better than whites. Although there was no one individual Negro composer of great public note, Negroes as a whole were granted the high quality of their musical contributions. There was more to come than the minstrel-show version of Negro music; but while the full vigor of his instrumental and vocal performance was still to be heard and accepted, the Negro was now something more than a happy child.

Chapter 4

THE BLUES

When the spiritual was transformed into the blues, the content shifted some; the emphasis was less on man's relation to God and his future in God's heaven, and more on man's devilish life on earth. All of the musical antecedents of late nineteenth-century song were summed up, however indirectly, in the blues. The spiritual was the dominant strain, but the work song, the patriotic anthem, minstrel words and melodies, and all the folk and art songs sung in America were compounded into the new form.

There is an interesting parallel to the blues in Byzantine music. Like the Byzantine, the music of the blues has its line of identifiable sources. We can show that Byzantine music derives from Syrian, Hebrew, and Greek sources, but, as scholars have come to understand in the twentieth century, it is essentially an independent musical culture. In the same way we can now understand that the blues is a form complete in itself, whatever its clearly marked origins, especially notable for its balance of intense feeling and detachment. This balance is the distinguishing mark of most of the great blues, of the fine blues singers, and of every sensitive jazz performer since the emergence of the blues.

In the popular song, the evolution of which is at least as long as that of the blues, there is no such balance, and the distinction between form and content is easier to make, since the major concern of popular-song composers and writers has usually been commercial. As one cannot in the blues, one can take for granted the verbal content of the popular song, chiefly a series of approaches to love, happy and unhappy, ecstatic and disastrous, chiefly sentimental, though sometimes, in the hands of rare masters, compassionate.

Most popular songs contain a verse of eight measures, which introduces the working situation, melodically and verbally, and a chorus, which is usually thirty-two measures long. The thirty-two-bar chorus is usually divided into the following simple pattern: the first eight bars state the basic figuration or theme; then these first eight bars are repeated, completing the first half of the song; then follows the eight-bar bridge or release, in which a considerable variation on the theme is effected (here there is usually a change of key, rhythm, and general phrasing); and then in the last eight bars there is a return to the original statement, a recapitulation. All of this adds up to a pattern that can be most easily remembered as A-A-B-A.

The first eight bars of the ordinary thirty-two-bar chorus usually can be broken down into two four-bar phrases in which the second four bars merely repeat the first with a very slight harmonic variation, so that the form can be stated thus: A-A'-A-A'-B-A-A'.

The variations on the basic A-A-B-A pattern of the thirty-two-bar chorus are numerous. There are such obvious but infrequently used variations as the sixteen-bar chorus, usually nothing more than an eight-bar theme and an eight-bar release (A-B); or a twenty-bar chorus (A-B-A); or sometimes a chorus longer than thirty-two bars, as a more complicated content seeks rudimentary form. All of these variations reinforce and redefine the basic thirty-two-bar popular-song chorus.

The basic blues form is a twelve-bar chorus, in which an initial four-bar statement is repeated with slight melodic and harmonic changes in the second four bars and then again with more significant variation in the last four bars. The lyric form of this chorus can be compared, as Richard Wright has put it, to a man walking around a chair clockwise (the first four bars), then walking around it again counterclockwise (the next four), and then standing aside and giving a full judgment upon it (the last four bars).

Harmonically the blues follows a simple chord pattern, that of most Western folk music. The first four bars are usually based upon the chord of the tonic (the first note of the scale); the second four bars are usually based upon the chord of the subdominant (the fourth note of the scale); the last four bars are usually based upon the chord of the dominant (the fifth note of the scale).

The blues melody derives from the blues chords, but it has a tonal concept all its own, based on the blues scale, which consists of the ordinary scale plus a flattened third note and a flattened seventh note, which are known as the "blue notes." Thus, in effect, you have a ten-note scale because both the natural form of the note and its flattened version are retained in the blues. In the key of C major, for example, the blues scale runs C–D–E♭–E–F–G–A–B♭–B–C; the flattened third is E flat and the flattened seventh is B flat.

This tonal content causes jazz's characteristic assault on pitch. From the flattened third and seventh notes of the blues scale, struck against or before or after the natural evaluations of those notes, comes a whole complex of pitch variations. Perhaps the most immediately comprehensible example of what Raymond Scott calls "scooped pitch" can be heard in the playing of alto saxophonist Johnny Hodges with the Duke Ellington Orchestra. Johnny does what so many other jazz musicians do, but his meticulous technique makes the practice much more understandable, as he moves from some division of a tone up to a note or by some division of a tone away from it. He may be anywhere from a quarter to say a sixteenth flat in approaching a given note; the same tone divisions may mark his departure from the note, sharpening the note. In the same way jazz singers slide into or away from a note, coming in sharp or flat, departing flat or sharp. The mastery of these musicians and singers is such that they do not produce glissandos, agonized slides over a series of notes, which obliterate all tonal distinctions. For all the apparent casualness, the seeming hit-or-miss nature of their playing or singing, they know what they are doing, and after a while you come to know too.

Most blues melodies use either the first five notes of the ten-note blues scale, or the second five; that is, again using C major as our demonstration key, a blues tune runs from C to F or from G to C (if it runs from C to F the flattened note is E; if from G to C the flattened note is B).

Typical examples of the blues, the best examples with which to start to become accustomed to the curious harmonic and melodic character of this music, are the records of the early blues singers. It is difficult to get their records today, but some of Bessie Smith's best sides are or will be available on long-playing records. In "Cold in Hand Blues" and "You've Been a Good Old Wagon," you get perfect examples of Bessie's singing an E flat against an E natural in the accompaniment, or a B flat against a B in the accompaniment; the E flat example is on "You've Been a Good Old Wagon," the B flat on "Cold in Hand Blues." And the two individual sides also illustrate the characteristic limited melodic range of the blues; "You've Been a Good Old Wagon" is built on the first five notes of C major, "Cold in Hand

Blues" on the second five. (Incidentally, on these sides you get the additional pleasure of listening to Louis Armstrong in 1925 when he was still playing cornet and was at the peak of his early style.)

Variations in the blues form are possible, both in its chord structure and in melodic line. Passing tones (tones out of the immediate harmony, not in the chords at hand) can be used to supplement the five fundamental notes of either half of the blues scale, as the ornaments of a melody or as integral parts of it. Instead of following the conventional division of the twelve bars of the blues into three repetitious four-bar segments or phrases, each division of four bars may vary considerably from the preceding phrase. The blues may be broken up into two-bar instead of four-bar phrases, so that in one blues chorus there will be six phrases instead of three. You may get two-bar phrases with two-bar fill-ins, as in Duke Ellington's "Jack the Bear," where the piano plays the essential two-bar phrase and the band plays the two-bar fill-in.

From the two- and four-bar phrases of the blues came the riff, which was the outstanding instrumental device of the so-called swing era. The riff is a two- or four-bar phrase repeated with very little melodic variation and almost no harmonic change over the course of any number of blues choruses.

Blues melodies are often exquisitely simple. In Ellington's "C Jam Blues" the four-bar main phrase consists of only two notes, G and C. The first two bars (or riff) are all on G; in the third bar the C is introduced in a slurred pair of eighth-notes. "C Jam Blues" is worth careful listening, to hear how ingeniously this seemingly empty pair of notes becomes a fresh, swinging blues.

Generally the blues bass is played in unaccented four-quarter time, the best example of which is the "walking bass." If you listen carefully to the Ellington recording of "C Jam Blues," you will hear a definitive example of the walking bass—1 2 3 4/1 2 3 4/1 2 3 4, over and over again, with brilliant chord or key changes to make room for the progression from tonic chord to subdominant to dominant, from C to F to G seventh over a series of scale-like phrases. Another very effective bass for the blues is the rolling octave bass, which consists of dotted eighths and sixteenths, syncopating up and down octaves.

"Stride piano," the particular pride and joy of Fats Waller and, before him, of innumerable ragtime pianists, comes from the blues. The trick in the stride bass is to play a single note for the first and third beats of the bar, and a three- or four-note chord on the second and fourth beats. The effect when the stride bass is poorly played is plodding and corny; but when this kind of piano is played by a Fats Waller or an Art Tatum the result is exhilarating.

The blues is usually played in unaccented four/four time or with stride accents, but it does, in one of its most prominent variations, make a departure from this structure. The variation? Boogie-woogie, of course. Boogie-woogie, contrary to the general impression, is merely a piano blues form which on occasion has been adapted for orchestral use. It goes back to ragtime and hasn't changed very much since its first appearance. It represents nothing more than a jazz conversion of the traditional basso ostinato device, the pedal-point or organ-point reiteration of a basic bass line. In boogie-woogie eight beats to the bar are usually emphasized, with single notes or triplets, following the fundamental harmony of the twelve-bar blues form. More conservative than most blues performers, boogie-woogie pianists almost never depart from the original key and usually play in the key of C. Cleverly orchestrated, the obstinate bass suggests the classical passacaglia form. As boogie-woogie is most often played, by such broad-beamed performers as Albert Ammons and Pete Johnson and Meade Lux Lewis, it is confined in its ornament to trills and tremolos in the right hand, and constricted rhythmically and harmonically.

Although the blues is the base, harmonically, melodically, and even to a degree rhythmically, of jazz as we know it today, it did not appear on paper under its proper name until 1912. Jazz was on the threshold of its formative years as an art and of its widespread recognition. It was given a considerable push on its way in the first published blues, W. C. Handy's "Memphis Blues," written originally as a campaign song for E. H. Crump, a mayoralty candidate in Memphis in 1909. Though Crump was a reform candidate, William Christopher Handy's "Mister Crump" certainly didn't indicate that; the words were, if anything, a mockery of the candidate's reform promises:

> Mister Crump won't 'low no easy riders here;
> Mister Crump won't 'low no easy riders here;
> I don't care what Mister Crump won't 'low,
> I'm gonna bar'l-house anyhow;
> Mister Crump can go an' catch himself some air!

"Easy rider" meant, and still does, a lover or pimp who hangs on to his woman parasitically; "barrelhouse" is a rough saloon, literally a house where barrels of liquor are tipped on end; used as a verb, it indicates spending a rough evening or day or life, or—as here—the music that reflects all of that. The tune written for these words in a sixteen-bar form—a cross between the blues and the popular song choruses but essentially the former—became the "Memphis Blues" in 1912. In 1914 Handy published his "St. Louis Blues" with its provocative Tangana rhythm, which is a kind of habanera or tango beat consisting of a dotted quarter, an eighth-note, and two quarter-notes.

All of these—the adroit balance of feeling and detachment in words and music, the formulation of a distinctive melodic line based on its own tonal concept, pliability as instrumental and vocal music—show why the blues has been the most enduring and persuasive of jazz forms.

Contrary to the average conception of the form, the blues claims all creation as its subject, ranging impressively from Mississippi floods to New Orleans *maisons* to the WPA and war and peace and other problems. But the blues is not only a music for melancholia. There is great joy in the blues too, a joy that sometimes retains a strain of nostalgia or carries a thread of yearning for money, for romance, for the moon. The joy is still there, however, and so too is the great cry that identifies these songs as songs of the times. Floods and floozies, unrequited love and unemployment, the blues describes them all.

The twelve-bar form we know as the blues came into its vigorous own in the early years of this century. Up and down the Mississippi— though its major sources were in New Orleans—the blues was sung and played by the Negro musicians of 1910 and 1920 and 1930. To white America, in showboats, in New Orleans and Chicago and New York night clubs, the Negroes brought their tales of weal and woe.

The blues was the base of the early great recordings of Louis Armstrong, whose trumpeting genius formed, in turn, the base for most of the hot jazz that came afterward. His early records are magnificent examples of the blues and the vitality of its composers and lyricists and performers. Unlettered, morally but not musically undisciplined, the wild musicians of Louis's, Kid Ory's, and King Oliver's bands created great jazz, great music—"Gully Low Blues," "Wild Man Blues," "Potato Head Blues"—out of the happy chaos of the New

Orleans Negro quarter before and during and after World War I. These blues tell you much about the life and times of the fabulous men who made that music.

The chronicle of the blues goes on through the great singers: the five Smiths—Bessie, Clara, Trixie, Mamie, and Laura; Ida Cox, Chippie Hill, Ma Rainey. This impassioned history gives you rough, untrained voices with a majesty and a power that have scarcely been equaled by the finest of Wagnerian singers. These women were sometimes impoverished, rarely comfortable financially. They sang for gin and rent money, and their masterpieces appeared on the so-called "race" labels of the record companies. Their records were thus bought mainly by their own people, and few of these singers reached the tiny affluence which would have given them a fair life. Only Bessie Smith scored financial success, largely because Frank Walker, then Columbia Records' race record director, saved her money for her.

At first you may dislike the harshness of Bessie's voice and of the voices of the other Smiths and Ma Rainey. You may be put off by the sometimes monotonous melodies. But, if you listen carefully, you will find a richness of vocal sound and of verbal meaning too. You will discover a touching stoicism in the face of disaster, touching because there are fear and sorrow in the laments of Bessie Smith or Ma Rainey, and passion as well—but all laughed or shouted away. And in the laughter and the holler you may discern the wisdom of the Southern poor Negro or white which puts the facts of nature in their proper place, which refuses to be overwhelmed by physical or mental torture. One feels these things, the blues singer says, but one can do nothing about them. And so she communicates the torture, but always with philosophical detachment. This is a vigorous and vital music; it calls a spade a spade, a flood a flood, and unemployment an unpicturesque evil. Along with spades, floods, and unemployment the sexual relations of man and woman are seen as both glorious and inglorious.

The rewards of fealty to the blues have come slowly. W. C. Handy, who wrote the enduring "Memphis Blues" and "St. Louis Blues," was not well off until his near-blind old age, when the stream of royalties from those blues classics began to flow in. Billie Holiday, perhaps the greatest of present-day blues singers, is a moderate night-club success, singing in the boxes and holes and caverns of New York, Philadelphia,

Chicago, San Francisco, and Hollywood. Billie's trueness to the blues is a cornerstone of her greatness. While she sings a pop tune with artistry, shaping a shabby phrase so it gleams as it never did before, she does just as well in the blues, in the basic jazz songs, which she sings with unmistakable conviction. "Fine and Mellow" and "Billie's Blues" are among her best songs, along with the evergreens of jazz, such fine songs as "The Man I Love," "Body and Soul," "Them There Eyes," and "Porgy."

The people who like the way Billie and other blues singers sing will follow them wherever they go, to after-hours joints in Harlem, to squalid little clubs in downtown New York, where the liquor tastes like varnish, where the prices, unlike the decor, are right out of the Waldorf and El Morocco.

Few other singers combine the attractions of Billie Holiday, who is not only a singer with a sumptuous style, but also a remarkably beautiful woman. There are other brilliant blues singers. There is Big Joe Turner, a fabulous fellow from Kansas City, who matches the stature of the men he shouts about in the blues. There is Jimmy Rushing, Count Basie's singer. It was his barrelhouse figure that inspired the song "Mr. Five by Five." Jimmy knows a thousand old and new blues, to which he has added countless variations of his own. One of the best of these is "Baby, Don't Tell on Me":

> Catch me stealin', Baby, don't you tell on me,
> If you catch me stealin', Baby, don't you tell on me,
> I'll be stealin' back to my old-time used-to-be.

> Thought I would write her, but I b'lieve I'll telephone,
> Thought I would write her, but I b'lieve I'll telephone,
> If I don't do no better, Baby, look for your daddy home.

He ends the blues with the amusing line, "Anybody ask you who was it sang this song, tell 'em little Jimmy Rushing, he been here and gone."

Jack Teagarden, a big burly Texan with an infectious Panhandle accent in his singing, has always been associated with the blues. One of the few white men to attain distinction in the form, he lapses into the twelve-bar chorus of the blues as a matter of course. He is identified irrevocably with W. C. Handy's "Beale Street Blues" and the lovely "I Gotta Right to Sing the Blues," which was the theme song of his big band of short but often distinguished life. He improvises beautifully with his trombone or his delicate baritone voice, making up words to ungainly measures when that is necessary, culling his rolling blues phrases from the cowhand. Such effective syllabifications as "mam-o" for mamma ,"fi-o" for fire, and "Fath-o" for Paul Whiteman (known to his familiars as Pops or Father) are Teagardenisms. Coming late to an engagement one night, he jumped onto the bandstand, where his orchestra was already playing. Noting the severe expression on the face of the manager of the place, he improvised this blues:

> Comin' through the Palisades I los' my way;
> Comin' through the Palisades I los' my way;
> Thought I was back on the road, workin' for MCA.

Jack's plaint is at a large remove from the vital central themes of the blues, but it indicates clearly how much a part of jazz the form had become by the late thirties. It was the blues that the instrumentalists played and the singers shouted and wheedled that sent jazz around the United States and across the world. It was the blues that Louie Armstrong played so persuasively and Bessie Smith sang so movingly that served jazz so well when it came to its Diaspora. There was, after all, something to disperse.

Chapter 5

NEW ORLEANS

Much has been written, colorful and full of enthusiasm, flamboyant and full of condemnation, about Storyville, from 1897 to 1917 the district of New Orleans marked out by statute for licensed prostitution. Like so much that has been written about jazz, a lot of this has been full of half-truths and whole truths out of context. It would be a gross distortion to say that Alderman Story's city within a city reflected nothing but high moral purpose on the part of the New Orleans legislators who founded it. It would be gross injustice to suggest that they were accepting the several filths of flourishing vice as a cheerful necessity. This district represents simply the first and the last attempt to license prostitution in an American city—a Catholic city—following a procedure made famous by many Catholic cities in Europe, most notably Paris, which didn't find it necessary to close its legally recognized brothels until after World War II. Whatever the merits of this solution to the problem of the oldest profession, for sixty years the attractions of Storyville and its antecedent quarters rivaled those of the cemeteries and the restaurants of New Orleans, and for almost half of that period music, side by side with loose ladies, soothed savage breasts.

The ordinance of March 10, 1857, which licensed prostitution, merits some close examination. In the words of the New Orleans Common Council's Ordinance Number 3267, "an Ordinance concerning Lewd and Abandoned Women," the specter of illicit though legalized sex comes immediately alive, for all the flat phrases and legal dryness. In the first of sixteen sections, the districts in which "it shall not be lawful for any woman or girl, notoriously abandoned to lewdness, to occupy, inhabit, live or sleep in any one-story house or building, or the lower floor of any house or building," were named. In the second section, it was declared "that it shall be the duty of all

35

police officers, policemen and watchmen to arrest any girl found in contravention of the foregoing section," and the punishment, "not less than thirty days' imprisonment," was set forth. The third and fourth sections defined the taxing and licensing system, which gave legalized prostitution budgetary importance; they deserve quotation in their entirety:

No. 1086. (3). That it shall not be lawful for any woman or girl, notoriously abandoned to lewdness, to occupy, inhabit, or live in any house, building or room situated within the limits described in the first section of this ordinance, and not in violation of, or prohibited by the said section, without first paying in to the city treasurer the tax imposed by this ordinance, and procuring from the mayor of this city a license to inhabit or live in or occupy a house, building or room within said limits as aforesaid —nor shall it be lawful for any person to open or keep any house, building, dwelling or room within the limits of this city for the purpose of boarding or lodging lewd and abandoned women, or of renting rooms to such women, without first paying the tax hereinafter levied, and procuring from the mayor a license so to open and keep a house, etc., as aforesaid. Every person failing to comply with the provisions of this section, shall pay a fine of one hundred dollars for each and every contravention, and in default of payment shall be imprisoned not less than thirty days. One half of the fine shall be for the benefit of the informer. Provided, that nothing herein contained shall be so construed as to authorize the issuing of licenses to occupy or inhabit any one-story house or building or the lower floor of any house or building situated within the limits described in the first section of this ordinance.

No. 1087. (4). That an annual license tax of one hundred dollars be and the same is hereby levied upon each and every woman or girl notoriously abandoned to lewdness, occupying, inhabiting, or living in any house, building or room within the limits prescribed in the first section of this ordinance, but not in contravention thereof—and an annual tax of two hundred and fifty dollars upon each and every person keeping any house, room, or dwelling for the purpose of renting to or boarding lewd and abandoned women, which said tax shall be payable in advance of the first day of February of each and every year.

The fifth section authorized the mayor to grant licenses, and the sixth prescribed fines for breaches of the peace by "any woman or girl notoriously abandoned to lewdness, who shall occasion scandal or disturb the tranquility of the neighborhood." In the seventh it was declared "that it shall not be lawful for any lewd woman to frequent any cabaret, or coffee-house, or to drink therein, under the penalty of not less than five dollars for each and every contravention, or of being dealt with as provided by the act concerning vagrants, at the discretion of the recorder before whom she may be brought." The eighth section served to alleviate the fears of those who suspected that sisters under the skin would be little concerned by differences of the skin:

That it shall not be lawful for white women and free women of colour, notoriously abandoned to lewdness, to occupy, inhabit, or live in the same room, house or building; nor for any free person of colour to open or keep any house, building or room, for the purpose of boarding or lodging any white woman or girl notoriously abandoned to lewdness, under the penalty of not less than twenty-five dollars for each and every contravention; in default of payment, the person so contravening shall be imprisoned not less than thirty days. One half of the fine shall be for the benefit of the informer.

Those who rented or hired houses, buildings, or rooms off-limits to prostitutes were ordered to be fined, if a petition signed by three "respectable citizens residing within the vicinity of any house, or building" should state "under oath" that the house, building, or room "is a nuisance," and that "the occupants thereof are in the habit of disturbing the peace of the neighborhood, or in the habit of committing indecencies by the public exposure of their persons, etc.," and "it shall be the duty of the mayor" to order the ejection of such offenders from the premises.

It was then provided that all such houses, buildings, dwellings, or rooms "shall at all times be subject to the visitation of the police of this city. . . . It shall not be lawful for any woman or girl notoriously abandoned to lewdness, to stand upon the sidewalk in front of the premises occupied by her, or at the alleyway, door or gate of such premises, nor sit upon the steps thereof in an indecent posture, nor accost, call, nor stop any person passing by, nor to walk up and down the sidewalk or banquette, nor stroll about the streets of the city indecently attired, under the penalty of not less than ten.dollars for each and every contravention."

The last four sections of this extraordinary ordinance deal with obstructors of this law, the enforcement of it by the police, the date when it was to go into effect (February 2, 1858); and, finally, all laws contrary to this one were repealed.

It was only in 1897, in a new ordinance sponsored by Alderman Story, that a specific district was set up to limit prostitution geographically. The earlier ordinance had restricted only operations, and had actually given the brothels and unaffiliated whores an unmistakably large swathe through the city in which to work. It was, then, from 1897 to 1917 (when the Secretary of the Navy shut down all red-light districts) that tourism descended upon prostitution in New Orleans and jazz came alive.

The district, a sizable chunk of New Orleans, was at first open to Negroes and mulattos, at least in certain sections, and they brought their trade and their music with them. In the last eight months of organized Storyville a restricted Negro district about half the size of Storyville proper was established. But for most of the two important decades Negro and white women, Negro and white musicians, worked side by side. Here in what their owners and residents invariably called palaces, châteaux, and maisons, in what are accurately named honky-tonks, in saloons, and in all the other entertainment places—except perhaps the "cribs," the tiny dwellings of the cheapest prostitutes—jazz was played. The well-placed white man in New Orleans looked down upon Storyville, publicly regarded it as a civic disgrace, whatever his private behavior; but at Carnival time, and especially on the day of Mardi Gras, this Orleanian lost none of his propriety and gained much in warmth by joining with the district in a celebration long since world-famous. The white Carnival had its King Rex, and the Negroes their King Zulu and their music, easily the most distinguished contribution to the jubilant festivities.

Visitors to the city, coming into the Southern Railroad Station on Canal Street, saw as much of Storyville as those who arrive in New York by way of One Hundred and Twenty-fifth Street see of uptown Manhattan. The view, just before arriving at the station, was of honky-tonks and cribs and palaces. Not far from the station one could visit the main saloon, the Arlington Annex, of the unofficial mayor of Storyville, Tom Anderson, who made this barroom, adjoining his Arlington Palace, his city hall. Anderson was the boss of the district, a member of the state legislature, the owner of a chain of saloons, and the head of an oil company. He was also the main instigator of that group of worthy Storyville citizens who pooled their resources and produced the official directory and guidebook of

Storyville, *The Blue Book*, which could be bought for twenty-five cents at the Arlington Annex after 1895.

The Blue Book was not the first of the guides to the bordellos, their madams and working personnel. In the 1880s and 1890s there was a weekly paper, the *Mascot*, which in its "society" column provided a sort of unofficial directory to what it called the "dames de joie." This was surely one of the strangest columns ever to appear in a newspaper. Some examples of its news items are:

Miss Josephine Icebox has been presented with a pair of garters and a belt made out of the skin of the cobra di cappello that escaped from the Wombwell menagerie, and was killed by a street car. The present was made to Miss Josephine by her lover in gratitude for having been saved from seeing snakes.

It is confidentially asserted that an heir is expected by her most gracious majesty, Queen Gertie. It is conjectured that the prince will have red hair. . . .

Mrs. Madeline Theurer has gone out of business on Barracks and Rampart streets. Mrs. Theurer enjoyed the good wishes of the ladies in the social swim. Although the lady has deemed it advisable to close her Barrack street chateau, still she will not abandon the profession entirely, but intends, in the near future, opening up in new quarters. It is safe to say that Mrs. Theurer can brag of more innocent young girls having been ruined in her house than there were in any other six houses in the city. . . .

In 1895 the *Mascot* reported in this column that "the society ladies of the city can now boast that they have a directory." It went on to explain:

In no other city in the Union can the dames de joie make a similar boast. Within the past week a little book, styled "The Green Book, or Gentlemen's Guide to New Orleans," has been freely distributed. In it are all the principal mansions de joie in the city (white and colored). The names of the madames of the house are given, as also are those of all the angels, nymphs and fairies. The color and nationality of the darlings are stated. Twenty thousand copies of the guide will be distributed during Mardi Gras. The price is twenty-five cents. The publisher's name does not appear.

It's colorful. It's amusing. It is also a picture of depravity, in which humans are reduced to inanimate things for sheer pleasure. Some jazzmen succumbed to the several lures of their surroundings; most didn't. Some became pimps, increasing their income from music by their industrious procuring; most were content to be paid for playing the music they loved. It cannot fairly be concluded that jazz must live in such an atmosphere. At times jazz has thrived on vice—and vice has lived luxuriously upon it. Music has always accompanied debauches; it has not necessarily reflected or condoned them.

Jazz musicians on the whole would probably prefer to live in a healthier environment than Storyville provided. Their wholesale departure from New Orleans after World War I was perhaps an attempt to find such an environment, as well as a search for new employment. The former was much less successful than the latter, but the struggle of sensitive jazzmen to achieve dignity has never ceased, and it has succeeded more often than the legends and the newspaper chronicles have ever suggested.

In 1895 or 1896 the first *Blue Book* appeared, and, shortly after, *The Lid, Hell-o,* and *The Sporting Guide* "of the Tenderloin-District, of New Orleans, La., where the four hundred can be found." *The Lid* explained itself: "No doubt you have read all about the 'lid' so it will be useless for one to further describe it. This little booklet is gotten up expressly for those who belong to that order of 'lid destroyers' who believe in making life as strenuous as one possibly can without injury to himself or pocket." *Hell-o,* through Tom Anderson, writing under an apposite pseudonym, stated:

To keep my friends from saying mean things while trying to get a connection with their girls—that is to say a telephone one, I have compiled this little book entitled "Hell-O"—please don't misconstrue the name and read it backwards.
Thanking you for your patience, I remain,
Yours,
"LITTLE SALTY"

The Sporting Guide explained: "This volume is published for the benefit of the upper 'Four Hundred' who desire to visit the Tenderloin District with safety and obtain the desired pleasure accruing from beauty and pleasure, which can be accomplished by following this guide."

But the most famous of the guides was *The Blue Book*, which was published regularly until 1915. In *The Blue Book* appeared advertisements for Tom Anderson's Annex, Cafe and Restaurant ("never closed, noted the states over for being the best conducted cafe in America, private dining rooms for the fair sex, all the latest musical selections nightly, rendered by a typical Southern darkie orchestra"), cigars, glassware and crockery, an attorney, a drugstore, a taxi company ("If you want to learn all the live places, while making the rounds, call up . . ."), beers and sparkling waters, Turkish baths, candies, an electric piano, the "king of piano tuners," all kinds of whisky, gin, wines, and a laundry.

The opening pages of several editions of *The Blue Book* set the tone of what it called the "Queer Zone":

PREFACE
"Honi Soit Qui Mal y Pense"

This Directory and Guide of the Sporting District has been before the people on many occasions, and has proven its authority as to what is doing in the "Queer Zone."

Anyone who knows to-day from yesterday will say that the Blue Book is the right book for the right people.

WHY NEW ORLEANS SHOULD
HAVE THIS DIRECTORY

Because it is the only district of its kind in the States set aside for the fast women by law.

Because it puts the stranger on a proper and safe path as to where he may go and be free from "Hold-ups," and other games usually practiced upon the stranger.

It regulates the women so that they may live in one district to themselves instead of being scattered over the city and filling our thoroughfares with street walkers.

It also gives the names of women entertainers employed in the Dance Halls and Cabarets in the District.

There is a certain wry humor about the quotation from the escutcheon of the British Royal Family, "Evil be to him who evil thinks." But the third page, opposite the advertisement for Tom Anderson's Annex, gets right down to "Facts"!

THIS BOOK MUST NOT BE MAILED

To know the right from the wrong, to be sure of yourself, go through this little book and read it carefully, and then when you visit Storyville you will know the best places to spend your money and time, as all the BEST houses are advertised. Read all the "ads."

This book contains nothing but Facts, and is of the greatest value to strangers when in this part of the city. The names of the residents will be found in this Directory, alphabetically arranged, under the headings "White" and "Colored," from alpha to omega. The names in capitals are landladies only.

You will find the boundary of the Tenderloin District, or Storyville: North side Iberville Street to south side St. Louis, and east side North Basin to west side North Robertson Street.

This is the boundary in which the women are compelled to live, according to law.

Thereafter the promises of the third page are fulfilled. First there is an alphabetical list of white prostitutes; then two pages of "Forty-five Late Arrivals"; then a page devoted to octoroons (only nine of these), with the two great landladies of the jazz era, Countess Willie Piazza and Miss Lulu White, in capitals; then an alphabetical list of two hundred and thirty-four colored prostitutes; finally a list of nine cabarets, with their dames de joie.

The dead seriousness of the neatly molded simple declarative sentences of *The Blue Book* makes quotation an almost irresistible temptation. Several examples, however, suffice to give the flavor of the advertisements for Storyville's landladies, the madams whose maternal interest in jazz surrounded its early musicians with a comfortable and sympathetic atmosphere and audience. Miss Lulu White's independently issued four-page "souvenir" booklet, published for her "multitudes of friends," and Countess Willie Piazza's ad in the sixth edition of *The Blue Book* are especially important for jazz. Lulu White, who ran the Mahogany Hall, a four-story house with tower and weathervane, found immortality in Louis Armstrong's "Mahogany Hall Stomp." She offered details of the hall's construction:

THE NEW Mahogany Hall,

A picture of which appears on the cover of this souvenir was erected specially for Miss Lulu White at a cost of $40,000. The house is built of marble and is four story; containing five parlors, all handsomely furnished, and fifteen bedrooms. Each room has a bath with hot and cold water and extension closets.

The elevator, which was built for two, is of the latest style. The entire

house is steam heated and is the handsomest house of its kind. It is the only one where you can get three shots for your money—
The shot upstairs,
The shot downstairs,
And the shot in the room.

She also included her autobiography:

This famous West Indian octoroon first saw the light of day thirty-one years ago. Arriving in this country at a rather tender age, and having been fortunately gifted with a good education it did not take long for her to find out what the other sex were in search of.

In describing Miss Lulu, as she is most familiarly called, it would not be amiss to say that besides possessing an elegant form she has beautiful black hair and blue eyes, which have justly gained for her the title of the "Queen of the Demi-Monde."

Her establishment, which is situated in the central part of the city, is unquestionably the most elaborately furnished house in the city of New Orleans, and without a doubt one of the most elegant places in this or any other country.

She has made a feature of boarding none but the fairest of girls—those gifted with nature's best charms, and would, under no circumstances, have any but that class in her house.

As an entertainer Miss Lulu stands foremost, having made a life-long study of music and literature. She is well read and one that can interest anybody and make a visit to her place a continued round of pleasure.

She said that, "in presenting this souvenir" to her "friends," it was her "earnest desire" to "avoid any and all egotism," and added, "While deeming it unnecessary to give the history of my boarders from their birth, which would no doubt, prove reading of the highest grade, I trust that what I have mentioned will not be misconstrued, and will be read in the same light as it was written." Finally she mentioned the fact that all her boarders "are born and bred Louisiana girls," and signed her words: "Yours very socially, LULU WHITE."
Countess Willie offered entertainment.

COUNTESS WILLIE PIAZZA

Is one place in the Tenderloin District you can't very well afford to miss. The Countess Piazza has made it a study to try and make everyone jovial who visits her house. If you have the "blues," the Countess and her girls can cure them. She has, without doubt, the most handsome and intelligent octoroons in the United States. You should see them; they are all entertainers.

If there is anything new in the singing and dancing line that you would like to see while in Storyville, Piazza's is the place to visit, especially when one is out hopping with friends—the women in particular.

The Countess wishes it to be known that while her mansion is peerless in every respect, she only serves the "amber fluid."

"Just ask for Willie Piazza."
PHONE 4832 MAIN
317 N. Basin

The Countess apparently was the first to hire a pianist, and there is a story, perhaps apocryphal, that his name, self-adopted or conferred by the customers ("club boys"), was John the Baptist. Another of the Countess's pianists was Tony Jackson, a showmanly musician who brought vaudeville into the brothel, and after 1908 became an established name in New York. He will be forever associated with his song, "I've Got Elgin Movements in My Hips with Twenty Years' Guarantee." Lulu White could also boast some fine pianists, notably Richard M. Jones, who died during the 1940s in Chicago, and Clarence Williams, who when he came to New York probably brought more of New Orleans with him than any other man, in his song-writing, record-making, and public performances. The most famous of the Anderson Annex pianists was Ferdinand Joseph (Jelly Roll) Morton, the Gulfport, Mississippi, musician, who will be remembered as long for his spoken jazz narratives as for his piano-playing and composing.

Lulu White's Mahogany Hall and adjoining saloon, at the corner of Bienville and Basin Streets, makes a good starting point for a tour of the area where jazz flourished from the late 1880s to 1917. Right before us, as we face south, is the Southern Railroad, a stretch of tracks leading along Basin Street to the terminal on Canal. A block east, on Iberville, is Tom Anderson's Annex, and back of it, on Franklin Street, the 101 Ranch, which had changed by 1910 from a kind of waterfront saloon, though some distance from the river, into one of the most impressive of the jazz hangouts, where King Oliver and Sidney Bechet and Pops Foster and Emanuel Perez played some of their strong early notes. Billy Phillips, owner of the 101, opened the Tuxedo Dance Hall diagonally across from the Ranch. The Tuxedo was the scene of many police raids and ultimately of Phillips's killing. Freddie Keppard played his driving cornet at the Tuxedo, and later Johnny Dodds was the featured clarinetist and Oscar Celestin led the band named after the hall, the Tuxedo Band, which in a later edition was still playing on Bourbon Street in New Orleans in 1951. Two blocks away from Lulu White's, at Liberty and Bienville, was the Poodle Dog Cafe—a name used in city after city; it was popular from 1910 through the early twenties as far north as Washington, D.C., where a café of the same name was the scene of Duke Ellington's first piano-playing job. North one block and east another, on Iberville, was Pete Lala's Cafe, much patronized for the music as well as the barrels of liquor, and where, at one time or another, Kid Ory and King Oliver and Louis Armstrong led bands. Lala also owned "The 25" club, a block down from the Tuxedo, another of the sometime jazz places.

Down the railroad tracks, as one goes away from the center of town on Basin Street, are cemeteries. Up Iberville and Bienville and Conti, going north, are cemeteries. If you follow the tracks, past the cemeteries, past St. Louis Street and Lafitte Avenue, you reach what is now called Beauregard Square, where now squats the Municipal Auditorium, graced with flowers and grass shrubbery. Now, in season, there are band concerts and rallies and public events of all sorts here. In 1803, Fort St. Ferdinand, built by the Spaniards on this spot, was destroyed in an attempt to wipe out yellow fever, thought to be caused by the stagnant water of the moats and the abundant filth of the city's ramparts. The park which replaced the fort was at first used as a circus ground, then enclosed with an iron fence and made into a Sunday-afternoon promenade ground and pleasance for Orleanians. For the city's Negro slaves, granted a half-holiday every Sunday, the new park was a wonderful gathering-place. Named Congo Square, the great open area was used by the Negroes for games, for singing to the accompaniment of tom-toms, for Voodoo ritual and ceremony. Here such of Africa as remained passed into Negro Creole life in America. Here were uttered the strange chants, the curious sounds, the ancient cries of the tribes, transformed, subtly but unmistakably, by French and Spanish culture: "*Pov piti Lolotte à mouin*"—softly, not clearly; "*Pov piti Lolotte à mouin*"— more firmly now, and clearer to the ear, repeated like the first line of the blues; then, twice, "*Li gagnin bobo, bobo*," the second time with a variation, *"Li gagnin doulè"*; then, again, the first line, sung twice; and finally, *"Li gagnin bobo, Li gagnin doulè."* The hypnotic effect must have been irresistible. The affinity with the remaining traces of Voodoo in Haiti, and in the rites of the Candomblé in Brazil is unmistakable—music, incantatory words, and dancing. The dancing, before the half-holiday celebrations ceased during the Civil War, attracted its share of tourists to sway and be moved in spite of themselves by the hypnotic beat.

The bamboulas, huge tom-toms made of cowhide and casks, were the bass drums, pummeled with long beefbones. Bamboo tubes produced a skeletal melody. Staccato accents were made by the snapping together of bones—the castanets. An ass's jawbone was rattled; the instrument is still used in Latin-American music and is known as the *guajira*, a word that means "rude" or "boorish," "rustic" or "rural" in present-day Cuban Spanish. Many Negro instruments, rhythms, and dances came to be used in Central and South America, leading eventually to the rhumba and the conga, the samba and the mambo, in Cuba, Argentina, and Brazil, where, as in New Orleans, music developed in numbers of Congo Squares, half-holiday games and chants and dances. The effect of Congo Square was twice felt in jazz; once directly, as it filtered through the tonks and the barrelhouses, the Storyville parlors and ballrooms; again indirectly, when bebop musicians went to Cuba to reclaim their earlier heritage.

By the end of the 1880s New Orleans Negro musicians were no longer playing jawbones, hide-covered casks, or bamboo tubes. As they grew more interested in the meaning and mechanics of music, they became more interested in the white man's instruments, which offered broader, fuller expression. These men, like many members of the American Federation of Musicians today, were part-time instrumentalists, who by day cut hair or served food or lifted bales or ran errands, but by night or on Saturdays or Sundays, for special or ordinary celebrations, played the instruments of the white man. The instrumentation of jazz at the end of the nineteenth century was in a sense conventional, although it was not the dance-music instrumentation familiar to most Orleanians. For the string trio (heard even in brothels) and the larger polite organization of bows and gut, Negro musicians substituted brass-band horns, cornet and clarinet and trombone, with an occasional roughening contributed by a tuba. Rhythm came, naturally enough, from drums and the string bass (more often than the tuba), and sometimes from the piano. These were the logical instruments, for the first large contribution to the new music was made by marching bands.

They marched (without the bass and piano) to wakes and from them in Negro New Orleans. They marched for weddings and for political rallies, when they were summoned away from their ghetto precincts. They marched again and again, just to march, for the pleasure of the members of the fraternal organizations and the secret orders with which their culture abounded. There were always plenty of other parades too—for the Fourth of July and Labor Day and Jackson Day and Carnival, for funerals and during election campaigns. And when the bands got going and the beat became irresistible, the followers, chiefly youngsters, fell in, dancing behind the musicians and keeping up the friendly, informal infernality. The bands played all the standard hymns, such as "Rock of Ages" and "Nearer, My God, to Thee" and "Onward, Christian Soldiers," and they made of some of them immortal jazz compositions, lifted forever from the parade or the funeral to the night club and the recording studio and the concert hall. And such a transfiguration as they turned out of "When the Saints Go Marching In" deserved the larger audience it finally found for its humors, at once delicate and assaulting, satirical and deeply religious. There were the "Saints" and the "Rock" and the "Soldiers" to move the deceased nearer to his God as he was brought to his resting place in the special section of the cemetery reserved for Negroes. Once he was interred, the music changed. "Didn't He Ramble?" the bandsmen asked rhetorically and followed the tale of a rambling townsman with their freely improvised, booming, blasting choruses, one after another, leading from the "Ramble" to Alphonse Picou's polka-like "High Society" and Jelly Roll Morton's tribute to a fellow Mississippian pianist, King Porter, after whom "King Porter Stomp" was named. Maybe they'd finish off with a rag, Scott Joplin's "Maple Leaf" perhaps, or the most famous of all, "Tiger Rag," fashioned from an old French quadrille. Whatever they played, the bands blew a mighty sound along the streets and through the alleys and into the squares of New Orleans. And when they were finished with parades they played for dances, little and big, and they brought with them into the makeshift and the more solidly constructed ballrooms and into the parks all the atmosphere of the marching band. Their dances looked and sounded almost

like the big ballroom blowouts of the twenties and thirties in Harlem
at the Savoy or the Renaissance, or in Chicago or St. Louis or any
other town where Negroes gathered to listen and to dance to their
music.

Jazz was absorbed into Negro New Orleans and passed on to
interested whites. It was taken up with that mixture of casual acceptance and rabid enthusiasm that is always found when an art form
becomes an integrated part of a culture. Whole bands were hired to
advertise excursions on the river, picnics by the lake, prize fights,
and dances; whole bands were lifted onto furniture wagons, bass,
guitar, cornet, clarinet, and drums, with the trombonist's slide hanging behind as he sat on the back edge, feet hanging down, slide hanging down, forming the "tailgate" of the wagon. Music was everywhere in the last years of Storyville and the first years of jazz.

Chapter 6

FIGURES OF LEGEND AND LIFE

They marched right up the streets, all the streets, and marched right down again. In the course of their spectacular strolls, New Orleans marching bands built a large and imposing repertory of music, much of which is still with us. For the music there had to be musicians; there were many, all kinds, all qualities, some of them personalities. Inevitably, it's the personalities who stick out, whose reputations remain, whose performances thread their way through the memories of men old enough to have heard them. But even in the memory borderland of fact and fancy, some musicians stand out for good reasons and must be accepted as the first vital figures of jazz. Others remained vigorous long enough between the two world wars to be heard and judged by a later generation. From these two sources—other men's memories and our own listening—emerges a large impression of the first jazzmen, one that has both logic and continuity.

Claiborne Williams was a cornetist and an entrepreneur. He was available for all occasions. Under his leadership were musicians who could play cotillion music for those Negroes who wanted to imitate white dances. But under his leadership too, cornetists, trombonists, clarinetists, drummers, and bass players marched and played the music of marching jazz. Constituting itself the St. Joseph Brass Band, this second and more important of the Claiborne Williams organizations offered one skillful jazz cornetist, William Daley, an impressive all-around drive, and the fine reliable sound of its leader's cornet.

The Williams bands flourished in the 1880s; so did those of John Robechaux. Robechaux was a drummer and, like Williams, a leader of several outfits. He booked his sweet band as he found demand. In the Excelsior Band, of which he was simply a part, there were two renowned clarinetists, the brothers Louis and Lorenzo Tio, who taught the music they played. At the turn of the century the Excelsior

49

featured two of the outstanding musicians of this era, clarinetist Alphonse Picou and cornetist Emanuel Perez.

The St. Joseph and Excelsior bands, two of the best of the 1880 crews, were close enough in time to the twentieth century to leave an identifiable mark. It must not be supposed, however, that these were the first or the only bands to march the New Orleans streets before 1900. These men followed others, whom they surely would have acknowledged if they had lived long enough to document their era. It is unfortunate that George Cable and Lafcadio Hearn, whose writing captured so much of New Orleans Creole life in the 1870s and 1880s, were not more interested in music, but the suggestion of its existence is always implicit and sometimes explicit in their books and articles.

In the years after Cable's and Hearn's era, from about 1895 to 1907, Buddy Bolden's Ragtime Band set the style. To begin with, he had Woody Warner on clarinet, Willie Cornish on valve trombone, Jimmie Johnson on bass, Brock Mumford on guitar, Louis Ray on drums, and himself on cornet. For the proper occasions he even sported a violinist, Tom Adams. They all were loud musicians, and they were vigorous, but they could play a pretty tune. Most important of all, they sported a brilliant cornet, the heroic voice of jazz, and to play it they had a leader fully armored in the personality that fitted the instrument.

Buddy Bolden's band fixed New Orleans instrumentation, the combination of one or two cornets, clarinet, trombone, bass, guitar, and drums, which was to set the sound patterns for jazz for years to come. Bolden, known as "the Kid" and "the King," was the early version of that indefatigable character so well known to later musicians who have grown up on their instruments through Saturday night functions and occasional midweek balls: he was an organizer, a man who always knew where a "gig," a one-night job, could be found. He played for picnics and for dances, for carnival crowds, for the strollers in the parks. When work was scarce for his own little band, he would move his three horns and three rhythm instruments into a bigger band with less permanent personnel and play with them for a night or a week, as the job demanded. The story persists that his lungs were so powerful that when he sat himself by an open window and barreled notes through his cornet his music could be heard for miles along the river. He was variously gifted:

cornetist, barber, editor and publisher of *The Cricket*, a gossip-mongering paper. His personality left an unmistakable imprint on the music that followed his; wherever he played in New Orleans, at the *Tintype* or *Economy* or *Love and Charity*, *Big Easy* or *Come Clean* dance halls, at picnic or parade, he drove his band through its paces and into the heads of musicians listening to him. In 1907 or 1908 he drove himself insane, as the word-of-mouth history has it, running wild at a parade. He was committed to an asylum and died there in 1931 or 1932 at the age of about seventy.

Buddy Bolden's band set the instruments and perhaps the harmonic and melodic order as well. To the cornet was assigned the lead part, the line identified as the melody; the trombone, particularly after the slide instrument replaced the valve horn about 1900, was a languorous counter-voice, punctuating the melody with character-istic smears and oozes; the clarinet, in vigorous contrast to the sus-tained trombone slides, maintained a hopping, skipping position, em-broidering decorative runs about the other lines. The rhythm instru-ments—drums, bass, and guitar—made up the engine that powered the jazz machine: their function was to keep the syncopated beat going in regular almost inflexible alternations of weak and strong ac-cents.

All of this added up to what has been described as polyphony, something of a misnomer for the crude counterpoint of New Or-leans jazz, since polyphony requires the simultaneous combination of several voices, each of a clear individuality, and the music which Bolden, his contemporaries, and his successors played was generally a sturdy mixture of the simplest variations on the key melodies, each man only tentatively for himself, and the end product dependent upon the chords to such an extent that the texture was more dominantly harmonic than melodic. What they did do, and apparently with great contagious gusto, was to administer just that touch of brash-ness, just that breath of spontaneity, just that drive, which together were to convert minstrelsy and worksongs, Congo Square blasts and cotillion refinements, into jazz. Early jazz had something less than polyphony or counterpoint, as we understand those terms in their original context—something less and something different—but on at least one level it had something more too.

Polyphonic music is a music of melodic lines played against each other; it moves from simple canonic forms, best illustrated by rounds

—such as "Three Blind Mice" or "Row, Row, Row Your Boat"—
to the enormously complicated and sophisticated maneuvers of eight-
part double fugues. In every case this music is conceived horizontally.
While its great baroque exponents, such as Bach or Buxtehude,
worked well within a harmonic frame, their linear thinking determined the shape and substance of their music. None of this can be
said for the so-called New Orleans polyphonists. However much
their present-day admirers may wish to confer contrapuntal glory
upon their favorites, the music of New Orleans at its pre-1917 best
appears to have been conceived harmonically, executed harmonically,
and to have proceeded from the same concern for chords which, in
a far more informed and organized fashion, has dominated the music
of swing and bop.

What appears to be a kind of rough polyphony in early jazz is
an improvised voicing of cornet, clarinet, and trombone not very
different from the scoring of two altos, two tenors, and a baritone
in the present-day dance band, although the sonorities may be coarser
in New Orleans jazz, the over-all texture thinner and tougher, the
harmonic freedom considerably less. The linear concept in the jazz
of Storyville and environs was contained in the polyrhythms, the rich,
ingenious pitting of one time against another in the two hands of the
piano or in two or more instruments. But New Orleans jazzmen did,
and their imitators and leftovers continue to, pull most of their
melodies out of the blues chords and a small stockpile of related
standard tunes. Whether they are playing a solo with organ harmony
in the background, or pushing a ride-out chorus to its obstreperous
end, their harmonic thinking is vertical, and their notes follow a
chord pattern. When, upon occasion, they may seem to those of their
critical supporters who are also enthusiasts for atonal music to have
scooped pitch and moved away from the confines of key and modula-
tion, it is probably nothing but the clumsiness of a performer with
an insufficient knowledge of his instrument.

Freddie Keppard is a musician to place beside Buddy Bolden. Here
we have a figure more of life than of legend, although the performances that gained him his early reputation were all before jazz was
recorded. When he got to Chicago he did record, in 1923, 1926, and
1927. In the 1926 records, with Jimmy Blythe's Ragamuffins and his
own Jazz Cardinals—in the first case backing Trixie Smith and in
the second with Papa Charlie Jackson as vocalist—one can gather

what he sounded like and perhaps some of the quality of Buddy Bolden's playing too. Through something less than high fidelity recording come the thrust and the exuberance, the rough tone, the rhythmic lift that pushed jazz into exultant being. Keppard dropped the violin for the cornet because he never learned to read music, but he had that grasp of the cornet that makes so much of the early music impressive. It would be silly to say, as some have of jazz musicians of this kind, that because he was unlettered he was a better musician, but there is no denying that some of the dramatic colors of jazz entered the music because of the lack of formal discipline in men like Freddie Keppard.

Freddie Keppard was the cornet mainstay of the great Olympia Band. Through most of its years, from its founding in 1900 to 1911, Keppard's cornet kicked the Olympia Band into powerful life. Beside him sat Alphonse Picou, embroidering clarinet lines around the cornet and trombone, Picou who made the clarinet part of "High Society" such a classic that thereafter it was played unchanged even by the most free-swinging improvising clarinetists. Picou is a fine example of the continuity of New Orleans jazz. His teacher was Lorenzo Tio, and, like Tio, he sometimes played clarinet in performances of French opera. His successor in the Olympia's clarinet chair was Louis de Lisle Nelson, known as Big Eye. Some of the tunes that Picou wrote, such as "Alligator Hop" and, the most famous of them all, "Muskrat Ramble," were later played by Nelson, and together they set the style that was to be expanded and embellished and carried across the country by Sidney Bechet, Johnny Dodds, and Jimmy Noone.

The valve trombone in the band was played by Joseph Petit, who was also the manager of the Olympia, a sizable saloon on Elks Place across Canal Street from the railroad terminal. He was later replaced by Zue Robertson, a relative of Buddy Bolden's and enough of a musical personality to influence many of his successors on his instrument, the slide trombone. The two most notable drummers of the Olympia, John Vean, known as Ratty, and Louis Cottrell, known as Old Man, introduced, one the first four-beat bass drum part, the other a more technical understanding of drums and drumming.

The journeys of Freddie Keppard take us to two of the other very important bands that thrived before the closing of Storyville. In 1911 the bass player Bill Johnson organized the Original Creole

Band, with Keppard and other Olympia musicians for its beginning. By 1913 the Original Creole Band had extended its vaudeville tours to cross-country proportions; for five years the band toured, reaching a substantial majority of the forty-eight states, going as far west as California, as far north and east as Maine. The band was notable for its cornet player, the redoubtable Keppard, and for a succession of clarinetists, starting with George Baquet, the only man in the band in his time who could read music. Baquet's skill was especially notable in the lower register, in which he carried the brunt of melodic responsibility. Keppard, a man with a large drinking and eating capacity, was a bustling showman on the stage; he could match Baquet's low notes on the cornet and then begin the first of many attacks on the high register which culminated in those screeching passages for dogs' ears played by Duke Ellington's trumpeter Cat Anderson and Stan Kenton's Maynard Ferguson. Baquet later was replaced by Big Eye Louis Nelson and Jimmy Noone, the last of whom was perhaps the most impressive not only of this trio of clarinetists but of all the New Orleans performers on that instrument. Keppard, in the course of his years with the Original Creoles, reported in to New Orleans from time to time. On some of those trips he would sit in with the Eagle Band, with which he appeared off and on from 1907 until about 1915. It was the most important of his New Orleans attachments, outside of the Olympians and the Creoles, although he was also heard to advantage in his occasional appearances with other bands around town and during his longer employment with the pianist Richard M. Jones at George Few-clothes' Cabaret and with his own band at Pete Lala's Cafe in 1915.

In its time, the Eagle Band made room for many of the most persuasive of New Orleans jazz voices. Its clarinetists included the talented son of Picou's teacher, Lorenzo Tio, Jr., Big Eye Louis Nelson, and, best of all, Sidney Bechet. Its cornetists, in addition to Keppard, included at various times Mutt Carey and Bunk Johnson. Bunk, whose immediate earlier work was with the Superior Band, from 1905 to 1912, led his musicians through the full range of jazz jobs. When they played a dance, they advertised, "The Eagle Boys fly high," and indeed they did, at Saturday night dances at the Masonic Hall, in their weekday and Sunday marches, and out of town at such places as Milneburg on Lake Pontchartrain, where there were good times out of doors, some of which were caught musically in the famous "Milneburg Joys." Never did the Eagle Band expand its size for its marching engagements; always you could hear the dancing lines of Lorenzo's or Sidney's clarinet, of Mutt's or Bunk's cornet, of Jack Carey's or Frankie Duson's trombone. Of them all, the men who established the firmest reputations were Sidney Bechet and, in recent years especially, Bunk Johnson. Bunk was rediscovered in 1938, when Louis Armstrong suggested that one of the writers for that invaluable symposium, *Jazzmen*, look him up to find out more than was known about early New Orleans jazz. William Russell found him in New Iberia, a small town near New Orleans, with his *Jazzmen* colleagues bought Bunk a new set of teeth, and listened long and sympathetically to his stories. In the next few years Bunk recorded, appeared on the West and East Coasts, and made a successful run at the Stuyvesant Casino in New York in the fall of 1945 and the winter of 1945–1946.

Known as "Bunk" long before the extravagant estimates of his prowess began to appear in the women's fashion magazines, and before the editors of *Jazzmen* bought him a lien on posterity along with his new teeth, William Geary Johnson had joined King Bolden at the age of sixteen. He brought a second cornet into play in the jazz ensemble and, if his mid-forties appearances can be trusted, a variety of restrained brass sounds. He was born in 1879, and his career extended from 1895 to 1931, with a revival from 1942 until 1949, when he died. In his earlier days he toured the South, the West, and the Atlantic States with minstrel shows and circus bands, played in several New Orleans outfits, and undoubtedly had some influence on most of the cornetists coming up in the Crescent City from the beginning of this century until the red-light district was shut down in November 1917. It is questionable that Louis Armstrong was his proud student, as has been claimed; not until Louis had been asked many times did he credit Bunk with even a mild tutorial interest in his blowing. Louis, always an agreeable questionee, was satisfied with what he regarded as the facts until interrogated to a standstill by Johnson cultists. For him, as he always said, it was Joe Oliver. "That was my only teacher; the one and only Joe Oliver."

Bunk's return to performance in 1942 brought listeners at least some quality of the music of which he had been an important part in his youth. It also served the enthusiasm of listeners who had inevitable limitations of age and place, who promptly linked Bunk and Buddy Bolden in a cornet pairing of equal importance with that of King Oliver and Louis Armstrong. As Morroe Berger cautions in his article on "Jazz Pre-History—and Bunk Johnson," "It is difficult to find ample justification for such categorical pronouncements." Berger goes on, in a discerning analysis of the size of Johnson's contribution, to point out that "in emphasizing Bunk's position in jazz history, the members of Bunk's admiration society naturally ignore that of early jazzmen who have some claims of their own." It must be remembered that Bunk Johnson was an old man when he reappeared on the jazz scene. It must also be remembered that Bunk had some glittering cornet contemporaries, not only Louis Armstrong but Freddie Keppard, Emanuel Perez, King Oliver, and Oscar Celestin. King Oliver we have been able to hear on records, and Oscar Celestin not only on records but in person—he was still playing in New Orleans in 1950.

Joseph Oliver was born in 1885. In 1900 he was a capable cornetist and was prominently featured in a children's brass band. On one of its tours he got into a nasty fight which left him with a scar on his face for life. The little brass band with which young Joe played made fair money, because in those days the interest in novelty bands was large in New Orleans and the near-by South. The way for novelty outfits had been opened by Emile Auguste Lacoume, Sr., better known as Stale Bread, who was a zither player. Stale Bread played with the Brunies Brothers and Rappolo, and in the late years of the last century he led a "Spasm Band," so called after the sound of its toy and improvised instruments: the harmonica, the zither, a bass formed out of half a barrel with clothesline wire for strings and a cypress stick for a bow, a banjo with four strings constructed from a cheesebox, a soapbox cut down to make a guitar, and anything from tin cans to barrels for drums. In 1903 Stale Bread had to leave the legitimate riverboat band he was then leading (which featured Lawrence Vega on cornet) because of an eye infection that blinded him.

After the early brass-band years Joe worked as a butler and doubled as a cornetist with marching outfits like the Eagle and Onward brass bands, in the second of which he shared solo cornet honors with Emanuel Perez. When he worked with these bands he paid a substitute to buttle for him.

Sometime after 1910 Joe made his way into Storyville and played with a variety of bands. One night he stood on Iberville Street, pointed across the street to Pete Lala's Cafe, where Freddie Keppard was playing, and farther down the street to the spot where Perez was entrenched, and blew the blues. Loud and true he blew and loud and clear he shouted, "There! That'll show them!" This exhibit of lung power and daring established Joe Oliver's majesty, and from then on he was "the King." King Oliver moved into Lala's with a band that featured Lorenzo Tio on clarinet, Zue Robertson on trombone, Buddy Christian on piano, and Zino on drums. By 1918 King Oliver was a major name in New Orleans jazz, and shortly after that he brought the name and the music for which it stood to Chicago; it was one of the most important moves in jazz history.

Oscar Celestin has, like Bunk Johnson, benefited from his longevity. As a cornetist he has been content with simple straightforward melodic lines, which demonstrate nothing like the invention of a Louis Armstrong or a King Oliver, none of the drive of a Freddie Keppard or Mutt Carey. Nonetheless, in the records he made on trumpet from 1924 to 1928, and again in his recent work, there has been a sufficient command of the sweetness of his two horns, trumpet and cornet, and an ease with jazz accents which make his long leadership of the band at the Tuxedo Cafe in Storyville quite understandable. With that band at various times were the clarinetists Lorenzo Tio, Jr., Sam Dutrey, Johnny Dodds, and Jimmy Noone; Johnny St. Cyr, the guitarist who later worked with Louis Armstrong, and the pianist Richard M. Jones. Armand J. Piron, an indifferent fiddler, was also a sometime violinist with the Tuxedo Band. More distinguished than Piron himself was the personnel he recorded with in 1923 and 1924 in New York, such able New Orleans musicians as the Junior Tio, the trumpeter Peter Bocage, the trombonist John Lindsay, and the drummer Louis Cottrell.

Of the remaining Negro cornetists of this period, two deserve more than passing mention. Thomas Carey, known as Papa Mutt or simply Mutt—no compliment to his visage—had a lasting association with the Eagle Band and played with various small combinations around Storyville. In eight record sides made with the trombonist Kid Ory for Rudi Blesh, from 1944 to 1946, Carey shows some vitality, if a limited invention, entirely understandable in a man whose playing years go back to the beginning of this century. Emanuel Perez played cornet with the Onward Brass Band, which goes back

to 1892 according to most estimates. He also played with the Imperial Band, which was in existence during the last four years of
the Onward Band, from 1909 to 1912, and in 1900 he sat beside Picou
in the Excelsior Band. Those who heard him said that his playing
demonstrated the evolution of jazz out of the first formal marching
bands, that though he was essentially a traditional brass-band cornetist, he evinced considerable jazz feeling in his placing of accents.
Of the generation before Louis Armstrong's, he apparently contributed much to the development of jazz styles on cornet.

Edward Ory, known as "Kid" for as long as he has been playing
professionally, is singularly famous among New Orleans trombonists,
and deservedly so. He made his jazz beginnings as an eleven-year-
old member of a kids' "string band" in La Place, Louisiana, where he
was born on Christmas Day, 1889. Later, when the child musicians
were able to buy instruments to replace their homemade ones, the
Kid was a professional and a distinguished one. On trips to New
Orleans after 1905, he sat in from time to time with the Buddy Bolden
band until Bolden was committed to the asylum. An eager student,
Ory pursued his music formally and informally, studying with
private teachers, hanging around New Orleans's best musicians, jumping in with both feet in 1911 when he brought some of his La
Place colleagues with him to stay in the big city. In 1915 he took
over the band at Pete Lala's Cafe and, with the important cooperation
of his musicians, made it perhaps the finest small crew in the city.
Joe Oliver was his cornetist, and Sidney Bechet played clarinet for
him; Henry Morton was on drums, and Louis Keppard on guitar.
When Joe left for Chicago he was replaced by Louis Armstrong.
When Sidney Bechet left to go on tour, Johnny Dodds took his
place. The standards were high. They stayed high until Ory left
for California in 1919, following the Original Creoles' drummer,
Dink Johnson, who had established his Louisiana Six out there. Ory's
band, by then known as Kid Ory's Brown-Skinned Jazz Band, did
well enough around Los Angeles until 1924, but it didn't receive
half the acclaim that the Kid's groups did after 1942, first playing
under Barney Bigard, then with Bunk Johnson, earning a radio
contract on Orson Welles's West Coast show of 1944, ultimately alternating between Los Angeles and San Francisco, where he became
a jazz fixture.

Between the first Ory excursion on the Coast and the second, there were several notable engagements. In 1924 Kid Ory joined Louis Armstrong in Chicago for a short stay and some distinguished records, the justly famous Hot Five and Hot Seven sides of 1925 to 1927. The list of Ory's and Armstrong's collaborations is a list of the most significant records of the years encompassed. "Wild Man Blues," "Potato Head Blues," "Gully Low Blues," "Ory's Creole Trombone," "Struttin' with Some Barbecue," "Hotter Than That," and "Savoy Blues"—to scoop up a 1927 handful—demonstrate the ease of the soloists and the staying power of the New Orleans forms. There were refinements, and these are evident in the very first records of Louis and Ory together in 1925 and 1926, "Gut Bucket Blues" and "Come Back, Sweet Papa"; there are longer, better sustained solos; the texture of the ensemble has changed, moving from a concerted grouping to more of a background for solos; but the essential pull of cornet, trombone, and clarinet is there, handsomely taken up by Louis, Ory, and Johnny Dodds. Ory left Louis to play with King Oliver, Dave Peyton, Clarence Black, and the Chicago Vagabonds, in that order, but neither in those appearances nor with his own bands in the forties, after he left retirement, does he show the cumulative power his solos always had with Louis. What he's never lost is the definitive slide—notes clearly out of a trombone— which the instrument had to have in New Orleans jazz, and the neatly filed short melodic phrases copied by a whole generation of trombonists.

Ory's clarinet confrere in the Armstrong days in Chicago was Johnny Dodds, to some the finest clarinetist in jazz, to others anathema. A native of New Orleans, a veteran of the Eagle, Tuxedo, and Ory bands there, he started his recording activity in 1923 with King Oliver. It reached an early peak with Louis, and was extended until June 1940, two months before he died, with various combinations of musicians under his own leadership. One of his best known couplings, "Wild Man Blues" and "Melancholy," shows off one of his most able devices, the alternation of rows of skipping notes and long sustained tones. Both tunes appeared again on Decca, eleven years after the first recording, which was made for Brunswick in 1927 with Louis, Earl Hines, and other Armstrong musicians. The 1938 sides, separately issued, were made with three members of the John Kirby band (trumpeter Charlie Shavers, drummer O'Neil Spencer, Kirby himself on bass), with Louis's ex-wife Lil

Armstrong on piano, and Teddy Bunn on guitar. It may be heresy to Dodds enthusiasts to say so, but there is a striking advance in the second recordings over the first. Dodds plumbs his chalumeau register, the lower range of the clarinet, with a touching melancholy, and moves his two-beat accents in beside the four-beat mastery of Shavers with no loss of style and a considerable gain of beat. He was forty-six when he made these sides and obviously capable of further development.

When it was that Sidney Bechet ceased development it would be hard to say, but unless one has an addiction for his jazz rather than an affinity, it must be admitted that at some point there was an end to his musical growth, and possibly at an early point. Perhaps his very early blossoming as a soloist accounts for the fixing of his style and ideas and playing patterns and sound at some mid-point in his career. He was a sometime guest with Freddie Keppard's band in his native New Orleans when he was eight, and a year later became a protégé of the clarinetist George Baquet. When he was thirteen he was playing with his brother's band and at seventeen he joined the Eagle Band. A year later he toured Texas with Clarence Williams and returned to New Orleans to join the Olympia Band under King Oliver. Chicago was next, in the summer of 1917, and it provided a series of jobs, with Freddie Keppard at the De Luxe Cabaret and with Tony Jackson at the Pekin. He went to Europe with Will Marion Cook's mammoth concert orchestra in 1919, stayed three years, then after three years around New York he returned to the Continent to stay until 1930. In Europe he led the orchestra at different times in three editions of *The Black Revue*, and toured Russia with a band that included the New Orleans trumpeter Tommy Ladnier. From 1928 on he was in and out of the Noble Sissle orchestra, in the United States and in Europe, until the end of 1938. Afterward, renowned as a clarinetist and soprano saxophonist, he played with his own little bands and made a variety of records for a variety of minor and major labels, but he certainly did not offer a variety of ideas.

No such repetition constricts his early records. With Clarence Williams' Blue Five from 1923 to 1925, Bechet played something approaching a long melodic line, scooping pitch on his two instruments in the way that Johnny Hodges later polished. Some of Bechet's best work appears on the Clarence Williams records that featured

Louis Armstrong on cornet and Charlie Irvis, who later joined Duke Ellington, on trombone. There is some persuasive reed blowing on "Mandy Make Up Your Mind" and "I'm a Little Blackbird Looking for a Bluebird," some of it on soprano and some of it on the sarrusophone, an instrument of the oboe family named after the French bandmaster Sarrus, who introduced it into the military band, where, except for such occasions as this one, it fortunately has remained.

Perhaps the most famous of Sidney Bechet's many records are those he made in 1932 with a band he called the New Orleans Feetwarmers. He and Tommy Ladnier match styles and tremolos effectively in the "Maple Leaf Rag," "Shag," and "I Found a New Baby." Teddy Nixon's trombone fits, and the rhythm section gets an apposite beat on these and the other three sides. Here, for some of us, Bechet's contribution to jazz ceases, and thereafter his quivering course through blues and the standard tunes of the jazz repertory becomes difficult listening. For others—a fair-sized audience in the United States and a majority of jazz listeners in Europe—his mastery was never more evident than in the years after World War II when his vibrato bounced careeningly through every performance. But it is no reflection on his appreciable contribution to reed styles to report that his latter-day oscillations set some people's teeth on edge, never so much as in his One Man Band record, in which he played clarinet, soprano and tenor saxes, piano, bass, and drums through "The Sheik" and "Blues of Bechet" for Victor.

Last of the clarinet masters of the first two decades of the twentieth century, and possibly the best, is Jimmy Noone. Born on a farm outside New Orleans, he came to his instrument later than Bechet, but early enough, at the age of fifteen, to develop a considerable skill by 1913, when he was nineteen. His teachers were Sidney Bechet and the Tio brothers, all of whom he replaced in different bands as he came of playing age and they moved around, in and out of New Orleans. He was in the Tuxedo Band for a while and played with Richard M. Jones at Fewclothes'. He played with Armand Piron's polite orchestra in the war years of 1917–1918, when Storyville had closed down, but earlier he had got his full playing experience in that quarter with the bands already mentioned, with Kid Ory, and with his own band at Frank Early's cabaret, where he shared leadership with the cornetist Buddy Petit. He toured briefly with the Original Creoles and was one of the first of the important Orleanians

to settle in Chicago, where he joined King Oliver in 1918, Freddie
Keppard briefly in 1919, and then Doc Cook's Dreamland Orchestra.
In the fall of 1926 Jimmy took his own band into the Apex Club,
earlier known as The Nest, in this year a club of some social distinction. While there he made twelve sides with Earl Hines on piano,
Joe Poston on alto saxophone, Bud Scott on banjo, and Johnny
Wells on drums. Eight of these fine 1928 performances have been
reissued in the Brunswick Collectors Series and offered as "a perfect
insight to an important period in American music—*Chicago style.*"
Technically these are Chicago records—they were made there; they
use Chicago musicians by adoption, such as Earl Hines; they include
saxophone, unheard of in New Orleans and proscribed after the
Diaspora in so-called New Orleans combinations, not by the musicians
themselves but by their critics. Actually these records are among the
best presentations of the abiding procedures and playing atmosphere
of New Orleans jazz. Without any brass, the clarinet and alto combination, with a decisive rhythm-section beat behind it, leads bright
ensemble figures ("Apex Blues," "I Know that You Know," "Four
or Five Times," "Monday Date"). Jimmy weaves his clarinet around
his ensemble, in and out of alto statements of the theme, in and out
of the ensemble ("Sweet Lorraine," "I Know that You Know,"
"Every Evening"). On several of the sides, notably "I Know that
You Know," he puts down a series of fast runs, scalar ascents and
descents, rehearsing the same figure over and over but with little
changes of chord or key and larger changes of register, all of which
suggest the Picou of "High Society," the Dodds and Bechet of innumerable performances; but he never fails in invention or technique as other players do. Like Johnny Dodds, Jimmy Noone recorded off and on through the twenties and thirties, made some sides
with Louis Armstrong (accompanying the blues singer Lillie Delk
Christian), and some with modern musicians in Chicago for Decca.
Like Johnny Dodds, Jimmy Noone had the adaptability to fit with
Charlie Shavers' trumpet and Pete Brown's alto; his new versions of
the "Apex Blues" (called "Bump It" in 1937), "I Know that You
Know," and "Four or Five Times" have all the cohesion of the old
ones made nine years earlier, and a new drive that came in with
swing as well. In November 1943, five months and three days before
he died, he made four sides for Capitol in one of recording director
Dave Dexter's impressive attempts to catch the fine older men of jazz

before it was too late. Working with Jack Teagarden on trombone, Billy May on trumpet, Dave Matthews on tenor saxophone, and a rhythm section of Joe Sullivan, Dave Barbour, Artie Shapiro, and Zutty Singleton, in up-tempo and ballad performances, Jimmy showed still the big, pure, and lovely tone, the controlled vibrato, neither too fast nor too slow, the same intelligent use of such devices as the trill and the register jump, the same facility over all the clarinet's range. No wonder he had such hordes of imitators, from Frank Teschemacher and Benny Goodman to Woody Herman, Joe Marsala, and Pee Wee Russell.

There were few pianists in New Orleans jazz of the quality of Keppard, Oliver, Armstrong, or Noone. There were, as a matter of fact, few pianists. The marching bands and the bands who played the advertising wagons couldn't use a pianist; the cabaret bands didn't want one very often. The major contributions of keyboard artists were made first in the bordellos and later wherever ragtime performances were in favor. Of the latter, more must be said in the history of the New Orleans migrations. From the bordellos a few men emerged: Richard M. Jones, who also led his own band at Fewclothes' but made his larger impression later on in Chicago; Tony Jackson, who found his place as a singer and pianist in New York; the first boogie-woogie crew, who must have influenced the second wave of C-major tremolists, the famous Chicagoans; and Ferdinand Joseph (Jelly Roll) Morton, who talked at least as well as he played piano and talked himself into a major role in jazz history.

The words and the music, the legend and the life of Jelly Roll fill a compendious series of Library of Congress records—now transferred to Circle long-playing records as *The Saga of Mister Jelly Lord*—and a book taken from them—Alan Lomax's *Mister Jelly Roll*. As the notes for the records have it, "the composite length of *The Saga of Mister Jelly Lord* is over seven hours—the length of three grand operas, five full-scale musical concerts, or fifteen complete symphonies—and it consists entirely of the talking, piano-playing, and singing of one man. . . . This would seem to signify that this one man was one of wide and varied genius, a man of towering stature in his field." It would rather, and it seems to me that it does, signify that Jelly Roll Morton was around a long time, played some, learned some, and talked more. He is an important exhibit; through his talking and playing much of our knowledge of Storyville life and musical times is substantiated, broadened, put to rights. He was something less than a great pianist; we can't even be sure he was an original one, so much of what he claimed as his own was obviously public domain in jazz or other men's doing. There was, for example, that famous 1938 article in *Downbeat*, in which he pre-empted the whole field for himself. It began: "It is evidently known, beyond contradiction, that New Orleans is the cradle of *jazz*, and I, myself, happened to be the creator in the year 1901, many years before the Dixieland Band organized." He went on to explain that the first stomp was his, "written in 1906, namely 'King Porter Stomp.' " When he "happened to be in Texas" in 1912, and one of his "fellow musicians" brought him a copy of the "Memphis Blues," he discovered that "the first strain is a Black Butts strain all dressed up," that is, the "strictly *blues*" of "a Boogie-Woogie player," and that the second strain was his ("I practically assembled the tune").

Jelly Roll's extravagances and exaggerations need no examination, or very little. They tell us more about the man than the music, show some of his humor and more of his pathos. But sandwiched in between the wild personal history and the overworked claims are much of the color of jazz and the mutual impact of jazz and Jelly Roll Morton. He was, as the Germans who have taken to writing about jazz would say, *echt* New Orleans, a real live Storyville piano player. He was born in New Orleans in 1885, brought up in Gulfport, Mississippi, and early turned to music—at seven, he said, working out on the guitar, and right afterward studying and playing the piano, "then considered the female instrument," Jelly Roll explained. With a certain diffidence he admitted that he was "always called a freak of a pianist" but hastened to add that he "always managed to pull the crowd any place I played." From him comes documentary evidence of the conscious use of French and Spanish materials, the shaping of an old French quadrille, much played in the Vieux Carré, into the rag known as "Tiger," the "mixture of Spanish with Negro ragtime," which, he said, "sounded great it seemed to the world, because when I played I was almost mobbed, people trying to get a peek at me." Where he played was Gulfport at first, then, on his return to New Orleans in 1909, wherever his two immediate mentors, Richard M. Jones and the St. Joseph Brass Band cornetist Sullivan Spraul, could find a job for him. In the year of his return he became the solo pianist at Tom Anderson's Annex and stayed, with side trips to Alabama, Georgia, and points north of New Orleans, some as far away as Chicago and Seattle, until 1915, when he moved to California. He stayed on the Coast until 1923, then spent five years in Chicago and seven in New York. He ran his own night club in Washington from 1936 to 1938. He returned to Los Angeles in 1938, to remain until his death in the summer of 1941.

Jelly Roll recorded off and on from 1922 to 1940. He made his epochal Library of Congress records in May 1938—epochal in the precise sense of the word: they recorded an epoch of jazz in which Jelly Roll's part was at first important. He saluted the Gulfport pianist King Porter in the "King Porter Stomp," which, in one form or another, had staying power in jazz until the forties, quickly and brilliantly adopted as it was by the first swing bands—Benny Goodman's, for example, and later Harry James's. He transformed the "Miserere" from Verdi's *Il Trovatore* into a workable jazz piano piece, perhaps the first conscious attempt to "jazz the classics." He set an Indian song to jazz, and many a French and Cajun tune was rolled off his keys. Playing cards were "jazzed" in his "Georgia Skin Game," and innumerable blues and rag variations were named and catalogued as his compositions—such tunes as "The Pearls," "Turtle Twist," and "Red Hot Pepper"; the latter, pluralized, named his most famous recording combinations from 1926 to 1930.

As a pianist he offered revealing insights into Storyville keyboard practice. The much discussed polyrhythms of ragtime found effective expression in his hands—three beats against four, dotted eighths and quarters against quarter-note accents, triplets against an even four or a syncopated two. One encounters enough uncertainty in identifying these rhythms in traditional terms to make clear the subtleties of the style; these are only suggestions of the contrasts in time. With this considerable rhythmic skill, however, went something less engaging, a plunking insistence on the beat, a reiterative melodic line that sometimes ragged rather than sparked a phrase, and a very limited harmonic imagination. If Jelly Roll Morton's understanding of jazz had obtained, and no other had developed, as his most ardent admirers seem to wish, jazz would have remained in a tight vise, of which the most striking example would be the ragged riffing of the least inventive swing musicians whose simple-minded recitals of two- and four-bar clichés helped to bring their own era to an untimely end.

Other men must be included in this group of sturdy Negro musicians. There is the trombonist George Filhe, whose first appearances go back at least to 1892, when he was twenty, who played with the Onward Brass Band, the Peerless, and the Imperial, and got to Chicago early, in 1915. In Chicago Filhe had his own band for a while, worked with such men as Emanuel Perez, Bechet, and the junior Tio, and contrasted his low-register looping and smearing with Bab Frank, who played the instrument for which "High Society" was originally designed, when it was a straightforward marching piece—the piccolo —and played it hot. Filhe made all the logical New Orleans connections—Carroll Dickerson, Dave Peyton, and King Oliver—then retired when jazz retired from prominence, along with so much else, in 1929.

A trombonist to go along with Filhe is Zue Robertson, who retired a year later, in 1930, after a wonderfully varied career. Zue, christened Alvin, was born in 1891, started on piano, switched to trombone at thirteen, did about a year on the road with Kit Carson's Wild West Show in 1910, and played with most of the New Orleans jazzmen— in the Olympia Band and with the touring Original Creoles, with his own band in Storyville, with Freddie Keppard, Bab Frank, the perky piccoloist, and Jelly Roll Morton in Chicago, and with King Oliver and Dave Peyton. From 1926 to 1929 Zue played piano again, and organ, at Harlem's distinguished theaters, the Lincoln and the Lafayette.

Two men used with special distinction the horn or tortoise-shell plectrum to pluck banjo and guitar strings in New Orleans jazz— Johnny St. Cyr and Bud Scott. St. Cyr is the redoubtable rhythm man who kept such a fine beat going for Jelly Roll Morton's Red Hot Peppers and Louis Armstrong's Hot Five and Seven; he proved then, as Allan Reuss and Billy Bauer did later with Benny Goodman and Woody Herman, that the plectrum beat is fundamental to a jazz rhythm section for sound, for evenness of accent, and to draw the other rhythm instruments together. Bud Scott, like Zue Robertson, did a lot of traveling on the road, was an important member of Kid Ory's first California band, and reaches back to the legendary music

—to Buddy Bolden, with whom he played when he was in his teens, in about 1906, to the Olympia Band, Freddie Keppard, and Jelly Roll. In Chicago he was with King Oliver and recorded with Jimmy Noone. In California he was an important part of the sporadic jazz revivals of the forties.

There have been lots of bass players, but none so famous as Pops Foster on what used to be called the string bass to distinguish it from the wind bass, the tuba, and sousaphone, which at first were used more frequently than the stringed instrument outside New Orleans. George Foster was born in 1892 and early learned to play the bass from his sister Elizabeth, after starting to play the cello. He was much in demand for advertising wagons, marching bands, and cabaret outfits; he put in time with the Eagle and Magnolia bands, Freddie Keppard, and Kid Ory, whom he later joined in California. Pops was one of the riverboat musicians who brought New Orleans music north, a sometime St. Louis musician, and for many years—with Luis Russell's band, which became Louis Armstrong's after 1935—the recognized leader of his profession. In the swing era too he was much on call for records with other men who were in demand at recording studios: he was reliable, he put down a good walking beat, he had learned to read music.

Pops's opposite number on drums, a popular recording musician much in demand in the thirties, is Zutty Singleton, who has long forgotten the Arthur James that originally preceded his surname. Zutty's genial qualities, his unfailing good humor, his big bass drum boom, paraded through a hundred sides or more, with Jelly Roll Morton, Sidney Bechet, Louis Armstrong, Red Allen, Mildred Bailey, Roy Eldridge, and his own recording band in 1935, 1940, and 1944. Born in 1898 in Bunkie, near New Orleans, Zutty began to play around the big town after the big time was over, but he played with some of the big men, with Big Eye Louis Nelson and John Robechaux's band, with the Tuxedo Band and the most famous of the riverboat leaders, Fate Marable. In Chicago he was with Jimmy Noone and Louis Armstrong among others, and with Roy Eldridge's memorable little band at the Three Deuces in 1935 and the next year. In New York he played with Fats Waller in 1931, with Vernon Andrade's popular Harlem band, and with Bobby Hackett downtown at Nick's. In Los Angeles Zutty has played with everybody who wanted to set a two-beat syncopation on the snare drums beside the bass drum four, and with more modern jazz musicians as well. He has again and again opened his capacious memory to part-time and full-time jazz historians and kept alive all-night sessions, scheduled and impromptu, as much with his good New Orleans humor as his good New Orleans time. He has no inflated opinion of the New Orleans music he has listened to and played, nor does he put it disparagingly in its place. He is one of the few direct links with the great city and its early great jazzmen who realizes that a beginning is a beginning, that this was an unusually good beginning, but that what came after was often good too—and sometimes better.

There is some of the same graciousness and perspicacity in the other famous New Orleans drummer who began in and went out from Storyville—Warren Dodds, Johnny's younger brother, best known as Baby because of that familial connection. Baby Dodds is older than Zutty by two years and closer to the first important bands by perhaps a decade. His playing experience before the 1917 closing order included stints with Willie Hightower's band, with Papa Oscar Celestin's band at the 101 Ranch, and a quartet at Fewclothes' Cabaret. His associates were some of the brilliant musicians and more of the less striking, whose skills must have been fair, judging by the work of one of them, Kid Shots Madison, a cornetist who came to prominence in the thirties and forties when a generation of young enthusiasts began once more to listen to New Orleans jazz on the spot. Baby Dodds was in the Eagle Band in its late years, worked the boats with Marable and Chicago with King Oliver, and during the last twelve years of his brother Johnny's life was with him most of the time. He played with Louis's wife Lil's band, with Louis and Kid Ory and Bud Scott, with Jimmy Noone, and with his own band. His recording activity has been large and full and, on the whole, impressive in the tradition that sets rim shots and gourd and bell noises on a par with the regular beat and sees perhaps as much comedy as drive in the central member of the rhythm section. In 1947, as a member of Rudi Blesh's broadcasting band, he played in a two-part radio battle of bands opposite a group that I organized. He listened with interest when he wasn't playing, and asked serious and probing questions of the finest of bebop drummers, Max Roach. He complimented not only Max but Charlie Parker, Dizzy Gillespie, Lennie Tristano, and Billy Bauer. Much of the time that the modern musicians were playing he just looked up and across the studio at them with a smile on his face and a warm expression in his eyes, as if to say what he later almost put into words, that he was proud to be a musician in the same music, that there were no terrifying differences between the old and the new, that good jazz was good jazz.

Chapter 7

LOUIS

In the second and third decades of this century musicians arose in New Orleans who transformed patterns, enlivened chords, extended the length of the melodic line, and intensified the central rhythmic drive of jazz. At least one of them, Louis Armstrong, demonstrated the individual splendor available to a sufficient talent in a restricted music. It is as a background for Louis and his successors that early New Orleans jazz has its most lasting interest.

It is not to disparage the achievement of the generations of Buddy Bolden, Bunk Johnson, and Freddie Keppard that I praise Louis Armstrong. His contribution is such, however, that it eclipsed the performances of his predecessors for many years. Without granting Louis the stature of William Shakespeare, it could be suggested that he arose from his background and learned from his predecessors as Shakespeare picked up the threads of Tudor drama. One can go too far with such analogies, but here there is a clear parallel. Individual greatness is not entirely self-generated. To understand Louis and appreciate his music, one must understand and appreciate the men who preceded and taught him.

Louis Armstrong's first big noise as a public performer was made on New Year's Eve in 1913 when he shot a pistol into the air in celebration of the coming year, which was to mark the opening not only of the First World War but of the career of the first major figure in jazz history. Louis's coming-out party was held at the New Orleans Waifs' Home, where he was sent for shooting off the pistol.

Louis's dates are easy to remember; they all coincide with major events. He was born on July 4, 1900; he was incarcerated in 1914; he led his first band in 1917, the year the United States entered the war and also the year that the New Orleans red-light district was shut up by order of the Secretary of the Navy. Like George M. Cohan be-

70

fore him, Louis was a Yankee Doodle Dandy, born on Independence Day. Cohan exploited his birthday for all it was worth—and it was worth a great deal in his illustrious career as musical chronicler of American patriotism. Louis has never paused in public to think over the significance of his birthday, but the date is a happy coincidence, and it is still more significant that that particular July Fourth was in the year 1900. For at the turn of the century jazz was rising slowly, laboriously, from its mangy manger, the sporting houses and muddy streets of New Orleans.

When young Armstrong burst upon the scene with a bang from his pistol, twelve and a half years later, he wanted to make a bigger noise than anybody else. It's questionable whether he did that night, but certainly he did when he began playing cornet in New Orleans bands a few years later. He made the biggest noise any single instrumentalist ever made in jazz; he made almost all the noises and riffs and tunes and tone progressions that shaped jazz and made it a legitimate art form instead of just parlor entertainment in New Orleans houses of joy.

At the city's Waifs' Home, Professor Peter Davis taught him to play the bugle for the Home's formal occasions, and then the cornet in the Home's brass band. And so, barely in his teens, Louis did just what all the adult jazzmen incubating jazz in New Orleans did. With his musical colleagues at the Home, Louis joined in performing a juvenile version of basic New Orleans jazz. He played for funerals and for basket parties; he marched up and down the city's streets and parks, "taking up," as he says, "all kinds of collections," matching the beat of the clinking coins with two and four to the bar. The Boldens and Johnsons and Olivers played for a living; Louis played for a penance, but it finally earned him a better living.

Sitting in his comfortable parlor in his home in Queens, New York, years later, Louis looked back over this part of his life and laughed. With very little solemnity and considerable humility he reviewed the basic facts, stated some vital opinions, and cleared up some myths and legends.

"Yes," he said, "it was Professor Davis taught me to blow cornet. I used to hang around Bunk and the other guys, but they were too busy to pay much attention to me. I never took a lesson from any of them."

He learned the lines and planes of jazz from the first king of jazz,

Joe Oliver. "Joe Oliver taught me more than anyone—he took up his time with me. If there's anybody who should get any credit—that is, *if* there is any—please give it to the great master of the olden days— Joseph King Oliver. . . . Yass Lawd. . . . There's the man that's responsible for my everything in the world of Swing-Jazz-Hot-Ragtime or any kind of music you might call it. . . . Joe used to call himself my stepfather, because I was like a son to him, he said. He sure acted like a father to me." Joe lived up to his self-assigned role with an enlightened musical paternalism for which jazzmen ever since have had cause to be thankful.

What was Louis's first professional job?

"If you count them honky-tonks, then it was Madranga's, at Franklin and Perdido Streets, a real honky-tonk, with Boogers on piano and Sonny Gobee on drums."

"It was all honky-tonks, one after another," until 1917, when a drummer "who was also a good businessman," Joe Lindsay, organized a little band with Louis. "We got all of King Oliver's extra work; Joe was looking out for his boy."

Then Joe left town, journeyed up the river to Chicago on the trip that jazz historians regard as epochal, the trip that started jazz on its way from the Crescent City to all the other cities of the United States. Louis took his place with the band that Oliver had led and left behind, the band that had been the King's and trombonist Kid Ory's. "It was kicks," Louis says. "Playing Joe Oliver's cornet parts made me feel important."

Louis Armstrong was important, then as later. Most of musical New Orleans was aware of his size as a jazz musician, greatly appreciative of the strength and clarity of his tone, the drive of his beat, and the resourcefulness of his melodic invention. He carried all these jumping assets from band to band: a year with Ory; another in Fate Marable's crew, playing the riverboats; then the Jaz-E-Saz Band with Picou and Sam Dutrey and Pops Foster and Baby Dodds; many months at the Orchard Cabaret in the French Quarter with Zutty Singleton's band ("I was the leader," Zutty says, "but Pops was teaching us all"); a year with Luis Russell and Albert Nicholas and Barney Bigard, among others, at The Real Thing, a cabaret on Rampart Street ("The music was almost as much fun as Ory's cooking," Barney says, extending Louis a compliment just short of the ultimate). Then Louis was ready for his own hegira up the Mississippi to Chicago. Joe

Oliver sent for him to play in his band. Louis felt that he was ready. "In those early years none of us bothered about reading; a good ear was enough. But by the time I got to Joe's band I could see those notes; "I was advancing," Louis recalls with pride. He joined the King Oliver band in Chicago at the Lincoln Gardens Cafe in July 1922, playing with Johnny Dodds on clarinet, Honore Dutrey on trombone, Bill Johnson clunking the banjo, Lil Hardin on piano, and Baby Dodds paradiddling and doodling on the drums. Louis himself played second cornet to Joe Oliver's first. Word got back to Louis's mother, Mary Ann Armstrong, that Louis was sick and didn't have a very good job. She rushed up to Chicago to see for herself. "One night I was sitting on the stand, blowing, when who should I see, coming through the jitterbugs, but Mary Ann. When she saw what a fine job I had and how big and fat and happy and healthy I was, she cried. She spent the rest of the night right on the stand with us and we all missed cues and muffed stuff, we were so happy."

In 1923 Louis recorded many sides with the Oliver band, playing the blues ("Sobbin'," "Riverside," "Canal Street," "Weather Bird," "Camp Meeting," "Working Man," "Krooked," and "Dippermouth"), and the stomps ("New Orleans," "Southern," "Chattanooga"), and the rags ("Snake," "High Society"). On the "Sobbin' Blues" he even got to play slide whistle; on the others he usually played second cornet back of Oliver's lead, an alternately delicate assist and blasting support.

Like the proverbial second fiddler, however, Louis began to feel a little out of things with King Oliver, even with the solos he got upon occasion. He was glad to accept Fletcher Henderson's offer in 1924. "I had my own part for a change. I enjoyed it. It was fine." Louis really rolls off that "finnnnnnnne" when he recalls joining Smack. He left Chicago gleefully for New York and stayed with Smack for much of 1924 and most of 1925, adding a voice of such authority to the illustrious Henderson band that the records made during his tenure have properly come to be known as Fletcher's Louis Armstrong Period. Three of the best of some forty sides he recorded with Fletcher are in the Columbia album of Henderson reissues—"Sugar Foot Stomp," "What-Cha-Call-Em Blues," and "Money Blues." There you can hear the lusty Louis who sat and blew beside Don Redman, Coleman Hawkins, Buster Bailey, and Big Green—a powerful sound for the time, a handsome suggestion of things to come.

"When them cats [the Henderson musicians] commenced getting careless with their music, fooling around all night, I was dragged, man. I went back to Chicago." Four more years of Chicago, four hectic, hurried years of Windy jazz. He went back to a band at the Dreamland Cafe and to studying music with renewed interest and vigor and attachment. The interest and vigor and attachment were due partly to the leader of the band, Lil Hardin, with whom he studied and whom he married. His earlier marriage, to smart little Daisy Parker in New Orleans, had been short-lived, although he still sees Daisy on trips back home.

From 1925 to 1929 Louis was a very busy man in Chicago. He was a recording name now. His sides with Smack and a batch with blues singers Bessie and Clara and Trixie Smith and Ma Rainey and Coot Grant and Maggie Jones and Sippie Wallace and Josephine Beatty and Eva Taylor and Virginia Liston, his work with Clarence Williams' Blue Five and the Red Onion Jazz Babies had made him a name. He was entitled to his own recording band. First the band was Lil's, Lil's Hot Shots: then it was Louis Armstrong's Hot Five in 1925 and 1926. It had the same personnel: Louis and Lil, Johnny Dodds, Kid Ory, and Johnny St. Cyr. It became the Hot Seven in 1927, with Pete Briggs on tuba and Baby Dodds added. It was the Hot Five again later in '27, and in '28 it reached its peak as a quintet, with Earl Hines and Zutty Singleton.

In '26 and '27 Louis played a lot of trumpet. He was a part-time sideman with the large orchestra at the Vendome Theatre which Erskine Tate led, and with Ollie Powers, and then, in the spring of 1926, he joined Carroll Dickerson's equally big band at the Sunset Cafe at Thirty-fifth and Calumet, which Joe Glaser owned. Earl Hines was on piano, and this is where he and Louis and Zutty formed their close musical and social partnership, a lasting association of sounds and ideas. It was at the Sunset too that they formed the business partnership with Joe Glaser which eventually made them all a lot of money. Louis took over the band at the Sunset when Dickerson left. Then he had a short try with his own Hot Six at the Usonia, where "We went in business; we went out of business." The attempt to buck the newly opened and successful Savoy Ballroom started on Thanksgiving Day of 1927; it flopped—his Hot Six died a cold death. Louis capitulated to the Savoy and Carroll Dickerson, rejoining the latter at the former. While he had unquestionably lost some *cachet* in reassuming his status as somebody else's featured soloist, his records were in such demand, there was such a commanding quality to his obbligatos for blues singers and choruses alone, that he was always on call for special jobs. He made numerous side-trips on Sundays to St. Louis, for a couple of days at a time to New York's Savoy Ballroom and to other places, to make extra money as an "Extra-Special Attraction—One Night Only—the Great Louis Armstrong!"

In the spring of 1929 Louis—or Pops or Satchmo or Gatemouth or Dippermouth, as he was variously called, depending on the juniority of the speaker or the degree of admiration for the cornetist's capacious lips—and a number of the boys decided to cash in. They elected Louis leader and cut out for New York in a caravan of battered cars, Louis's Ford with glistening yellow wire wheels leading the procession. They arrived in time to greet the stock market crash.

When they got to the big city the only work they could find at first was a job substituting for Duke Ellington at the Auburn Theatre in the Bronx. Duke's bass man, Wellman Braud, set that. But they didn't have to struggle. Shortly afterward, with a band hastily enlarged, came an engagement at Connie's Inn uptown, where they played through the first months of the depression. Then on to California—Louis's first trip West—to front Eddie Elkins' band, with Lawrence Brown on trombone, and "a little kid, a seventeen-year-old cat named Lionel Hampton, on drums."

The next year, 1931, Louis made his first trip back to New Orleans since leaving in 1922, with "a great band, a bunch of cats I picked up in Chicago on my way back from the Coast." They played the Suburban Gardens, an aptly named spot on the outskirts of town. ("I did my own radio announcing and everything!") He hit New York, played some dates as a single, recorded with Chick Webb's band for Victor. Then back to the Coast to take over the band led by alto saxophonist Les Hite, the same one Elkins had led, at the Los Angeles Cotton Club.

This was 1932. In the summer of that year Louis went to Europe for the first time, then came back to New York after four months to do some more work as a single out of Chicago and New York. The next summer he went back to Europe with his third wife, Alpha, to stay until January 1935. Europe was a success, with one sad experience —at the Holborn Empire Theatre in London, where Louis split his lip and played through one whole show, his shirt front covered with blood. "Mmmmmmmm, my chops was beat." He left behind at least one record he wants to hear again, his two-sided "On the Sunny Side of the Street." During the Nazi occupation of France Louis heard that Hugues Panassié had buried a large number of records as a precaution; he said, "That cat'd better unbury that record. If I tried a million times, I'd never make a 'Sunny Side' as good as *that* one."

Leonard Feather, reminiscing years later about Louis's trips to Europe, wrote:

There are few musicians in jazz history who owe more of their fame to Europe than Louis Armstrong. Though Louis was a big name in his own country for many years before his first transatlantic trip, nothing that had happened to him over here could compare with the wild acclaim that greeted him when he first poked his personable head around the edge of the curtain on a memorable first night at the London Palladium in the summer of 1932. . . . Nobody knew what kind of a band Louis would have with him. All they knew was that this almost mythical American figure, whose voice and horn had enlivened a Parlophone record every month or so, was coming miraculously to life. As it turned out, the band assembled for Louis was nothing and nowhere. Later on he toured with two other combinations, one an all-white group which included most of the clique of Scottish musicians, many of whom for some mysterious reason were hipper than the Englishmen. Louis and Alpha were lionized wherever they went. . . .

Louis's success in Great Britain was not entirely unqualified [however]. One noted and dyspeptic critic, Hannen Swaffer, wrote a bitter diatribe in a London daily describing how the "veins in Armstrong's neck stuck out like a gorged python" while he played, and failed to understand how people could consider that his performance of "Tiger Rag" was music. . . .

Louis did a lot more through his visits than merely play a couple of successful tours. He paved the way for the other great American Negro musicians who came over in the following five years; he stimulated the interest and raised the standards of English musicians who need their encouragement at first hand rather than through records. He made countless friends and made the same impression on everyone he met, that here was a man who, not blessed with the educational qualifications of the more fortunate, made his way in life through a combination of great artistry and a heart of unalloyed gold.

When he got back to the States Louis picked up Luis Russell's orchestra and for the next ten years, with one or another variation of the original personnel, he toured America from coast to coast, from the downtown Connie's Inn in New York to the California Cotton

Club. In various sojourns on the West Coast he was featured in several movies, including Mae West's film *Every Day's a Holiday*, *Going Places*, *Pennies from Heaven* with Bing Crosby, *Cabin in the Sky*, *Atlantic City*, and *New Orleans*. Orson Welles, an ardent Louis fan, once had an idea for a film biography of Louis, but it never materialized.

He made many records for Decca after 1935, most of them good. His band has been everything from awful to good, but he himself has almost always been wonderful, a musician's musician of taste and extraordinary skill, whose exquisite trumpet tone, easy melodic variations on the melodies at hand, and marvelous gravel-throated singing style remain the identification of a large and original jazz personality. Occasionally, for one reason or another, Louis has not sounded absolutely right. At one point it was because he was kicking away sixty-five pounds and, in coming down from 230 to 165, he suffered pain and a resultant lack of physical control. At another time it was "beat-up chops" again. At one memorable point, the 1944 *Esquire* concert, it was poor matching of musical styles—his against Roy Eldridge's, Art Tatum's, and Coleman Hawkins'—and poor physical condition. But even at that concert, as records will attest, there were Armstrong moments. There will always be, as long as that inspired Satchel- or Dipper- or Gatemouth wraps itself around a horn.

And there will always be warm friendships in his life, deep family loyalty, and a close attachment to those who have been good to him. Two Joes retain his greatest respect and admiration: Joe Oliver, who sponsored him musically, sponsored and fostered and fathered him; and Joe Glaser, his employer of the Sunset Cafe days in Chicago in 1926 and 1927 and from 1935 on his manager and one of his closest friends. "I can confide in him," says Louis; "I can trust him. He was a wonderful employer twenty years ago; he's a great manager today." The feeling is mutual; Glaser swears by Louis; he would do just about anything for him, a kind of dedication that most people who get to know Louis well sooner or later feel toward him.

Good friends, good food, easy living—these simple but not always easily attainable comforts command Louis's life, and over them all looms music. He loves playing it and singing it. And he loves talking about it, running over his own experiences and discussing all kinds of music with infectious enthusiasm in his rumbling, syllable-crumbling bass voice, with rich diction and ready laugh. But Louis is loath to choose an all-star band, not at all sure that there are "bests" on any horn. "I'm not drastic, like some of the critics," he says. "Each of the cats has his style, and there are lots of wonderful ones, lotsa styles that send me." He likes Johnny Hodges and Benny Carter on alto; Lester Young and Coleman Hawkins on tenor; Benny Goodman, Artie Shaw, and Prince Robinson (a "fine cat from the old school") on clarinet; with Carney ("of course") on baritone; Teagarden and George Washington on trombone; Tatum and Wilson and Earl Hines ("Pops") on piano; Al Casey and Lawrence Lucie on guitar ("that's all I've heard"), and Pettiford ("a very good man") on bass. On drums, "there's a million."

Trumpet? "You know what King Oliver said to me? 'You gotta play that lead sometimes. Play the melody, play the lead, and learn.' And that's what I like to hear, sometimes anyway. Some of that fantastic stuff, when they tear out from the first note and you ask yourself 'What the hell's he playing?'—that's not for me. Personally, I wouldn't play that kinda horn if I played a hundred years; you don't have to worry about my stealing those riffs. So you see, I like a trumpeter like Shelton Hemphill, with Duke. He takes his music serious. He's the best first man of our race, best we have. Then there's Red Allen. And, because I believe in going ahead, all right, there's Roy [Eldridge]. I really give Roy credit; he's trying to lead 'em all."

What about the musicians Louis played with when he first started? How would they stand up today? How *do* they stand up today? "Most of us," Louis says, "the musicians of that time, couldn't stand the gaff today—the pace is too fast for 'em today. They wouldn't hold your interest now the way they did then. You can't go back thirty years, man. It's all right for a novelty. But missing notes and not caring nothin', not a damn, about 'em, you can't play music like that nowadays. Take me back thirty years—I could play that stuff with one finger! Why, I'd live forever! But why should I go back? I want to stay up with the times. Every once in a while I lay an old-fashioned phrase on 'em, but music's better now than it used to be, it's better played now. Whether it's arranged or improvised, the music of today is way ahead of what it used to be. We've advanced a lot since the early days. Music should be played all kinds of ways, anyway. Symphonic stuff, beautiful things, everything goes. If there are people who want to omit arrangements, omit scored backgrounds, omit any kind of music, you tell 'em I said, 'Omit those people!' "

Chapter 8

ACROSS THE TRACKS

When you hear a battered old upright piano clanking away in a barroom scene in a Western motion picture, you're probably listening to ragtime. This is the music so long thought to be directly responsible, all by itself, for jazz. This is the music that was actually a part of jazz. This is the music that Jelly Roll Morton and all the piano professors played in Storyville. This is the music that Buddy Bolden played and that another one of the fathers of New Orleans jazz, Papa Jack Laine, picked up and shaped into a tradition all its own.

Ragtime isn't very difficult to understand, though sometimes it is difficult listening for ears trained to another kind of jazz. Basically, it's a series of syncopations, syncopations on the off beats, the weak second and fourth beats of the bar, by the right hand against syncopations emphasizing the strong beats, the first and third of the four in the bar, in the left hand, syncopations that don't stop, that keep going and changing and moving ahead from the first bar of a ragtime performance to the last. Ragtime is essentially a piano music. It was picked up by all the other instruments and moved around to all the voices of the jazz band, but it started on the piano, and it achieved its greatest distinction as piano music.

The genesis of ragtime is the same as the beginning of all of jazz— in hymns and hunting songs, spirituals and coon songs, minstrelsy and marches. But the place in which it had its most significant early impetus was not New Orleans; it was played in the "tenderloin," the red-light district, the "sporting men's" home of another town. The town was Sedalia, Missouri, a Western town by Eastern standards, with a main street that was convertible from agricultural commerce by day to sporting life by night. The man who more than any other was responsible for the quality and success of ragtime was Scott Joplin.

Scott Joplin, who settled in Sedalia in 1896, published more than fifty ragtime compositions, but he is best known, now as during his lifetime, by the second to reach print, his "Maple Leaf Rag." Both this and the first to be published, "Original Rags," came out in 1899. Joplin wrote a variety of music—songs that suggest Stephen Foster's ballads, waltzes, what he called a "Mexican Serenade," and music for the slow drag, the dance evolved by Negroes to be done to ragtime— as well as an instruction book called *School of Ragtime*. An intelligent man and proud of his heritage, he called one of his rags, "The Chrysanthemum, an Afro-American Intermezzo." In 1903 his first opera was performed in St. Louis. Called *A Guest of Honor*, it was described by its composer as "A Ragtime Opera." In 1911 his unperformed opera, *Treemonisha*, was published by John Stark, his publisher and patron and good friend. A three-act opera, it retains the Aristotelian unities: it takes place during the morning, afternoon, and evening of one day; all of it is laid on a plantation in Arkansas; and it has one story line. The narrative, which Joplin identified in parentheses on the title page as a Story Fictitious, is of a Negro couple named Ned and Monisha, who deal intelligently with their freedom after the Civil War. The title refers to a baby found by Monisha under a tree before her cabin, named after herself and the tree, who is educated and grows up to be a leader of her people.

Scott Joplin died in 1917, the year Storyville was closed and ragtime lost its following, a year pivotal in the large and the small for the American people. In the years before Joplin's death in the Manhattan State Hospital in New York, a generation of able ragtime pianists grew up: Tom Turpin, Louis Chavuin, Ben Harney, Scott Hayden, James Scott, and Luckey Roberts, the flashy ragtimer Duke Ellington imitated so successfully that traces of the imitation still remain in his playing and gestures. Jelly Roll Morton and Tony Jackson, who figured in other aspects of the jazz story, were essentially adept ragtime pianists. James P. Johnson, the New Jersey boy who grew up to be a considerable jazz pianist and Fats Waller's teacher, is entirely in the ragtime tradition. The list is long and impressive, and the music these men wrote and the way they played other men's music are still part of jazz, at this point so subtly interwoven with the music of the modern players who did not grow up as ragtimers that it can be identified only as contrasting rhythms, one of the abiding graces of jazz form.

There were special places that ragtime pianists made their playing homes; two were the Maple Leaf Club in Sedalia and the Rosebud in St. Louis. As the Royal Gardens Cafe in Chicago was immortalized in the "Royal Garden Blues," and as the Savoy Ballroom in Harlem was immortalized in Edgar Sampson's "Stompin' at the Savoy," so Scott Joplin made the Sedalia club famous in the "Maple Leaf Rag" and the St. Louis cafe famous in his "Rosebud March." In these places and others ragtime players fashioned their repertory, one that was played and made a permanent part of jazz by white musicians. Joplin's "Maple Leaf Rag" and Joseph Lamb's "Sensation Rag" are two of the most famous rags still played by Dixieland musicians. Eubie Blake, one of the most talented of the musicians to be influenced by Joplin and Lamb and the other ragtime composers, wrote the score for the enormously successful all-Negro musical of 1921, *Shuffle Along*. Noble Sissle, later famous as a band leader, constructed a superb ragtime lyric for one of the songs in that show, "I'm Just Wild About Harry," which has the lilt and drive of the great rags.

The first distinguished white band in New Orleans, the direct predecessor of the more famous Original Dixieland Jazz Band, was Jack Laine's Ragtime Band, which was gathering musical ideas and skill and an audience at the end of the nineteenth century and beginning of the twentieth, at the same time the music after which it was named was maturing. Laine, who was born in 1873, and his son Alfred enlisted at one time or another up through the First World War the talents of just about all the white jazzmen in New Orleans and environs. His Reliance Brass Band, and later his Ragtime Band, played carnivals, marches, just about all the functions a band that could keep you dancing or marching could play. Two Negroes, Dave Perkins and Achille Baquet, wandered into the Laine band for long periods, but were apparently so white of skin and so blue of eye that they passed unnoticed except as musicians. It was with Laine's band that the famous Dixieland tune, "The Livery Stable Blues," emerged; then it was known as "Meatball Blues." They also played the ragged quadrille called "Tiger Rag"; they called it "Praline," after the famous New Orleans sweet and bumpy raggy candy. It was Laine's outfit that got most of the "advertising-wagon" work; its ragtime accents, its blary sound, told all New Orleans about a forthcoming prize fight, about a restaurant, about a dance, about a Sunday night social, about some new kind of food or furniture. And the "tailgate" trombonist was always perched on the back seat of the advertising wagon, tossing his slide out behind the other musicians so he wouldn't hack their necks or spear their eyes in the cramped quarters behind him.

Papa Laine, in 1951 a handsome white-haired man in his seventies, still remembers his hectic, happy life of four and five decades ago. He was a kind of small-town Meyer Davis, leading some bands, contracting others. At one time he had two or three brass bands going for him and several outfits that played for dancing. He ran a minstrel show at times and played music for the circus. He himself was a drummer; Lawrence Vega was his cornetist, Achille Baquet his clarinetist, Dave Perkins his trombonist; Morton Abraham played the guitar, and Willie Guitar played the bass. In his Reliance Band he had the famous clarinetist Alcide Nunez, known as "Yellow" to his intimates—because of his complexion, not his character. These musicians are remembered with affection by Laine, their leader, and by others who heard them: Vega for his felicity of phrase, sweetness of tone, and drive; Baquet for his punchy staccato playing; Perkins for that brash style which came to be known as barrelhouse or gutbucket; Abraham for his poignancy, possibly out of his Mexican background; Guitar for his wit, on and off the bass, some of which may have been coincidental, such as the fact that he lived on Music Street. In 1951 Nunez was still known around Chicago, where he had come in 1914, for his blues and ragtime skill on the clarinet.

A band which consisted largely of ex-Laine musicians and which preceded the Original Dixielanders to Chicago was Brown's Dixieland Jass Band; as early as 1915 it played at the Lambs' Cafe in the Windy City. This band was a direct outgrowth of an outfit that backed the old vaudeville act of Frisco and McDermott; it was Frisco who sold the Brown band to Chicago cafe owners. In Tom Brown's outfit Larry Shields made his first Northern appearance and demonstrated some of the wooden-toned clarinet authority that later became quite famous with the Original Dixieland group. The six-piece band, in addition to the clarinet (first Gus Mueller, then Shields) and the leader's trombone, consisted of Ray Lopez on cornet, Arnold Loyocano, who doubled on bass and piano, and the drummer Bill Lambert. Most important, it was with this band that "jazz" emerged as a term to describe the semi-raucous, always rhythmic, and quite infectious music these men played. When the band came to Chicago, directly from New Orleans, the word "jass" had a semi-sordid sexual connotation. Chicago Musicians Union officials decided that the competition was neither necessary nor tolerable. They thought that labeling this group a jass or jazz band would be a very successful smear. But their attempt to disparage the Brown band failed; the term caught on, and Brown's Dixieland Band became Brown's Dixieland Jass Band, an exciting purveyor of a new kind of music with a new name as virile as the sounds it described.

When Yellow Nunez came up to Chicago in 1916 he brought up most of the future members of the Original Dixieland Jazz Band: Dominick James (Nick) LaRocca on cornet, Eddie (Daddy) Edwards on trombone, Henry Ragas on piano, and Anton Lada on drums. The band played briefly at the Casino Gardens in Chicago, and during this engagement Nunez and Lada left the band because of a disagreement over money, and perhaps because they thought they were better suited to a band entirely their own.

Lada and Nunez sent to New Orleans for a trombonist (Charlie Panelli), a banjo player (Karl Kalberger), and a pianist (Joe Cawley). They took their new musicians with them to the Athenia Cafe, where they ran at least half a year in 1915, then came to New York to play at Bustanoby's Restaurant, at Thirty-ninth Street and Broadway. In New York they took the name of the Louisiana Five and made a series of records for the Columbia, Emerson, and Edison companies. Some were in the laughing tradition, "Be-Hap-E" and "Clarinet Squawk"; some were closer to sorrow, "Blues My Naughty Sweetie Gives to Me" and "Weary Blues." The Louisiana Five boasted an able clarinetist in Nunez and an unusually well-equipped drummer in Lada. After the Five disbanded, in 1924, Lada went on to write some fine Dixieland songs, to spend five years in Hollywood as musical director of two radio stations, and then to settle down as a songwriter and reminiscent musician.

When Shields joined up in place of Nunez, the Dixieland Jass Band, first at the Schiller Cafe, then at the DeLobbie Cafe, was all set except for an exchange of drummers, Tony Sbarbaro (Spargo) for Johnny Stein, who had been the first replacement for Lada. With Daddy Edwards as manager and Nick LaRocca as musical guiding hand, the ODJB made off for New York and the glamorous Reisenweber's just off Columbus Circle, replacing the Brown band, which was first offered the job. The ODJB was an immediate success. Dancers found its music infectious, party givers found jass to their liking as a noisy background for noisy drinking and talking. The Victor and Aeolian companies both recorded the band.

Its first two Victor record sides, made in February 1917, summed up the band's music: there were the inevitable "Livery Stable Blues" (née "Meatball") and "Dixie Jass Band One-Step." A few days later, the band had the date at which its best-known recording, Nick LaRocca's "Tiger Rag," was made. There were also the "Ostrich Walk," "At the Jazz Band Ball," "Sensation Rag," and "Skeleton Jangle," all classics today, all still played wherever musicians indulge in Dixieland. At later record sessions in 1918, before it went to Europe, the band originated its famous "Clarinet Marmalade," "Fidgety Feet," and "Barnyard Blues." No other tunes that came out of its members' heads ever hit again like these. It had only one other record side that was quite such an epoch-making affair, and that was some years later when the declining band recorded "Margie," with "Palesteena" overleaf.

There were changes in this band before it left for Europe. Pianist Henry Ragas, who was, in one of the unfortunate jazz traditions, an enormous drinker, died in his hotel room in February 1919, and was replaced by several men, who in turn made way for J. Russell Robinson. Daddy Edwards had no eyes for Europe, so Emil Christian took over his trombone role.

The band got to England in March 1919, and was featured in the musical *Joy Bells*, which was otherwise noteworthy only for its most successful song, "The Bells of St. Mary's." The band played at places like Rector's and the 400 Club and became something of a pet diversion of London society.

When it came back to New York after nearly two years of England and Paris, the band began to struggle some and to make a few changes of style and personnel. At last the saxophone made its appearance, played by Benny Krueger, who doubled on alto and tenor saxes. The Dixielanders went commercial in the most invidious sense; they were soon a "true fox trot band." They played what was popular and what was successful, and by the time they got to the Balconades on Columbus Avenue at Sixty-sixth Street in 1923 they were more distinguished for their old tunes, which they still played, though with little of the old energy—"Tiger Rag," "At the Jazz Band Ball," "Jazz Me Blues" and of course the "Livery Stable Blues"—than they were for the actual quality of their performance. Frank Signorelli, who

figured in bands of some jazz importance for the next ten years, replaced Russell Robinson on piano; Larry Shields and Nick LaRocca
went South, where they found Robinson on the police force, and
Daddy Edwards followed them shortly after and wound up coaching
various athletic teams at the New Orleans YMCA. Just before the
Dixielanders broke up, Bix Beiderbecke wandered into the Balconades
and heard them play the tunes that he was to play and reinvigorate in
the following years.

The Original Dixieland Band had not been a great success in its
home town, New Orleans, which is why it assumed the "Dixieland"
tag rather than the name of its home town. This name has ever since
been associated with music that is more or less a direct product of
their performances. What they played was often deliberately funny,
imitating animal sounds in the "Barnyard Blues," human sounds in
most of the other pieces. Theirs was a kind of comedy drama without
dialogue, but full of amusing, identifiable sound, marked for farcical
conflict and belly-laugh climax. It is today a good deal less contrapuntal in its structure, and it has lost its drive because the greater
jazzmen who followed discovered that playing a straight unaccented
four-to-the-bar gets a much better beat than the weak-and-strong
playing, the so-called two-beat, of the Dixie musicians. With the exception of the Lunceford two-beat, which wasn't even vaguely Dixieland but depended on dotted strong beats—anticipations, as they are
called—for its drive, two-beat jazz has lost its fire. It sustained musicians for about ten or twelve years after the dissolution of the Original
Dixieland Jazz Band and then collapsed of its own inherent rhythmic
weakness.

But today, if one listens to the records of the Original Dixieland
Band without prejudice, it is almost impossible to deny the extraordinary vitality and the linear strength of the music that went along
with the comedy. Regarded only historically, the records are exciting. They reflect the contagious conviction of the five musicians; the
skill of a facile clarinetist, Larry Shields, in the Picou tradition, with
surer technique and larger musicianship; and above all, close attention
to the oldest business in music, that of setting melodic line against
melodic line. With none of the sophistication and very few of the
resources of the baroque masters who created their intricate counterpoint out of the heritage of the Gregorian chant, the New Orleans
boys nonetheless understood the essential strength of linear writing.

When, through the din of pre-electric recording, you hear LaRocca's cornet play the melody lead, Shields echo it an octave higher, Edwards underscore it an octave lower, and the piano give it a kind of ground bass, you feel the essential strength, the musical trueness of this form. Relying on trite melodies, the Dixielanders were fortunate in having the blue notes of the blues and the intense steadiness of rhythm that has always characterized good jazz. These things, expressed in a rough counterpoint, make the Original Dixieland Jazz Band still hearable today, in spite of the crudities of such originals as the "Tiger Rag" and the inanities of "At the Jazz Band Ball" and "Jazz Me Blues."

The New Orleans Rhythm Kings came up to Chicago four years after the Original Dixielanders. They differed very little from the Original Dixieland Jazz Band; their music was much the same, their ensemble drive was much less, but two of their soloists were more gifted than any of the Dixielanders. Paul Mares was the leader of the band, which opened in 1921 at Friars' Inn on the near-north side of Chicago, a couple of blocks away from Michigan Avenue and the Art Institute. Mares was the leader, but no star. His outstanding men were Leon Rappolo, the clarinetist, and George Brunies, the trombonist. Mares played trumpet, Jack Pettis played the saxophones—chiefly C-melody—Elmer Schoebel was the pianist and arranged such of the numbers as were arranged, Lew Black played banjo, Steve Brown bass, and Frank Snyder drums. The band played at Friars' Inn for more than two years, and before it was finished as an organization it had the distinction of bringing Ben Pollack into the band picture as its drummer and offering numerous examples in each of its instrumentalists to the distinguished jazz musicians who grew up in Chicago in the next decade. Today the Rhythm Kings' records offer little but Rappolo's clarinet and Brunies' trombone; the ensemble sounds weak and the inspiration lags. When you realize that these musicians played together for four years after the last vigorous performances of the Original Dixieland group, it is no compliment to them to mark the lack of originality. Remaining members may take great pride, however, in the fact that they nurtured Leon Rappolo and played with Brunies when he was at his best.

Leon Joseph Rappolo was born in New Orleans on March 16, 1902, the son of a concert artist, the grandson of a clarinetist, and from the very beginning a character about whom legends inevitably grow. He started as a violinist and switched to clarinet in emulation of his grandfather; he took some lessons and at fourteen decided he was good enough to play in a pit band. He ran away from home to prove his professional stature, and joined the band that was playing for Bea Palmer's act on the Orpheum Circuit; she was one of the big names of 1916 vaudeville, and her husband-pianist, Al Siegel, has since been associated with a large number of successful popular singers only vaguely related to jazz. Rappolo was found by the police of Hattiesburg, Mississippi, and, in accordance with his parents' orders, brought back to New Orleans. There, a few years later, he played at the Halfway House with Albert Brunies' band, which trained one Brunies brother after another—but none of brother George's quality —on various jazz instruments. In this band Leon started and, after his trip to Chicago, ended. With the Halfway House orchestra he played some guitar and snare drum as well as clarinet, and he quickly won the admiration of all the musicians he played with and many he didn't. Just before the New Orleans Rhythm Kings opened at Friars' Inn they persuaded Rappolo to join them, and he stayed with them a couple of years until, sick in mind and wandering in responsibility, he went back to New Orleans to join the Halfway House orchestra of Albert Brunies again. After a brief stay, it was obvious that a mental hospital was the only safe place for Rappolo, and he was incarcerated in one until his death in 1941.

The legends about Rappolo are numerous and just about all unproven. The best known is about his performance on telephone wires while a friend listened, his ear on one of the poles, applauding each well-turned telephone-wire phrase. From stories like this and from Rappolo's unquestionable clarinet authority, engendered by a large tone and a sense of phrasing, came an enormous reputation. Fortunately we have some recorded proof of Rappolo's skill to sustain it.

We don't have anything but a few oldsters' words for the alleged brilliance of Emmett Hardy, the trumpeter and cornetist who played briefly with the New Orleans Rhythm Kings at Friars' Inn, and on riverboats, where they say he was Bix Beiderbecke's strongest and most direct influence. The influence apparently lay in Hardy's preciseness and sweetness of tone and soft attack—all qualities of Bix's playing.

George Clarence Brunies, who was born two years before Rappolo in New Orleans, also came of a musical family. He joined the New

Orleans Rhythm Kings when the band started in 1919, and stayed with them through their most important years, leaving them in 1923, two years before the last records of this group were made. From the very beginning his style was molded by an enormous tone, made burly by his pulverizing slide technique and his cheek-contorting blowing. For twelve years, from 1923 to 1935, Brunies languished in the Ted Lewis band, never, even at its best, a jazz orchestra of any distinction. Finally, with the success of the hit song "The Music Goes Round and Round" at Christmastime in 1935 and the subsequent sensation that Benny Goodman caused, ushering in the big-band "swing" craze, there were jobs again for the New Orleans tailgate artist in legitimate jazz bands. With the New Orleans Rhythm Kings, at the beginning of his career, as later, Brunies made funny noises with his horn and topped the infectious caterwaul with a clown act in which he slid the trombone over its various positions with his foot, lying on the floor to do it and thereby performing a feat that was as amusing, and as successful musically, as Joe Venuti's nimble bowing of the four strings of the fiddle at once. In later years, guided by a numerologist, Brunies changed the spelling of his first name, dropping the final e, and removed the e in his second name, to end up with the name of Georg Brunis. His playing remained unchanged, blowzy as ever, funny as ever, and just as strongly dependent upon a two-beat rhythm.

The line between the humor of these Dixieland musicians—the ODJB's animal imitations or George Brunies' clowning—and pure corn is a very thin one. To the undiscriminating ear it is sometimes difficult to tell the difference between the clumsy, grossly syncopated excesses of the clarinetists Boyd Center and Fess Williams and the trumpeter Clyde McCoy, on the one hand, and the dramatic, sometimes touching, sometimes amusing two-beat cadences of Shields, Rappolo, or Brunies. There are two kinds of music, however, of which the pseudo-Dixieland, really corny musicians are entirely incapable. None of them can ever achieve the poignancy, the searing pathos of a first-rate Dixieland ballad or blues, the kind of torch that in later years was carried by Jack Teagarden on trombone and Bobby Hackett on cornet and trumpet. None of them, not even Spike Jones, who knows better and is satirizing rather than imitating Dixieland, is capable of the lilting humor of Dixieland at its best, when it is burly and boisterous and wonderfully ribald all at once. George

Brunies' tailgate flatulence is amusing in those ways. Whole choruses of ODJB records and ensemble sections of New Orleans Rhythm Kings records are delightful in such a fashion, in knockdown and dragout choruses, at the ends of performances, the so-called ride-outs, and again in the turbulence and tumult and general good humor of a well-performed "Clarinet Marmalade" or "Jazz Band Ball" or "Ostrich Walk." These are the qualities that the white New Orleans musicians had, which became the Dixieland canon: humor sometimes tongue-in-check, sometimes burlesque, and a pleasant nostalgia that sometimes became a more meaningful sorrow. Whatever the final limitations of their style, the music that these musicians brought to Chicago was rich in at least two of the eternal emotions.

Chapter 9

DIASPORA

Thou . . . shalt be removed into all the kingdoms of the earth. (Deuteronomy 28:25.)

The keelboats couldn't have done it. They were only forty to eighty feet long and seven to ten feet across, and they had very few passenger cabins—when they had any at all. It took three or four months to get upstream from New Orleans to Louisville, though the return trip could be made in a month. The keelboatmen of the first decades of the nineteenth century were characters all right; they flung themselves against the river, they danced, they fiddled, they flirted, they fought anybody and everybody—Indians, river pirates, and townsmen. They produced a great legendary figure, Mike Fink, the king of the keelboatmen, and they carried one of the important early strains of American music a long way. The keelboatmen did well by the boating songs and the levee songs, but there weren't enough of them, and their boats were too small, to carry a freight as heavy as jazz, or even its musical ancestors, the spirituals and the worksongs and the minstrel melodies. But the steamboats were big enough and went far enough often enough; they were the logical vehicles of jazz dispersion.

When the *New Orleans* left Pittsburgh for the Gulf of Mexico, in 1811, the steamboat arrived on the Mississippi River. By the middle of the 1820s a hundred or more steamboats were chugging along the Mississippi and the other rivers of the Middle West. By the late 1830s the steamboat route reached along the upper Mississippi to what is now St. Paul; excursions became popular all along the Mississippi— splendid day's outings, more varied and energetic in their entertainment than any other obtainable. Depending on which excursion you took and from where, you might see Indians and the beginnings of new settlements, and if there wasn't adequate entertainment on the

90

boat you could always go ashore to dance and sing and laugh or watch others do so. The Mississippi steamboats were handsome; they had their own distinctive architecture and interior decoration. Mark Twain, whose *Life on the Mississippi* fixed the riverboat forever in American literature, was fervent about the look of the boats. The cabins were hospital-white, with that antiseptic shine that only sailors know how to get, carried right down to the porcelain knobs on all the doors. There were filigree work and gilt, the glittering prisms of chandeliers, and in the ladies' cabins, as Twain described them, "pink and white Wilton carpet, as soft as mush, and glorified with a ravishing pattern of gigantic flowers." Although frayed a little here and there, not quite so glittering, the white streaked a bit, most of this luxury was preserved in the steamboats of the first decades of the twentieth century, and businessmen who took the long trip or families who boarded for short excursions still expected remarkable entertainment and got it.

The names of the first New Orleans jazz musicians to play the riverboats are unknown today. But sometime about the end of the first decade or the beginning of the second of the twentieth century, a band we know something about began to play the boats. The leader was "Sugar Johnny," a powerful cornetist whose playing in all senses of the word sent him to early retirement and obscurity. He was done for by drink and ladies and those loud bursts of sound that only the most disciplined brassman can get away with. He had two capable men, Roy Palmer on trombone and Laurence Dewey on clarinet; Louis Keppard on guitar, Wellman Braud on bass, and Minor Hall on drums. Braud was a St. James, Louisiana, boy who had played violin in string trios at the Terminal House and Tom Anderson's Annex in Storyville. Hall—not to be confused with the other famous New Orleans drummer of that name, Fred "Tubby" Hall—made his biggest splash a few years later with King Oliver's band in Chicago; he was nicknamed "Ram." Sugar Johnny's band settled in Chicago in 1916, after doing its share of the vaudeville circuit, and added, on piano, Lil Hardin, a smart young woman from Memphis who had come to Chicago to finish the work in music she had begun at Fisk University and had been lured away from her classical studies by jazz.

The biggest of the riverboat orchestras, and the most important for jazz, was put together in St. Louis by the pianist Fate Marable. Essentially a dance and show band, Marable's often made room for the most distinguished of New Orleans musicians—Louis Armstrong, Pops Foster, Johnny St. Cyr, Baby Dodds, and Picou. Known at times as the Jaz-E-Saz Band, this group swung vigorously down the river. Davey Jones, who played the mellophone, a curious combination of French horn and cornet, moved around that sweet and soft instrument almost as fast as Louis Armstrong did on the cornet. Percie Sud is recalled by Duke Ellington as a cornetist who "ended up by stealing everybody's stuff, so slick was he," but Louis played too much to steal more than fragments. One of the stories about Louis's playing with Marable, almost certainly true, was that he used to start playing his choruses at Alton, Illinois, fifteen miles out of St. Louis, and would still be playing them when the boat tied up at the St. Louis dock. Boyd Atkins, who played soprano sax and clarinet with Fate for a while, is famous for his authorship of "Heebie Jeebies," which he and Lionel Hampton freshened in later years, and for at least one record side with Louis Armstrong, his riverboat colleague, "Chicago Breakdown," on which he played the soprano.

All the strands were tied together in Chicago. The riverboats brought one crew of New Orleans musicians; others came and went by other means, and eventually settled down. Before Sugar Johnny's group settled down at the Dreamland Cafe, George Filhe, the New Orleans trombonist who in 1913 had arrived in Chicago as a cigar-maker, organized a six-piece band at the Fountain Inn in 1916. Like so many of the other bands of the period, Filhe's group played at the Arsonia Cafe after it had finished its regular job at the Fountain. In 1916 Emanuel Perez took a five-piece band into the Deluxe Cafe on State Street near Thirty-fifth, the crossroads of the jazz world in Chicago. After hours Perez's New Orleans quintet played at the Pekin theater-cabaret, up on State near Twenty-sixth Street, home for fifteen years before that of every kind of Negro entertainment—the drama, the musical revue, vaudeville, dance bands, and singers and jazz groups. The best of these bands, the one that really set the jazz pace, was the one that the bass player in the Original Creole Band, Bill Johnson, formed in 1918.

The Original Creole musicians found themselves in Chicago in 1918 after a long tour with the *Town Topics Revue*, which the Shuberts had sent on the road. They had had all they could take of the road and, like musicians in dance bands many years later, looked around for jobs that would permit them to remain in one place, namely Chicago, for a long time. Johnson found a job at the Royal Gardens Cafe on Thirty-first Street near Cottage Grove. He took two men who had played with the Original Creoles, Jimmy Noone and trombonist Eddie Venson, added pianist Roddy Taylor and New Orleans drummer Paul Barbarin. Then he sent down to jazz's home town for his cornetist, Joe Oliver. Oliver was an after-hours doubler too; in the early morning he went into the Dreamland Cafe, where he played with Sidney Bechet and Weldon Braud and others come up from the Crescent City. In 1920 Oliver made the famous move to the Dreamland with Johnny Dodds and trombonist Honore Dutrey, the bass player Ed Garland, Fate Marable's drummer Minor Hall, and the pianist who had joined Sugar Johnny in Chicago, Lil Hardin. In 1921, in California, where Oliver spread the jazz word, Baby Dodds replaced Hall on drums. In the middle of 1922 Louis Armstrong left the Jaz-E-Saz riverboat band to settle down with King Oliver; with him, jazz came to stay in Chicago.

They were all there. Freddie Keppard and Jimmy Noone were playing together at the Royal Gardens in 1920, and two years later joined Doc Cook, originally Charles L. Cooke, about a mile north at the Dreamland Cafe. In 1922 there were a lot of fine bands around the south side of Chicago, the Negro section. At the Red Mill Cafe trumpeter Tommy Ladnier, trombonist Roy Palmer, and pianist Teddy Weatherford, Earl Hines' idol, were the better half of a six-piece band. Bands that never recorded, like Junie Cobb's, with the clarinetist Darnell Howard, later a fixture in the Earl Hines band and in Chicago clubs, were playing viable jazz in the New Orleans tradition. Trumpeters very well spoken of by those who heard them, such as Bobby Williams and Willie Hightower, Bob Shaffner and Cliff Matthew, were carrying on the heroic traditions of New Orleans cornetists, were receiving something like adulation from their friends, but never a record contract. W. C. Handy and Jelly Roll Morton joined forces long enough about this time to make some Midwestern tours out of Chicago, but not to record.

At the ballrooms and the parks and the municipal pier, indoors and outdoors, big bands were playing concert music and dance music and giving the New Orleans soloists their share of free rides. Charles Elgar's Creole Band played the Dreamland Ballroom for five years until 1922, and when he moved on to the Green Mill, on the north side, Doc Cook took over with men like Freddie Keppard and Jimmy Noone in his band. Cook, who had been in charge of the music at Riverview Park from 1918 to 1921, stayed four years at Dreamland before moving on for a little more than three at the White City Ballroom, where he was the object of the musical affection of most of the young white jazzmen growing up in Chicago in the decade between 1920 and 1930. But the biggest of these big band leaders was Erskine Tate at the Vendome Theatre from 1918 to 1929. His musicians' names read like a roll call of the best in Chicago in that decade: Freddie Keppard and Louis Armstrong and two other celebrated trumpeters, Ruben Reeves and Jabbo Smith; pianists Teddy Weatherford, the man to whom he meant so much, Earl Hines, and Fats Waller; clarinetists Darnell Howard, Buster Bailey, and Omer Simeon. The swinging Vendome syncopaters took over the stage for shows as long as two hours between movies and showed their audiences how a band as large as fifteen pieces could retain the improvisatory spirit of New Orleans jazz. Some of that quality is evident in the single record made by the band in 1926, "Stomp Off, Let's Go," and "Static Strut."

Along with the brilliant Negro jazz bands, from 1914 on the founding fathers of white Dixieland were playing around Chicago. First there was Tom Brown and His Jass Band; then came the Nunez-Lada group, and shortly afterward the Original Dixieland Band. Full fruition of this music came when the original members of the New Orleans Rhythm Kings met clarinetist Leon Rappolo in Davenport, Iowa, and succeeded in bringing him with them to open at Friars' Inn.

After the New Orleans Rhythm Kings, one more white band held the stage as jazz made its way from the brothel to the box office. This was the Wolverines' Orchestra, organized in late 1923. It played in New York in 1924, at the Cinderella Dance Hall, at which time Bix Beiderbecke, its star, went over to the Balconades to hear the Original Dixielanders, and Red Nichols went over to the Cinderella to hear Bix. But their story is a part of Bix's and must be dealt with later, in that context.

The blues singers came through Chicago from time to time too, and sometimes stayed for long runs. Probably more than any other group, these singers sent jazz down the main streets and back lanes, into the front parlors and hall bedrooms of America. Looking at them and listening to them, it wasn't hard to see and hear the majesty so often imputed to these women. Almost as soon as they began to record in 1923, they found a huge audience, sympathetic, moved, if not always aware of the size of the contribution.

Mamie Smith was the first to record, in 1920, with Johnny Dunn's Original Jazz Hounds, a fair group with a singer who was better than fair. But Ma Rainey, who didn't come to records until 1923, was the first of the giants and the mother of them all. She was thirty-seven in 1923 and a veteran of the tent shows, the cabarets, and the meeting houses, all the places where one sang on the Negro circuit. A plump woman with a rich, round voice, Gertrude Rainey never left the meaning of her blues lyrics to the imagination. She banged home her sad, usually sexual tale, when she was "Countin' the Blues," chanting the Frankie and Johnny saga in "Stack O'Lee Blues," pointing out that "Yonder Comes the Blues," singing about such varied boy friends as those in "Titanic Man Blues," "Icebag Papa," or "See See Rider," the famous Negro characterization of a male low-life, that no-good who battens on women.

Ma Rainey had a pupil who, not uniquely, eclipsed her teacher. Ma found this pupil, Bessie Smith, on one of her trips with a traveling show through Tennessee. Student and teacher worked well together; the result was the most magnificent of all the blues voices. From Ma Rainey, Bessie Smith learned the intricacies of blues singing, the carefully placed two-bar fill-ins and introductions, the little melodic variations, the tricks of voice and rhythmic accent, the twists of phrase with which to untwist the double meanings. Bessie was not shy before the crudest facts of life, but she had more to sing about. Her heart went into the plaints addressed to God ("Salt Water Blues," "Rainy Weather Blues," "Back Water Blues," "Cemetery Blues," "Golden Rule Blues") and to man ("Mistreatin' Daddy," "Careless Love," "Do Your Duty," "Sweet Mistreater," "A Good Man Is Hard to Find"). Perhaps the most famous of her records is the two-part "Empty Bed Blues," full of an almost terrifying loneliness. But no one record is Bessie's best; of her more than one hundred and fifty records, more than half are masterpieces. In a voice that, differently trained, would have been superb in opera, she often gives the stature of art to commonplace blues. And for her, too, some of the best musicians of the twenties and early thirties played their very best: Louis Armstrong, Joe Smith, Jimmy Harrison, Coleman Hawkins, Fletcher

Henderson, James P. Johnson, Jack Teagarden, and Benny Goodman all appear behind her and stay tastefully though inventively back of her. The suggestion of awe in their playing is understandable: Bessie Smith in a recording studio, as on a stage, was the Empress of the Blues her publicity called her. She strode the boards the way she rode her voice, with that overwhelming certainty that only the very great, no matter what the field, can assert. Her death in 1937 in Mississippi, when there was some doubt about taking her to a white hospital, echoed the tragedy of the lives she had sung so imperially.

There were four other Smith girls, none of them relatives of each other or of Bessie, who sang the blues and sang them well: Clara Smith, Laura Smith, Trixie Smith, and the first of them, Mamie Smith. Ida Cox, like Ma Rainey, made many records with Lovie Austin, the woman pianist, and her Blues Serenaders; Ida deserves the implied compliment. Bertha Hill, better known as "Chippie," was accorded the handsome assistance of such musicians as Louis Armstrong, Johnny Dodds, and Richard M. Jones; her throaty extravagances were also deserving. Not quite as much can be said for the other singers of the blues who were supported by fine jazz musicians—such women as Sippie Wallace, Lillie Delk Christian, Alberta Hunter, Victoria Spivey, and Ethel Waters. The first records made by Ethel Waters, in 1924 and 1925, are more distinguished for the backing by the lovely cornet of Joe Smith, with sometime solos by such men as Buster Bailey and Coleman Hawkins, than they are for her singing. Her real quality can be assayed by her 1932 record with Duke Ellington, "I Can't Give You Anything but Love" and "Porgy," in which her rich tones and insinuating vibrato make good tunes into better. There is more of the same on the coupling she made in 1933 with Benny Goodman, "I Just Couldn't Take It, Baby" and "A Hundred Years from Today." The kind of thing she does in these records, and that Adelaide Hall did in hers with Ellington, is the result of the application of the blues personality to the ballad. Softened some, and a good deal more sentimental, jazz appeared in the popular song. It infiltrated so much of the entertainment world that it became difficult to tell where jazz left off and commerce began. In singing popular ballads, many jazz singers balanced their musical accounts and made listening to trivial songs a pleasure.

The great commercial overhauling of jazz was only suggested and barely begun in the early twenties. Nevertheless, it was by increasing transfusions of box-office plasma that jazz made its way around the country. For about another decade the best of the instrumentalists were able to maintain their integrity because their music was still taking shape. The Chicago youngsters who roamed the South Side in search of jazz instruction were able to exploit much of what they learned when they played in clubs run by gangsters and other over-lords of the Prohibition era who were not too commercially demand-ing. In the same way, New Orleans musicians far from home in Cali-fornia and New York brought a fresh commodity to audiences who demanded little to go with their liquor except the beat and the new sound, which these musicians undeniably had. Still the big bands were growing, the bands that sweetened their jazz or made it symphonic, and musicians like Bix Beiderbecke, seeking fairly profitable and regu-lar employment, had to join them. The synthesis of the various New Orleans jazz strains was being made with that same curious combina-tion of backroom secrecy and brazen outdoor openness that attended the making of bathtub gin and open-still corn whisky. The Jazz Age was upon us, and nobody but the court jesters of the period, the jazz-men who played the music after which it was named, had any glim-mering of what it was about.

Chapter 10

THE JAZZ AGE

Jazz was written about in the 1920s chiefly as a symbol, a symbol and a symptom and a handsomely crunchy epithet with which one could dismiss either the era itself or one group of its volatile citizens. The group was not always the same. Sometimes it was the inhabitants of Fitzgerald's Princeton and the Ritz-Carlton Hotel and long, sleek cars. Sometimes it was T. S. Eliot and/or Irving Berlin, who were interchangeable in several of the jazz categories of the time. Sometimes it was John Dos Passos, John Howard Lawson, E. E. Cummings, H. L. Mencken, Sinclair Lewis, Al Jolson, Fanny Brice. Sometimes the Italian Futurists. Sometimes the Jews. Sometimes the radio industry. Only occasionally was it the Negroes (also only occasionally granted the dignity of a capital N). And every now and then "Jazz" meant the music itself, but only every now and then, for the music itself was not much discussed. Jazz was not to be analyzed; it was to be accepted as an American symbol, as *the* American symbol, and what it symbolized was unmistakable— ". . . as unmistakably American as the sound of a jazz band." The simile was H. L. Mencken's.

As early as 1921 cries of "Enough," "No more!" and "Jazz is dying" were raised in all quarters, from the musical magazines to the literary weeklies, monthlies, and quarterlies. Clive Bell summed up the literary attitude succinctly in his piece, *"Plus de Jazz,"* which appeared in his American outlet, the *New Republic*, in 1921. *"Plus de Jazz!"* No more jazz! Bell attributed the exclamation to an obscure journalist sitting with "perhaps the best painter in France" and "one of the best musicians . . . in a small bistro on the Boulevard St. Germain." Bell recorded the talk among the three because "Jazz is dying, and the conversation . . . is of importance only as an early recognition of the fact." Yes, he added, "Jazz is dead—or dying, at any rate—and

98

the moment has come for someone who likes to fancy himself wider awake than his fellows to write its obituary notice." Whereupon he modestly did so, listing the characteristics of the deceased: ". . . a ripple on a wave . . . its most characteristic manifestation is modern painting [but] only the riff-raff has been affected."

"Italian Futurism," Bell declared, "is the nearest approach to a pictorial expression of the Jazz spirit. The movement bounced into the world somewhere about the year 1911. It was headed by a Jazz band and a troupe of niggers [sic], dancing. Appropriately it took its name from music—the art that is always behind the times. . . . Impudence is its essence, . . . impudence which finds its technical equivalent in syncopation: impudence which rags." Then he cited "the determination to surprise" and its "grateful corollary—thou shalt not be tedious," acknowledging the brevity of "the best Jazz artists" as "admirable," reminiscent "of the French eighteenth century." However, "Jazz art is soon created, soon liked, and soon forgotten. It is the movement of masters of eighteen." No irony or wit is in jazz, but "childish" fears and dislikes "of the noble and the beautiful. . . . Niggers can be admired artists without any gifts more singular than high spirits; so why drag in the intellect?" Bell admitted a ten-year domination of music and literature by jazz and again cited the Italian Futurists as the only painters to have been affected by the movement, evidenced in "their electric-lit presentation of the more obvious peculiarities of contemporary life and their taste for popular actualities."

In underlining the impudence, determination to surprise, and brevity of jazz, Bell touched upon genuine qualities of the art. In suggesting that the Futurists were its pictorial representatives, he was on less secure ground and his "electric-lit" image did not support his argument as effectively as would have a description of the adumbral lines which surrounded Balla's dogs and Marinetti's figures, the syncopated movement of the Futurists.

He had an easier time with Stravinsky. "Technically, too, he has been influenced much by nigger rhythms and nigger methods. He has composed ragtimes. So, if it is inexact to say that Stravinsky writes Jazz, it is true to say that his genius has been nourished by it." And "the Jazz movement has as much right to claim him for its own as any movement has to claim any first-rate artist. Similarly, it may claim Mr. T. S. Eliot—a poet of uncommon merit and unmistakably in the great line—whose agonizing labors seem to have been eased somewhat by the comfortable ministrations of a black and grinning muse." Eliot's jazz qualities, it appears, are his "demurely irreverent attitude," his prim insolence, his "playing the devil with the instrument of Shakespeare and Milton," his provocative use of the emotion of surprise—"like Stravinsky, he is as much a product of the Jazz movement as so good an artist can be of any." However, "Eliot is too personal to be typical of anything, and the student who would get a fair idea of Jazz poetry would do better to spend half an hour with a volume of Cocteau or Cendrars. In prose I think Mr. Joyce will serve as a, perhaps, not very good example; . . . with a will, he rags the literary instrument: unluckily this will has at its service talents which though genuine are moderate only." Virginia Woolf "is not of the company" but "Jazz has its master" in Stravinsky, "its *petits maîtres*—Eliot, Cendrars, Picabia, and Joyce . . . and *les six* . . . chaperoned by the brilliant Jean Cocteau."

In sum, Bell offered two major conclusions: (1) "He, at any rate, who comes to bury Jazz should realize what the movement has to its credit, *viz.*, one great musician, one considerable poet, ten or a dozen charming or interesting little masters and mistresses, and a swarm of utterly fatuous creatures who in all good faith believe themselves artists." (2) "The age of easy acceptance of the first thing that comes is closing. Thought rather than spirits is required, quality rather than colour, knowledge rather than irreticence, intellect rather than singularity, wit rather than romps, precision rather than surprise, dignity rather than impudence, and lucidity above all things: *plus de Jazz.*"

Waldo Frank made the broadest sweep in his outline of the jazz movement. "Jazz music" (jazz was still an adjective to its derogators, only occasionally a noun), said Frank, "is the art which is part reflection and apology of our chaos and part rebellion from it." He cited Irving Berlin and asserted in the next sentence, "Alike is the poetry of T. S. Eliot. . . . Aristocratic sentiment, a vague oriental wisdom are subtly disarrayed to bear the mood of a meager modern soul. Aesthetically and culturally, there is little to choose between the best of Berlin and 'Mr. Prufrock' or 'The Waste Land.' " Frank went on in his 1929 *Rediscovery of America*—and here the prefix should be removed, for these were surely initial discoveries, if not inventions: "In this group also belong the works of John Dos Passos

and John Howard Lawson. . . . Lawson is as satisfied to let his
characters shout Revolution, as Al Jolson to mutter Mammy." A
remarkable comparison, quickly succeeded by another: "A better
performance, but still of the same class, is the 'Him' of E. E. Cummings. . . . In this play, as in his lyrics, Cummings has found for
the popular dance and jazz an equivalent in terms of the highest im-
pressionistic art of Europe"—hence, really, no equivalent at all.
"The nostalgia of T. S. Eliot and Berlin is feeble; it is the refrain,
dissolved in our world, of early nineteenth-century romantics (Musset
and Nerval—Schubert and Robert Franz). . . . Of this class also
is the rhetorical art of H. L. Mencken. To understand his appeal one
must think of Jolson shouting Mammy, of Miss Brice's Yiddish Indian, of the vaudeville performer, Cummings, who at the sight of a
girl in a bathing suit, tears off his shirt, devours his straw hat and
breaks a grand piano. . . . The art of Sinclair Lewis is of this family.
. . . His tune is plaintively self-suffering, rather than sadistic."

Frank explains it all. "Its dominant trait justifies calling it 'the
family of jazz'; for the trick in the jazz dance or song, the jazz
comic strip, the jazz vaudeville stunt, of twisting a passive reflex to
our world into a lyrical self-expression is in all these arts. Eliot and
Berlin, Cummings and Lewis have the same appeal. The fact that
some have a small audience and some a large, is due to a mere difference in their idioms: another proof of the essential likeness of all
American 'atoms'—high-brow or low. Devotion to our chaos under-
lies and directs the shallower rebellion from it. Servitude is perhaps
the precise word. In ideal and emotion, these men are measured by
the dissolute world from which they yearn to escape. Their nostalgia
is but the perfume of decay. Their art reflects what they hate because *they* are reflections; its lyric glow is our world's phosphor-
escence."

One could describe Eliot's "demurely irreverent attitude" and his
"mood of a meager modern soul" in support of one's vigorous association of his poetry and the jazz movement, but the actual direct
influence of jazz on his working method was never delineated, though
there were few stronger influences in his rhythms. From *The Waste
Land:*

> O O O O that Shakespeherian Rag—
> It's so elegant
> So intelligent.

Only occasionally did Eliot indicate so strongly the early source of
his rhythms of ragged futility. No other poem reflects the influence
as clearly as *The Waste Land*, but surely the last lines of "The Hollow
Men" are a kind of jazzed-up nursery rhyme:

> This is the way the world ends
> This is the way the world ends
> This is the way the world ends
> Not with a bang but a whimper.

The use of lower-case letters, set in jagged lines, words broken
in halves and quarters to maintain a regular beat, suggests a taste
for jazz syncopation on the part of E. E. Cummings, if something
less than the full-scale avowal of jazz faith with which Waldo Frank
debited him.

Hart Crane, who wrote most of his cryptic descriptions of modern
tragedy in a slum bedroom overlooking the Brooklyn Bridge, with
jazz records spinning a comparative consonance to his verbal dis-
sonance, shows no immediate musical influence, but one of his most
frightening images springs from the "family of jazz" and its mechanical apparatus:

> The phonographs of hades in the brain
> Are tunnels that rewind themselves . . .

When Carl Sandburg and Vachel Lindsay used the music, they
called it by its name. It runs through Sandburg's verse in syncopated
rhythms, repetitive patterns, obviously drawn from jazz; it appears
at its clearest—and worst—in the crude sentimentality of his "Jazz
Fantasia." Lindsay, at his best, managed what Louis Untermeyer
called "an infectious blend of rhyme, religion, and ragtime." He
loved to chant his own poetry and left directions as marginal notes
for his long poems, indicating either dramatic action or the rise and
fall and emotional quality with which he wanted various sections
to be read or sung or chanted. He snapped his rhymes, exterior and
interior, with the one-two precision of a Dixieland band's marching
beat; he rolled his vowels with the fervor of a revival meeting, having taken much inspiration from both bands and musicians and re-
vivalist singers and shouters. His Negro Sermon, "Simon Legree,"
concluded on a jazz note:

And old Legree is fat and fine:
He eats the fire, he drinks the wine—
Blood and burning turpentine—
Down, down with the Devil;
Down, down with the Devil;
Down, down with the Devil.

His Study of the Negro Race, "The Congo" ("Being a memorial to
Ray Eldred, a Disciple missionary of the Congo River") opens like
a jazz lyric; its rhythmic refrain acknowledges a New Orleans source:

Fat black bucks in a wine-barrel room,
Barrel-house kings, with feet unstable,
Sagged and reeled and pounded on the table,
Pounded on the table,
Beat an empty barrel with the handle of a broom,
Hard as they were able,
Boom, boom, BOOM,
With a silk umbrella and the handle of a broom,
Boomlay, boomlay, boomlay, BOOM.

Then, on the next "Boomlay, boomlay, boomlay, BOOM," an explanation:

A roaring, epic, rag-time tune
From the mouth of the Congo
To the Mountains of the Moon.

Directions for the reading of "The Daniel Jazz" cite "a strain of
'Dixie'" and "a touch of 'Alexander's Ragtime Band.'" And the
form suggests the blues as the work spins itself out in a series of
tercets directly related to the lyrics Bessie Smith and Ma Rainey
sang.

Whatever Lindsay's failures, one of his conspicuous successes was
his keen understanding of the primitive jazz forms, his adaptation of
the devices of the spiritual, the folk song, and the blues, sprung on
the meter of the jazz band.

The Negro poets who won such a large audience for their work,
good, bad, and indifferent, in the intense days of the so-called Negro
Renaissance, smack in the middle of the twenties, also caught some
of the feeling for jazz that was so much a part of their lives. Most
of them accepted it cheerlessly, as most of them accepted the world

104 A HISTORY OF JAZZ IN AMERICA

of prejudice into which they had been born. James Weldon Johnson, the senior member of the group, told a rough tale in his three books, *The Autobiography of an Ex-Colored Man*, *Black Manhattan*, and *Along This Way*, published in 1912, 1930, and 1933, respectively—told it with compassion and concern for oppressor as well as oppressed. In his poetry he caught some of the rhythmic movement of his own people, especially in the seven sermons in verse that make up his 1927 volume, *God's Trombones*, but here, as in his song-writing collaborations with his musician brother, J. Rosamund Johnson, his most direct influence was the spiritual, for he came of the generation that felt its strongest tie to the old South, its first American home, in the spiritual.

There was more of the new Harlem in Claude McKay, a Jamaican who came to the United States in 1912, rose through the occupations available to Negroes (Pullman portering, waiting on table, acting as busboy and kitchen helper) to a position of some importance in the radical literary movements of the twenties, most prominently as associate editor of *The Liberator*. His novels, *Home to Harlem* (1928) and *Banjo* (1929), caught some of his new home and its instruments; a sonnet, written in 1921, "The Harlem Dancer," said much about the clubs in which jazz was played in New York:

> Applauding youths laughed with young prostitutes
> And watched her perfect, half-clothed body sway;
> Her voice was like the sound of blended flutes
> Blown by black players upon a picnic day.
> She sang and danced on gracefully and calm,
> The light gauze hanging loose about her form;
> To me she seemed a proudly swaying palm
> Grown lovelier for passing through a storm.
> Upon her swarthy neck black, shiny curls
> Profusely fell; and, tossing coins in praise,
> The wine-flushed, bold-eyed boys, and even the girls,
> Devoured her with their eager, passionate gaze;
> But looking at her falsely smiling face,
> I knew her self was not in that strange place.

The writing was self-conscious, adorned with bromidic ornament, flushed with social protest, an almost academic demur which every Negro was expected to file in his creative activity, whether he wrote novels or poetry, painted, composed music, or simply flung his hips at his partner's pelvis as they laced legs and raced feet around "The Home of Happy Feet," the Savoy Ballroom uptown in New York, or its opposite number of the same name in Chicago.

Aaron Douglas, who was the official graphic artist for the New Negro movement, spilled blacks and whites and grays across his lithographs in cartoon-like action, setting a lynch rope carefully over the heads of an undulating dancer and a saxophonist whose body was twisted in imitation of the dancer. Langston Hughes commented with expert bitterness on the relations of the white man and the Negro in his novel, *Not without Laughter* (1930), which could best be explained—both the title and the story—by a line from the introduction to his second volume of poems, *Fine Clothes to the Jew* (1927): "The mood of the *Blues* is almost always despondency, but when they are sung people laugh."

Hughes' first book was the traditional slim volume of verse, *The Weary Blues*, published in 1926. He used the A-A-B blues lyric form for all it was worth, and a lot more, converting its three-line simplicity into a six-line stanza, and killing some of his best lines with approximations of Negro dialect that suggested Ku Klux Klan caricatures and motion-picture and theater stereotypes far more than the writing of a sensitive Negro poet. At his best he caught some of the most winning irony of the migrant Negro, properly expressed in the blues structure:

> Once I was in Memphis,
> I mean Tennessee,
> Once I was in Memphis,
> I mean Tennessee,
> But I had to leave 'cause
> Nobody there was good to me.

His pictures of jazz life were less adroit, missing the understatement that sparked his most distinguished blues of weariness. The usual people:

> Charlie is a gambler
> An' Sadie is a whore.
>
> Play that thing,
> Jazz band!
> Play it for the lords and ladies,
> For the dukes and counts,
> For the whores and gigolos . . .

The usual sounds:

> So beat dat drum, boy!
>
> He made that poor piano moan with melody.

The usual message:

> To keep from cryin'
> I opens ma mouth an' laughs.
>
> You know that tune
> That laughs and cries at the same time.
>
> Won't be nothin' left
> When de worms git through.

Critic Russell Blankenship called him "a jazz singer crooning in modern parlance the old, old woes of the black man. Much of his poetry sticks in one's memory just as a haunting jazz phrase flashes again and again into the mind."

Countee Cullen, the most sophisticated in background, in use of words, in choice of subject, of the Negro poets, left no "haunting jazz phrase," but he did manage some startling images, notably the tree in the South.

> (And many others there may be
> Like unto it, that are unknown,
> Whereon as costly fruit has grown.)
> It stands before a hut of wood
> In which the Christ Himself once stood—
> And those who pass it by may see
> Nought growing there except a tree,
> But there are two to testify
> Who hung on it . . . we saw Him die.
> Its roots were fed with priceless blood.
> It is the Cross; it is the Rood.

With the last lines of *The Black Christ*, written at the very beginning of 1929, Countee Cullen ended the era of the New Negro. With poetry such as this, the Negro's work was within a few volumes of being accepted as something less than freakish; literacy was no longer quite so remarkable, even in this subject people. But recognition of the Negro's most effortless product, his least self-conscious expression, was still a long way off in 1929. His flowing articulation was only aped and mimicked and distorted by the white man until well into the thirties; Benny Goodman and the Swing Revolt waited another six years.

Typical of the cold shoulder and rough treatment accorded jazz in the twenties, as a musical expression rather than a symbol of futility and fashion, was the attitude of Paul Rosenfeld. After James Huneker, only Rosenfeld had the equipment and the equilibrium, the ease and the warmth, necessary to receive all the arts in America at once— all but jazz, that is. In his *Port of New York*, Rosenfeld paid eloquent attention to the 1924 arts and artists, fourteen of whom he toasted in as many chapters and an epilogue, as evidence of "the movement of life in America . . . an America where it was good to be." In his *Musical Chronicle*, covering activity within the art of notes and chords from 1916 to 1923, the principal interest was European, radiating from the music of D'Indy, Bloch, Casella, Milhaud, Strauss, Mahler, Prokofiev, Bartok, and Schoenberg, among others, with a nod in the direction of one of Rosenfeld's favorite American composers, Leo Ornstein. When he summed up the philosophy of the first book and the narrative of the second, in a brief volume in Lippincott's One Hour Series, *An Hour with American Music*, Rosenfeld made a definitive statement about jazz. His feeling was so strong that he opened his book with a seventeen-page castigation of jazz, the first of eight chapters and almost an eighth of the book.

"American music is not jazz," Rosenfeld wrote. "Jazz is not music. Jazz remains a striking indigenous product, a small sounding folk-chaos, counterpart of other national developments." He explained what music is—"the representative work, say, of Bach and Beethoven, Mozart, Wagner and Brahms, primarily is what jazz from the beginning is not: the product of a sympathetic treatment of the sonorous medium. *Music* is a chain of temporal volumes released by sensitive manipulation of an instrument. . . . In works like the last sonatas and quartets of Beethoven, the fantasias and fugues of Bach, *Tristan und Isolde* of Wagner, the logic is so universal that we have the impression these pieces existed since the beginning of the world, and must persist till doomsday." The product he recommended might possibly be "still small in worth," Rosenfeld admitted, "But it exists; it swells. New creative talents appear with every year; and while they may yet seem uncertain and anything but overwhelming, they have added a new interest and excitement to life, filling it with the vibrance of gathering powers." He was describing the music of Edgar Varese, Carlos Chavez, Aaron Copland, Roy Harris, and Roger Sessions. Yet every one of his words could be applied just as well to the jazz musicians and singers whose careers and art were just then taking shape. In the light of the subsequent performances of the composers he named who were working in classical forms, and of the jazzmen working at the same time toward the organization of a new music, it could more convincingly be said that the *hot* musicians had surely "added a new interest and excitement to life, filling it with the vibrance of gathering powers," while their confreres, working in more traditional forms, out of borrowed molds, created no more than "a striking indigenous product, a small sounding folk-chaos, counterpart of other national developments."

The twenties were the *Wanderjahre* for jazz. There were no important jobs anywhere, and everywhere people mistook Paul Whiteman and Irving Berlin and Al Jolson and Ted Lewis and Cole Porter and Vincent Lopez for jazz artists. Fletcher Henderson pieced together enough work as an accompanist for blues singers, a composer of sorts, and an arranger of more than sorts to rise above failing record companies and the mistaken impressions of white audiences. He had a band of considerable strength by 1924, one that set a style and made a lot of reputations and came most completely into its own under the aegis of Benny Goodman and an entirely different set of musicians when Benny built the Kingdom of Swing around Fletcher Henderson's music in 1935 and 1936. Duke Ellington commuted from Washington, D.C., to New York until he managed to strike a Harlem club-owner's fancy in 1923, and a substitute's job at the Cotton Club in 1927 finally made fact of what had been four years of Harlem fancy.

Louis Armstrong had been building a reputation since 1922, when he made his debut in Chicago with Joe Oliver's band at the Lincoln Gardens, until 1928, when he came to New York to stay. He was something of a legend among musicians and enough of a name among Negro and white followers of jazz to draw crowds wherever he played. The Immerman brothers, who ran Connie's Inn up in Harlem for white tourists, put him at the head of Luis Russell's band. Between 1922, when Satchmo left New Orleans, and 1928, when he arrived in New York, he had accomplished much.

Fletcher Henderson, Duke, and Louis dominated the jazz of the twenties along with pianist Earl Hines and a few youngsters out of Chicago and near-by Midwestern towns and cities. The youngsters, most of them anyway, were helped along by their connections with the big names of the time, the pseudo-jazzmen with whom the music of jazz was irresistibly associated in the twenties. Bix Beiderbecke made a reputation of a sort as a cornetist with the Wolverines from 1923–1925. He was helped along by his brief hitch in Chicago with Charlie Straight's band at the Rendezvous, and a lot more by the year he spent with Frankie Trumbauer's band in St. Louis, which ended with the hiring of both Bix and Tram (Trumbauer) by Jean Goldkette for the hot section of his sweet-and-hot combination. A year with Goldkette, who had a name, and Bix was hired by Paul Whiteman, who had the biggest name of them all.

Paul Whiteman, called "Pops," sometimes called "Fatho'," played a paternal role in the jazz of the period, a role he was highly conscious of and which his associates and employees accepted so completely they called him by his two nicknames as automatically as they called Charles Lindbergh "Lindy," Clara Bow the "It Girl," George Herman Ruth "Babe," and Mary Louise Cecilia Guinan "Texas." In the late twenties his fatherly domain included some of the most distinctive sounds in jazz, those produced by Bix, by Jimmy and Tommy Dorsey, Joe Venuti, and Eddie Lang. His singers included the Rhythm Boys, the threesome from which Bing Crosby emerged, and Mildred Bailey. And those of his musicians who were not distinguished jazzmen at least had a large reputation as such; Red Nichols and Frankie Trumbauer were more famous as recording artists than the talented musicians they hired to play under them, but it was for the performances of Bix, Venuti, and Lang that discriminating people bought and held on to Nichols and Trumbauer records. Whiteman needed the subsidiary reputations of his musicians and singers to maintain his holding-company position as King of Jazz, but it wasn't Bix or Nichols or Trumbauer, Bing or Mildred Bailey who built that position for him, and none of them did much more than fill out the gigantic shadows cast by the Fatho's Gargantuan figure. The man who succeeded in making Whiteman King of Jazz was just as synthetic a jazz musician, but his music was compounded of a substance immediately and unyieldingly engaging to the American people. From February 12, 1924, when George

110 A HISTORY OF JAZZ IN AMERICA

Gershwin's *Rhapsody in Blue* was introduced by Whiteman at New York's Aeolian Hall, the two men were indissolubly associated in the public mind. Their positions at the heads of their professions were assured, the bandleader's for at least another eleven years, the composer's for more than a quarter of a century.

Whiteman, who had made his first trip to Europe in 1923, was well aware of the snob appeal added to his music by that successful tour only three years after starting his band. For the Aeolian Hall concert he underscored that appeal many times. The auditorium itself was, of course, one of the two major concert halls in New York, consecrated, like Carnegie Hall, to classical music. But merely bringing jazz into more respectable surroundings wasn't enough; it had to have the right sponsors. These were more easily forthcoming than Whiteman had at first hoped. "While we were getting ready for the concert," he explained in 1926 in his book, *Jazz*, "we gave a series of luncheons for the critics, took them to rehearsals and explained painstakingly what we hoped to prove. . . ." What they hoped to prove was "the advance which had been made in popular music from the day of discordant early jazz to the melodious form of the present, . . . [that] modern jazz . . . was different from the crude early attempts—that it had taken a turn for the better." The critics were doubtful, at the rehearsals anyway, but a long list of distinguished musicians, financial and literary figures, doubtful or not, were willing to lend valuable aid. "I trembled," Whiteman said, "at our temerity when we made out the list of patrons and patronesses for the concert. But in a few days I exulted at our daring, for the acceptances began to come in—from Damrosch, Godowsky, Heifetz, Kreisler, McCormack, Rachmaninoff, Rosenthal, Stokowski, Stransky. We had kindly response, too, from Alda, Galli-Curci, Garden, Gluck and Jeanne Gordon. Otto Kahn and Jules Glaenzer agreed to represent the patrons of art on our roster and the prominent writers we asked were equally obliging. These included: Fannie Hurst, Heywood Broun, Frank Crowninshield, S. Jay Kaufman, Karl Kitchin, Leonard Liebling, O. O. McIntyre, Pitts Sanborn, Gilbert Seldes, Deems Taylor and Carl Van Vechten."

According to Whiteman, the concert cost eleven thousand dollars and he lost "about seven thousand dollars on it. . . . I didn't care. It would have been worth it to me at any price." He was quite right. The sugar coating which had been carefully applied to all the jazz on the program—and there wasn't much to begin with—went down well with the audience there that night and with the critics. Popular songs like "Whispering" and "Limehouse Blues," "Alexander's Ragtime Band" and "A Pretty Girl Is Like a Melody," a suite of four serenades written for the concert by Victor Herbert, dance versions of "The Volga Boatmen" and "To a Wild Rose," with symphonic outbursts between choruses—such music was custom-tailored for any audience. There was nothing "crude" about it, nothing strident to betray its origin in the "discordant early jazz"; there was no mistaking Whiteman's point; he had proved what he had hoped to prove—"the advance which had been made in popular music . . . to the melodious form" of Berlin, MacDowell, Herbert, and Gershwin.

The *Rhapsody in Blue*, along with four piano numbers composed or arranged and played by Zez Confrey, represented the most serious attempt to concertize jazz. Confrey, whose listeners found most engaging the tinkly trills and rippling arpeggios of his "Kitten on the Keys," simply adapted some of the more obvious bravura embellishments of Liszt, Leschetizky, Tausig, and other nineteenth-century composers of musical melodrama to a few of the more obvious devices of ragtime. Gershwin, who went along with Confrey in his mating of the surface tricks of two musical forms, was a little bolder in his selection. The *Rhapsody* shows some influences from the early writing of Debussy, and Ferde Grofé, who orchestrated Gershwin's piano score for him, went farther along Impressionist lines; that brought Gershwin's classical line almost up to date for New York's audiences and critics, to whom Stravinsky was frightening and Schoenberg unthinkable in 1924. To justify his image—"in blue"—Gershwin employed the blues scale from time to time, dipping into flattened thirds and sevenths, against their natural intonation or directly after, and suggesting the blues thereby; Grofé added more to the jazz conviction of the *Rhapsody* with his use of the brass smears and "dirty" reed inflections then much favored by jazz musicians. A merger of jazz and the classics had been effected, as far as Whiteman and his audiences were concerned, and the press looked on as cheerfully as it did at the acquisition of new companies by Standard Brands and General Foods, or the combination of automobile manufacturers into industrial empires like General Motors.

The *Herald's* W. J. Henderson said, "Mr. Gershwin's composition proved to be a highly ingenious work, treating the piano in a manner calling for much technical skill and furnishing an orchestral background in which saxophones, trombones and clarinets were merged in a really skillful piece of orchestration. If this way lies the path toward the development of American modern music into a high art form, then one can heartily congratulate Mr. Gershwin on his disclosure of some of the possibilities. Nor must the captivating cleverness of Zez Confrey be forgotten. . . ." For the *Tribune's* Lawrence Gilman, "Mr. Whiteman's experiment was an uproarious success. This music conspicuously possesses superb vitality and ingenuity of rhythm, mastery of novel and beautiful effects of timbre." But "How trite and feeble and conventional the tunes are, how sentimental and vapid the harmonic treatment." Deems Taylor of the *World* criticized "the occasional sacrifice of appropriate scoring to momentary effect and a lack of continuity in the musical structure" but found "at least two themes of genuine musical worth" and "a latent ability on the part of this young composer to say something in his chosen idiom." Olin Downes, in the *Times*, had much to say for "remarkably beautiful examples of scoring for a few instruments," for music that was "at times vulgar, cheap, in poor taste, but elsewhere of irresistible swing and insouciance and recklessness and life; music played as only such players as these may play it—like the melo-maniacs that they are, bitten by rhythms that would have twiddled the toes of St. Anthony." Gilbert Gabriel of the *Sun* thought the *Rhapsody* justified its title because of "a degree of formlessness in the middle section. But the beginning and the ending of it were stunning. The beginning particularly, with a flutter-tongued, drunken whoop of an introduction that had the audience rocking. Mr. Gershwin has an irrepressible pack of talents."

The success Gershwin had tasted in 1919 when Al Jolson sang his song "Swanee" in the musical comedy *Sinbad* was very large financially, gratifying theatrically, but not of the quality or the size of the fame and favor he enjoyed after the *Rhapsody*. His *Concerto in F*, written to Walter Damrosch's commission and first performed by that conductor with the New York Symphony Orchestra in 1925, bore the marks of its piecemeal composition: Gershwin had written more than he needed, and he chose and rejected measures on the basis of a performance of the manuscript by musicians he hired to run it through for him in a theater rented for the occasion.

Like the *Rhapsody*, the *Concerto* was most moving in passages devoted to the nostalgic tunes Gershwin turned out with facility. Its orchestration, Gershwin's own, took another step from the dance band toward the symphony orchestra. He essayed his most adventurous step in *An American in Paris*, four years later, in which the lessons the composer had learned from intense listening to the music of Ravel and *les six* were poorly applied to an undistinguished set of themes—using French taxi horns and another fine blues melody.

Constant Lambert, contemplating the effects of symphonic jazz ten years after the *Rhapsody in Blue* had made its debut, summed up his impressions by running down Gershwin's work. "The composer, trying to write a Lisztian concerto in jazz style, has used only the non-barbaric elements in dance music, the result being neither good jazz nor good Liszt, and in no sense of the word a good concerto. Although other American composers, and even Gershwin himself, have produced works of greater caliber in this style, the shadow of the *Rhapsody in Blue* hangs over most of them and they remain the hybrid child of a hybrid. A rather knowing and unpleasant child too, ashamed of its parents and boasting of its French lessons." It would be hard, as well as unnecessary, to dispute Lambert's disappointed dismissal of this progenitor of a large musical family, one of the members of which was Vladimir Tostoff's *Jazz History of the World*, played at one of Jay Gatsby's "intimate" large parties. "When the *Jazz History of the World* was over, girls were putting their heads on men's shoulders in a puppyish, convivial way, girls were swooning backward playfully into men's arms, even into groups, knowing that someone would arrest their falls." However much the meager nature of Gershwin's music may have eluded critics and audiences trained to listen to traditional composers, its effect upon them was essentially the same as Vladimir Tostoff's *Jazz History of the World*'s upon the Great Gatsby's swooning girls. Within a few years an annual Gershwin concert was a certain sell-out at the Lewisohn Stadium summer concerts of the New York Philharmonic Orchestra, and then at other summer concert series around the country.

There were other Gershwins, other Tostoffs. Without exception, they were siphoned off by the movies and radio, in both of which the demand for new composers and arrangers was insatiable. Al Jolson's *The Jazz Singer* in 1927 put words and music in the mouths of screen actors and actresses and set a sound track alongside the flickering frames. Scales were ascended and descended as flights of stairs were ascended and descended, great pseudo-jazz crescendi accompanied the swelling of tears, sudden mock-syncopated sforzandi announced dramatic twists and turns. The scoring was brighter and larger and infinitely more varied than the tinny adaptations of Rossini, Waldteufel, and Ethelbert Nevin with which organs and pianos had set scenes and closed them, described everything from the pop of Lon Chaney's limbs in and out of their sockets to the smack of a Theda Bara kiss; but nothing in the opulence of the new movie music could hide its essential likeness in emotional and tonal range to the music of the movie console. Subtlety was simply out of the question. In 1928 it was estimated that twenty million people went to the movies every day, and, right or wrong, twenty million people were not interested in the delicate perceptions of cinema jazz composers.

Radio listeners were not so numerous as moviegoers in 1928, but the development of the communication channels Guglielmo Marconi had discovered was as impressive to chart as attendance at the film palaces. From 1920's few thousand sets, crudely put together by home engineers, the industry had filled demands for seven million by 1928. From 1920's one station, KDKA in Pittsburgh, the number of transmitters had grown to close to a thousand eight years later, even after Congress had withdrawn many licenses because of practice "not in the public interest." There were millions of sets, many more millions of listeners; the blare of a prizefight commentary, the scream of a murdered woman in a detective drama, the yawp of political speeches, and wow of static were almost commonplace sounds in American homes. Even more familiar sounds to radio listeners were the voices of popular singers and the lilt of dance bands; in the early days of broadcasting, music, and particularly popular music, was the standard fare. The time on ten small stations in 1928 was divided this way: of a total of 294 hours, 28 were devoted to talks, 77 to serious and semi-serious music, 189 to what was then called "syncopation." On ten large stations, the proportion inclined even more dizzily in favor of "harmony and rhythm": of 357 hours in toto, 56 went to talks, 42 to "classics and semi-classics," 259 to the music of such exotic organizations as the South Sea Islanders, the A. & P. Gypsies, the Anglo-Persians, the Cliquot Club Eskimos, the Ipana Troubadours, the Happiness Boys, Rudy Vallee, and Roxy and His Gang. The quality was poor, the pretension bold, the confusion abundant. "All over the country the trombones blare and the banjos whang and the clarinets pipe the rhythm," Charles Merz, in *The Great American Bandwagon*, described radio in 1928. "Oom-pah-pah, oom-pah-pah, I got the blue-hoo-hoos, I got the blue-hoo-hoos, I got the oom-pah-pah, the oom-pah-pah. . . . If it is true that from twenty to thirty million Americans are listening in on the radio every evening, then for a large part of that evening they are listening in on the greatest single sweep of synchronized and syncopated rhythm that human ingenuity has yet conceived. This is our counterpart of the drum the black man beats when the night is dark and the jungle lonely. Tom-tom." Twenty years later such a description of the music of Ipana and Cliquot Club, of Roxy, Vallee and A. & P. Gypsies seemed silly. But jazz was not jazz in the twenties; it was everything else.

Jazz was "the hopeless comment of the 'Beale Street Blues' " to Francis Scott Key Fitzgerald, when he substituted the real thing for the cotillion orchestra and polite quartet that accompanied high society drags. But above all, jazz was the new anthem for Fitzgerald, a rallying cry for millions of Jazz Age Americans, as the song written by the ancestor after whom he'd been named had aroused hundreds a hundred and fifty years before. Jazz achieved its meaning in the pages of Fitzgerald's novels and in a few of the lines between lines of the social and literary arbiters of the time. It wasn't understood by its listeners, most of whom preferred the synthetic product of Paul Whiteman, the nasal reductions of Rudy Vallee, the tinkly distillations of toothpaste troubadours, to the ruder, richer, more demanding, and often more delicate music of the men who really played jazz and the women who sang it. A chronicle of jazz in the Jazz Age not only can but must, much of the time, neglect the music itself, for the music itself remained virtually undiscovered until the Swing Renaissance of the middle thirties, when Salvation Army stockpiles and cellar bins yielded the considerable beauty sometimes slipped, more often slugged, into record grooves by Duke and Smack and Pops, by Bix and the Dorseys, a blues singer named Bessie Smith, and a kid clarinetist out of Chicago named Benny Goodman.

Jazz was hopeless comment, unmistakably American; it was impudence, it was Stravinsky, Eliot and Joyce, Irving Berlin and E. E.

Cummings; the refrain of early nineteenth-century romanticism dissolved in our world, the perfume of decay, an autumn wind high in the lonesome treetops, "a roaring, epic, ragtime tune," more often Gershwin than Ellington; the symbol of an era caught between illusion and disillusion, an ode to futility, and unmistakably the sound of Americans. Futility was the subject of odes in the twenties, and jazz played the tunes of despair and destruction of a culture passing with elaborate gestures into desuetude. But just on the brink of limbo, with something really hideous, the Great Depression, before them, the American people followed a jazz spiritual's advice, to "look down, look down, that lonesome road," and discovered insight where earlier there had been only insult, perception in perdition, wealth, in the most vivid of popular song images, amid poverty. There was valuable self-criticism along with the withering contempt of the nay-sayers; there was valid self-respect along with the willful exaggeration of the yea-sayers. If one could forget that Bruce Barton had made Jesus the founder of modern business and the Apostles the first great advertising men, one could look back to a literature that was coming alive, rising impressively out of the sloughs of adolescent despair. If one could distinguish H. L. Mencken from Jolson shouting "Mammy," the girth of Whiteman from the dimension of Armstrong, take jazz directly rather than in symphonic synthesis, then one could hear a vital native music making the first grunts and sighs of meaningful communication on the level of art. "Out of a picture-frame," Paul Rosenfeld said, and it is permissible to add, out of some magazines and a few books and a pile of phonograph records, "there comes an intimate address to the American in us. . . . We may not know it; but the long prelude to the new world is over; the curtain is about to be rung up."

Chapter 11

CHICAGO

The most far-reaching and positive contributions to jazz in the twenties were made in Chicago. One must go there to see and hear what had become accepted, and to discover how the changes that were being made took shape all around the confounding, clumsy, crudely elegant, and brilliantly shabby town.

First of all, of course, there was the diaspora—the early attempts at migration from New Orleans, most of them doomed; the later trips up the river when finally Louis Armstrong made the music stick. After 1910, the Original Creole Band came; it returned before World War I and made a small impression, mostly on local musicians who weren't as good as their competitors from the South. Jelly Roll Morton was making a career for himself, some of it musical, during various stays in Chicago. Sugar Johnny and Minor Hall, Roy Palmer, Wellman Braud, and Lil Hardin played around town, apart and together. Sidney Bechet and King Oliver and Paul Barbarin played at the Dreamland Cafe and the Royal Gardens. Freddie Keppard was a distinguished representative of "N'Oryins," one of the few who did not play at any time with the big bands. Some of the big bands were minstrel shows organized as orchestras, some of them theater orchestras; some of them, like their successors all over America, were mixed outfits that played all kinds of popular music. Louis Armstrong put in some time with Carroll Dickerson and Erskine Tate, who led two of the biggest; and Sidney Bechet ornamented Will Marion Cook's thirty-six-piece band, which also featured twenty banjos!

King Oliver and Louis Armstrong played together and separately, and together and separately made the most decisive impact upon Chicago musicians. When Jimmy Noone and Johnny Dodds and Earl Hines also began playing in Chicago, the influence was complete,

117

and jazz in Chicago was set to go the several ways that New Orleans performers at their best suggested and invited.

The key year in many ways for Chicago musicians was 1922. That was the year Louis joined King Oliver; it was the year that Bix Beiderbecke began to play around Chicago at various little joints; the New Orleans Rhythm Kings were ensconced at Friars' Inn; Muggsy Spanier was blowing around town, a kid with talent, sitting in with established older men and with other talented youngsters; the Goodman kids, Benny and Harry, were beginning to show some jazz skill and were earning money from time to time on their instruments, Benny most notably as an imitator of Ted Lewis; and finally, in this impressive list, five students at Austin High School on the West Side put themselves together as a band—Jimmy McPartland on cornet, his brother Dick on banjo and guitar, Jim Lannigan on piano and bass, Bud Freeman on C-melody sax, and Frank Teschemacher on clarinet. Before many years had passed they were joined by the Goodmans, Dave Tough (whom they picked up at Lewis Institute), Floyd O'Brien (whom Dave Tough picked up at the University of Chicago), Mezz Mezzrow, Fud Livingston, Jess Stacy, Jack Teagarden, Red McKenzie, Eddie Condon, Joe Sullivan, and Gene Krupa. These musicians were all part of the Chicago picture at one time or another; to attempt to separate the pure voices from the contaminated, as "Chicago style" enthusiasts have so often done, is to end up with all of Frank Teschemacher's bad notes and crippled phrases and none of the drive that he and his Austin Gang associates communicated so attractively.

Tesch is alternately a bore and an unforgivable noise in many of his recorded performances, but simultaneously he is a "swinging fool," to use an expression which, like the music, sprang as much from his playing as anybody else's in the late twenties and early thirties when the beat began to take over and big bands became the inevitable consequence of the fascination with heavy time. Well, the big time was Tesch's, and Benny Goodman picked it up as much from him as from the general drive around him. The big time was also the Austin kids' and their friends'. Two-beat music was moving out for a lot of musicians; the sure way to prove it is to listen to the records made by the Chicago Rhythm Kings and the Cellar Boys, to the Charles Pierce sides and the Chicago dates played by Red McKenzie and Eddie Condon. The new jazz was in steady four/four time, or moving toward it, away from the heavy syncopations of weak and strong beats. The new jazz that was Chicago's jazz was compounded of many strains, so many strains that even the old beat had to change to make way for them, and the bands had to get bigger and the music had to face a period almost as much of torture as of joy before the accomplishment which made a good deal of it, if not all, worth while.

It was Tesch who turned a bunch of enthusiastic record listeners into jazz musicians. The Austin gang used to spend its spare moments across the street from the high school at a drugstore called Spoon and Straw. Four of the five high school boys were violinists of a sort; Lawrence Freeman, Bud to his friends, wasn't sure whether he was a tap dancer or a drummer. All of them were positive that some of the most exciting music they had ever heard was on the records of the New Orleans Rhythm Kings, which they listened to with an attention they never paid to their high school teachers. These records were impressive sides that Rappolo, Brunies, and their associates had made in the studios of the Starr Piano Company in Richmond, Indiana, for the Gennett label. Tesch convinced his fellow schoolboys that "Tiger Rag" and "Tin Roof Blues" and "Shimme Shawabble" were within their reach. He showed them how much he could do with "Clarinet Marmalade" and "The Maple Leaf Rag" and convinced them that there was something they could do too. When Dave Tough, who really was a drummer, showed Bud Freeman that his instrument was the C-melody saxophone and not the traps, they had formed a band.

The band the kids made, with Dave North now on piano, they called the Blue Friars, after the inn which was the playing home of their idols, the Rhythm Kings. They picked up a few jobs around town and in the summer of 1924, their first playing year as a group, they went to work at Lost Lake, not far from Chicago. When they came back to Chicago in the fall, there were no jobs until Jimmy McPartland found a promoter, Husk O'Hare, to front them and to find them work. O'Hare was no musician but he got them work, including some time on radio station WHT, where they were known as O'Hare's Red Dragons. When they went to work at the White City Ballroom, where Doc Cook later took over with his big band, they took the name of Husk O'Hare's Wolverines, after the band with which Bix was making his reputation. They added Dave Tough's friend Floyd O'Brien on trombone, and filled out the band for Saturday night performances with Mezz Mezzrow or Fud Livingston—

which gave them a three-man saxophone section. What they played together was obviously more than ordinarily effective jazz; most of the good jazz musicians around Chicago came in at one time or another to listen, to enthuse, and to encourage. The band returned the compliment in whatever time they could find before or after work; they went all over town, listening to Louis and Jimmy Noone and Johnny Dodds, to Bix when they could, to Earl Hines, and to all the other fine musicians who were making Chicago the center of jazz in the 1920s.

On weekends the band opposite them at White City was Sig Myers' Orchestra. Not distinguished as a whole for its personnel or performance, the Myers band did have Arnold Loyocano, who had originally come north from New Orleans with Tom Brown's band, on bass, and Muggsy Spanier on cornet. Muggsy, christened Francis, was the man. Born in Chicago on November 9, 1906, by 1924 he had done a vast amount of gigging around and playing short and long engagements with first rate jazzmen. He had teamed up for a while with Bix and had listened with an avid ear to Joe Oliver, Keppard, and Louis, all of whom influenced his driving cornet. When Jimmy McPartland left to take over Bix's job in New York with the original Wolverines, Muggsy Spanier replaced him with O'Hare's Wolverines. Jimmy, a cornetist of lovely tone and matching ideas, was the only logical man to replace Bix; Muggsy, a cornetist of searing tone and punchy phrase, was, as it turned out, the only logical man to replace Jimmy.

After the White City job Tesch and Muggsy took most of the band into the Midway Garden, a few blocks away at Sixtieth Street and Cottage Grove. Jim Lannigan and Bud Freeman joined Art Kassel, who led a commercial outfit, in which tinkly sounds passed for jazz; however, it offered some compensation besides money to its new musicians in the men who sometimes played with the band, such men as the Rhythm Kings' pianist Elmer Schoebel and bass player Steve Brown, and clarinetists like Danny Polo and Benny Goodman. Jess Stacy joined Muggsy and Tesch one night, and they had a fine new pianist. Jess came from Cape Girardeau, Missouri, where he had worked in a music store, listened with rabid attention to Fate Marable's band, with Louis and the Dodds brothers, when it came to town on the steamboat *Capitol*, and later had played on the *Capitol* himself with Tony Catalano's Iowans from Davenport. Jess, a quiet and sensitive musician, followed the Chicago pattern in his listening to and learning from Earl Hines. All of Tesch's band listened and learned; as often as possible they sat in with the great jazzmen, where they played or where they lived.

Muggsy and Tesch jammed frequently with Wingy Manone and Eddie Condon. Wingy, born Joseph Manone in New Orleans in 1904, picked up the name by which he is best known when an early accident took one of his arms. After a wandering trumpet career in the South, he came to Chicago in 1924 and settled down at the Cellar, where he was often joined in jam sessions by other jazzmen. Condon, born a year later than Wingy in Goodland, Indiana, came to Chicago ten years later with the family he saluted so amusingly in his autobiography, *We Called It Music*. He started playing the banjo before he got to high school, and by the time he hit the upper grades he was already playing jobs. In 1921 he went to stay with his brother Cliff in Cedar Rapids, Iowa, and the day after he arrived he went to play with a band led by Bill Engleman, who was a businessman but liked music so much he had a dance band. Then Eddie moved on to Waterloo, Iowa, where one Hollis Peavey wanted "to play jazz music" and needed a banjo for the band he was forming. Eddie played up and down the northern Mississippi—Wisconsin, Minnesota, Iowa —with Peavey's Jazz Bandits and then was offered a job in Syracuse, New York, playing with Bix Beiderbecke and Pee Wee Russell. It was an exciting assignment; through Bix's playing Condon first realized the size of jazz. Just before they left Chicago, Pee Wee and Eddie accompanied Bix to the Friars' Inn, where Bix sat in. Then, says Eddie, "It happened." He suddenly realized that all music was not the same, "that some people play so differently from others that it becomes an entirely new set of sounds." After the Syracuse job Eddie came back to Chicago, a veteran at seventeen, to play with various groups around town, with college boys, with the Austin gang and others who joined Wingy Manone at the Cellar, at the Three Deuces, at all the other places where white musicians were allowed to play.

Joe Sullivan became the regular pianist with the Chicago musicians. At seventeen, in 1925, he had already picked up a substantial musical education at the Chicago Conservatory of Music and in speakeasies, smoky back rooms, musicians' amateur and gangsters' professional ginmills. He had a keen ear and a honky-tonk touch, and he soaked up the several piano-playing traditions of the New Orleans professors and the Sedalia and St. Louis ragtimers, Earl Hines' piano trans-

122 A HISTORY OF JAZZ IN AMERICA

formations of trumpet styles, and the alternately dapper and delirious rumbles of the boogie-woogie pianists. In Joe's playing, so vital a part of the so-called Chicago-style records, all these strains met and were woven into a handsome jazz tapestry.

Boogie woogie was at its vigorous best in Chicago in the middle twenties. Jimmie Yancey, in a sense the founding father of boogie woogie, had settled down in Chicago after a singing and dancing career that took him as far as a command performance before King George in London. He was much in demand for rent parties, those paradoxically joyous occasions when eviction was eluded by passing the hat to sympathetic celebrants. He rolled all around the town, on his feet and on the piano keyboard, and picked up a lot of imitators and a few capable students. Pine Top Smith, who learned his tremulous trade from Yancey, gave the whole species a name in his 1928 recording of "Pine Top's Boogie Woogie." In that famous record he gave the chords of the tonic and the dominant a noisy ride and in his accompanying patter explained a dance that was to be performed to the music, with an audible leer to his words, making clear the sexual meaning of the music. There is no question that the atmosphere in which boogie woogie was played was stimulating to the gonads, but it is difficult to hear the atmosphere in the music, except with verbal suggestion. In spite of its rolling rhythms and multiple climaxes, boogie woogie is essentially a virtuoso exploitation of the polyrhythms of ragtime, a series of bass rumbles and treble tremolos that sometimes mask melodic and harmonic commonplaces. There is charm and humor in the playing of Yancey, Pine Top, and their successors, but not necessarily a sexual enchantment. There is also a kind of bordello flavor in the playing of Pine Top and such of his contemporaries as Will Ezell, "Speckled Red" (Rufus Perryman), Montana Taylor, Hersal Thomas, Romeo Nelson, Turner Parrish, Cow-cow Davenport, Jimmy Blithe, Lemuel Fowler, and the still-active "Cripple Clarence" Lofton. But in the best of them, Yancey, Meade Lux Lewis, Albert Ammons, and Pete Johnson, the abiding quality is of a tricky and witty pianism.

Ammons and Lewis were both drivers for the Silver Taxicab Company in 1924, both apprentice blues pianists, both beginning to get the boogie-woogie beat. They both played the house parties and the jug celebrations; they both were formidable pianists and rent-party entertainers. Ammons became a band pianist as well as a soloist and made lots of trips into the South, on one of which he brought the Chicago transformation of Storyville piano back to its home ground, New Orleans. Lewis drifted away from music and became a car washer in a Chicago South Side garage. Both were rediscovered in 1935, when John Hammond, single-handed, brought boogie woogie back and, with Ammons' help, found Lewis in a garage. Both were brought back to records in January 1936, Albert with his fine Club De Lisa band, Meade Lux Lewis as a piano-celeste and whistling soloist. In these records they demonstrated their rhythmic skill, showing how much could be done within the rigid confines of boogie woogie. Listening to them, one could hear the triumphant part played in jazz by rhythm. Listening to them, one could hear the massive influence of rhythm upon musicians in Chicago in the twenties.

Rhythm was the boss in Chicago jazz. Under the successive ministrations of the New Orleans immigrants and the West-Side natives, jazz moved from a few fixed syncopations to a wealth of rhythmic devices. The accents within the jazz measure moved from two weak and two strong to an even four. Phrases, choruses, whole performances were better integrated because of the rhythmic change. It was almost as if these jazzmen, building a new art, were aware of rhythm as the Irish poet William Butler Yeats understood it:

The purpose of rhythm, it has always seemed to me, is to prolong the moment of contemplation, the moment when we are both asleep and awake, which is the one moment of creation, by hushing us with an alluring monotony, while it holds us waking by variety, to keep us in that state of perhaps real trance, in which the mind liberated from the pressure of the will is unfolded in symbols.

The Chicago musicians never articulated their understanding of rhythm in quite such terms, but there was in them as in Yeats a kind of belief in the mysticism of "the beat." Without ever falling into the trance of the African tribe or the Irish poet, they were able to free their minds from the pressure of musical consciousness, in order to do as Yeats suggested the artist do—"seek out those wavering, meditative, organic rhythms, which are the embodiment of the imagination, that neither desires nor hates, because it has done with time, and only wishes to gaze upon some reality, some beauty." The beat became a second nature; it did hush with "an alluring monotony" and hold awake with variety. The rhythmic breadth of the Chicago musicians can be heard in the first records made together by Muggsy and Tesch.

Charles Pierce was a South-Side butcher in Chicago who loved jazz and implemented that love by using the money he made from meat to support a first-rate jazz band which played weekends and made records. In October 1927 Pierce took Muggsy and Tesch and seven other musicians, including himself on saxophone, into the Paramount Studios in Chicago to make their memorable "Bull Frog Blues," "China Boy," and "Nobody's Sweetheart." On all these sides there is a drive, the rhythmic integration stringing solos together. There is more of the same on the November and December dates made by a more select group of musicians. Under the name of the Jungle Kings, Muggsy combined with Tesch, Mezz Mezzrow on tenor sax, Joe Sullivan, Eddie Condon, Jim Lannigan on tuba, George Wettling on drums, and Red McKenzie as the vocalist, to make "Friars Point Shuffle" and "Darktown Strutters' Ball." Wettling was a well-trained and experienced drummer from Topeka, Kansas, who had studied some of the finer technical points of jazz with Mezzrow in Chicago. McKenzie was a St. Louis bellhop who played a comb with tissue paper over it and made appealing noises alongside the kazoo played by Dick Slevin and the banjo played by Jack Bland in the Mound City Blowers, with Frankie Trumbauer on alto sax on some of his record sides, and Eddie Lang on guitar on others made in 1924. Unfortunately, none of McKenzie's happily influential singing appears on these records.

Red McKenzie, a dapper little man whose tongue was cogent with words as well as with hair combs, had come to Chicago, with his Blue Blowers as a novelty threesome, in Gene Rodemich's successful band. In that year, 1924, Isham Jones, the most able and best equipped of the leaders of sweet bands, got the Blue Blowers a Brunswick recording date, and Brunswick took them from there to Atlantic City, where Red met Eddie Lang. The Blue Blowers played the Palace in New York in the summer of 1924 and then went to London to play a date at the Stork Club there. Back in America, Red did pretty well, playing around the country. A friendly, amusing, and talented man, he made many friends, among them recording officials. He arranged the first date on Okeh for Bix Beiderbecke, Eddie Lang, and Frankie Trumbauer, the date at which they recorded their inspired "Trumbology" and their lovely "Singin' the Blues." He also arranged their date for Paramount in October of that same year, 1927, and, in December, the Okeh date made by McKenzie and Condon's Chicagoans. For that last date Jimmy McPartland was back, having had a couple of years' run with the Wolverines, of which he became nominal leader in 1925, and having played a great deal around Chicago, using many of the original Blue Friars musicians. Bud Freeman, by this time an adept at tenor sax, Tesch, Joe Sullivan, Jim Lannigan, and Gene Krupa joined Condon—but not McKenzie, who neither played nor sang on any of the sides.

They played "Nobody's Sweetheart" again, as well as "Sugar," "China Boy," and "Liza." They played with the ebullience inevitable at such a reunion of musicians. Standing on soapboxes, they poured all they had learned into the recording microphone, and it was much. The beat was almost an even four-four; the ensemble was both fluid and clean. Gene Krupa, then just moving into the select circle, was a native Chicagoan who showed at eighteen, as later, a considerable technical skill but a heaviness as well. Frank Teschemacher, who scored several of the ensemble passages, showed, especially in the brilliant middle passage of "Nobody's Sweetheart," that he was moving along in his jazz ideas and had gone past the point at which only unscored improvisation was acceptable.

There was more of the same spirit and skill and progress in the next date made by these musicians, on the fourth of April, 1928, under the name of the Chicago Rhythm Kings. The personnel differed in the substitution of Muggsy for Jimmy, Mezz Mezzrow for Bud, and the addition of McKenzie as a vocalist. Again the ensemble and the soloists worked brilliantly together; again Tesch's thinking dominated the sides. Here Tesch's inspiration, as well as his occasional clumsiness, can be heard; here is his uninhibited drive which carried every other musician along with him. And on these sides, too, is Red's appealing voice, that languorous vibrato, that refashioning of the ballad line which could make even of a pallid melody a touching, poignant tune.

Recording was opening up in the second half of the twenties; the record companies were finding an ever-increasing audience for their wares. In 1926 sales of records in America reached a dizzying new high of 151,000,000 disks. In Chicago, on June twelfth of that year, the Consolidated Talking Machine Company (Okeh Records) celebrated the phenomenal success of records with a "Cabaret and Style Show" at the Coliseum. For about ten thousand people, Okeh's Chi-

cago recording manager, the pianist Richard M. Jones, gathered together the stars of his label. There were the big bands—Carroll
Dickerson's Sunset Cafe Orchestra, Charlie Elgar's Arcadia Ballroom
Band, Dave Peyton's Peerless Theatre Orchestra, Doc Cook's Dreamland Ballroom Orchestra, Erskine Tate's Vendome Syncopaters. Al
Wind brought down his Dreamland Cafe band, King Oliver the
Plantation Cafe Orchestra, and Louis Armstrong led his Hot Five
through an actual recording as the climax of the evening, after Butter-
beans and Susie, Lillie Delk Christian, Chippie Hill, Lonnie Johnson,
and Richard M. Jones had demonstrated their individual talents as
singers and instrumentalists. Earlier in the year there had been an
"Okeh Race Records Artists Night" at the same Coliseum. In September 1927 twelve recording bands played a glittering program until
five o'clock in the morning at Riverview Park Ballroom. The record
industry's success had built a large and clamoring audience for jazz.
When, in 1928, Tesch, McKenzie and Condon, Joe Sullivan, Jimmy
McPartland, Bud Freeman, Jim Lannigan, and Gene Krupa went to
New York to play with Bea Palmer, it was natural that they should
record with a variety of bands. Tesch made his remarkable "Shim-
Me-Sha-Wabble" and "One Step to Heaven" with Miff Mole's or-
chestra, with Red Nichols on trumpet, Miff on trombone, Sullivan,
Condon, and Krupa. Then Condon made a date under his name with
Tesch, Sullivan, and Krupa. Finally Tesch was invited to play with
a band assembled under the famous recording name of The Chocolate
Dandies, consisting of Nat Natoli on trumpet, Tommy and Jimmy
Dorsey, Don Redman, George Thomas, Frank Signorelli, and Stan
King. He appeared on one side, the famous "Cherry," playing tenor
sax.

   With the records came fame of a kind, and with the fame a variety
of job offers. Jimmy McPartland joined Ben Pollack, who had also
snared Benny Goodman some years earlier when Benny was playing
in California. Jim Lannigan joined the Chicago Symphony Orchestra,
which recognized his ability on the bass. Tesch went to work with
Jan Garber's Guy-Lombardo-style band, no fair berth for his talents,
although he later made two good sides with Ted Lewis, along with
Muggsy Spanier and George Brunies. When the depression came in
1929, the great years of Chicago jazz were over, although Tesch continued to play until his death in 1932. With the coming of radio the
name-band era inaugurated during the peak recording years was fully

under way. Popular tunes, novelty acts, and the bands associated with them had caught the public's fancy, and there wasn't much of an audience for the little groups that played the big jazz. Tesch spent most of the last three years of his life playing with bands like those of Garber and Lewis.

In the last years of the Hoover administration there were still some jobs, still some record dates. In October 1929 Tesch made two sides with Elmer Schoebel and his Friars Society Orchestra, playing "Copenhagen" and "Prince of Wails." The next year, in January 1930, he made "Wailin' Blues" and "Barrelhouse Stomp" with the Cellar Boys, Wingy Manone's band, with Bud Freeman on tenor sax, Charlie Melrose on piano and accordion, and George Wettling on drums. Two years later, in January 1932, he was playing in a little band under the trumpeter Wild Bill Davison. But he was not long for the band or this world. One night he and Wild Bill were driving to work in a leisurely fashion. A truck crashed into their car, throwing Tesch clear of the machine but killing him on the spot, while Wild Bill was only dazed.

Tesch's earlier colleagues accepted his death as an inevitable tragedy. Cruel fate, they felt, had killed the man as it had killed his music three years earlier.

Chapter 12

BIX

Many of the great men of jazz died prematurely, but almost all of them had brought their music to maturity before they died. Not so Bix Beiderbecke. Bix lived twenty-eight years, and even before he died he had passed into legend. There was something about the little round horn in the little round face, something about the quality of his tone and the character of his melodic ideas that hit all the men who played with him and many who listened so hard that they awarded him a kind of immediate immortality. But he did die—young and only half-grown as a musician.

By 1938, when Dorothy Baker's highly fictionalized and best-selling life of Bix, *Young Man with a Horn*, was published, he had taken on some of the qualities of a minor god, and to many musicians he was and still is jazz incarnate. The last paragraph of *Young Man with a Horn* begins, "The sun was in Rick's face," as if to indicate that when he died a kind of special light shone down from Heaven for him, and as Rick had this golden quality in the book, so did his progenitor's playing, according to the hosts of musicians and fans who have kept the name of Bix Beiderbecke alive. To see them sit around a phonograph and listen to beat-up copies of old Paul Whiteman records on which Bix plays, or to some of Bix's own records in even worse condition, is to watch men transfixed.

Leon Bismarck Beiderbecke ("Bix" was an abbreviation of his middle name) was born in Davenport, Iowa, on March 10, 1903. From a background that was steeped in music, Bix caught the fervor early. He came of a wealthy German-American family, which was in the lumber business. His sister was a pianist, and his mother played both the piano and the organ; Bix took piano lessons as a matter of course, and his parents fondly believed he would be a concert pianist. When his Uncle Al, a Davenport band leader and cornetist, visited his family,

Bix insisted on being taught the rudiments of the horn. Uncle Al didn't take him seriously, but Bix bought himself a cornet and began to play it anyway.

Like the Chicago kids who congregated at the Spoon and Straw, Bix had an ice-cream-parlor headquarters, Maher's, where he could usually find his cornet when he had absent-mindedly misplaced it. All his life Bix was absent-minded. As Eddie Condon later recalled, he was always losing his cornet or stepping on it—"I can't remember how many horns he'd run through." He even dressed absent-mindedly, and often had to borrow a coat or a tux because he had forgotten his own. Condon described his old friend as "a guy with a nonchalant, almost vacant look on his face, with his hat way back on his head, just about ready to topple down."

At high school in Davenport, Bix thought and dreamed cornet when he wasn't playing one. When he had the horn in his possession, he sped out to Poppie Gardens, near Geneseo, Illinois, in his Ford touring car, to sit in with the Carlisle Evans band and, even in those beginning days, impress them. When the riverboat *Capitol* steamed into Davenport, Bix would jump on board and get up steam himself on the calliope. When Louis and the Dodds boys played he listened intently, then went home to try out their ideas for himself. Emmett Hardy, who played in some of the white riverboat bands, was also an influence, contributing, some say, the concept of sweet round tone that Bix made into a vital jazz trumpet and cornet tradition.

His parents, no longer quite so set on a concert career for him, sent Bix to Lake Forest Academy in the Chicago suburb of the same name in 1921. He spent almost a year at Lake Forest, and before he left had aroused something more than the academic interest of the headmaster. He was the creator and leader and star of the school band, and widely popular among the students, but he was out before the school year was out. He used to sneak downtown when he could to play with musicians and soak up some of the gin they left. He was outstanding as a music student, but wasn't interested in any other subject. He spent much of his time on campus listening to Original Dixieland Jazz records and particularly picking out Nick LaRocca's cornet solos. Before he was asked to leave school he knew most of the standard Dixieland jazz numbers and many of LaRocca's original ideas.

Shortly after leaving Lake Forest he took his first professional job, on a Lake Michigan excursion boat that traveled between Chicago and Michigan City (for a while this band had young Benny Goodman, in short pants, playing a little clarinet). From the excursion boat job and others around Chicago came the personnel of the Wolverines, a small outfit which followed the amended Dixieland instrumentation —a tenor saxophone added to the basic horns, cornet, clarinet, and trombone.

Founded by pianist Dick Voynow, the Wolverines adopted their name for a job they got late in 1923 at a roadhouse near Hamilton, Ohio, the Stockton Club. Bix played cornet, Jimmy Hartwell was the clarinetist, Al Gande the trombonist, and George Johnson played the instrument foreign to New Orleans jazz, the tenor. The rhythm section consisted of Bobby Gillette on banjo, Min Leibrook on bass, and Bob Conzelman (soon replaced by Vic Moore) on drums, in addition to Voynow.

The Wolverines with Bix achieved a degree of popularity at Midwestern university dances and did fairly well in some theaters around Indiana, Ohio, and Kentucky, as well as at odd dance halls and ballrooms. Their Stockton Club job came at the beginning of one of the noisiest and bloodiest of the Prohibition gang wars. A fight among bootleggers and their gun-happy friends started at the club on New Year's Eve 1923. To cover the frightening clamor, the Wolverines played "China Boy" loud and furious for more than an hour. The story of Bix's succession of relaxed choruses in this bloody and roaring setting is a major part of his legend.

At the University of Indiana the band was so popular it played ten weekends in a row, giving pleasure to many, especially to Hoagy Carmichael, who was an undergraduate there, and, as a member of the campus band, was beginning his own career as pianist, singer, and composer. On one of the band's appearances at the university, Hoagy got them to play at the Kappa Sigma house on the afternoon of the evening they were to play for the fraternity dance. Bix didn't pick up his cornet for more than four notes—a break in a chorus of the "Dippermouth Blues," King Oliver's classic—but such four notes! Hoagy, describing the great moment, exults:

The notes weren't blown—they were hit, like a mallet hits a chime, and his tone had a richness that can only come from the heart. I rose violently from the piano bench and fell, exhausted, onto a davenport. He had completely ruined me. That sounds idiotic, but it is the truth. I've heard Wagner's music and all the rest, but those four notes that Bix played meant more to me than everything else in the books. When Bix opened his soul to me that day, I learned and experienced one of life's innermost secrets to happiness—pleasure that it had taken a whole lifetime of living and conduct to achieve in full.

When Vic Berton, who was a drummer and booker around Chicago, heard the Wolverines, he quickly booked them into theaters in the Indiana-Kentucky circuit and got them a two-month job at the Municipal Beach Pavilion in Gary, Indiana, where many Chicagoans could hear them. During this engagement Bix concentrated as much on piano as on cornet. Before the band went to the beach, in 1924, it made its first records in a crude studio in Richmond, Indiana; the walls were of boards, electrical connections stuck out everywhere, and a large horn protruded through a velvet drape under the ornate letters which proclaimed the studios those of Gennett Records. In March the band made "Jazz Me Blues" and "Fidgety Feet," in May, "Oh, Baby," "Copenhagen," "Riverboat Shuffle," and "Susie." Bix's eloquent performances stuck out on those records like the plugs and the wire on the studio walls. When the summer was over the band made three more sides, "I Need Some Pettin'," the title of which employed a newly coined name for a very old practice; the transformed quadrille "Tiger Rag," a New Orleans and Chicago jazz classic; and the tune that celebrated a place, "Royal Garden Blues."

In October 1924 the band made its entry into New York, one that was hardly triumphal. It played at the Cinderella Dance Hall off Times Square, then as in later years the acme of ten-cents-a-dance emporia. Bix left the band while it was in New York, but not before Red Nichols had come to pay homage with his ear and later with his cornet, and not before Bix had made some more records with the Wolverines, two with George Brunies on trombone, "Sensation" and "Lazy Daddy," two without him, "Tia Juana" and "Big Boy," on which Bix played piano.

Bix went from the Wolverines in New York back to Chicago, where he played some with the Charles Straight orchestra and jobbed around town a bit. (The exchange was even. Jimmy McPartland went from Chicago to New York to join the Wolverines.) He played an Indiana prom with the Jean Goldkette band. He did a week at the Riviera Theatre in Chicago, billed with Frank Quartel; the two of them played trumpet and concertina as the Pepper Boys. Their act was right in the old vaudeville tradition; Bix sat at the bottom of the stage and blew up to Frank, or vice versa. They did as much posing as playing. Bix was doing his serious playing where he did his listening, at the Apex where Jimmy Noone and Earl Hines were, at the Sunset Cafe where Louis was, at the clubs and theaters where Bessie Smith sang, and at all the other places where you could hear and sometimes play with the great men. There is a story about a night when Bix and Louis played a Battle of Cornets over on the South Side. After hearing Bix, the story goes, Louis put down his horn and cried, saying he could never play like that.

In the course of his happy wanderings around Chicago Bix made a couple of sides with some friends, Min Leibrook and Vic Moore from the Wolverines, the trombonist Miff Mole, the composer-pianist Rube Bloom, and the man most insistently paired with Bix after this date in December 1924, Frank Trumbauer. Under the name of the Sioux City Six, they did "I'm Glad" and "Flock o' Blues" for Gennett. In March of the next year Bix and Tommy Dorsey and the clarinetist Don Murray took a rhythm section with them into the Gennett studio to do "Davenport Blues," in honor of Bix, and "Toddlin' Blues."

In September 1925 Bix joined Frank Trumbauer's band at the Arcadia Ballroom in St. Louis. For almost a year he made at least a hundred dollars a week; this was big money for him and good money for most musicians of the period when a hundred dollars had a large negotiable value. With Trumbauer he formed a lasting musical attachment; they made many records and personal appearances combining Bix's cornet and the leader's C-melody or alto saxophone. With Trumbauer, Bix played concerts and explored some of the resources of French Impressionist music, which influenced his piano playing and writing considerably, though not his cornet. He began to fool around with short piano pieces, pastiches strongly reminiscent of Debussy and Ravel; some of these later emerged as "In a Mist," "Flashes," "In the Dark," and "By Candlelight"; of these he recorded only "In a Mist," also known as "Bixology," which he did as a piano solo.

The French Impressionist composers and their American disciples and imitators made a great impression upon Bix's generation of jazz musicians. When Frank Trumbauer recalls his days with Bix he remembers the Impressionist music.

BIX

Not a young man with a horn. Not responsible for the many literary attempts to describe a beat-it-down, jivin' cat, that everyone might think constituted the immortal personality of the Bix that I knew.

Bix was an intelligent young man, a fast thinker, and well versed in many things, and, much to the surprise of many people, he was an ardent student of Debussy, Stravinsky, Cyril Scott, and Eastwood Lane—knew their symphonies like most jitterbugs know their Goodman, studied them and loved them and, strange to say, understood them. We sat for many hours, with Bix at the piano, playing his conception of Eastwood Lane's *Adirondack Sketches,* of which "The Land of the Loon" was his favorite, and also mine, and if you have heard "In a Mist" or "Candlelight," you can readily realize the musical influence inspiring his work.

When Frank recalls Bix's playing he describes it in Impressionist terms, reminiscent of the outdoor scenes of Manet and Renoir, suggestive of the warm natural colors of the poet Paul Verlaine. Whatever his execution in words, Frank's intention—and Bix's—is the same as that of the Impressionists.

To describe in print the work of Bix is almost like trying to describe the color in the beautiful flowers that we see all around us, or the beautiful clouds we see in the sky, or the varicolored leaves in the fall [which] make an impression so indelible on our minds. Still, these things relatively have an association with anything artistic. You just can't measure it with a yardstick.

It was another sixteen years before the impact of Impressionism was again so directly felt in jazz. Much of the music of radio and movie studio orchestras in the twenties and thirties sprang from Debussy and Ravel and their American imitators. Paul Whiteman's so-called symphonic jazz and Andre Kostelanetz's swollen scores borrowed from Impressionist sources. So did the music Johnny Richards composed for Boyd Raeburn's band in the mid-forties, and Stan Kenton's tone poems for piano and orchestra are in the same tradition. But improvised jazz with a steady beat didn't go right to Bix's inspiration, the Impressionists, until the formulators of bebop did their first playing at Minton's in 1941. It's interesting to speculate upon Bix's possible arrival at music like bop perhaps a full decade before Charlie Christian, Dizzy Gillespie, and Charlie Parker—if he had kept his health and lived.

In the spring of 1926 Jean Goldkette offered both Bix and Frank jobs in his large orchestra, and the offer was too good to turn down. It was a good band, for a semi-symphonic dance band, and it offered a musician the freedom to blow some of the time, Bill Challis's knowing arrangements, and some capable colleagues, as well as the money. Don Murray, a fair clarinetist, was the reed soloist. Ray Ludwig and Fred Farrar played able trumpet, and Sonny Lee played somewhat better trombone—he was soon to be replaced by just as good a man, Bill Rank. Steve Brown, the Original Dixielander, was on bass, and Irving Riskin, whom everybody called Itzy, played the piano and made the jokes. Chauncey Morehouse was the drummer and he justified his imposing names in his complicated approach to the hides. Later he fooled around with a scale full of tuned drums and mastered the talking and singing scalar beats.

Bix was growing rounder all the time, in face and body and cornet sound. He was the natural leader of the jazz group Goldkette sported within his big sweet band and enough of a pianist to be featured in the sweet outfit too. Of the two sections, the jazz was clearly the better, with Bix and Frank, Pee Wee Russell on clarinet, Sonny Lee, Ray Ludwig, Itzy, and Chauncey. But on records it was the big band that drew attention. Bix played on all the records from the fall of 1926 to the fall of 1927 but took only two solos, on "Slow River" and "Clementine (from New Orleans)." On such sides as "My Pretty Girl" his legato cornet could be heard through the staccato jerks and snorts of the ensemble, and his fans listened hard for those moments of grace.

On "Clementine" Bix's colleagues almost matched him. Eddie Lang, the guitarist, had come to the band from his native Philadelphia via the Dorsey Brothers' Scranton Sirens, the Mound City Blue Blowers, and a variety of gigs around Atlantic City and New York; he was a quiet man with a loud guitar voice, well trained musically as a violinist and well equipped intuitively. Eddie's swinging plucking stayed close to Bix in style and authority through the Goldkette months. So did the swooping fiddling of Joe Venuti, like Lang an Italian who had grown up in Philadelphia. Joe's birth at sea en route to the United States was a splendid subject for his quick and unstoppable wit, which was both loud and funny in its articulation. He had joined his four strings to Eddie's six in Philly, then had moved with his compatriot to the Scranton Sirens, and had come to Goldkette just before Bix.

Another of the considerable Goldkette talents was Danny Polo, a clarinetist of wide playing experience who joined up for the February 1927 records. Danny's playing then was strictly Storyville—notes of short valuation tied together in skipping phrases reminiscent of Picou, suggestive of Dodds and Bechet. New Orleans was the major influence then; the Trumbauer alto sax hopped and skipped and jumped, and so did Don Murray's clarinet and the Goldkette reeds as a team. Frank Teschemacher's drive had not yet been heard enough nor understood nor imitated.

Bix's roommate when they were both playing for Goldkette was the pianist Itzy Riskin. Itzy's firmest impression of Bix was of a great musician and a great person, not of a virtuoso cornetist. "He was the most easy-going guy I ever met. . . . As long as I knew him, I never heard Bix say a bad word about anybody! Even without his playing you could love and admire him for that alone. . . . He certainly was the greatest natural musician and the grandest guy any of us will ever know."

About Bix's ability on the cornet, Itzy had qualifications. "There were probably scores of cornetists who, technically speaking, could play rings around Bix, but there never has been one or will be one who can approach him when it comes to innate musicianship on his horn." But Itzy made a philosophical judgment. "After all," he said, "there's a big difference between being a straight, perhaps almost soulless instrument, and a person whose very soul breathes music that's translated so beautifully through the medium of a horn. Bix's heart was far ahead of his lips." As further evidence, Itzy offered Bix's piano playing:

That Bixian feeling pervaded through the man's piano playing as well. His improvisations were the most moving passages I've ever heard. I remember one night in an Indiana cafe after work when Bix hit a chord that was so beautiful that somebody (I think it was Hoagy Carmichael) became so excited that he threw a chair at him!

Funny thing about Bix's piano playing: he could play only in the key of C and he had great difficulty in reading—something which he seldom bothered to do anyway. And don't get the idea that Bix was the greatest reader in the world when it came to cornet, either. He was, I should say, only an average reader, if that.

While the Goldkette band was in Cincinnati Bix's failings as a sight-reader or any other kind of reader of music were embarrassingly demonstrated. Bix and some of his colleagues were invited to listen to a band of youngsters who were proud of the accuracy of the transcriptions of Goldkette records their talented arranger had made. There the records were, note for note, right on the nose. After they had played a while they asked Bix to sit in. Bix agreed, as Itzy said, "in his usual gracious manner." The performance went along, and Bix sounded fine with the imitation Goldketters until they came to a jazz cornet passage. Bix stopped. The band stopped. He couldn't make anything out of the notes before him. The notes were his, notes he had improvised and which the arranger had copied down accurately, but Bix couldn't read what he himself had created.

Bix was an unorthodox cornetist. Self-taught, he followed his own dictates in fingering the horn, and he raised all the parts written for his instrument from its own key, B flat, to the piano key, the simple center and beginning of the evolution of keys, C major. Even if he had been able to read well, his need to transpose everything into C would have played havoc with his playing, and if he had mastered the problem of sight-reading, his fingering would have gotten in his way. Too, his C-major predilection gave him a concept of pitch that verged on the twelve-tone formulations of the Schoenberg school of composers. He thought in terms of the C-major octave and the accidentals, sharped or flatted notes; it was inevitable that he should warm to the augmented chords and whole-tone scale of Debussy and Ravel, steps toward the eventual dissolution of fixed tonality, of thinking in terms of key.

The Goldkette band broke up in 1927—too many prima donnas and too many expensive musicians; it was almost impossible to meet the payroll. Though Goldkette himself continued to lead bands in late airings out of Chicago, and to make some additional appearances, his great years were over. Adrian Rollini, the bass saxophonist and fountain-pen virtuoso (he actually played jazz of a sort on a made-over fountain pen), took many of the ex-Goldkette musicians to New York for the opening of a new club, the New Yorker. Bix, Venuti, Lang, the pianist Frank Signorelli, Chauncey Morehouse, Bill Rank, and Fred Farrar went into the club, which lasted for all of two weeks. When it closed they all joined Paul Whiteman, who was better able than Goldkette to support such well-paid names. Bix went into the four-man trumpet section, sitting with Charlie Margulies, the technician of the group, with Henry Busse, whose speech with a German accent seemed to be reflected in his playing accents, and with Goldy Goldfield, the roly-poly little man who was the comedian in the band. Bix was paid three hundred dollars a week apart from records, a lot of money then or now as a regular salary for a musician.

Bix made many records with the Great White Father; on some you can hear him play beautiful solos; on others his lovely tone stands out as brass lead; on still others he is unnoticeable. He pops up for moments just as Whiteman's other stars do. On "San" and "Mississippi Mud," "From Monday On," "You Took Advantage of Me," "Sugar," "Coquette," "Changes," "Ol' Man River," and "Back in Your Own Backyard," Bix played with Tommy and Jimmy Dorsey, Eddie Lang, and Joe Venuti again. On "San" he and the Dorseys all played trumpet. On some of his forty-five sides with the band Bix did not try; the quality of the songs varied a great deal. On about a third of the sides he was working with songs that had already or were to become jazz classics, tunes especially notable for their chords or melodic lines, tunes easily adaptable to solo or ensemble jazz. These are the songs noted, in which the quality of his associates was brought into play alongside Bix, and the Whiteman band justified its reputation and income.

A portion of Whiteman's "Sweet Sue," a twelve-inch record, gives us one of Bix's best solos. After a muddy concerted ensemble, a treacly celeste and violin, and a whispered tenor vocal, Bix sails in with authority and full rhythmic spread, but with all the measured sweetness that doesn't change the mood so much as enhance it. But one can't go to the Whiteman or the Goldkette records to hear the Bix about whom Hoagy Carmichael, Frank Trumbauer, and Itzy Riskin raved. This man appears on the Frankie Trumbauer records for Okeh and on his own sides for the same label. Under Trumbauer's leadership he made over forty sides, some of which have become jazz classics. These include the 1927 "Singin' the Blues," the exquisite "I'm Coming, Virginia," "Way Down Yonder in New Orleans," and "For No Reason at All in C," on which Bix played both cornet and piano. On "Wringin' and Twistin' " he again played the two instruments in a trio that included Trumbauer and Eddie Lang. On "Cryin' all Day," a neglected Trumbauer record, all of the simple, handsomely constructed beauty of Bix's cornet moves solemnly in solo and more vigorously in the ensemble. Of the records he made under his own leadership in 1927 and 1928, six are first-rate of their kind: "Royal

Garden Blues," "Goose Pimples," "Thou Swell," "Louisiana," "Wa-da-da (Everybody's Doing It Now)," and "Ol' Man River." On all of these records the prevailing spirit and style is Dixieland, in which Bix's soft tone and subtle phrasing stand out almost as much as a glockenspiel would; but there is no doubt that Dixieland jazz was what Bix liked and what he wanted to play, whether or not his own style was best suited to it. On "Sorry," "Somebody Stole My Gal," "Thou Swell," and "Since My Best Gal Turned Me Down" Bix can be heard at his Dixie best.

Bix was a heavy drinker. There are stories of great bouts, of great drunks and great hangovers. After a couple of years of Whiteman, he was often an unreliable musician. Whiteman sent him on a cure at the end of 1929. He was out of the band for a year—but at full salary. As Trumbauer explained, praising his old boss, "in the case of illness, not only Bix, but various other members of his organization too numerous to mention, received full salary, and this group includes myself, for all the time off, and were met with a hearty handshake and 'I hope you're feeling better' when they returned again to the Whiteman fold." But the cure didn't cure Bix. He returned to the band for a short while, then left again, trying as unsuccessfully to play radio jobs as he was trying to quit drinking. He had never been a fast reader, and there was just enough in radio to be played at sight or at second seeing to keep him from relaxing and indeed from playing satisfactorily. At times he was in such poor health he could play nothing faster than half-notes—his lips wouldn't function. By the spring of 1931 he was a physical if not a mental wreck. He played the Camel cigarette radio program one night and couldn't make it and never played it again. He played four nights with the Casa Loma orchestra and didn't do much better. From the piano in his room in the Forty-fourth Street Hotel he led many drunken parties, improvising, imitating, and playing lots of music. Babe Ruth was sometimes in attendance; he was close to Bix and affectionate about his cornet playing as Bix was about Babe's ball playing. As many musicians as could squeeze into the room gathered there.

In 1930 he made his last recordings, five led by Hoagy Carmichael and another three under his own name with Joe Venuti, Benny Goodman, Pee Wee Russell, Jimmy Dorsey, and Gene Krupa. Of the Carmichael sides, two feature Benny Goodman, one Tommy Dorsey and Duke Ellington's growl trumpeter Bubber Miley, one Bud Freeman on tenor sax, one Jimmy Dorsey on clarinet, one Jack Teagarden on trombone; Eddie Lang was the guitarist and Gene Krupa the drummer on most. The Carmichael sides include two of Hoagy's most famous songs, "Rockin' Chair" and "Georgia on My Mind." The other three sides were indifferent novelties sparked by Teagarden, Jimmy Dorsey, Venuti, and Lang.

Bix kept busy through the spring and early summer of 1931, auditioning for a European job and making promises to himself to straighten out. But he never did straighten out. In June 1931, his health ruined by drinking, he insisted on playing a job at Princeton, which was too much for him. He came down with a severe cold. It deepened into pneumonia. On August 7, 1931, he died.

Paul Whiteman paid an expansive tribute to his former employee a number of years after Bix's death. "Bix was not only the greatest musician I've ever known but also the greatest gentleman I've ever known," Whiteman said. "But hang it, I can't tell you why." Maybe, he continued, it was because "Bix was just one marvelous guy, quiet, unassuming, never worrying much about anything, and taking everything as it came." Whiteman explained that Bix was extremely polite. When he came down from the stand he'd exclaim to the kids waiting there to greet him, "Well, how's everything down there?" And he'd accompany the words with his warm, almost bashful smile. He was nice to everybody. "Despite his greatness, he was anything but a big-headed, fluff-you-off fellow." That was part of his great gentlemanliness. There was also the dimension of his musicianship. "Somehow or other he gave you the impression that he was constantly striving for something that was just out of his reach. His continual searching for some sort of ultimate created almost a mystic halo about him— it gave you the feeling that here was a genius who knew of something beautiful to strive for and that, even though he might never reach it, he was far above you merely because he could sense that beauty for which he was reaching. . . . And I just can't describe that tone, those notes and phrases, and, least of all, the feeling with which he played. To me, there's never been a soloist like him, and let me tell you, I'd give my right arm if I could live to hear another Bix. I think my arm's safe, though!"

Extravagant? Perhaps. But all the reports check. Compare Whiteman's words and Trumbauer's and Carmichael's and Riskin's. Speak to one of Bix's intimate friends, such as Jimmy McPartland, who knew him well off and on during the great playing years from 1924 to 1931. Jimmy in those days could drink as much as Bix; in 1951 he still could play as well as Bix, not just in imitation of him. Jimmy doesn't reach so obviously for the unreachable, but the sound is Bix's and the ideas come from some of the same sources. "That was the only way for us," Jimmy said. "Maybe we thought we saw it when we were drunk. Sometimes we even heard it when we played. It was elusive, beyond our grasp, but we knew it was there and we knew that it went something like that—like the way Bix played it." That way was a fertile compound of a jazz beat and a round and beautiful tone that never accepted a distorted sound or a rough edge on a note as real. It was one of the important ways of jazz. It brought into the music a concern for constructed beauty that was as attractive on the surface as within.

Chapter 13

NEW YORK

For a long time New York has been a symbol to a large proportion
of Americans of all that's wicked and woeful in the world. For almost
as long it has been the center of art in America, but, its decriers will
tell you, only because of its banks and bankers. Gotham is one of
New York's many names, and Gotham was a village in England whose
people were proverbial for their follies. Wall Street is one of New
York's many streets, and Wall Street is an avenue whose people are
proverbial for their moneybags—some of them worn right under the
eyes. But New York has other names and other streets.

To the jazz musician the dearest of the names for the big town is
the Apple; the apple has been for centuries a symbol of special en-
dearment as well as Eve's temptation in the Garden of Eden. New
York is the apple of many a musician's eye. Most cherished of New
York streets for musicians was Fifty-second Street, *the* street for
many years. And there are other sanctified thoroughfares: Lenox and
Seventh Avenues for several blocks here and there uptown in Harlem,
where the various ballrooms have been or are ensconced; One Hundred and Twenty-fifth Street, where the bands have blown at the
Harlem Opera House and still blow at the Apollo; Broadway, where
the big presentation houses give stage room to a fair share of jazz, and
Birdland carries on still for forlorn Fifty-second Street. All of this
adds up to a considerable hot geography; jazz has had several homes
in Gotham. For more than thirty years jazz has matured in New York,
and for twenty of the thirty with growing distinction.

A detailed examination of New York jazz does not yield a "style"
in the sense that chroniclers have defined the styles of New Orleans
or Chicago or Kansas City jazz, and yet something very close to a
music that is New York's own emerged in the forties and fifties. The
movement that is variously labeled "progressive" or "modern" or

141

"new" jazz is a New York movement. Its motion spins from the early steps of musicians in Kansas City and St. Louis, Chicago, Tulsa, and Pittsburgh, but its permanence was established in New York. Here bop was born; here Lennie Tristano made his home and organized his school; here the sounds we lump together and call "cool," because they are so relaxed and restrained, so unlumpy, found adherents and skilled representation. Jazz musicians came to New York to make experiments and stayed, and so did the principle of experimentation in jazz. The keynote of jazz in New York has been experimentation.

But first an audience had to be found. Traditionally the leader of American cities in the arts, as well as in population figures, New York was a sad fourth or tenth or twentieth in taking up jazz when that ill-clad, ill-housed, ill-fed music first offered itself.

While Gotham had had vision in spotting new writers and painters, and had even extended a sort of refuge to the modern classical composers, it was purblind to the efforts of the Original Dixieland Jazz Band and King Oliver and the other pioneers in jazz. These men did all right in their native New Orleans, and then all the way up the Mississippi River to Chicago. But New York was content with a desultory ragtime and the music of revues and operettas.

In Harlem there were a few men of distinction who knew how to kick a tune and why, who played in the bordellos and the boîtes— the first not nearly so numerous as in New Orleans, the second not nearly so glamorous as in Paris. Bubber Miley, who is credited as the inventor of the growl style of trumpet playing, was playing uptown at the beginning of the 1920s. Jimmy Harrison, a gifted trombone player, was around. So were Edgar Sampson and Benny Carter. Charlie Johnson was beginning his fifteen-year engagement at Smalls' Paradise, with a band that sheltered most of the great names in Harlem at one time or another.

But downtown it was Victor Herbert and Irving Berlin and "Typhoon," "foxiest of fox trots." The Original Dixieland Jazz Band came to Reisenweber's in 1917 and played the "Tiger Rag" and the "Sensation Rag" and the "Ostrich Walk." But in 1917, though they were regarded as "interesting" attractions, Nick LaRocca's trumpet and Larry Shields' clarinet didn't catch New Yorkers' fancies particularly. The band's records sold; "Livery Stable Blues" went over a million copies; you still get worn ODJB disks in scrap drives. But it was London, not New York, that really went wild over the New

Orleans gang. When they finished their tour abroad they came back to more receptive audiences.

Then Harlem really woke up. Mamie Smith was singing the blues with a fine little band at the Garden of Joy, One Hundred and Fortieth Street and Seventh Avenue, atop a huge rock. Count Basie was playing piano in a little band at Leroy's. Tricky Sam was playing trombone at the Bucket of Blood. And there were the pianists: James P. (Johnson), Willie the Lion (Smith), and Seminole, "whose left hand was something to listen to," Duke Ellington says. Fats Waller was a baby musician then, in the early 1920s. Bessie Smith's imperial command of the blues was being established in Harlem theaters and cafes.

Clarence Williams came to New York after the First World War and published songs ("Royal Garden Blues," for example) and got himself a couple of record dates—the Blue Five—and he was in. W. C. Handy and William Pace organized a record company—Black Swan—and got themselves a great star, Ethel Waters, and then a pianist, Fletcher Henderson, and then a bandleader—Fletcher Henderson again—and they were in, for a while anyway.

Before Ethel Waters there were two Negro entertainers who captured New York, Bert Williams and Florence Mills. In a sense, Williams set the style. He was *the* minstrel man; though Negro, he performed in blackface. His characterizations satisfied the stereotyped public conception of the Negro: he was the "darky" from the "Deep Souf"; he was "coal black Joe." That he was also a great deal more escaped the notice of most of his audiences. After all, he came from the West Indies, whence came so many servants and day laborers and that funny corruption of the British accent. After all, he wore tattered clothes and a beat-up stovepipe hat and huge bedraggled shoes with flapping soles. He was respected, he was a headliner, but nobody except his own people and a few sensitive whites made a serious attempt to understand him and his background and what he was doing. It was not much bruited about that his grandfather had been the Danish consul in Antigua, where Williams was born, and that his name was his grandfather's. His large audiences at the Ziegfeld Follies from 1910 to 1919 did not know that he studied with the brilliant pantomimist Pietro during summers in Italy. Few knew that he had at least a passing skill on all the musical instruments. But he was a successful comedian, even in the Negro musicals of 1903 (*In Dahomey*), 1906 (*Abyssinnia*), and 1909 (*Mr. Lode of Koal*). When he made his debut in the 1910 Follies, the same edition of the Ziegfeld beauty contest in which Fannie Brice made her first appearance away from burlesque, he found an attentive audience but few admirers who penetrated the façade of what the dramatic critic Bide Dudley called a "slouch Negro."

Critic George Lemaire described Bert Williams' "great art, his sureness of vocal method and his perfection of pantomime":

He had very eloquent hands, which even the grotesque cotton gloves could not hide.

I am sure that if Bert Williams had suddenly found himself deaf and dumb he would have been able to command the high place that he held in the theater just the same, because of his thorough mastery of pantomime. I have seen him silently rise from his chair, while a group of us were sitting, and go to a door, admit a lady in gesture, order a whole dinner, with various bits of comedy to the waiter, pay the check and escort her out. It would be a perfect gem in its completeness. He could turn his back on his audience and convey more than thousands of actors can do with every trick known to show business.

Heywood Broun detailed one of Bert Williams' great narratives, a ghost story:

We could see the old Negro feverishly turning the pages of the Bible. The cats from the fireplace took form before our eyes. Sparks dripped from their jaws and wind howled outside the cabin. All this was built by a tall man, his face clownishly blackened with burnt cork, who stood still, in the center of the stage, and used no gesture which traveled more than six inches. The first cat came out of the fireplace and paused to eat some live coals. It was a friendly little cat. The next cat, the size of a Saint Bernard, ate some coals, spat out the sparks, and said, "When are we gwine to begin?" The third cat, as big as a Shetland pony, and slobbering fire, made the same inquiry, to which the other two replied, in unison, "We cain't do nothin' till Martin comes." At which point the old preacher said, "When Martin gits here, you tell him I was here, but I'm gone."

His skills were handsomely framed in the Ziegfeld Follies by such lovely ladies as Lilyan Tashman, Ina Claire, Peggy Hopkins Joyce, and Marion Davies. In his last Follies, in 1919—dated for the next year as all the Ziegfeld Follies were—his co-stars were Eddie Cantor, W. C. Fields, Eddie Dowling, Marilyn Miller, Charles Winninger, Ray Dooley, Van and Schenck, and Fannie Brice. Even in such select company he shone; through the outrageous dialect and the ridiculous get-up spoke the melancholy voice of the American Negro.

In the early twenties Florence Mills was the enchanting symbol of the spells Negro entertainers could weave over white audiences in New York. The "Little Blackbird," as she was known in Harlem, came downtown with the variously attractive Noble Sissle and Eubie Blake musical, *Shuffle Along*. The cast was exciting, the singing and dancing different from anything hitherto heard or seen downtown, but only the individual stars, the team of Miller and Lyles, and Florence Mills, duplicated their uptown success. Florence Mills brought her graciousness and warmth to another all-Negro revue, *Dixie to Broadway*, in 1924; its seventy-seven performances almost tripled the run of *Shuffle Along* on Sixty-third Street. She became the great attraction at the Plantation Club at Fiftieth Street and Broadway, where Duke Ellington heard her. Later, when Duke came to write three Portraits of Great Negro Personalities of the Theater —Bert Williams, Bill Robinson, and Florence Mills—he saved the softness and the sweetness for her, rescoring Bubber Miley's lovely melody, "Black Beauty," which had served Duke as a piano solo, for Harold Baker's rich trumpet and the full band.

Ethel Waters first came downtown as Florence Mills' substitute. She was twenty-three in 1923, when she moved into the Plantation and almost single-handedly made "Dinah" into a kind of national anthem. She has often told the story of her childhood, most recently in her autobiography, *His Eye Is on the Sparrow*. Illegitimate, part of a large family, impoverished almost to extinction, she had the worst of Chester and Philadelphia, Pennsylvania. She has summed up her experience in three sentences: "I've stolen food to live on when I was a child. I was a tough child. I was too large and too poor to fit, and I fought back." Her formal education was in the hands of nuns; her informal in the back streets frequented by prostitutes, and later, when she was sixteen, in a second-class Philadelphia hotel where she worked as chambermaid and laundress for $4.75 a week. Talked into going on the stage by two neighborhood boys, she made her first appearances singing the blues in Negro theaters. After an apprenticeship in the Negro clubs through the South, she found a series of club jobs in Harlem, where she made a considerable reputation for herself, not only with her nominal Negro audience but with white pub-crawlers who came uptown—a few to admire, more to gape and to get drunk. She described her work in those years for the columnist Earl Wilson: "When I was a honky-tonk entertainer I used to work from nine until unconscious. I was just a young girl and when I tried to see anything but the double meaning in songs, they'd say, 'Oh, my God, Ethel, get hot!' " The serious songs, as she explained, were all for Florence Mills. When she moved to the Plantation, she took advantage of the new opportunity, not so much to sing "serious songs" as to add her distinctive throb to the torchy ballads then in vogue.

When Ethel Waters, capitalizing on her Plantation Club success, took a band out on the road to accompany her in one-night and longer appearances, she sent for Fletcher Henderson. He was the logical man to organize the band; he knew everybody who was anybody worth speaking of musically, and besides most of the good musicians played for him sooner or later. He had them on the record dates he led or supervised; they played for him either at the Roseland Ballroom or at the Club Alabam, both on Broadway.

Fletcher, son of a Cuthbert, Georgia, schoolteacher, had studied chemistry at college. But music was irresistible to him; and his command of the piano and of all the forms of jazz and popular music was equally irresistible to those who heard him and hired him when he came to New York just after the First World War. In 1919 he went into Roseland for the first time; he kept coming back until 1935. When the Black Swan record company, for which he had done all kinds of odd accompanying and supervising jobs, broke up, he moved his several talents into other record studios. With some of the brilliant men of his dance band, cornetist Joe Smith, trombonist Big Charlie Green, clarinetist Buster Bailey, banjoist Charlie Dixon, he accompanied Ma Rainey on the Paramount label. Alone or with one or more of his musicians, he backed Bessie Smith on almost fifty of her epochal Columbia sides. Alone, he made three piano solo sides for Black Swan, and then ten times as many orchestra records for the same label and for Emerson, Edison, Paramount, and Puritan.

With his Club Alabam orchestra he began his properly famous series of recordings for Vocalion and associated labels. His trumpets, Howard Scott and Elmer Chambers, were notable chiefly for their contributions to the concerted ensemble drive. The rest of his personnel reads like a Who's Who of Harlem jazz for the next two decades. Charlie Green played the trombone—funny trombone, less like Kid Ory than like George Brunies. Don Redman fitted his long face and little body beside the suave figure of Coleman Hawkins; his alto sax was the brilliant counterpart of Hawk's tenor. Fletcher led the band from his piano, his moon face and gentle smile a trademark. The rhythm section consisted of banjoist Charlie Dixon, bassist Bob Escudero, and drummer Kaiser Marshall. On and on the records came. Louis Armstrong filled out the trumpet section in 1924, and in the same year Buster Bailey added his clarinet to the saxes of Don and Hawk. The next year the two Smiths, Russell and Joe—no relation—replaced Chambers and Scott; when Louis left, the brass was reduced to a two-man trumpet section until Rex Stewart joined in the spring of 1926. At the end of that year Jimmy Harrison came in on trombone. In 1927 Don Redman left, not to be replaced satisfactorily until the next year when Benny Carter became Fletcher's star soloist. When Benny joined the band Joe Smith was out, suffering from the paresis that killed him at an early age. Bobby Stark was the new trumpeter. Benny Morton was in on trombone for a while and was later replaced by Claude Jones; neither recorded with the band in 1929—there wasn't much record work either before or right after the crash. The New Orleans trumpeter Tommy Ladnier was in for a while too, in 1926 and 1927.

No one record of this great Henderson era deserves to be commended above the others, though the eight sides reissued by Columbia in its series of Hot Jazz Classics albums offer a fair sampling of the quality of the band. In that album the inevitable sweetness of Joe Smith's cornet and trumpet can be heard on "What-Cha-Call-Em Blues" and "Snag It," although there is a better representation of his sound and ideas in his recording of "I Want a Little Girl" with McKinney's Cotton Pickers. Louis's participation in the Henderson band can be sampled in the aforementioned blues, in the superb vehicle he fashioned along with King Oliver, "Sugar Foot Stomp," and in "Money Blues." In the last, the size and splendor of Coleman Hawkins on the saxophone can be heard, as well as on the 1927 "Hop Off" and in two sides made with the 1932–33 edition of the band, "King Porter Stomp" and "Can You Take It?" On those sides, with the exception of the last, Bobby Stark's searing trumpet rides through along with Hawk, suggesting some of the characteristic drive of

Henderson's brass section. More of the same can be heard, with Rex Stewart, Charlie Green, Joe Smith, Hawkins, and Fats Waller featured, in Fletcher's own composition, "Stampede."

Drive was the overwhelming point of Fletcher Henderson's music. And there was plenty of competition to establish the point, each soloist vying with the others in half-serious and sometimes dead earnest instrumental battles. Fletcher scored his arrangements to give the same quality to section choruses, so that brass and reed phrases sounded like spontaneous solo bursts. With this band, the exciting reiteration of two- and four-bar phrases, usually built on a blues pattern, became a basic big-band jazz formula. All of this drive and reiteration had become ordinary jazz currency by the time swing appeared, but none wrote it better than Fletcher, which is why Benny Goodman sent for him when the Goodman band was on its way to success.

Few bands afterward could boast such soloists. Don Redman poured his perky personality into his alto; Benny Carter gave that instrument breadth and inimitable variety. Rex Stewart, like Big Green, was a humorist, but he could also play with the vigor that Bobby Stark showed or the sweetness of Joe Smith. Jimmy Harrison and Benny Morton were stylists; for them the trombone was sometimes witty but more often poignant.

The great figure in the Henderson band was Coleman Hawkins. Until Lester Young came along with Count Basie, there was only one way to play tenor sax, the way Hawk played it. Just two men recaptured the Hawkins flavor, Chu Berry and Ben Webster; to them came naturally the Hawkins sound, audible breathing and great swoops of swollen phrase tied together with a languorous vibrato that gave their tenor jazz both piquancy and power. Hawk's suaveness of appearance and smoothness of language cried for Continental appreciation, which they received when he moved to Europe for five years in 1934. He spoke in a round deep bass-baritone voice, usually using few words but carefully pointed. When he wanted to he could be charming; he was also capable of a high seriousness, and his conversation sometimes took a learned musical turn. He began to study cello in 1912 at the age of five, after rudimentary piano instruction by his mother. At nine he took up the tenor saxophone, and in three years at Washburn College in Topeka, Kansas, he was a zealous student of all the technical branches of music—harmony, counterpoint, composition. Surely his early mastery of the cello in St. Joseph, Missouri, where he was born, played a significant part in the development of that large lovely mellow tone he affected on the tenor. Certainly his playing experience at Washburn and with local bands in Topeka was an excellent preparation for his first professional job of consequence with Mamie Smith's Jazz Hounds, whom he joined in Kansas City in 1923. He spent about a year accompanying Mamie, one of the blues-singing Smith girls, playing alongside trumpeter Bubber Miley and making with him and others dozens of sides for Okeh backing Mamie. In 1924, when Mamie's Jazz Hounds arrived in New York, Hawk joined Fletcher.

Smack, as Fletcher has been called since his college days, when he had a roommate named "Mac," had a remarkably well-educated band. Don Redman was born in 1900 at Piedmont, West Virginia; he picked up the trumpet at three, played in a kids' band at six, and began to study the piano at eight. At Storer College he studied all the instruments and, like Hawk, addressed himself seriously to the problems of traditional music. He studied some more, privately and at conservatories, in Boston and Detroit before he joined Fletcher Henderson in 1925.

Benny Carter, who replaced Don Pasquall, who had replaced Redman, was also a college man. Benny was born in New York City in 1907, went to Wilberforce University, where he did not specialize in music but did play in the college band led by Fletcher's pianist brother, Horace. His professional experience before joining Smack included a short stretch with Duke Ellington. Buster Bailey, christened William in Memphis, Tennessee, in 1902, was a music student in high school, and later, when he moved to Chicago, had several private teachers, the most important of whom was Franz Schoepp, the Chicago Symphony clarinetist who also taught Benny Goodman. Before joining Fletcher, Buster played with W. C. Handy's orchestra and the Vendome Theatre orchestra under Erskine Tate for three years from 1919 to 1922. Trumpeters Rex Stewart and Bobby Stark were both fine musicians and conversationalists; their early education and experience, in Washington and New York respectively, peppered their rich talk of music and musicians.

Fletcher Henderson and his musicians made a large niche for themselves in jazz history. They also helped bring New York alive to jazz.

Duke Ellington helped too. He came to New York in 1923. He and Sonny Greer, "a very fly drummer," as all his Ellington associates called him, and Toby Hardwick came up to New York from Washington, D.C., with Wilbur Sweatman's band, one of the first important colored organizations. The work wasn't so good or so regular, and there was a lot of free time for free playing at the uptown cafes. Duke used to walk the streets with a pianist named only Lippy ("Lippy had heard so much piano that he couldn't play any more"), and James P. and Fats and the Lion, and walk and walk and ring doorbells. Lippy would get the bunch into homes where there were pianos. And they would play. All night long they would play, Duke and Fats and James P. and the Lion. The days, when they should have earned money, were not as good as the nights, when they didn't want to earn money but just wanted to play and did.

Duke went back to Washington until, a few months later, he was able to reorganize his own band for a short session at Barron's in Harlem. Then came the Hollywood Club, downtown, in September of 1923. Its name was soon changed to the Kentucky Club, the South having a certain cachet on Broadway in night-spot names, because the South was where the music came from and Broadway was waking up to the music. After four years at the Kentucky Duke was a name on Broadway. The Cotton Club was the next step, and Duke was a name in America. There were records for Victor, under the band's right name, and for Columbia and Brunswick and Melotone as the Jungle Band, and Joe Turner and His Men, and Sonny Greer and His Memphis Men, and the Harlem Footwarmers. There was radio, first over WHN locally in New York and then, with a nod of thanks to Ted Husing, over CBS, throughout America. New York was finally aware of jazz, and the great jazz was beginning to come from New York.

The white bands of distinction were later in arriving. Paul Whiteman played the Palais Royal from 1920 to 1923, but that wasn't the great Whiteman band, it was only the first. Paul Specht had some pretty good men in his popular outfits, and Red Nichols was with George Olsen. Vincent Lopez was ensconced at the Hotel Pennsylvania from 1919 to 1924. And there was a lot of good booking time and money for the bands that rented out by the evening; that's where Meyer Davis broke in, and that's how Jan Garber got his start. Fred Waring was just emerging with the Pennsylvanians. And from the same state came the Scranton Sirens, with two boys who blew more than any sirens New York had ever heard—Tommy and Jimmy Dorsey. Eddie Lang came into that crew after a while too, to play some magnificent guitar.

From these groups and others some great men were poured into the record vats. Red Nichols took over, and so did Phil Napoleon; the trumpeters led the record dates then; they played the instrument of jazz authority. Napoleon's Original Memphis Five (1923 to 1928) played some fair-to-middling music, with Jimmy Lytell's clarinet and Frank Signorelli's piano impressive, and Milfred Mole (better known as Miff), a Long Island boy, a talented, well-trained trombonist. Miff had a couple of dates himself, with his Molers, which was the toothsome name they thought of for pick-up crews he led.

But over and above Napoleon and Mole, as leaders, there was one great white record-dater, Ernest Loring Nichols. The Nichols group was called the Five Pennies. With penetrating music, the Nichols band called the turn on New York and American jazz for many years after 1925. The Dorseys and Fud Livingston and Miff were among Red's first recruits. Then, in later years, came Benny Goodman and Joe Sullivan and Jack Teagarden and Glenn Miller, as the Ben Pollack band, on from Chicago in 1927, contributed its share. Nichols made so many records that nobody up at Brunswick or its successor, Columbia, ever really knew exactly how many, or whether they were all issued, or if not, where some of those discarded masters were. Nichols became a great name on records; his Pennies incubated the jazz bands of ten years later; the fairly tight, routinized Nichols sessions set the style for the men who stepped out of and away from these dates to become the biggest bandsmen of them all, Tommy Dorsey and Jimmy Dorsey and Benny Goodman and Glenn Miller.

There was lots of music in Red Nichols' home in Ogden, Utah, where he was born in 1905: his father was a professor of music at Weber College. Red's first instrument was the cornet, which he began to play at the age of four; at five he was good enough to play in public. He left the Culver Military Academy in Indiana, where he had studied some music, to play trumpet in the George Olsen band. He left Olsen to join Johnny Johnson and come to New York to play at the Pelham Heath Inn in 1923. When Johnson went to Florida, Red took over the band, which had some fine jazz musicians in it. He started to record with Sam Lanin's Red Heads, named after the Nichols sorrel top, in February 1925, and later, without Lanin's sponsorship, the band became known on records as the Redheads. The headwork was impressive: there was Red's head, pianist Arthur Schutt's, Jimmy Dorsey's, and Miff Mole's. Miff had made his instrumental beginnings on the violin and then the piano and had played trombone with the Original Memphis Five for a couple of years before he and Red put their heads together in such dance bands as Johnny Johnson's, Sam Lanin's, Roger Wolfe Kahn's, and all the Nichols organizations, on and off records. Miff's was a sensitive melodic style; his sweet phrases complemented Red's more vigorous lines handsomely, adding variation to the New Orleans–Chicago trumpet-trombone patterns. Miff was the old man in the band, twenty-six when they first began to record; his was a steadying and an enriching influence.

Red Nichols' records are the counterparts in distinction and quantity of Fletcher Henderson's sides. Under many recording names, Red introduced some of the most distinguished white jazz musicians to a large listening public. Besides the Redheads, and his most familiar recording group, Red Nichols and His Five Pennies, Red led bands under the names of the Louisiana Rhythm Kings, the Wabash Dance Orchestra, the Charleston Chasers, the Hottentots, the Midnight Airdales, the Arkansas Travelers, Red and Miff's Stompers, The Goofus Five, and the New York Syncopaters. The dates Miff Mole led were signed Miff Mole's Molers.

Pee Wee Russell, born Charles Ellsworth, Jr., in St. Louis in 1906, came from the University of Missouri and Chicago small bands to make his first appearance on records with Red in 1927 in "Ida" and "Feelin' No Pain." Babe Russin came from Pittsburgh, Pennsylvania, and engagements with the California Ramblers and Smith Ballew, to play tenor sax with Red Nichols. Adrian Rollini, nominally a bass saxophonist, introduced his "goofus" on the same date on which Pee Wee first recorded. The goofus, which was adopted as a recording name for dozens of sides, was a Rollini invention, a kind of toy instrument with the look of a saxophone and the sound of a harmonica or concertina. Dick McDonough and Carl Kress were Red's regular guitarists and set a high standard for all future rhythm sections; Eddie Lang made many sides with Red too, setting a standard for solo guitar that was not even approached again until

Charlie Christian appeared with Benny Goodman's Sextet. The Chicago musicians appeared often with Red: the drummers Dave Tough and Gene Krupa, the pianist Joe Sullivan, and the tenor saxist Bud Freeman. The Dorsey Brothers also popped up on many sides, especially Jimmy, who surely made his most lasting contribution on Nichols' records, playing a kind of darting, devilish, driving clarinet. Fud Livingston, a clarinetist much like Jimmy Dorsey in his playing manner, and Benny Goodman were frequently featured. When the trumpet section was enlarged for records, Manny Klein and Charlie Teagarden added their mellifluous sounds. Arthur Schutt made his first record appearances on piano with Nichols and established a lasting reputation as a technically facile and generally resourceful pianist, a reputation which led him to Hollywood studio bands. But the biggest and the best of Red's associates, apart from Miff, was Jack Teagarden.

Welden John Teagarden was born in Vernon, Texas, in 1905, of a part-Indian family. He began to play trombone when he was seven, worked some with his father in the cotton-gin business and as a garage mechanic in Oklahoma City, then went to San Angelo, Texas, to work as a motion-picture projectionist. In his time off from the projection booth he played with local bands, sitting in on jam sessions as often as he could find them. He moved to San Antonio, Texas, to play with a band at the Horn Palace, and then in 1921 joined Peck Kelly's Bad Boys in Houston, playing with the legendary leader-pianist, Pee Wee Russell, and Leon Rappolo at various times. He was a happy man with a feeling for jazz that amounted to an addiction; he used to carry around Louis Armstrong's records of "Cornet Chop Suey" and "Muskrat Ramble" in his instrument case or under his overcoat, and would play them any time he got within sight of a phonograph. He loved to play and played with such contagious warmth that audiences loved to hear him. With Willard Robison's band in Kansas City and with his own outfit in Wichita Falls, Kansas, with Doc Ross and with the St. Louis bands of Herbert Berger and Johnny Youngberg, Jack blew his lusty jazz and his melancholy ballads. There were always lots of jokes and lots of liquor and such incidental good times as that ride down Santa Monica's streets when the Doc Ross band was known as Ranger Ross's Texas Cowboys and Jack gave credence to the name by his secure seat in the saddle of a white horse, his trombone over the pommel and his chaps bright red. When Jack came to New York in 1927 he was immediately snapped up for records by Willard Robison, Roger Wolfe Kahn, Sam Lanin, and Red Nichols. In 1928 he joined the Ben Pollack band but continued to record with Red as often as possible. The Red Nichols records would be a significant ornament in jazz if only for Jack's salubrious trombone solos.

The quality of the various Red Nichols recording outfits can be established by listening to the sides in the albums Decca has issued in its Brunswick Collectors Series, now transferred to long-playing records. These include the justifiably famous "Ida," "Peg o' My Heart," "Indiana," "Dinah," "Shim-Me-Sha-Wabble," and "Tea for Two." On "The Sheik of Araby" Jack Teagarden demonstrates his way with melodic improvisation in two choruses after he has interrupted a saccharine singer. Benny Goodman swings through "China Boy," "The Sheik," the "Wabble," "Indiana," "Dinah," and also enlivens "Peg"; Jimmy Dorsey warms "Buddy's Habits," "Boneyard Shuffle," "Washboard Blues," "That's No Bargain," "Tea for Two" and "I Want to Be Happy." Teagarden is on all eight sides of the first volume, and needless to say, Red is on all the sides. The size of Red's contribution must not be measured only by the quality of the musicians he brought to records or by the effective, sketchy ensemble writing or by the generally fine performance of his musicians; Red's own playing is a considerable part of the accomplishment of these records. For reasons difficult to ascertain, his playing has often been disparaged. But the most casual hearing of his records makes clear why he was given so many record dates, became so popular, and drew so many distinguished musicians to play with him. He played ballads with a sweetness that suggests Bix Beiderbecke, although it is not of that unique excellence. He plowed his way through jazz figures with a brass authority and rhythmic integrity worthy almost of Louis Armstrong. He was neither a Bix nor a Louis, but he was close enough to each to deserve high praise, and both as a soloist and a leader he maintained jazz standards over hundreds of sides that few other recording musicians could equal.

As the twenties became the thirties, New York took over for the nation in earnest. Jean Goldkette came through with his band, the first really big one with good musicians in it, Bix Beiderbecke and Bill Rank and Frank Trumbauer and Don Murray. Jean Goldkette left New York with precious few of the good musicians. Paul Whiteman took most of them, including Bix and Bill and Frank. Wingy Manone came up to New York with Jack Teagarden. Jack Teagarden left New York with Ben Pollack and he too ended up with Paul Whiteman.

Paul Whiteman had sensed that there was something up around • 1924, when he gave the *Rhapsody in Blue* concert at Aeolian Hall. From then on he recruited from the jazz ranks and organized a more capacious and varied music. From his big outfit, which never played much besides the abortive product they used to call "symphonic jazz," there came the little bands that made the records, Bix's and Frankie Trumbauer's. The New York jazzmen all played with Nichols, and were joined by such itinerant Chicagoans as Gene Krupa and Joe Sullivan and Pee Wee Russell and Bud Freeman, who had left Windy City jazz followers in their debt for a lifetime and come to settle in New York.

An attitude, if not a style, was born and prospered. There is an identity to New York jazz at least comparable with that of the New Orleans and Chicago product, perhaps more striking than that of Kansas City. The vivid coloring of the New York music is not alone from jazz, as it comes close to being in the Kansas City picture. It has been so much around and about, like the sidewalks and the lamp posts, as almost to escape notice and elude chronicling. Clearly, however, New York is central to this history: without it, some major jazz causes would have had minor effects, and this music would have been without its constantly experimenting laboratory.

Chapter 14

THE CRASH

The future of the United States looked more than good in 1928; according to the members first of Calvin Coolidge's cabinet and then of Herbert Hoover's, we were entering a "new economic era." The fantasy life of the nation was peopled with millionaires and set in country clubs and great manor houses, and since so many did get rich quick there was no reason why everybody couldn't. But on Tuesday, October 29, 1929, in the course of 16,410,030 transactions, the average prices of 50 leading stocks fell almost 40 points. Thousands who had bought on margin were not able to support their purchases in the unprecedented and frantic unloading of stocks, and they were wiped out. The country was entering a five-year period of deep depression, and although the dreams were of manor houses and country clubs, reality refused to adjust itself to fantasy. Keeping pace with zooming unemployment, the slums grew larger and jazz musicians found themselves without jobs.

The full flush of American fantasy life was not really discovered until the depression. Escape was the order of the day from 1929 to 1934. The detective story, which had done very well from 1926 to 1929, did much better from 1930 to 1934. Sound had been added to motion pictures in 1926, and in 1927 dialogue had been added in Al Jolson's *The Jazz Singer*. In 1932 the three-color process called Technicolor was as much a reality as the sound track. With words and music and color, motion pictures were able successfully to circumvent "problems." American audiences wanted no part of their troubles when they sank into movie-palace horsehair, nor did they want a music that deserted their narcotized retreats. America wanted the music that was played in the country clubs of its dreams, and it got it.

There had been successful purveyors of country-club music, soft, sometimes sedate, sometimes bouncy, before the depression. Art Hickman gained a large following with that kind of music during the years of the First World War. Isham Jones and George Olsen led such bands, and Paul Whiteman began his career with such an outfit in Hickman's bailiwick, California, in 1919. Vincent Lopez added what seemed to be a virtuoso exploitation of the piano to the festivities; Ted Lewis did business with a battered top hat and a tooth-clenched, insistent question, "Is everybody happy?"; Ben Bernie led his band with a cigar and through his Broadway talk made his audiences feel they were a part of the glamorous life of show business in New York. There was showmanship in these bands and innocuous well-sugared sound, but never so sweet as when Guy Lombardo and Rudy Vallee took over in the first years of the depression.

Guy Lombardo began his career in London, Ontario, where his Italian parents presented him with almost enough brothers to fill out a dance band. He found his first audiences through a Cleveland radio station and built his huge following through radio when he was ensconced a few years later at the Granada Restaurant in Chicago. There was some appeal in the name of the band, the Royal Canadians, a happy bit of nomenclature in the days when H.R.H. the Prince of Wales was almost as popular as His Honor, the princely James J. Walker, Mayor of New York City. There was more appeal in the music itself, a shrewdly mixed anodyne topped with a generous helping of saccharine saxophone. There have been many explanations of the sound of the Lombardo saxes—that the reeds are ingeniously notched by the saxophonists, that a special kind of paper is inserted under the reeds; several disgusted musicians have suggested that the bells of the saxophones are filled with everything from warm milk and melted butter to thick molasses and corn whisky. Guy himself insists that his success comes from his choice of songs, songs whose abounding sweetness or novelty tricks assure their catching on with the public. But the writing for and playing of his saxophones must be credited as the chief causes of his commercial glory. Insensitively sharp and out of tune, yes, but also soft and at least on the edge of mellowness, the Lombardo saxophones effected a change not only in popular taste but in jazz as well. Few bands were untouched by the Lombardo sounds after Guy's opening at the Hotel Roosevelt in New York in 1930. Although they rejected his ricky-ticky beat with distaste and made great fun of his flea-bite cymbal-beat codas, Harlem bands adopted his saxophone voicing almost to a saxophone man. Louis Armstrong did not hesitate to name Guy Lombardo's as one of his favorite bands.

The enormous favor which Rudy Vallee enjoyed after 1929 resulted from his satisfying the same would-be country-club audience that Guy Lombardo serenaded. The Vagabond Lover, as Rudy came to be known, rested with a more conventional merging of violins and saxophones, a gentle joining of related colors that soothed audiences and supplied his megaphone murmurings with a subdued background. Like Lombardo's, Rudy Vallee's success came through his radio broadcasts, and radio saved him later when there was no longer a public clamor for "crooning" and his considerable skill as a *conferencier* could take over. The emphasis he and others put upon his college background at the University of Maine and at Yale was almost justified, for he analyzed his depression audiences and the music they wanted with the cool precision of a good academic mind and the equally cool practicality of a good businessman. Of jazz he said:

I knew that the vogue for "hot" bands was really appreciated only by musicians and by a few individuals who were interested in "hot" band arrangements and who at places where these bands performed were of a nature to allow this music to work them into a frenzy of dancing. I knew also that to play "hot" music one must have brass. *Although I do enjoy* this so-called "hot" music, when properly rendered, and get as great a kick as any musician out of Red Nichols, Frank Trumbauer, Joe Venuti, Eddie Lang and other masters of that style, I realized that it was over the heads of the vast majority of people who, after all, are those who buy the records and sheet music.

Of the choice and performance of his repertory, he said:

The clever orchestra leader is he who makes his program up of a few sweet soft tunes, with occasional vocal choruses among the instrumental, followed by a wild peppy tune, played ever so softly, because *pep* is not *volume*, and loud raucous notes have never delighted the ear of anyone.

He kept all of these things in mind when he moved from the Heigh-Ho Club to the Villa Vallee and from the smaller vaudeville circuits to the Palace Theatre and ultimately the Paramount Theatre, "the theater that had always been my goal to appear at, once we had entered into showdom."

As a result of Rudy Vallee's spectacular success, the vocalist became a necessary adjunct of a dance band, even one that was primarily concerned with improvised jazz. At first all dance-band singers imitated Vallee's use of the megaphone, which he painstakingly explained he used only because, "although my voice is very loud when I speak or shout, yet when I use it musically it is not penetrating or strong, and the megaphone simply *projects the sound in the direction in which I am singing*." One of those who adopted the megaphone was Will Osborne, who was helped considerably by Rudy himself. Others, because they were unable to imitate Vallee or because they had singing personalities of their own or, in a few cases, because they had the taste and skill, extended the range of crooning and converted what was essentially an enfeebled and sometimes nasalized singing style into something closer to the jazz tradition. Such singers were Bing Crosby and Russ Columbo, who in 1931 competed with each other for the public's fancy over the rival CBS and NBC radio networks. The fullness of their baritone voices and the richness of their intuitive untrained musicianship were handsomely employed in the exploitation not only of the plug songs of the moment but also of the tunes which were beginning to become classics in jazz and popular music. Bing had lived and worked with Bix Beiderbecke and the other distinguished musicians of Paul Whiteman's jazz days. Russ had played violin in the Gus Arnheim band at the Cocoanut Grove in Los Angeles when Bing was singing there. Their natural voices were so much alike that at times they were indistinguishable from each other. Their personalities, however, were not the same: the Crosby charm was compounded of an irrepressible wit and a romantic undertone, the collegian's balance of the comic spirit and seriousness; the Columbo enchantment was all romantic to fit his dark attractions, much like those of Rudolph Valentino. Bing Crosby went on to become the most magnetic musical personality America ever had. Russ Columbo died young, when a hunting gun he was cleaning went off accidentally and killed him instantly. The effect of their jazz-inspired singing was to act as a kind of reagent to the dominating treacle of Guy Lombardo and Rudy Vallee in the early thirties.

Ben Pollack arrived in New York at about the same time that Rudy Vallee did, in 1927. Rudy had graduated from Yale; Ben had graduated from Chicago and California jazz, by way of the New Orleans Rhythm Kings and countless dance bands. Gil Rodin joined the first Pollack band in California at the Venice Ballroom when Ben took over Harry Baisden's orchestra; Gil nurtured the Pollack band through its tumultuous Chicago days, bringing Harry and Benny Goodman into the organization and acting as referee in numerous disputes between the two Bens. Pollack himself was responsible for bringing Glenn Miller up and for maintaining a driving Dixieland beat he had developed in his days with Paul Mares, Leon Rappolo, and George Brunies. He had been one of the first drummers to drop the novelty effects, the cowbells and the gourds and the wood-blocks, to concentrate on keeping the rhythm steady and the beat inspiring. All of Ben Pollack's band benefited from his craft, his extensive and intensive experience, and his good taste. As a result, his Chicago band, at its peak at the Southmoor Ballroom, was a swinging wonder —even without Benny Goodman, who had left to rejoin Art Kassel, with whom he was always sure of enough money and regular work to support his large family. Benny rejoined, after some of Gil Rodin's typical persuasive eloquence, in time to make the first records with the Pollack band. Glenn Miller, who was impressed with the sound of the Roger Wolfe Kahn band, convinced Pollack that the addition of two violins would make an effective ornament for the first sides, and Al Beller, Ben's cousin, was hired along with Victor Young, the lantern-jawed prodigy who rose very quickly as arranger, composer, and leader of record dates, after his short stint with Pollack. Those first two sides were in fact an uninteresting capitulation to Glenn's commercial instinct, but thereafter not a Pollack side was recorded without some fine solo jazz.

Just before the band got to New York, after stays at the Rendezvous and the Black Hawk in Chicago, Benny Goodman, his family obligations once more on his mind, along with his differences with the sturdy little drummer-leader, left again, to join Isham Jones. In New York Gil Rodin again went on the prowl for good musicians and this time came up with two of the players who had impressed him so in the Charles Pierce and McKenzie-Condon recordings, cornetist Jimmy McPartland and saxophonist Bud Freeman. Jimmy remained with Pollack for several years; Bud left after a few months. The quality of the band's personnel, however, remained uniformly high. When Glenn Miller decided that he wanted to play at New York's Paramount Theatre with Paul Ash, who had briefly fronted the Pollack band in Chicago, and wouldn't go to Atlantic City for

the band's Million Dollar Pier engagement, Jack Teagarden was
hired. The Pollack musicians were jamming musicians, and they sat
in with little bands all over New York. On one of their jaunts around
Manhattan Island they heard Jack for the first time, playing with
Wingy Manone, with whom he had made the migration to New
York from Texas. They decided Teagarden was a must. So was
Frank Teschemacher, who was in town between jobs. And Benny
Goodman came back again, the lure of New York having overcome
his latest reticence to play with Pollack. On that Atlantic City job,
the Pollack saxes thus were the three reed giants of the Austin High
gang: Benny, Tesch, and Bud. When Gil Rodin had recovered from
a tonsillectomy, however, Tesch left the band to go back to Chicago.

The Pollack band was a playing band. Whether at the Million
Dollar Pier or at the Park Central Hotel or the Silver Slipper in
New York, it had few considerations except those of jazz. The band
played all the tunes that Vallee sang and Lombardo mellowed, but
with the vitality and the freshness that musicians like Benny Goodman, Jimmy McPartland, and Jack Teagarden could not help bringing even to the sleaziest tunes. When they weren't recording for
Victor with their leader, Jack and Benny and Jimmy were making
records for Perfect and Cameo under the name of the Whoopee
Makers, and for Brunswick with song publisher Irving Mills, who
labeled the band organized to exploit his tunes as his Hotsy-Totsy
Gang. They also made sides with Jack Pettis, the tenor saxophonist
who had been a member of the New Orleans Rhythm Kings with
Ben Pollack. Through all these many sides the Chicago organization
of jazz sounds obtained; following the practice of the ODJB and
the Rhythm Kings, of the various Teschemacher outfits and Bix's
little bands, it was each man for himself in the ensemble and all
by himself when his solo came up. Without any permanent arranger
of Fletcher Henderson's caliber, the Pollack musicians, whether playing with Ben or as a recording collective, relied chiefly on their own
large individual talents. The big band arrangements were simply
skeletons to be filled out by the soloists, and so by the most elementary conversion of soloists' phrases to band sections, the Pollack
orchestra, and Bob Crosby's band after it, managed to retain all the
small Dixieland band flavor with two and three times as many musicians.

The Ben Pollack band developed into the organization Bob Crosby later fronted when swing became the thing, after Benny Goodman and Jimmy McPartland had left. Both musicians quit when they were heavily censured by Pollack for leaving dust on their shoes after a handball game they had played on the Park Central roof just before the nightly show at the hotel. They were replaced by two men Jack Teagarden recommended, his cornetist brother Charlie and clarinetist Matty Matlock, who was then playing with a band in Pittsburgh. Ray Bauduc had come in on drums when Ben decided he wanted only to front the band, because he said he was "sick and tired of having people come up to the band and ask when Ben Pollack's going to come in." Nappy Lamare had been taken out of a small relief band at the Park Central when Dick Morgan, Pollack's original guitarist, quit. Eddie Miller, who had been playing alto with Julie Wintz's band, took over Babe Russin's chair; Russin had been in for a short time in place of the original man in the chair, Larry Binyon, and then decided that, like Glenn Miller, he didn't want to leave New York. So the nucleus of the Bob Crosby band was formed when Ben Pollack went out on the road in 1933. Charlie Spivak and Sterling Bose joined on trumpets, and Joe Harris came in on trombone when the band was playing at the Chicago Chez Paree. After a New England tour the band came back to Billy Rose's huge Casino de Paree, went down to the Hollywood Dinner Club in Galveston, Texas, and ended up at the Cotton Club in Los Angeles, where it broke up on November 1, 1934; Ben made some noises about cutting down the brass section and finally decided that he wanted to settle down in California.

The best arranger Ben Pollack ever had writing for him was Don Redman. The ex-Henderson alto saxophonist had been with McKinney's Cotton Pickers in Detroit in 1927; in 1928 and the next year he provided a fine batch of manuscripts for Pollack. As few others in the history of jazz, he was able to satisfy the fantasy-minded public's conception of melodious dance music and at the same time to provide jazz musicians with swinging figures upon which to improvise. As few others during the dog days, he kept jazz alive.

When William McKinney asked Don Redman to come out to Detroit in 1927 to take over the musical direction of his band, the Cotton Pickers were best known as a show band. They cut up a great deal and made some stabs at glee-club arrangements but had little in the way of musical distinction. Don took over at the Grey-

THE CRASH

stone Ballroom, following the Jean Goldkette band when it went on the road. He brought Bob Escudero (bass, tuba), Cuffey Davidson (trombone), and Prince Robinson (sax) into the band, and added his muscular arranging touch to a library badly in need of reshaping. The showmanship of the band remained a great asset, but it was put on a musical footing.

The earliest records made by McKinney's Cotton Pickers show the band's sharp coming of age under Redman. The fine jazz it was beginning to play is obvious in "Milneberg Joys"; its supply of ballad manuscript from Redman is illustrated by "Cherry." Soloists of great quality were still limited at this point, however, except for the trombone of Claude Jones, Don's own supple efforts on alto and clarinet, and the tasteful, resourceful trumpet of John Nesbitt, who was also an able arranger. When Joe Smith joined, the band assumed importance, ranking with Duke's and Fletcher's. On "Gee Ain't I Good to You" you can hear some typically lovely Joe Smith cornet and a typically simple and charming vocal by Don, and you can appreciate Don's always maturing arranging powers. His scoring for the saxes was growing more colorful, his brass was beginning to sound like the powerhouse sections of the swing bands.

The Cotton Pickers did good business at the Greystone. They did so well, in fact, that when they had to fulfill recording dates with Victor in New York or Camden only Don and Joe Smith were permitted to leave the band. So Don started organizing recording dates in New York under the name of McKinney's Cotton Pickers, and a couple of times as the Chocolate Dandies, featuring such stellar jazzmen as Coleman Hawkins, Benny Carter, Fats Waller, the Dorsey Brothers, and Tesch. He hastily put together arrangements for these men, and some fine records were made. "If I Could Be with You One Hour Tonight" and "Baby, Won't You Please Come Home?" made in 1930, with their lovely sax chorus introductions, illustrate the pattern of the Redman arrangement. Just about always he opened with a chorus by the saxes, prepared the way for the vocal with a trumpet or trombone solo, scored some easy riffs back of the singer, and either carried the singer to the end of the arrangement or climaxed the vocal with a clean rideout ensemble chorus. "Rocky Road," one of the best of the McKinney records, departs interestingly from this pattern. Like "I Want a Little Girl," it is a superb showcase for the talented trumpet of Joe Smith, who plays on this side in his vaunted growl style. Redman himself sings one of his most appealing vocals and plays a fine alto chorus. The whole gets a fine beat, building to its key saxophone chorus after the middle vocal. There are beautiful or provocative moments on almost every McKinney record made under Redman's musical direction. He tried out every sort of scoring, soloists against one or two or three sections, guitar introductions, celeste interludes, straight ballads or ballads with a spirited rhythmic background. Don himself played and sang his high-pitched, infectious vocals just often enough to be marked as an all-around musician of distinction. As a result of such scoring and playing, the forceful McKinney Cotton Pickers of 1928 to early 1931 were to all who heard them at the Greystone in Detroit, or on records, an inspired band.

While at the Greystone with McKinney, from 1927 to 1929, Don was also doing some arranging for the Ben Pollack and Louis Armstrong bands and some recording with the latter organization in Chicago. Don made a routine of traveling to the Windy City once every week or so to bring in a new arrangement for Pollack and to rehearse it with the band when it was in town; after several hours with Pollack he would rush over to work with Louis at the Savoy Ballroom, and then to record with the seven-piece Armstrong Savoy Ballroom Five. Louis recorded three originals of Don's, "Save It, Pretty Mama," "Heah Me Talkin' to Ya" and "No One Else but You."

Since he was doing all this work for other leaders, Don decided in 1931 that he wanted his own band. A man of quick decision, he picked himself and his horn up and left McKinney forever; he also left behind him a fine home in Detroit. The Cotton Pickers never again sounded so good, even during their brief moment under the recording supervision of Benny Carter.

For the nucleus of his new band Don took over the Horace Henderson orchestra. He had added to it several times in several sections by the time he opened at Connie's Inn for his first engagement in October 1931. When he made his first sides in September and October, the band was an impressive organization, showing the subtleties and size of Redman's growth as arranger and leader. These initial sides were the bizarre "Chant of the Weed," the powerful "Shakin' the African," and the delightful "I Heard" and "Trouble, Why Pick on Me." Few of the subsequent records by the Redman band ever eclipsed the popularity and success of "Chant of the Weed" and "I Heard," but almost all of Don's recorded work achieved respect and admiration among fellow musicians, and he continued to produce work of even quality. The saxophone choruses remained experimental, distinguished by difficult but delightful unison and harmonized voicings.

Soon after its formation the band played several weeks of the Chipso air commercial with the Mills Brothers and then toured the country as part of the Mills Brothers unit. Harlan Lattimore was Don's vocalist from 1931 through 1935 and made a few appearances later on. Lattimore was an excellent baritone; his warmth and phrasing, mixed with Bing Crosby's singing manner, set the style that has since become accepted for all male singers with a band that has any jazz feeling. Harlan projected his feeling with taste and never muffed the meaning of words or music to exhibit one of his vocal elaborations. "Underneath the Harlem Moon," "Tea for Two," "If It's True," "Lazybones," and "Lonely Cabin" were his hits. On them you hear his languorous vibrato articulated in handsome masculine tones.

The chief soloist of the Redman band, outside of Don himself, was Benny Morton. His soulful trombone and flow of ideas dominated record after record made by Redman until 1937. His sweet tone and subdued playing complemented the style of Sidney De Paris on trumpet excellently. Bob Carroll on tenor, Claude Jones on trombone, Shirley Clay on trumpet, Edward Inge on alto, and Horace Henderson and Don Kirkpatrick on piano were other soloistic assets of the band.

Don was reunited with Ben Pollack when they both played Billy Rose's theater-restaurant, the Casino de Paree, in 1934. By then the Redman band had seen its best years; it retired almost exclusively to theaters, with one last year at the downtown Connie's Inn that later became the Cotton Club, and some one-nighters. But Don's writing remained consistent. He developed his swing choirs, the first to sing "jive" lyrics against the straight background of standard songs ("Stormy Weather," "Exactly Like You," "Sunny Side of the Street," "The Man on the Flying Trapeze") with Benny Morton supplying the straight backgrounds on trombone. A short session with the short-lived Variety label of Irving Mills produced the best of his swing choir work, and some work before and afterward for

Vocalion also showed the inspired Redman arranging pen at work. In its last two years, 1938 and 1939, and into part of 1940, his band recorded for Victor and Bluebird, showing off fewer soloists, more and more complicated writing. The saxes played tremolo; Don featured himself on alto a great deal to make up for the absence of soloists; the trombones and trumpets were assigned complex figures. The final results of all this were oblivion for the band and the emergence of Don Redman as full-time arranger for other leaders. In 1938 he arranged the famous recording of "Deep Purple" that went so far to establish the Jimmy Dorsey band as a jukebox favorite. He did "Hold Tight" for Jimmy, and a great many numbers for Louis Armstrong and Ella Fitzgerald, as well as some for Charlie Barnet, Jimmie Lunceford, Paul Whiteman, Fred Waring, and Harry James. Several of Count Basie's best arrangements were Don's.

The men who worked for Don say that no matter how you came into one of his bands, you left a musician. They seem sure that he carried enough in his head to fill the books of another twenty orchestras, and that the music he wrote and arranged and led was consistently ahead of its time. This diminutive man, who began his musical career as a cornetist at three, saw his way through a half-dozen instruments, as many bands, and the most varied abilities and activities; Don Redman was a style-setter and a pacemaker in jazz.

A career parallel to Don Redman's and similarly important in the preservation of jazz was that of Chick Webb. He was perhaps the greatest of jazz drummers, a gallant little man who made his contribution to jazz within an extraordinary framework of pain and suffering. His musical contribution ranks with that of the other great jazz dead: Bix, Tesch, Bunny Berigan, Chu Berry, Jimmy Harrison, Tricky Sam, Jimmy Blanton, Charlie Christian. His gallantry ranks high in jazz. His life carried him through the first years of the swing era; his music, along with that of Duke Ellington, Don Redman, and Ben Pollack, carried jazz through its deluge.

Chick Webb was born crippled, but that didn't seem to bother him and it very rarely bothered others. He was born on February 10, 1909, in Baltimore, Maryland, into a poor family, a family-conscious family; Chick remained close to his mother and grandfather for most of his life.

His first job was peddling papers, when he was nine. He was already following the parade bands around Baltimore and saving up for his own set of drums. When he finally got the drums he evolved a set of exhibitions which could be counted upon for a good Saturday night return, say a dozen dollars. The first steady drumming job to come Chick's way, after he had worked the Chesapeake Bay excursion boats for some time, was with the Jazzola band. The Jazzola band was not much musically, but it was important for two of its men, Chick Webb and John Trueheart, the guitarist. Chick and Trueheart met in the Jazzola band and remained close friends ever afterward. When Trueheart left for New York Chick wanted to go badly. But his friend returned quickly, out of luck. They decided to try again, together.

In New York Trueheart, luckier this time, got an out-of-town job, while Chick moseyed around town. He got to know Bobby Stark. And that fine trumpeter got to know Chick's drumming and got Chick a job in the band he played with, Edgar Dowell's. Chick clicked and sent for Trueheart. The two of them made sixty dollars apiece a week—"a fortune!" said Chick, who saved all but ten dollars of it weekly. Then the band broke up, and Chick was out of work for a year.

Playing Sunday sessions at Smalls' Paradise with Toby Hardwick, Johnny Hodges, Benny Carter, and Duke Ellington, Chick began to get around among the topflight musicians. Duke and he spent a lot of time together, and when the Ellington sextet landed its Kentucky Club job Duke found an opening at the Black Bottom Club for Chick to lead his own band. But Chick refused; he just wanted to play, not lead. Johnny Hodges wouldn't hear of the refusal, and Chick found himself leading a band.

The first Chick Webb band was a quintet: Trueheart on guitar, of course, Hodges on alto, Don Kirkpatrick on piano, and Bobby Stark on trumpet. The band played an engaging, relaxed jazz. After five months Duke helped it to another job at the Paddock Club, this time with a payroll for eight. Elmer Williams came in on tenor sax, to stay with Chick for many years, and one Slats, a fine trombonist, joined up. This was 1928.

Chick Webb's Paddock Club band didn't read music but it cut the Fletcher Henderson and King Oliver bands in one-night Battles of Music at the newly opened Savoy Ballroom in Harlem. It impressed the listeners so much that although it was booked for a year it played on and off at the ballroom for ten. There were changes during that important decade, but the quality of Chick Webb's music on the Savoy stands remained constant. No matter what he played elsewhere, there was a certain meaning for Chick in the ballroom called "the Track"—because it looked like a racetrack—and this was Chick's musical home. He left the ballroom after his first year and stayed away for almost two years before coming back under Moe Gale's aegis; but after he came back he never left for such a considerable period again.

After some time on the road in 1928 Chick and his band went into the Rose Danceland at One Hundred and Twenty-fifth Street and Seventh Avenue; they were a success. They stayed a year and a half, until Chick received an offer for a try at vaudeville. The try flopped. The band was badly presented in a setting that wasn't right for it. Chick wanted to go back to the Savoy, which had refused the band after its road tour because Chick insisted on adding men. Chick struggled for more months than he liked to remember. Fletcher Henderson "borrowed" Trueheart and Bobby Stark for an audition, and only Trueheart returned. The band broke up, but still Chick didn't give up. He had his choice of big bands to play with: Duke, Smack, any band he wanted, but he wanted his own band. Everybody recognized his drumming greatness; Chick by this time recognized his own leading talent and he was determined to express it.

A number of fine musicians recognized that leading talent too, and persuaded Chick to pick up sticks in front of them: Toby Hardwick, Hilton Jefferson, Elmer Williams on saxes; the legendary trombonist Jimmy Harrison; Louis Bacon, Louis Hunt, and Shad Collins on trumpets; Elmer James on bass; Trueheart and Kirkpatrick. The new Chick Webb band won Moe Gale's favor, and he booked it into the Roseland Ballroom, where it did very well. After something more than a year there, Chick went out on the road again, and Claude Hopkins went in. Hopkins was a smash hit with his tinkling piano and Lombardo-like band, and the management insisted on his staying. Benny Carter joined Chick's band, then left it, taking a number of its men, and Chick was discouraged and struggling again. His band was out of work for seventeen months and very low in spirits. Then Jimmy Harrison died. Chick didn't know where to turn. Fortunately the Savoy did. They signed him up again, and in 1930 Chick Webb was safely ensconced once more at the big ballroom at One Hundred and Fortieth Street and Lenox Avenue.

Things began to break for Chick. He went on the road once more, with the *Hot Chocolates* revue touring company. The band seemed really set for big and important things, with an effective personnel, some fine arranging, and the unique encouragement that a full stomach and new clothing give.

The next time Chick went back into the Savoy he went back for good. He went back determined to build the best orchestra ever. He went back with a good band that got progressively better. Edgar Sampson joined up on alto, and the saxes consisted of Pete Clark, who took most of the clarinet solos as well as lead alto, Sampson on alto, and Elmer Williams on tenor. The trumpets were Renald Jones, Mario Bauza (lead), and Taft Jordan; Sandy Williams was on trombone, a fixture with the band until Chick's death; Elmer James was on bass, Joe Steele on piano, and Trueheart on guitar. Sampson's joining the band meant a lot. It meant a full-time arranger, for one thing. Originals like "Don't Be That Way," "When Dreams Come True," "Blue Minor," and "Stompin' at the Savoy" sprang from Sampson's fertile pen, and Chick was really on his way. Edgar Sampson became the band's official greeter. If you came up to the Savoy during those years from 1931 to 1935, he was the man you could talk to most easily, the musician who'd explain to you about the music the band played, about the men who played it, and anything else you might have thought of to bother a working musician. Sampson's good nature and his freely extended good will earned him the affectionate nickname of "the Lamb."

For years the commercial attraction with the band was Taft Jordan, a dark man whose infectious grin popped on and off with the rapidity of an alternating neon sign. His big stock in trade was imitating Louis Armstrong, with a gravel voice and a relay of his own tricky gestures. He capped this with trumpet solos phrased Louis-like. Taft at his best was a compelling trumpeter. You can hear him playing on Chick's delightful theme, "Get Together," and singing and playing much like Louis on "On the Sunny Side of the Street."

Sandy Williams and Bobby Stark, inseparable friends and constant companions, kidded everybody all the time, kidded on and off the stand, kidded without respect for convention or propriety, and kept all the boys laughing all the time. As a trombonist, Sandy offered a powerful barrelhouse tone and jabbing phrases that punctuated Sampson's tunes with brilliant effect. When Bobby joined the band the trumpets really picked up as a team; his incisive, inspired solos supplied a necessary bite.

When John Kirby was with the band, during most of 1934 and part of the following year, the rhythm supplied the Webb band was at its best. Chick laid down a consistent bass beat that he rarely departed from, and decorated it with superb brushwork. Trueheart's musicianship was of a piece with his personality, unpretentious but firmly grounded in the principles of good guitar playing. His shyness never permitted him to take a solo, but few were his equal in giving a rhythm section definition. When Trueheart was forced out of the band in 1936 by a lung condition verging on tuberculosis, Chick saw to it that for more than a year and a half, as he convalesced, he received his regular salary. Trueheart was more than Chick's good friend and the band's fine guitarist. He stomped off tempos for the band at the beginnings of all numbers. He had much to say in organizing "head arrangements," the on-the-spot compositions of the whole band, and helped to put together sets. Much of the direction and execution of the Chick Webb band of the middle thirties, just before it became famous, should be credited to John Trueheart.

Elmer Williams was the finest soloist Chick ever had on a saxophone. His booting tone and well-organized ideas helped put the sax trio of the early years on a footing with the brass. You can hear some short but effective Williams tenor on "Don't Be That Way" and "On the Sunny Side of the Street." After Elmer left the band, at the end of 1934, came Ted McRae, a youngster with a pretty tenor tone, who added an effective voice but just wasn't in the same class with Elmer. Altos never meant too much in Chick's bands, except in the early days when Johnny Hodges was playing for him. Edgar Sampson played good section sax and added a friendly solo every now and then. In the late years Hilton Jefferson was again in the band, an impressive, penetrating, flowing lead man. Hilton had been in for a short while in 1934, but his major work with Chick was in 1938 and 1939. Louis Jordan was a fair alto soloist, somewhat stereotyped in his ideas but contagiously enthusiastic and always driving. Wayman Carver on flute and later Chauncey Haughton on clarinet were effective soloists, whose best work was done with the short-lived small band Chick put together in imitation of Benny Goodman's chamber groups. The combination, called the Little Chicks, was made up of clarinet, flute, bass, drums, and piano.

At an amateur night at the Apollo Theatre in Harlem one Wednesday in 1934, Chick came down to see if anyone of genuine vocal ability might pop up. His vocals were being handled in the quivering tenor made popular uptown by the work of Orlando Robeson with Claude Hopkins' band. Chick's boy was Charlie Linton, and no particular distinction attached to his imitative work. So Chick sat through some ordinary singing, dancing, and comedy until a nervous but personable girl came on to sing "Judy," a popular song then. She moved the audience and she moved Chick. He decided Ella Fitzgerald was the girl for him and hired her forthwith.

Chick brought Ella home to live with him and his wife. He clothed her, directed her life, brought her along with the band, and built everything around her as the long-sought, at-last-found commercial attraction the band needed. Here was a naturally gifted singer with an extraordinary feeling for singing the way a good jazzman plays, improvising, first rhythmically, in later years melodically. She had a little girl's natural stage presence and great communicable warmth. Ella Fitzgerald gave the final push needed to make the band the real success it soon became.

The end of 1937 was the beginning of Chick's peak period. Van Alexander was writing catchy arrangements, and the band's records were moving up. Ella was a big attraction, and Moe Gale got Chick, Ella, and the Ink Spots a sustaining program on NBC, "The Good Time Society," which stayed on the air almost half a year. The brass section was becoming famed as a unit. The boys in the band referred to Taft, Mario, Bobby, Sandy, and Nat Story (the second trombone) as the Five Horsemen. Crowds collected around the bandstand at the Savoy to hear them get off and to clamor for Taft's exhibitionistic "St. Louis Blues" and "Stardust," for Chick's fantastically driving solo on "Tiger Rag," for encore after encore from Ella.

Chick wasn't much of a reader, though he could follow a score, having taught himself the rudiments of sight-reading. As a musician, however, he was remarkable. He'd always stand at the side during rehearsals of new numbers and have section bits, figures, solos played over and over again until he was familiar with every bar in every arrangement. On the stand, if a musician or a section muffed something, he'd turn around and hum the right passage correctly, note for note, to the single or group offenders. After an exhilarating night of playing, if he was pleased with a solo, he'd walk up to somebody in

172   A HISTORY OF JAZZ IN AMERICA

the band, say Sampson, tug at his jacket pocket—which was about where Chick reached up to—and begin, "Say, Sampson, did you hear that solo of Sandy's?" and, sliding a mock trombone with his hands, he'd sing over the whole solo in question. It might have been eight or thirty-two bars, improvised at the moment, but Chick's phenomenal musical memory kept it with him.

In early 1938 Chick Webb's band went into Levaggi's, a restaurant in Boston that had never before booked a jazz band, much less a colored one. The band did well. It came out of Levaggi's for one-nighters and theaters and went back for the early summer. When it returned it was an established band. "A-Tisket, A-Tasket," Ella's general idea for a swing-nursery rhyme, particularized by Van Alexander, had swept the country, and Chick's and Ella's record had been the brush that swept it. On the back of "A-Tisket" was "Liza," a fortunate coupling that showed off Chick's drumming and helped make the little man almost as famous as his singer. In August the band went into the New York Paramount Theatre. The future was assured. The scuffling was over.

But Chick was sick. He'd been sick for sixteen years and wouldn't admit it. Tuberculosis of the spine, seriously complicated by a misery-making case of piles, was moving through his small hunchbacked body. When the band went into the Park Central Hotel in New York—the first colored band ever to play it—in December 1938 Chick was in bad shape. When it left that spot for the Paramount again, in February 1939, Chick was so sick he used to faint after shows. But he still wouldn't admit it. "I'm gonna be *so* well in another couple of months," he'd say. The band went off on an ill-advised tour of one-nighters, just after it had played its last New York date under Chick at the Apollo. Chick was so sick he almost always appeared with a literally gray face. But he was looking forward to a stationary summer spot. "Besides," he said, "I've gotta keep my guys working."

The last engagement Chick Webb ever played was on a riverboat just outside of Washington. He was so miserably ill then that he had to be rushed to the Johns Hopkins Hospital in Baltimore—"just for a check-up," Chick insisted. He wouldn't let his publicity man give the news to the press. "I'm tired of them always reading about me being sick in bed," Chick said.

He was operated upon on the ninth of June, 1939. The doctors knew he wouldn't live and marveled at his ability to hold on through the week until the sixteenth. Chick was determined to live. But finally he realized his condition. On Friday he told his valet to "go home and get some sleep, 'cause I know I'm going." The valet tried to argue with him. But Chick knew the answer that always quieted his faithful valet-chauffeur and assistant-in-chief. "Ain't I the boss?" he asked. The valet went home.

At eight o'clock on the evening of the sixteenth, with his relatives and close friends around him, Chick asked his mother to raise him up. Raised, he faced everybody in the room, grinned, jutted his jaw, and announced cockily, "I'm sorry! I gotta go!"—and died.

Chick Webb left a formidable musical record behind him. He left vital memories and strong affections, but most of all he left a tradition of faith in his men and the music they played, of faith in himself and responsibility to all who worked and played with him, a tradition of musicianship and leadership.

Chapter 15

DUKE ELLINGTON

When one generalizes in writing or talking about jazz, one must always make an exception of one man. Whether the generalization is of time or place or prevailing attitude, it rarely fits the special case of Duke Ellington. In the first years of his career he and his musicians played the blues, and his particular piano style was clearly ragtime, but the total effect of the music he wrote and played at the time cannot be so neatly categorized. He took a serious beating in the years leading up to the depression, but he sailed serenely through the most bedeviled years in the modern era when jazz and its musicians were taking an unholy cuffing. He profited by the enthusiasms and rediscoveries of the swing era, but he had long been recognized as a serious musician by the time Benny Goodman came along. As a composer of large stature and the leader of an incomparable organization of talented individuals, he had been favorably received almost from the day he stepped into the Cotton Club in December 1927. The achievement was unmistakable; no such transformation of the basic and elemental in jazz had ever before been effected.

Duke started out to be a painter and achieved sufficient distinction in the medium in high school to be offered a scholarship to Pratt Institute in New York. But in 1917, before he turned eighteen, he left high school; in just a few months he would have graduated, but the lure of music was too much to be denied. To begin with he was strictly a ragtime pianist, imitating the flashy look of Luckey Roberts as he lifted his hands in wide arcs from the keyboard, imitating the striking sound of all the ragtime pianists he heard around his native Washington. He had not had much training beyond a few lessons at the piano from his mother, which began at the age of seven, and some instruction in the rudiments of music by Henry Grant, his music teacher in high school, who noticed that the boy had a fresh interest in melody and an originality in his harmonization of tunes. Duke learned more playing his first job at the Poodle Dog Cafe, where he composed his first tune, "The Soda Fountain Rag." Whenever possible he used to play at a local lodge hall with the other youngsters in his part of town who were learning the obvious and the devious ins and outs of improvised jazz. Among his associates at the True Reformers Hall in 1917 and the next two years were Toby Hardwick, who was playing bass fiddle then, Arthur Whetsel, the cornetist, who was a premedical student at Howard University, and the banjoist Elmer Snowden. Whenever possible Duke played one of the five pianos in Russell Wooding's huge band, a strictly commercial organization that had little use for Duke's fanciful ideas. His great fun was playing with the little bands, the gig outfits that played the choice one-nighters that popped up from time to time, especially on weekends, around Washington. He played with such bands as those led by Lewis Thomas, Daniel Doy, and Oliver Perry, better known as Doc. Duke learned much from all of them, but most from Perry, who was most encouraging. While playing with Doc, Duke put an ad in the telephone book explaining that he was available, like Doc and Thomas and Doy and Meyer Davis, for all sorts of musical engagements. Duke got his share of jobs and began to shape his personnel; he shifted Toby Hardwick to C-melody saxophone, and moved Whetsel, Snowden, three brothers named Miller, and a drummer behind him. William Greer, known variously as Little Willie and Sonny, came to town to play at the Howard Theatre in the pit band and soon after quit to join Duke. Then they all quit Washington to join the bandleader Wilbur Sweatman in New York; Sweatman had sent for Sonny, but Sonny wasn't being sent for unless he could bring Toby and Duke along with him. The job with Sweatman was short-lived—once again Duke's irrepressible improvisation got him fired—but the Ellingtonians had discovered New York, and Washington was never again more to them than the place where they were born and did their first playing.

In 1923, the year after the frustrating experience with Sweatman, four of them were sent for again, this time by Fats Waller, who had met them when he played with a burlesque show in Washington in the spring of that year. Duke went back up to New York with Toby, Sonny, Whetsel, and Snowden; their anticipations were high. When they got to New York they found bad news awaiting them: there

were only promises, no job. But then the singer and mistress of cere-
monies, Ada Smith, stepped in. Known as Bricktop—the name under
which she later opened a very successful nightclub in Paris—she had
a reputation and she had connections. She got the boys a job at a
night club run by a politician and man-about-Harlem, Barron Wilkins.
Barron's was a sumptuous and select uptown club, patronized by the
downtown great of show business, by Harlem's own Bert Williams,
and by Jack Johnson, the heavyweight champion. Barron's was in a
basement at One Hundred and Thirty-fourth Street and Seventh
Avenue but, according to the musicians who began to drop in regularly to hear the Washingtonians, Duke and his boys raised the roof.
They played much rousing jazz and won their followers that way;
they kept them with their soft and subtle transmutations of blues and
ragtime phrases. Their clothes matched the rough jazz; their personalities, especially their speech, were more like the handsomely fashioned quiet music they played. They were naturals for Broadway
with such an intriguing combination of the loud and the soft in music
and manner; six months after they opened at Barron's they moved
into the Hollywood Cafe at Forty-ninth Street and Broadway.

At the Hollywood they were once again taken up by show folk.
Once again their variations on traditional jazz themes caught hold.
The variations were more spectacular at the Hollywood, which
shortly after their arrival was renamed the Kentucky Club. They had
a solid rhythm section, with the addition of silent, self-assured
guitarist Freddie Guy. They had what they called a "jungle-istic"
voice in the trombone of Charlie Irvis, who growled gruffly and sug-
gestively on his horn, using a large bottlecap for a mute. Playing at
a place called the Kentucky, playing jungle-istic music, they were
ripe for the attention of Bohemia and Park Avenue, then both suddenly enthusiastic about the talents of the Negro—rooted, they
thought, in the jungle.

Bubber Miley joined up in late 1924 with his extraordinary variety
of growls, more reliable and controllable than Irvis's, with the aid of
a plumber's plunger as a mute. Bubber had a ready smile and a
chortling laugh and got both into his trumpet playing. He was a
New Yorker who had grown up with Bobby Stark, Freddy Jenkins,
and Benny Carter in the rough setting they called the Jungle on Sixty-
second Street, but James Miley had learned a lot about the South
from his mother and had listened long to the music of Southern

Negroes. From a spiritual, a hosanna, that his mother had sung, he constructed the lovely melody which was his solo in his own "Black and Tan Fantasy," one of the first great successes of the Ellingtonians. From the sound of trains and the conversations in them, from the sound of organs and choirs and Negro churches, from the general hubbub of night clubs and the particular cries and grunts of night-clubbers, from anything and everything he heard around him, Bubber made his music. Duke was making what he called "conversation music" and was well aware of its potential qualities, and he knew too that his best talker was Bubber Miley. Bubber set the style which Joe Nanton enlarged when he joined the band for its short stay at the Plantation Club between engagements at the Kentucky, in the spring of 1926.

They called Joe Nanton "Tricky Sam," in amazed admiration of the ease with which he got out of hard work. He joined several months after Cootie Williams, replacing Charlie Irvis; they were both set the task of imitating the eminent growlers who more than anybody else gave the Ellington music its striking identification. Tricky was a charmer with a high-pitched voice and a stream of facts, gleaned from the World Almanac and other reference works, with which he was glad to amaze you once you broke down his shyness. Cootie was a handsome man who had come to New York from Mobile, Alabama, in 1928 with Alonzo Ross's band, and had played briefly with Chick Webb. He had a husky bass voice that sometimes sounded like the trumpet growls he was learning to master. Both Tricky and Cootie made magnificent contributions to the records Duke was beginning to make in large numbers in the late twenties. Bubber continued to make records with Duke after he left the band, so that Cootie wasn't heard until early 1929 by the large audience that was buying Ellington records. Tricky began to record with the band as soon as it moved to the Vocalion label in late 1926, after it had made a series of rather ordinary sides for Perfect, Gennett, and Blu-Disc.

From the first Vocalion side, the band's theme, "East St. Louis Toodle-oo," its own special qualities were apparent. The "Toodle-oo" was Bubber's, a definitive demonstration of his growing melodic line, here a kind of middle-tempo plaint in which the accents were those of speech—a mildly demonstrative, elegantly phrased speech. The Ellington musicians knew that "Toodle-oo" was something special, and they recorded it again and again, for Vocalion, for Brunswick, for Columbia, for Victor. They knew that Bubber's "Black and Tan Fantasy" was a musical achievement too, and they gave it several plays in different recording studios. The appropriately named "Fantasy" shifted mood several times, chiefly to make room for the various plunger effects of Bubber and Tricky. In all of the Ellington versions of this adventure in musical—and, be it admitted, racial—colors, the original pattern was followed: the melodic phrases fashioned by Duke and Bubber gave way to growl solos by Bubber or later by Cootie Williams or, still later, by Ray Nance, then by Tricky; the growl solos gave way to the ironic quotation of the theme of the Funeral March movement of Chopin's B-flat-minor piano sonata. The concluding bit of Chopin was Duke's bitter-sweet racial philosophy. To him, as to so many children all over America, it was the melody usually sung with the words, "Where will we all be a hundred years from now?"

Harry Carney joined the band in June 1926, on a one-nighter just outside Boston, and used his high school playing experience to great effect in the enlarged saxophone section, first as an alto saxist, then as the best of the baritone saxophonists, when Duke recorded for Victor in October of that year. On two sides, "Creole Love Call" and "The Blues I Love to Sing," the saxes played lovely obbligatos for the lovely soprano voice of Adelaide Hall, whose wordless vocal on the "Love Call" was almost an obbligato in itself. Adelaide Hall made only two other sides with Duke, tunes from the *Blackbirds Revue* in 1933, but her measured amatory acrobatics were enough to make her 1927 collaboration with Duke a jazz classic.

The band recorded first as Duke Ellington and His Kentucky Club Orchestra, then dropped the cabaret identification, but when it was such a signal success as a last-minute replacement for King Oliver at the Cotton Club uptown in 1927, it became obligatory to name its new playing home on records. Under the names of Duke Ellington and His Cotton Club Orchestra, the Whoopee Makers, the Harlem Footwarmers, Six Jolly Jesters, the Ten Blackberries, and simply Duke Ellington and His Orchestra, it recorded steadily, regularly, and wonderfully from 1927 to 1932. There were significant additions to the band, most notably in 1928 when Barney Bigard, Johnny Hodges, and Freddy Jenkins joined up. Barney, who was born in 1906 in New Orleans, had studied with the great New Orleans teachers, the Tio brothers, had played with King Oliver and Charlie

Elgar in Chicago after leaving New Orleans, and had also put in some time with Luis Russell before joining Duke, with whom he stayed twelve years. His impeccable clarinet playing in person and on such record sides as "The Mooche," "Blue Light," "Subtle Lament," and more particularly "Clarinet Lament" gave the New Orleans conception of his instrument a new life and a varied expression. Johnny Hodges, born the same year as Barney, in Cambridge, Massachusetts, had played some around Boston and with Chick Webb before joining Duke, had listened assiduously to the playing of Sidney Bechet, and, with Ellington, developed an alto and soprano saxophone sound with which to express ideas like Bechet's. Called "Rabbit" by the Ellingtonians because of his amusing facial resemblance to a bunny, Johnny's playing suggested nothing so cute, though he was capable of a delightful lilt when it fitted. Essentially, however, his was the band's elegant voice; with an awesome technical ease and an incomparable beauty of saxophone sound, he traveled up and down and around melodic lines, scooping pitch in his own unique way, but never, in those days, lapsing into empty sound. Freddy Jenkins the band called "Posey" because of his elaborate gestures and grimaces when he took a solo. He was a left-handed trumpet player with a real gift for soft muted solos and a flashy talent too on hand cymbals, which he used as a clattering commentary in the band's more effervescent moments.

While Duke was at the Cotton Club he and his band made a movie short subject called, after the music it featured, *Black and Tan Fantasy*, in which the mood of Bubber's piece was made visual with a considerable use of low-key lighting. In 1930 the band journeyed out to Hollywood to play a part in Amos and Andy's first movie, *Check and Double Check*, and to feel individually insecure in the simulated atmosphere that surrounded the two black-faced white men, even though the players were treated as visiting celebrities on the RKO lot. They were celebrities: in Europe their records were being listened to and written about as works of art; in the United States, when jazz was given critical attention, Duke was always singled out along with Louis Armstrong to exemplify the best of the native music. By 1932, when Lawrence Brown and Ivy Anderson joined the band, "hot collectors," as those who were building jazz record libraries were being called, were getting into vigorous arguments over the merits of the new additions and that of 1929, Juan Tizol. Lawrence, who had studied science at Pasadena Junior College and played with the Les Hite band when Louis Armstrong fronted it, was a further confirmation of Duke's growing taste for a languorous and luxurious music which had first been demonstrated when Tizol was hired. Tizol was a Puerto Rican who played the valve trombone with symphonic brilliance; he sweetened the sound of the brass section and also brought into the band Latin-American rhythmic accents, not in his trombone playing but in his shaking of the maracas, the rattling gourds which several other Ellingtonians quickly picked up. The addition of Lawrence brought the band a musician who could play sweet or hot, whose vast technique and big tone permitted him to extract any and all the possible playing effects from the sides of his trombone, from beautiful ballads to bumptious two-beat jazz. There could be no doubt about the over-all quality of the Ellington orchestra after the additions of 1932. The individual musicianship and colors of his six brass, four saxes, and rhythm gave Duke for the first time an adequate palette with which to express his matured ideas. Now, too, he had a singing voice always there, always ready, always good.

It was Ivy Anderson's fortune to have a voice and a personality that fitted an orchestra and an era so tightly that she was and will be remembered as long as the music and the time are remembered. Her life, like her songs, was a medley, a puzzling mixture. She was born in Oklahoma and educated at a convent in California, and she was as sophisticated a singer as jazz has produced. She had had some serious vocal coaching and sang in night clubs and revues, including *Shuffle Along*. With her neat coiffure, her impeccable clothes, her refined and delicate features, and her exquisite manner went an improper, rough voice, an impudent gesture, a sardonic smile that, in bewildering combination, tumbled audience after audience into her lap in the course of eleven years with Ellington.

She sang first, briefly, with Anson Weeks's band, and was featured at the Grand Terrace in Chicago. Then she joined Duke Ellington in February 1931. She left the Duke in 1942, suffering from asthma, the condition which killed her seven years later at the age of forty-five. After leaving Duke she worked irregularly; she made her final appearance in New York to raise the last few dollars necessary to buy an apartment house in Los Angeles, which was to have been her security.

Since her departure there have been many other singers with Duke, some of merit, some just barely able to discharge their vocal responsibilities, but good or bad, successful or not, none has ever replaced Ivy. Her sound on records was such that she made certain words and phrases indelible: "It Don't Mean a Thing if It Ain't Got that Swing," "Stormy Weather," "My Old Flame," "Oh, Babe! Maybe Someday," "It Was a Sad Night in Harlem," "All God's Chillun Got Rhythm," "A Lonely Co-ed," "Killin' Myself," "I Got It Bad and that Ain't Good," "Rocks in My Bed"—those are Ivy's songs. They are her songs not because she sang them first with Ellington, but because she embraced them, hugged them tight, possessed them, and then shared them with her listeners.

Ivy sang "Stormy Weather" in the *Cotton Club Parade* of 1933, as they called the annual show at Harlem's most important night club; she also sang "Raisin' the Rent," "Happy as the Day Is Long," and "Get Yourself a New Broom." These fine songs, written by lyricist Ted Koehler and composer Harold Arlen, were typical of the music Duke recorded when he wasn't recording his own brilliant compositions. His chief provender, however, during the Cotton Club years, were his own three-minute masterpieces. His soloists made many contributions in the way of little figures, two-to eight-bar phrases, around which Duke could score a whole composition. "Sophisticated Lady," for example, the famous coupling on records with "Stormy Weather," was mostly Toby Hardwick's tune, which Duke whipped into a thirty-two-bar chorus and made into a smash hit. Bubber's lovely "Black Beauty" was material both for the band and for a charming piano solo in which Duke wove tricky, raggy, endlessly inventive variations around the Miley theme. Harry Carney contributed "Rockin' in Rhythm," an extraordinary rhythmic exercise like Duke's own "Jubilee Stomp," "Saratoga Swing," and "Saturday Night Function." In the six minutes of the two sides of "Tiger Rag," the band sounded more like Fletcher Henderson's than Duke Ellington's, but the solos by Freddy Jenkins, Barney, Carney, Johnny Hodges, Bubber, and Tricky were Duke's voices and sounded like nobody else's. There were the mood pieces, in which plaintive melodies were given apposite sonorities, soft clarinet, low muted trumpet, restrained growls inflected as if they were heartfelt sobs. "Misty Mornin' " and "When a Black Man's Blue" are typical of the mood pieces; "Mood Indigo" is the most famous of them, with its exquisite combination of trumpet and trombone, both muted, and the clarinet in its lowest register. On the two sides of the twelve-inch recording of "Creole Rhapsody," Duke served notice that he was not forever to be content with the three-minute form. Still, through the thirties, Duke's medium was the ten-inch record, and to it he adapted all his composing ideas and skills. It is difficult to think of such tightly molded pieces as "Echoes of the Jungle," "The Mystery Song," and "Blue Ramble" as anything longer or shorter than they are; each orchestral statement, each solo is precisely where and as long·as it should be.

Duke's success was almost without limits; certainly no jazz band of this quality sold so many records or pleased so many audiences. To most jazz musicians there was a kind of infallibility about the Ellington band; they regarded each new record as a definitive musical pronouncement. But Duke himself was not satisfied: there had been too many business complications; his organization had got too large for comfort; he wasn't at all sure that he had achieved anything much. Short of quitting, there seemed only one expedient measure, a trip to Europe. In the spring of 1933 the Ellington band embarked for England, where it spent many weeks before a brief appearance in Paris. Everywhere he went Duke was received with such adulation and ceremony that it was inevitable he should rub noses (figuratively) and indeed play some jazz (literally) with two future Kings of England, the Prince of Wales and the Duke of York. The European trip gave him confidence again, made him realize that if his music could please discriminating audiences and stir controversy it was more than a complicated means of making a living. He came back to the United States set to double or triple his activity.

In the autumn of 1933 Duke took his band south for its first trip into the world of rigid double standards. To everybody's delight, the band was received as it had been in Europe. The marks of racial discrimination were unmistakable, but the band was not affected much more than it had been in England, where there had been one or two minor incidents.

After this very successful Southern tour, Duke went out to Hollywood to make a couple of movies for Paramount and to play at Sebastian's Cotton Club, where Lawrence Brown had got his start in the Les Hite band. In the mystery-musical film, *Murder at the Vanities*, the band played its own variation on Coslow's and Johnston's variation on Liszt's "Second Hungarian Rhapsody," renamed "Ebony Rhapsody." In short appearances in Mae West's *Belle of the Nineties* it took two lovely songs, "Troubled Waters" and "My Old Flame," and made them lovelier with the help of Ivy Anderson. The band also played some fine music in a short film, *Symphony in Black*, which apart from the Ellingtonians was nothing more than a rehearsal of Negro stereotypes.

On the way out to the Coast, in Chicago, the band recorded Duke's musical trainride, "Daybreak Express," which integrated railroad sounds and music more successfully and less synthetically than the French composer Arthur Honegger did in his famous "Pacific 231." Some of the success of the swinging express was its necessary compression to fit the three-minute record form; once again Duke took advantage of a mechanical limitation. Another important recording made in Chicago was "Solitude," which, coming so soon after "Sophisticated Lady" and rivaling the latter's success, added much to the public's conviction that Duke was one of its favorite composers of popular songs. After Hollywood, in the fall of 1934, Duke made one of his many switches from one record company to another, back to Brunswick from Victor. He recorded "Solitude" again, "Moonglow," a song based on one of his own figures but accruing royalties for another composer, Toby's lovely "In a Sentimental Mood," and two brassy little triumphs, "Showboat Shuffle" and "Merry-Go-Round." In September 1935 he reached the magnificent climax of his first decade of recording with the two records of a four-part composition, "Reminiscing in Tempo."

The title, "Reminiscing in Tempo," is a clue to the piece's construction. It rambles rhythmically over a series of related melodies. In it Duke reminisces about jazz and the places in which jazz can be played and all the things that can be done with jazz. He also soliloquizes, as he has explained, beginning the ramble "with pleasant thoughts." Then, he says, "something gets you down." The end comes when "you snap out of it, and it ends affirmatively." Something did get Duke down; his mother had died in May of the same year. Something did snap him out of it; the coming of the swing era brought Duke a larger audience and, if possible, a more intense interest in every twist and turn and divagation of his music. "Reminiscing in Tempo" was greeted with an astonishing furor of praise and condemnation. Some found Duke's reminiscing inflated, even pretentious, a lamentable departure from the three-minute form in which he had been so notably successful. Others, those who crowded the Urban

Room of the Congress Hotel in Chicago in the spring of 1936, those who wore out copy after copy of the two-record "Reminiscing," cheered the adventurousness of the work and listened long and hard enough to discover more expansive and better-developed form in all the qualities that had endeared Ellington to them.

It was for this second audience that Duke ordered his concertos, three minutes in length but, like "Reminiscing in Tempo," more ambitious in form. Barney's concerto was "Clarinet Lament"; Cootie's, "Echoes of Harlem." When the first two concertos did well, Duke fashioned two others, "Trumpet in Spades" for Rex Stewart, who had brought his perky cornet into the band in 1934, and "Yearning for Love," which didn't exhibit Lawrence Brown's capacious talents nearly as well as the earlier "Sheik of Araby" or the later "Rose of the Rio Grande." For his disapproving, mildly disaffected fans, Duke provided a series of good old-fashioned jam sessions, "In a Jam," "Uptown Downbeat," "Harmony in Harlem," and revived his very earliest jazz pieces, "East St. Louis Toodle-oo" and "The Birmingham Breakdown," to both of which he affixed the adjective "new."

Swing had come along in 1935, apparently to stay forever. In celebration of the enthusiastic jazz revival, Duke named two of his works "Exposition Swing" and "Stepping into Swing Society." It was difficult to decide who had stepped into whose society, but clearly the Ellington musicians were at home in the new music. Other bands noisily claimed swing as their very own, but every musician who played big-band jazz knew that almost his every phrase had in some way been shaped by Duke Ellington and his musicians.

Chapter 16

SWING

On February 2, 1932, Duke Ellington brought his Famous Orchestra, as the record labels have it, into a New York studio to record three sides. One of them became a jazz classic, "Lazy Rhapsody." One of them, "Moon over Dixie," had almost no interest for Ellington fans, then or now. One of them, "It Don't Mean a Thing if It Ain't Got that Swing," named the whole era that was to follow in three years. Ivy Anderson sang it with all the strength and joy which her first work on records had to have; in her swinging singing and the band's similar playing the title was handsomely demonstrated. In December 1935 a bright little novelty record, with almost no discernible meaning except the implicit joy in its title and the execution of the meaning thereof, inaugurated modern jazz in general and the first few years of it in particular. The record was Eddie Farley's and Mike Riley's "The Music Goes 'Round and 'Round"; the era which was beginning was called Swing.

Maybe it was the swing away from the worst years of the depression that made the Christmas of 1935 the logical time to start the new era. Maybe the American people, or that group interested in the dance anyway, had had enough of Guy Lombardo and Hal Kemp and all the more pallid versions of jazz. Maybe this was simply proof that jazz would never die as long as fresh talent was available. Whatever the reason, it was the freshness of the music that Benny Goodman and his musicians played that made swing as inevitable as the success of "The Music Goes 'Round and 'Round" was incalculable. Benny was the logical man to take charge of the new music. Of all the talented musicians who came out of Chicago, he was clearly the most polished, the most assured, the most persuasive stylist. Of all the instruments with which one could logically front a jazz band, his was the last to reach public favor. Of all the clarinetists to achieve esteem, if only

185

among jazz musicians, he was clearly the most generally able and specifically facile.

Before Benny, Sidney Bechet and Johnny Dodds and Jimmy Noone had established certain clarinet procedures, but none of them, in spite of their individual and collective ingenuities and skills, had the kind of sound that made Benny's success so certain. Popular success in the band business has, like popular success in so many other kinds of popular culture in America, always depended upon some novelty interest. Benny's graceful, skillful maneuvering of clarinet keys certainly had such interest to dancers and listeners alike in 1935. It didn't matter what he played—"The Dixieland Band" or "Hooray for Love," "King Porter Stomp" or "Yankee Doodle Never Went to Town"—it was that infectious compound of lovely sound and moving beat that made Benny his large audiences. Sound and beat were both fashioned over many years of playing experience, most notably on the records with Ben Pollack from 1926 to 1931, and then with various bands such as Red Nichols and the Whoopie Makers, Irving Mills' Hotsy Totsy Gang, Jack Pettis, and various combinations under Benny's own name. When Benny became a success as a band leader he could look back to a career that was traditional for jazz and had ranged over most of the possible styles of the middle and late twenties and early thirties. His playing experience moved all the way from short-pants imitations of Ted Lewis to every possible kind of dance, radio studio, night club, ballroom, and one-nighter job. None of the problems he had to face were new to him.

Benny Goodman's first impact upon the country at large was the third hour, which Benny had all to himself, of the three-hour National Biscuit program which was sent over the National Broadcasting Company network every Saturday night. Working with most of New York's first-rate white jazzmen, with many of whom he had shared stands before, Benny put together a startlingly good band for radio. He had made records with the Teagardens, trumpeter Manny Klein, Joe Sullivan, Artie Bernstein, and Gene Krupa; his standards were high. In his broadcasting orchestra he had the trombonist Jack Lacey, the lead alto saxophonist Hymie Schertzer, Claude Thornhill on piano, and George Van Eps on guitar. After a dismal showing at Billy Rose's Music Hall, a theater-restaurant which was distinctly not the right setting for his kind of music, he put together a band with which to go out on the road, and improved on his radio personnel. Gene Krupa became his drummer, Jess Stacy his pianist, Ralph Muzillo and Nate Kazebier his trumpeters. Though his saxophones and trombones were something less than the combinations of the best musicians that his previous recordings had suggested he might have, as sections they were well disciplined and swinging, on the whole the abiding virtues of the Goodman band that played the music called swing.

"Swing," as some of us knew then and all of us know now, was just another name for jazz; it was a singularly good descriptive term for he beat that lies at the center of jazz. It certainly described the quality Benny's band had. With Fletcher Henderson as his chief arranger, Benny's music had a quality that only the very great big bands had had before, and it reached more people than jazz had ever dreamed of for an audience. Fletcher's writing was such, so tight, so adroitly scored in its simplicity, that each of the sections sounded like a solo musician; the collective effect was of a jam session. With such an effect, it was possible to record essentially dreary material like "Goody Goody" and "You Can't Pull the Wool over My Eyes" and give it something more than a veneer of jazz quality. A big-band style was set that was never lost again, as the distinguished qualities of New Orleans and Chicago jazz had been, at least to the public at large, after their peak periods. After the emergence of the Goodman band, all but the most sickly commercial bands tightened their ensembles, offered moments of swinging section performance and even a solo or two that were jazz-infected. Kay Kyser, in his last years as a working bandleader, hired Noni Bernardi to lead his saxes, and Noni, who had played alto with Tommy Dorsey, Bob Crosby, Charlie Barnet, and Benny for a while, converted not only his reeds but the band itself from a series of ticks and glisses into a dance orchestra of some distinction, with jazz inflections that had some of us looking forward to each new record. When Harry James became a successful trumpeter-leader as a result of a crinoline and molasses version of "You Made Me Love You," the essential swing style was preserved and some first-rate jazz sandwiched in between nagging laments and rhapsodies and pseudo-concertos for trumpet and orchestra. Charlie Spivak paid occasional respects to his jazz background, and there was some fair jazz in the music of the Dorsey Brothers after they split up and led their separate bands; in the band of the ex-society leader, Al

Donahue; in radio studio groups; even in more than a few territory bands, those minor-league outfits that build a name and a public only within an easily negotiable geographical area.

Benny's success was far more than a personal one; his influence was lasting; his way was others' too. When Benny turned a poor road trip into a jubilant roar of approval at the Hollywood Palomar Ballroom, the cheers were not only for his band but also for the school of jazz it represented. Other bands playing music even vaguely related to Benny's were almost equally well received for a while, and it became expedient to identify one's jazz as "swing." Fortunately some of the bands that benefited from Benny's success were deserving, and a few of them developed and expanded the way of playing jazz called "swing."

Bob Crosby, Bing's singing younger brother, took over the distinguished remnants of the Ben Pollack band in 1934, and it, more than any other band, large or small, brought New Orleans jazz back to life. Bob had as his band's centerpiece one of the best musicians ever turned out by that city, Eddie Miller, and, to match Eddie's tenor, Matty Matlock's clarinet; Yank Lawson's trumpet; Nappy Lamare's personality, vocals, and guitar; Bob Haggart's bass; and Ray Bauduc's drums. After the demise of the band the Dorseys led together in 1935, Tommy turned soft-spoken ballads into a big business and Jimmy tried several things, finding their chief musical success with a semi-Dixie style built around Ray McKinley's drums, and box office appeal with alternately up-tempo and medium or slow vocal choruses by Helen O'Connell and Bob Eberle. Charlie Barnet, who had had a New York playing and recording career like Benny's, if shorter, moved a step beyond the others in his band's performances of Duke Ellington manuscript; and Woody Herman, identified like Charlie with the squat little Fifty-second Street bandbox, the Famous Door, played the blues and pops and sang standards handsomely.

Fifty-second Street came to enthusiastic life shortly before Benny bowled over the Coast and then took over Chicago. The lifeblood in his trio and quartet, Teddy Wilson, had been an interlude pianist at the old Famous Door, across the street from Barnet's and Herman's later headquarters. The kind of performance Benny's small units made popular after Teddy drove out to Chicago to play a concert with the Goodman musicians in March 1936 was a Fifty-second-Street session: any number of instruments short of a big band could be com-

SWING

bined as long as the beat was steady and the time allotted sol...
pansive. There were all kinds of groups along Fifty-second Street's
two playing blocks in the thirties and early forties: Red McKenzie
and Eddie Condon, together and apart, at first with Bunny Berigan,
then with the cast that became Nick's permanent two-beat repertory
company, Pee Wee Russell, Max Kaminsky, Wild Bill Davison,
George Brunies, and George Wettling; Fats Waller, before Benny
hit and carried him along with the others who played that kind of
music; John Kirby, an Onyx fixture with Charlie Shavers, Buster
Bailey, Billy Kyle, and O'Neil Spencer, the Spirits of Rhythm, and
Frankie Newton's band; singers like Billie Holiday and pianists like
Art Tatum, who eventually became the Street's major luminaries.
Perhaps the most significant of all the bands was the one that, even
more than the Goodman band, typified, expanded, and carried swing
forward—Count Basie's.

The Red Bank, New Jersey, pianist William Basie, who had started
as a drummer, had become a Kansas City jazzman, working with
Bennie Moten, then with his own twelve-piece band at the Reno Club.
Benny Goodman and John Hammond heard the band out of a short-
wave station, W9XBY, recognized extraordinary skills in the jumping
rhythm section and the fresh patterns of Lester Young's tenor solos.
With Benny's help, John, the most articulate and influential of the
jazz critics of the thirties, did something about it. Basie moved to the
Grand Terrace in Chicago, made records for Decca, and came on to
New York's Roseland Ballroom in 1936. He picked up fans and followers as he went from club to record date to ballroom; the best of
the swing styles was clearly his; the bridge to later jazz was built.

The illustrious solo moments of the Basie band were those of
Lester Young on tenor and Harry Edison on trumpet, but they weren't
fully appreciated until some years after the band had passed its peak.
The real star was what Paul Whiteman called Count's "All-American
Rhythm Section" in a 1942 article in *Collier's*, selecting the best musicians in jazz. Freddy Greene was a guitar rock; Joe Jones' drum
tempos and Walter Page's bass intonation were neither as steady
nor as consistent; and Basie himself provided only piano decoration,
albeit charming. It was a unit, however, one which took fire from
Joe's cymbals and warmth from Walter's strings, got good guitar
time, and was capable of sustaining a string of choruses all by itself,
with the titled head of the band and the section tinkling on the off-

190　　A HISTORY OF JAZZ IN AMERICA

beats. "I don't know what it is," one of the Basie veterans once said. "Count don't play nothing, but it sure sounds good!"

There were others in the band who sounded good, too: Benny Morton, whose trombone was languorous always and often lovely; Dickie Wells, who made funny noises into fetching phrases on the same instrument; Vic Dickenson, who carried the sliding humor further. The famous Basie trumpeter when the band was most famed, from 1936 through 1942, was Buck Clayton, whose identifying grace was delicacy. When joined with a subdued Lester and Dickie and the rhythm section for a Cafe Society Uptown engagement, Buck's muted trumpet set the style for the small band within the large and pointed to Basie's major achievement: the ability to keep the roar implicit and the beat suggestive. At other times, it was all ebullience, a genial fire stoked by rotund Jimmy Rushing's robust blues shouting, the brass section's stentor and the saxes' strength. Men like the late Al Killian, of the leathery lungs, passed through the trumpet section. Tab Smith, an insinuating alto saxist of the Hodges school, replaced Earl Warren, the band's original ballad singer and lush reed voice, for a while. Several tenors tried at various times to duplicate the furry sound of Hershal Evans, who died early in the band's big-time career—most notably and durably Buddy Tate. Jack Washington was a baritone player of some distinction—and power, the key quality of an organization that for a while blasted every other band out of the way.

Jimmie Lunceford's showy musicians moved into prominence earlier than the Basie musicians—and moved out earlier. With the death of Lunceford in Oregon on July 12, 1947, the last edition of a once-great organization, already fading badly, was washed out completely. But the style remains, firmly embedded within the grooves of a select number of phonograph records.

Jimmie, a Fisk University graduate, recruited the nucleus of his first band at a Memphis high school, where he was an athletic instructor. He picked up Sy Oliver in the early thirties and his style was set, never to vary importantly until his and his band's demise. That style, sooner or later, influenced almost every important band in jazz. It was the most effective utilization of two-beat accents discovered by any jazzman; it made a kind of impressive last gasp for dying Dixieland, with its heavy anticipations, its almost violently strong and whisperingly weak beats, its insistent, unrelenting syncopation.

There were about eight years of prime Lunceford, beginning with the Cotton Club engagement the band played in 1934, ending with the exodus from the band of Willie Smith in 1942. At first the band played flashy, stiff instrumentals in the Casa Loma manner, such Will Hudson specials as "White Heat" and "Jazznocracy." These and other Hudson pieces were used in turn by Glen Gray's Casa Loma Orchestra, a group of Canadian musicians who excited some enthusiasm in the year just before Benny Goodman took over, more because of their shrewd balance of ballads and mechanical jazz than because of any real musical quality. When Sy Oliver became Jimmie's chief arranger in 1935, the parade of two-beat specials most irresistibly associated with Lunceford's name began: "My Blue Heaven," "For Dancers Only," "Margie," "Four or Five Times," "Swanee River," "Organ Grinder Swing," "Cheatin' on Me," " 'Taint What You Do," "Baby, Won't You Please Come Home," etc. Bill Moore, Jr., showed up to replace Sy when the latter left to join Tommy Dorsey; Bill left a vital impression on the band's books with his "Belgium Stomp," "Chopin Prelude," "Monotony in Four Flats," and "I Got It" (the last backed on records by Mary Lou Williams' sensitive "What's Your Story, Morning Glory").

Coupled with the instrumental style of the band, which, much as it emphasized its hacking two-beat, depended upon section precision, was a singing manner. Jimmie's boys whispered, wheedled, cozened, rather than sang. Out of the first husky efforts of the Lunceford Trio (Sy, Willie, guitarist Al Norris) grew the individual vocalists, Oliver and Smith, Joe Thomas, later Trummy Young. Their rhythmic attack at a low volume held a brilliance of innuendo which never failed to grab an audience's attention (for example, Trummy's "Margie," Sy's "Four or Five Times," Willie's "I Got It," Joe's "Baby, Won't You Please Come Home" and "Dinah") as Jimmy Crawford's brilliant drumming grasped its pulse.

The band's soloists were always secondary to the arrangements in Lunceford's heyday, but some genuinely distinctive individual sounds did emerge from the group. Trummy Young played a wistful trombone. Willie Smith's agile, enthusiastic alto remains the most in favor, but there are tenormen who swear by Joe Thomas's soft tone, and those of us who followed the band eagerly in the mid-thirties remember with pleasure the solo trumpeting of Eddie Tompkins, who was killed in war maneuvers in 1941. Eddie can be remembered for other things, too: when the trumpet section consisted of his horn, Sy's, and first Tommy Stevenson's, then Paul Webster's, it was a high-flying unit, not only in the screeches it sometimes played in tune, but in its instrumental gymnastics, in its wild flinging of its three trumpets into the air in perfect unison.

At its zenith, Lunceford's was *the* show band, whether in its military formations on the stage or ballroom stand, in its multiple doubling of instrumentalists as singers, or its comparatively precise performances. Even after it passed from the serious consideration of musicians and critics as a contemporary jazz outfit, its old records retained interest, its old appearances stirred a nostalgic tear. Jimmie never did much more than wave a willowy baton, smile tentatively, and announce the names of his soloists and singers, but he held title to one of the genuinely distinctive swing bands.

Some of the powerhouse quality of the Lunceford band was picked up by its most slavish imitator, Erskine Hawkins and the Bama State Collegians. The self-styled Gabriel of the trumpet never did as much with the youngsters he brought from Alabama State University to New York as he might have. But he was luckier than most of the men who brought flashy outfits into New York for one or two or a dozen appearances in the late thirties and early forties, to leave an impression of crude strength and undeveloped talent and no more; he at least made enough of a reputation to be confused with Coleman Hawkins by some of the unknowing; he had a hit record grow out of one of his band's original works, "Tuxedo Junction." The Jeter-Pilar band came in from St. Louis several times and always charmed its listeners, but never had the soloists or the scores to make the charm linger. The Sunshine Serenaders came in from Florida and made a lot of attractive noise, but never with an identity all its own. The Harlan Leonard band blew in from Kansas City, and its breezy airs and brassy competence, coupled with the booming impression of the Jay McShann band and Count Basie, gave the impression for a while that there was such a thing as a Kansas City "style." But when these were compared with the Andy Kirk band, so very different really, so much more timid, so much more a matter of Mary Lou Williams' writing and playing talents, the style disappeared along with the comparison.

SWING

There was more of the Kansas City style—if Leonard and Mc-Shann and Basie were representative of it—in bands that had rarely if ever seen the Missouri metropolis. The massive Mills Blue Rhythm Band, bumping along behind the solos of Red Allen on trumpet and J. C. Higginbotham on trombone, was an example of this sort of jazz. Willie Bryant's swinging group of 1935 and 1936, with first Teddy Wilson, then Ram Ramirez on piano, with Puddin' Head Battle on trumpet, had much of the same spirit, some of it because of its leader's sprightly announcing and singing wit. The minor outfits—Billy Hicks and his Sizzling Six, Al Cooper's Savoy Sultans, Buddy Johnson's band—all had it in varying measure. Cab Calloway bought it when he began to fill out his sections with men like Milton Hinton on bass, Chu Berry on tenor, and Cozy Cole on drums in 1936 and 1937 and then Jonah Jones on trumpet a few years later. When Cab began to buy manuscript from men of the quality of Don Redman, he had a band to compete with Basie and Lunceford and even Ellington. If his box office could have matched his budget, if his personal public and the new band's following could have been coupled, his contribution to jazz history might have equaled his flamboyance and his fervor as a singer.

The white bands got the first swing customers; the Negro outfits followed close behind. About the same time that Basie was emerging as a national figure, so were the bands at the Savoy Ballroom in Harlem—Teddy Hill's and Chick Webb's; so was Jimmie Lunceford, with his precision scoring and precision musicians; so was the band that Jimmie followed at the old Cotton Club, Duke Ellington's. Duke was almost as much in demand for rhythm and hot-club concerts as Benny; his experiments, such as the four-part "Reminiscing in Tempo," were the subject of violent controversy among musicians and aficionados; his tone colors were adopted by all kinds of bands and musicians. Along with the Negro bands themselves, individual Negro musicians and singers were beginning to be accepted, even with white bands. Benny Goodman added Lionel Hampton to his trio and made it a quartet. Later, in the first of several reorganizations of personnel after short-lived retirement, Benny took on Cootie Williams and Sidney Catlett, and Charlie Christian was his featured guitarist and perhaps the very best musician he ever had.

Artie Shaw showed himself something more than an imitator of Benny when he signed Billie Holiday as his singer, and, though this was not an altogether successful arrangement, the hiring of Lips Page for Artie's comeback band in 1941 and Roy Eldridge in another return edition in 1944 proved entirely satisfactory on all counts. These were instances in which Artie's threats to revolutionize jazz and the business attendant upon the music leaped beyond words into inspired deeds. It was not always that way, partly because Artie's attempts at the sublime were undisciplined, partly because the sublime was not always accessible, even to the impeccably disciplined of jazz.

The first attempt, after an early success as a radio studio and jobbing clarinetist in New York, was with a combination of solo jazz instruments, rhythm section, and string quartet. In various combinations in 1936, it failed commercially, and musically too, because of a certain protective pallor that approached indifference. The new few editions of the stringless Shavians led to a simple swinging skill by 1938, best illustrated for the public by the fabulously successful recording of "Begin the Beguine," best demonstrated for musicians by the authority of soloists like Georgie Auld on tenor, Les Robinson on alto, Chuck Peterson and Bernie Privin on trumpet, and Artie himself on clarinet, with a formidable assist the next year by young Buddy Rich on drums. Then in the fall of 1939 Artie ran away from a choice engagement at the Hotel Pennsylvania in New York, ran to Mexico because, he said, he was sick of the spectacle and the corruption of the jazz business. In a few months he was back with a lot of strings and at least one shrewdly chosen Mexican song, "Frenesi," which made his lush fiddle sound popular on records. With the strings, Artie made a variety of attractive dance records through 1942. With Billy Butterfield at first, then with Roy Eldridge; with Johnny Guarnieri on harpsichord at first, then with Dodo Marmarosa on piano, Artie recorded some small band jazz, riffy but fresh. The first group of small band sides made in 1940, the second made in 1945, joined to the 1938–1939 big-band jazz, represent Artie Shaw's swing contribution. Like his own playing, these alternately move and plod, occasionally catch fire and hold the torch brilliantly.

The accomplishment of the swing era, 1935–1940, is difficult to evaluate. Its achievement was of the magnitude of that in the New Orleans period. It found an audience for every variation on what was essentially the New Orleans-Chicago theme with an added Kansas City seasoning, and although some of the less talented and more backward recipients of the success Benny Goodman brought them made ungrateful critical noises, they were restored to jazz life in the process. No-body, least of all Benny himself, thought that a conclusion had been wrought and an end to the development of jazz accomplished. Some, as a matter of fact, musicians and audiences both, suddenly became aware of music outside jazz and became humble about the hot music, the improvisation, the beat. But, whatever the limitations, the clichés, and the hollow repetitions, a new vitality had been discovered, continuity with Chicago had been established. Such was the convic-tion of vitality that, in 1950, when jazzmen were casting around again for a renewal of their forces and an enlargement of their audiences, they looked back with excited interest at the swing era—whatever the term "swing" itself meant, whatever the countless kinds of music that had masqueraded under its name.

Confusion surrounded the use of the two terms "swing" and "jazz" as soon as swing became popularly accepted. There was one school of thought, of which critic Robert Goffin was the most rabid exponent, that believed "swing" denoted the commercialization and prostitution of real jazz, that it had partly supplanted jazz, and that it consisted only of written arrangements played by big bands, whereas jazz consisted only of improvised music played by small bands. Another school of thought held that good jazz, whether played by one man or twenty, must have the fundamental quality of swing, a swinging beat, and could therefore legitimately be called swing, and that despite the different constructions put on the two terms by some critics, both words stood for the same musical idiom, the same rhythmic and harmonic characteristics, the same use of syn-copation. Confusion regarding the meaning of the word "jazz" de-veloped even among musicians themselves. A leader of a big band, telling you about his three trumpet players, for instance, would say, "This one plays the jazz," meaning that the man in question handled the improvised solos. Yet many musicians began to use the adjective "jazzy" to mean "corny," and some of them began to narrow down the meaning of the noun "jazz" to denote corn.

Before the word "swing" became popular there was none of this confusion. Fletcher Henderson and others played arrangements with big bands more than twenty years before the official arrival of swing as a jazz style, and nobody thought of calling his music anything but jazz. Yet during the swing era the same kind of music played by big bands was considered by the Goffin school to be something apart from and interfering with jazz—just as, still later, the same type of critic deplored bebop and cool jazz and disparaged these developments in the evolution of jazz as departures from and betrayals of the pure tradition.

The truth is that there is absolutely no dividing line between swing and jazz. Roy Eldridge hit the crux of the matter at the height of the controversy. "Difference between jazz and swing? Hell, no, man," he said. "It's just another name. The music advanced, and the name advanced right along with it. Jazz is just something they called it a long time ago. I've got a six-piece band, and what we play is swing music. It's ridiculous to talk about big bands and small bands as if they played two different kinds of music. I play a chorus in exactly the same style with my small band backing me as I did when I was with Gene Krupa's sixteen pieces."

Fletcher Henderson agreed with Roy, though he made a slight distinction: "There is a certain difference in the technical significance; swing means premeditation and jazz means spontaneity, but they still use the same musical material and are fundamentally the same idiom. To say that a swing arrangement is mechanical whereas a jazz solo is inspired is absurd. A swing arrangement can sound mechanical if it's wrongly interpreted by musicians who don't have the right feeling, but it's written straight from the heart and has the same feeling in the writing as a soloist has in a hot chorus. That's the way, for instance, my arrangement of 'Sometimes I'm Happy' for Benny was written—I just sat down not knowing what I was going to write, and wrote spontaneously what I was inspired to write. Maybe some arrangements sound mechanical because the writers studied too much and wrote out of a book, as it were—too much knowledge can hamper your style. But on the whole, swing relies on the same emotional and musical attitude as jazz, or improvised music, with the added advantage that it has more finesse."

Many devotees of earlier jazz, whose nostalgic yearnings for the old idols of a dying generation involve an indiscriminate contempt for anything modern, claimed that swing musicians paid too much attention to technique and too little to style, that the fundamental simplicity of jazz was lost in the evolution of swing. Theirs was an unrealistic argument. It is true that much of Louis Armstrong's greatness lay in the pure simplicity of his style and that he often showed a profound feeling for jazz without departing far from the melody;

it is also true that such swing stars as Roy Eldridge, whom most of the fans of the old jazz despised, made vast technical strides and played far more notes per second in their solos. But it is true too that there were times when Louis's playing was complicated, and there were New Orleans clarinetists whose music was just as involved and technical as some of the jazz played by later musicians. More important, really good jazz musicians of any period or style have never used their technique as an end in itself; they use it as a means to achieve more variety, more harmonic and rhythmic subtlety in their improvisations. If somebody like Jelly Roll Morton had been blessed with a technique even remotely comparable with Earl Hines' or Art Tatum's, he would undoubtedly have been a far finer pianist, and it wouldn't have changed him from a jazzman into a swingman, because basically there is no difference between the two.

Most people who like jazz of any style, school, or period admire Duke Ellington, whatever their reservations. Do they consider his music swing or jazz or both or neither? If the devotees of early jazz were to follow their theories through consistently and logically they would have to say that an Ellington number was swing while the arranged passages were being played, but as soon as a man stood up to take a sixteen-bar solo, it became jazz. If, as so often happened with the Ellington band, a solo that was originally improvised was so well liked that it was repeated in performance after performance until it became a regular part of the arrangement, then would it still be jazz? The question becomes even sillier when you realize that music such as Charlie Barnet's, Hal McIntyre's, and Dave Matthews', and that of other prominent swing musicians, written in exactly the same idiom as Ellington's, sometimes using identical arrangements and sometimes entirely different arrangements in the same style, was passed off or ignored by these jazz lovers as "commercial swing" of no musical interest.

Since the word "swing" was accepted by the masses and couldn't be suppressed, it might have seemed logical to let the term "jazz" fade out of the picture entirely and to call everything swing from 1935 on, whether it was Benny Goodman, Louis Armstrong, Eddie Condon, or Duke Ellington. But that word "jazz" has a habit of clinging. It has figured in the title of almost every book written on this type of music, from Panassie's *Le Jazz Hot* on; an important exception, curiously enough, was Louis Armstrong's book, *Swing*

That Music. Louis, although he has always been one of the chief idols of the nostalgic jazz lovers, liked the new word and used it frequently in preference to "jazz." Of the distinction between the two terms, he said, "To tell you the truth, I really don't care to get into such discussions as these. To me, as far as I could see it all my life, jazz and swing were the same thing. In the good old days of Buddy Bolden, in his days way back in nineteen hundred, it was called ragtime music. Later on in the years it was called jazz music, hot music, gutbucket, and now they've poured a little gravy over it and called it swing music. No matter how you slice it, it's still the same music. If anybody wants to know, a solo can be swung on any tune and you can call it jazz or swing."

Benny Carter, always a thinking musician, expressed essentially the same sentiments in different words, in an ordered argument: "I don't think you can set down any hard and fast definition of either 'jazz' or 'swing.' Both words have been defined by usage, and a lot of people use them in different ways. For instance, a lot of musicians use the word 'jazz' to denote something that's old-timey and corny. As I understand it, though, 'jazz' means what comes out of a man's horn, and 'swing' is the *feeling* that you put into the performance. Well, the jazz that comes out of the horn happens in so-called swing performances too. So even if 'jazz' and 'swing,' as words, do mean two separate things, as musical elements they're very often combined in one performance, and to talk about swing having replaced jazz, or followed it, is just nonsense."

Red Norvo wanted to junk the old word. "The word 'swing' doesn't signify big bands playing arrangements—that's the most obvious thing in the world. My records with the Swing Sextet and Octet had no arrangements, but they were swing, just the same as other records I made which did have arrangements. 'Swing,' to me, stands for something fresh and young, something that represents progress. Jump is another good name for it, too. I certainly hope it isn't jazz we're playing, because jazz to me means something obnoxious, like that Dixieland school of thought."

Lionel Hampton was differently concerned about the names people called his music. In his years with Benny Goodman (1936–1940) he was content with "swing," particularly when used as a verb to describe his own performances with the Goodman Quartet and those of the various groups of musicians who recorded under his leadership in the distinguished jazz series he made for Victor. Both Lionel as an individual and his pickup bands swung. So did his first big band, organized in late 1940—partly because of his own spectacular drive; partly because of his guitarist, Irving Ashby, a much more sparkling musician then than later with the King Cole Trio; partly because of Lionel's other soloists, especially the violinist Ray Perry. Later editions of Lionel's band intensified this concern of his with the beat. The band that played a concert at Symphony Hall in Boston in the winter of 1944 and at Carnegie Hall in New York in the spring of 1945 was an overwhelming organization which swamped the thirty-odd strings Lionel gathered for the concerts and almost accepted discipline. But in spite of a few subdued solos from the gifted but generally noisy tenor saxophonist Arnett Cobb and a dynamically versatile brass section, all the music ultimately gave way to wild exhibitions by the many drummers who passed through the band and by Lionel himself. It was engaging for a while, but after a few years of the frenzy of "Flying Home," "Hamp's Boogie Woogie," and "Hey-Ba-Ba-Re-Bop" one could listen only for the occasional moments of Milt Buckner's chunky piano chords or a random sax or brass solo of distinction. Lionel called his music "boogie woogie," "rebop," "bebop," or "swing," as the fashion suggested, but at its best it was only the latter, and at its worst it was a travesty of the other styles, if any representation of them at all. Finally, those who were interested in music came only to hear Lionel play vibes and were best satisfied with his slow, insinuating ballads, especially his big-band "Million-Dollar Smile" and the lovely set of solos with organ and rhythm accompaniment, released by Decca in 1951.

The music that will longest be associated with Hamp is not his own band's, in spite of its charged moments, but rather the combinations of other men's musicians he led in the Victor studios in Hollywood, Chicago, and New York from 1937 to 1940. His first date featured Ziggy Elman, and so did his last significant session but one before recording with his own men. Ziggy was typical: he was a lusty trumpeter with a personality perfectly attuned to the manners and might of swing. Cootie Williams was another of the same stripe. So were Red Allen and J. C. Higginbotham, Benny Carter, Chu Berry, Johnny Hodges, King Cole, and Coleman Hawkins, on their instruments. There was the memorable "One Sweet Letter from You," with Hawk, Ben Webster, Chu, and Benny Carter. There was "On the Sunny Side of the Street," to some still Johnny Hodges' best side. There was Ziggy's best playing on records, whenever he appeared with Lionel. Finally, there was the electrifying Hampton, welding the disparate personalities, topping the unified groups, epitomizing an era and its way of joining talents and styles.

Lionel Hampton has always found a large audience for his music, the combination of audiences that made swing. As few other bandleaders after the swing era, he held that combination of audiences. But within a decade after his band made its first appearance, it was no longer of musical significance as a band; its final effect upon jazz —as with most of the important swing bands—was the effect of its soloists, especially Hamp himself.

Chapter 17

THE SIDEMEN

If it accomplished nothing else, the swing era produced one lasting effect. The enthusiastic acceptance of the new cause by college and high school youngsters and their immediate elders focused attention on the sideman.

All jazz bands, large and small, have a nominal leader and sideman. As with the word "jazz" itself, the origin of the term "sideman" cannot be accurately traced, but its meaning is obvious. Like so much of jazz nomenclature, it is a descriptive word: inevitably the members of a jazz band sit to the left and to the right of center, a center sometimes occupied by a playing leader, sometimes by the drummer or a whole rhythm section. When sidemen take sides, left or right, in a big band, they fall into solo or section chairs and are prepared to take up a set of varying chores. In a small band everybody is a soloist. When swing came along its enthusiasts began to pay attention to the least members of the bands for which they had enthusiasm. The hot men, as they called the soloists, moved in an aura of acclaim hitherto reserved for a very small number of acknowledged great. The effect was cumulative and retroactive: hot collectors sifted through their records to find unappreciated beauties in a trumpeter here, a clarinetist there, a drummer somewhere else. Bix Beiderbecke, the biggest sideman jazz has known, was rediscovered; the records on which he had played suddenly became valuable collector's items. On records and off, in one-nighter and ballroom and hotel appearances, new bands were listened to avidly, with the hope that some new genius would pop up in brass or reed or rhythm sections. The apotheosis of the sideman was complete.

A considerable impetus to this new interest in the sideman was provided by the writing of two men. John Henry Hammond, Jr.,

202   A HISTORY OF JAZZ IN AMERICA

who had learned much about jazz as a record collector in his years
at Hotchkiss and Yale and more in his trips from Connecticut to
New York to hear the sizable jazzmen in person, had become an
indefatigable writer and organizer of jazz record dates by 1935. In
his short-lived jazz column in the Sunday *Brooklyn Eagle* he set a
model for all future writers about jazz. With fervent adjectives
and accurate judgment, he called attention to the fine musicians
playing with Fletcher Henderson and with Benny Goodman. He
helped Teddy Wilson to get the Brunswick contract which accounted
for perhaps the most significant series of jazz record dates in the
swing era. He was almost personally responsible for the emergence
of Count Basie's remarkable band from a Kansas City night club.
Some of the best musicians of the period owe their professional existence to his efforts.

George Simon joined the staff of *Metronome* in 1935, fresh
from Harvard and the little jazz band he had led from the drums in
the New England houseparty territory. George went to work with
a special interest in the complexities of the large band and the abilities
of its musicians. He set up a rating system for bands, based on the
report-card letters A to D, and the words which preceded his rating,
"Simon Says," became famous among musicians. George's reviews set
a style in jazz criticism; a summary of the basic qualities of a given
band, its musical style and commercial appeal, would be followed
by a painstaking analysis of each of the sections, paying equal attention to the sound of, say, the saxophone section as a whole, to the
lead alto saxophonist, and to the jazz soloists, be they alto and tenor,
or two tenors, or alto, tenor, and baritone. He revealed the inner
workings of a jazz band to his readers, stressing the large responsibility
of the musicians who never took a solo but whose work, good or
bad, was so important a part of the ultimate effect of a band's performance. He emphasized the delicate balance of the scored arrangement and the improvised performance, making less mysterious and
more meaningful the electric effect of the Benny Goodman band and
other swing outfits.

In the band which Benny took across the country in the fall of
1935, to score such a resounding success at the Palomar Ballroom
in Hollywood in early 1936, there were at first few stars. Benny's
band was the perfect example of the brilliant coordination of individuals to make up sections and sections to make up an orchestra

that the first jazz critics were writing about. Bunny Berigan made some records with Benny but didn't go out on the road with him. Nate Kazebier, who played the trumpet solos, was not of Bunny's stature, but he did have a pleasant tone and his solos swung. Joe Harris, who had come over from the disbanded Ben Pollack orchestra, had an attractive barrelhouse edge to his trombone playing. Dick Clark was a fair tenor, but it was rather the sax team, with Toots Mondello's or Hymie Schertzer's rich lead alto sounds, that gave this instrument distinction in the Goodman band. Gene Krupa made interesting faces as he chewed his gum and sweated his way through drum solos, but—much as these intrigued fans—they were less important than the overwhelming drive of the rhythm section as a whole, especially contributed by Jess Stacy's piano and Allan Reuss's guitar, and taken up by the whole band; this drive gave to Benny's music its distinguishing quality. Jess was a fine soloist too, and Helen Ward contributed throbbing ballads suggestive in style of Ethel Waters' best singing, and finally there was the superlative clarinet playing of the leader.

Benny's best work, however, was not with the big band, but with the trio he formed with Teddy Wilson and Gene, and with his quartet, formed when Lionel Hampton joined on the vibraphone in the summer of 1936 in Los Angeles. In the trio and quartet records Benny's Chicago training and Teddy's vast experience, reaching from Tuskegee study to Detroit, Chicago, and New York playing, made the difference. Teddy had worked in the Erskine Tate, Jimmy Noone, Benny Carter, and Willie Bryant bands, and had accompanied the Charioteers, the most musicianly of the vocal groups of the thirties. Teddy had a style essentially his own, compounded of some of the staccato elements of Earl Hines' piano playing, the various drifts of other men's ideas which inevitably make their way into the jazz soloist's playing machinery, and a way of fashioning fill-in runs of his own between phrases that gave his every performance lift and integration. His precise articulation on the keyboard proved just the right complement to Benny's swooping cadences and sweeps across the clarinet registers. Lionel Hampton, a Louisville, Kentucky, boy who had grown up in Chicago and had played exclusively in Los Angeles before joining Benny, added a ringing vibraphone note to the chamber unit of the Goodman organization and a power-drive on vibes and drums all his own. None of the many records these musicians made together, with Dave Tough replacing Gene for eight sides and Lionel drumming on one, was bad.

Gordon Griffin, better known as Chris, joined Benny in the spring of 1936; Ziggy Elman joined in September of the same year; and before the year was out, in December, Harry James filled out the trumpet section. That trumpet section, with first Murray McEachern and then Vernon Brown on trombone, a succession of tenor saxophonists (Vido Musso, Babe Russin, Bud Freeman, and Jerry Jerome), Jess on piano, Gene and then Dave Tough on drums, and an inspired leader, made the band great. No single record caught the enormous impact of that band, although the two-sided twelve-inch "Sing, Sing, Sing" and such ten-inch instrumentals as "Bugle Call Rag," "Somebody Loves Me," "Roll 'em," "Sugar Foot Stomp," "Don't Be that Way," and "Big John Special" suggest its quality. There is more of it in the four twelve-inch long-playing sides, issued in 1950, of the Carnegie Hall concert of January 16, 1938. Most of that concert is on those records, which capture with remarkable fidelity the band itself, Jess Stacy's five lovely choruses in "Sing, Sing, Sing," and the inspired collaboration of musicians from the Count Basie, Duke Ellington, and Benny Goodman bands, and Bobby Hackett—a collaboration that thrilled all of us present that glittering night. This was Benny's achievement, the matching of equal talents on all the jazz instruments with little concern for box office and much for musicianship. To a greater or lesser degree, insofar as they matched that achievement, other bands and musicians made a permanent or transient impression during the swing era.

During these years a bandleader did not have to be much concerned with box office; as long as his musicianship and that of his sidemen were better than average, the box office was his. Benny provided the spark; those who followed kept it going, and they spread their collective light over all three jazz audiences—the first and perhaps the last time that phenomenon has occurred. The three jazz audiences are made up of groups of varied size and commercial importance. The first, usually called by musicians who cannot reach it "the great unwashed," consists of members of America's middle-class majority, those whose entertainment consists chiefly of novelty, whose escapist predilections were so much in the ascendant during the depression years. The second group, mixed in quality and source, but essential for jazz success, is the compromise group; it will take a certain amount of musical quality, prides itself on its intellectual broadmindedness, likes to dance the latest dance and to be *au courant* with the latest musical idea, but must have that idea presented to it as a novelty. This group requires less thick sugar coating than the first and will often be receptive to music which is anathema to the first, but for all practical purposes the appeal to both is the same. The third and last group, the group which has kept jazz alive through its worst days, consists of the diehard fans, college boys and those slightly older, who combine analytical skill with taste, know what they want and where to find it, and make it possible for the experimental jazz musician to find an audience if not a living. Somehow, in the swing years, all three of these groups combined to form a large and generally appreciative audience for jazz. Sometimes members of the first group showed an interest in the finer points of jazz and even looked for the distinguishing marks that separated quality from quantity. The new jazz titillated musical nerves that had been drugged almost into insensibility by what the jazz musician calls the Mickey Mouse and "cheese" bands, the purveyors of pre-digested pap. For half a decade it jostled the huge numbers of the first and second groups, made some into jitterbugs, others into at least mildly comprehending listeners, and made it possible for the skilled jazzman to play with pleasure and for profit and to build a reputation more or less commensurate with his talent.

The wide acceptance of a free jazz expression brought into jazz, for several years at least, a new growth of styles and development of stylists. There was a self-confidence abroad, as a result, that turned small jazz musicians into medium-sized ones and medium-sized ones into great ones. Sidemen who without this general encouragement would never have thought of becoming bandleaders tossed other men's music and jobs aside and went out with their own bands —sometimes to lose thousands of dollars, occasionally to make many more thousands of dollars. Woody Herman fronted a group of musicians from Isham Jones' sweet dance band who had decided to form a cooperative organization. The Herman band's greatest distinction, until new blood took over and turned it into perhaps the best of all the white bands in the mid-forties, was Woody's profound feeling for a torchy vocal. There were also such soloists as Joe Bishop, who played the fluegelhorn sweetly, and Neal Reid, whose trombone accents were amusingly guttural.

In the Bob Crosby band, Eddie Miller played the clarinet a bit and sang some, but more important, his tenor saxophone lines, in their organized length and smooth, unvibrating line, anticipated the mature conception of that instrument that developed in the early days of bebop, as a result of Eddie's and Lester Young's and Bud Freeman's pioneering. Throughout its history the Crosby band featured Matty Matlock on clarinet, Nappy Lamare on guitar, Bob Haggart on bass, and Ray Bauduc on drums, as well as Eddie. At various times it had such biting Dixieland trumpeters as Yank Lawson and Muggsy Spanier, and the extraordinary trumpet variety that Billy Butterfield provided. From 1938 to 1940 Irving Fazola enriched the band with his exquisite clarinet tone and perhaps the most polished concept of the New Orleans reed tradition. Warren Smith and Floyd O'Brien were variously responsible for the barrelhouse trombone sound, and the piano, important to the band after Bob Zurke joined in 1936, grew less honky-tonk when Joe Sullivan came in in 1939 and a good deal less so when Jess Stacy brought his suave keyboard ministrations in to replace Joe. The Crosby band was easily the best of those which consciously and occasionally conscientiously endeavored to keep the New Orleans and Chicago traditions alive in the late thirties.

Several of the men Tommy Dorsey featured in the years from 1935 until December 1939, when the band was revised along powerhouse lines suggestive of Jimmie Lunceford's band, were authentic Dixieland and Chicago voices too. At different times such trumpeters as Max Kaminsky, Bunny Berigan, Pee Wee Erwin, and Yank Lawson kept a spirited conception alive in a band that had been dedicated to more commercial pursuits by its leader. First Joe Dixon and then Johnny Mince challenged Benny Goodman's clarinet leadership with a more distinctly Dixieish line than any Benny ever played once he took out his own band. Dave Tough joined Tommy a few months before Bud Freeman did, and left a few months earlier, lasting from the early spring of 1936 to the end of 1937. The most exciting moments in the Dorsey band's performances before its revision in style—apart from Tommy's tonal mastery of the trombone—surely belonged to Dave and Bud. They imparted to Tommy's small band, the Dixie outfit he called the Clambake Seven—in cheerful adoption of the term used by jazz musicians both in annoyed disparagement of a poor jam session and in warm approbation of a good one—a freshness and a fervor which cut through the trivial material that was on the whole the Seven's basic feed. Brother Jimmy, elder of the two Dorseys, made over the remnants of the Dorsey Brothers' band into an effective accompaniment for Bing Crosby on his radio program and a fair commercial Dixieland band, which was at its best in such novelties as "Parade of the Milk-Bottle Caps" and "A Swing Background for an Operatic Soprano." Freddy Slack played some ingenious boogie-woogie piano for Jimmy, and Ray McKinley, a two-beat drummer with Ray Bauduc's kind of skill, kept the weak and strong accents in good order, especially when he took some of Jimmy's musicians into Decca's Los Angeles studios and made four knock-down-and-drag-out sides in March 1936.

There was some Dixieland flavor in the music of the Red Norvo band, but, as always with Red, it had the individual identification of a richly talented, always experimenting, always developing musician. Kenneth Norvo, nicknamed after his red hair, had, like so many jazz musicians, started as a pianist, but in high school he became a xylophonist. He joined a touring Chautauqua organization when he was seventeen and then went into vaudeville with a band called the Collegians. He did a stretch in Chicago with Paul Ash's theater band and then went into vaudeville for himself. After short stints with his own band in Milwaukee and as part of a radio-station band in Minneapolis in 1928, he played with Victor Young and Ben Bernie for a while in Chicago, then did more than a year at NBC as a member of its Chicago studio band. In 1931 he joined Paul Whiteman and stayed with him for three years, after which time he extended his repertory, married Mildred Bailey, and formed plans for his own band. Red had made xylophone solo records accompanied by such men as Jimmy Dorsey and Benny Goodman, had led two first-rate pick-up bands through two different sessions, and had brought the nucleus of his medium-sized dance band to records —first under his own name, then under the name of the Len Herman Orchestra, then as Ken Kenny and His Orchestra, then under the name of his trumpeter Stew Pletcher—on several different labels before he inaugurated the superb series recorded for Brunswick from 1936 to 1939. At first the band featured the delicate sounds made by Stewie, Herbie Haymer on tenor saxophone, Red, and his incomparably gifted singer, Mildred Bailey. Then Hank D'Amico joined to fill the saxophone section to the full complement of the thirties—

quartet size—and to add a lovely clarinet voice. Through this change
and the eventual addition of a second trombone, the imaginations of
Red and his sometime trumpeter and sometime arranger, Eddie
Sauter, wefe allowed full play. The beat of the band was essentially
in two, but the harmonic transformation of such familiar tunes as
"I Know that You Know," "Liza," "Remember," and "Russian
Lullaby" bore no resemblance to Dixieland. Eddie's sometimes witty,
sometimes brash, usually gentle, and always unhackneyed arrangements showed the mark of discipline derived from such composers as
Stravinsky, Prokofiev, and Bartok, mixed with and expressed through
a distinctly American personality. Out of his fresh manuscript, solos
leaped delicately into place and Mildred's voice arose with that extraordinary grace of phrase and impeccable intonation that regularly
distinguished her singing. She and Red were billed as Mr. and Mrs.
Swing and justified the sobriquet not with the volume which audiences were coming more and more to expect of a swing band in
the late thirties but with the subtlety and sagacity of their rhythmic
ideas.

The resolute Dixielanders of the period found their haven at Nick's,
first on the west side of Seventh Avenue in Greenwich Village, and
then across the street, when the crowds it attracted enabled the
titular owner of the two-beat emporium to build new quarters at
Tenth Street and Seventh. Here Eddie Condon led the band he called
the Windy City Seven or the Chicagoans or simply his own, always
featuring the wry squeaks and sometimes amusing departures from
pitch of Pee Wee Russell's clarinet, usually with George Wettling
on drums, Brad Gowans or George Brunies on trombone, Artie
Shapiro on bass, and Max Kaminsky on trumpet. Here Bobby
Hackett made his New York debut, startling audiences with the accuracy of his imitations of Bix Beiderbecke on the cornet, the instrument to which he had switched in Boston after leaving his native
Providence and his first instrument, the guitar. His soft sound and
melodic imagination, so much like Bix's, stood out on the first records
that Milt Gabler made for his own label, Commodore, named for his
music shop, international headquarters for serious jazz record collectors. Though Bobby's colleagues on those first Commodore dates
were such eminent Nicksieland musicians as Brunies, Pee Wee, Bud
Freeman, Jess Stacy, Artie Shapiro, Wettling, and the redoubtable
Eddie Condon, with Jack Teagarden added for three sides, it was

his playing that made the records of more than passing significance. When Bobby made his own dates, with some of the same musicians, for Vocalion, it was he who once again dominated the performances. One doesn't slight even such a musician as Jack Teagarden if one points to Bobby's commanding authority on these records; so powerful an echo of Bix, with almost as rich a melodic gift, was hardly to be expected so soon after his death. Even after Bobby joined Horace Heidt for a little less than a year and Glenn Miller for longer, between 1939 and 1942, his deft melodic variations, up and down and around figurations, and always with continuity, were of unceasing sweetness and high style.

Bunny Berigan was another trumpeter with overtones of Bix in his playing, but his style was essentially his own. He plumbed the lower depths of the trumpet and found an expansion of ideas in his bottom notes that no other trumpeter was able to use to such advantage. Bunny, who died at the age of thirty-three in 1942, started to play the trumpet in Fox Lake, Wisconsin, where he was born. His grandfather came home one day with a trumpet, handed it to Bunny, and said, "Here, this is you. Play, you!" Bunny's first jobs in his teens were with local bands, and it was with one of them that Hal Kemp, when he was passing through Wisconsin in 1928, heard Bunny. A year and a half later Hal sent for Bunny to join his band, the best of the treacly outfits that served depression fantasies; it employed an effective series of reeds, played by its saxophonists in imitation of a Debussyan sound, and also boasted a fine pianist and arranger, John Scott Trotter, who later joined Bing Crosby as permanent conductor and arranger. Bunny played with Paul Whiteman during one of the Whiteman band's many appearances at the Biltmore Hotel in New York in the early thirties, and then began to gig around New York with a band that played college and society engagements. He graduated, with many of his associates of those bands, into radio work. He did a lot of recording in 1933 and 1934 with the inventor of the goofus, Adrian Rollini, who was much in demand at the record studios. He recorded the famous "Mood Hollywood" with the Dorsey Brothers in 1933 and with them, too, accompanied Mildred Bailey on eight fine Brunswick sides in the same year. In 1935, his big year as a part of pick-up recording dates, he made the memorable four sides that the Casa Loma band's arranger, Gene Gifford, arranged and led, with Matty Matlock, Bud Freeman, Claude Thorn-

Dick McDonough, Wingy Manone, and Ray Bauduc. In 1935 he also made Glenn Miller's first date, with the fine trombonist Jack Jenney, Johnny Mince, and Eddie Miller; with Jack and Johnny, Chu Berry,. Teddy Wilson, Gene Krupa, George Van Eps, and Artie Bernstein, the bass player, he made, under the leadership of Red Norvo, four sides, including the superb coupling of "Bughouse" and "Blues in E Flat." With Benny Goodman that year he made just under two dozen sides, among them "King Porter Stomp," "Jingle Bells," "Stompin' at the Savoy," and "Blue Skies," on all of which he takes brilliant solos. In 1935 and 1936 Bunny was also a staff musician at CBS, for which he led a series of jazz units, the most famous of which was the group known as Bunny's Blue Boys. He was a featured performer on the Saturday Night Swing Club, which went on the CBS network in 1936, one of the best jazz programs, sustaining or sponsored, ever to become a regular feature on a radio network. He was part of many radio and record bands accompanying singers—but none so impressive as Mildred Bailey, one of whose Alley Cats he was, with Johnny Hodges and Teddy Wilson, on the four sides recorded under John Hammond's supervision for English distribution; and Billie Holiday, whom he accompanied on four sides in 1936, with Artie Shaw and Joe Bushkin. That was the year he was also a Fifty-second-Street regular, appearing at Red McKenzie's club and sitting in at other places, showing off his long and large and almost unquenchable drinking and playing capacity. At the end of 1936 Tommy Dorsey was looking around for someone skilled enough to give his brass section the proper lift; logically enough, he settled on Bunny Berigan. Bunny settled on the Dorsey specialties like one of the early pioneers; he made "Marie" and "Song of India," "Melody in F," "Liebestraum," and "Who'll Buy My Violets" into his own vehicles, making it possible for jazz fans to endure the glee-club chattering in tempo that sold the records to millions. While with Tommy, Bunny continued to make records under his own name; these and his fetching performances on the Dorsey sides made him a record name, and he soon took advantage of his fame by forming his own band. In that band, which opened at the Pennsylvania Hotel in April 1937, were some fine young musicians: the talented arranger and pianist Joe Lippman; a jumping tenor saxophonist down from Canada, Georgie Auld; one of the very best of bass players, Arnold Fishkin; a couple of fine trumpet players, Benny Goodman's brother,

Irving, and Steve Lipkins; and a veteran drummer, George Wettling. Bunny joined Victor's select swing circle; his records enjoyed a full-size publicity campaign along with those of Benny Goodman, Tommy Dorsey, and Fats Waller. With those eminent recording stars, he contributed two sides to the twelve-inch album *A Symposium of Swing*, one of the most ambitious efforts of the time to capture the full flavor of a jazz band. To that album Bunny brought his inimitable singing and playing of "I Can't Get Started" and "The Prisoner's Song." Thereafter he had almost two years more of recording for Victor, but less and less success. He continued to play beautifully, made a lovely Beiderbecke album, playing some of Bix's own tunes and others associated with Bix, and was generally impressive in person too. But drink, as it had for so many other jazz musicians, was beginning to do for Bunny. He was irritable, subject to roaring arguments; his musicians and he were not getting along together. In February 1940 he junked his band and rejoined Tommy Dorsey. For six months he was an ornament of the band and helped Tommy regain some of the popularity he had begun to lose. But six months was all that an irritable Bunny and an always high-tempered Tommy could take together. When they broke up there was nothing left to do but start a band again, and Bunny went back to the road. He was in no condition to manage the strain and stress of one-nighters; his constant refuge was the bottle. There were several breakdowns and a siege of pneumonia in Pennsylvania before his band came in to play a job at Manhattan Center in New York on June 1, 1942. Bunny didn't play with his band; he was in Polyclinic Hospital, dying of cirrhosis of the liver. Benny Goodman, who was playing at the Paramount Theatre, brought his sextet over to Manhattan Center to help out. Bunny's friends went to visit him at the hospital, among them the bass player Sid Weiss. Bunny looked up at Sid, a slight little man. "And they tell me *I'm* sick," he said. "Looks like you should be here instead of me." That was the afternoon after the job at the Center. That night Tommy Dorsey, who was playing at the Astor Hotel, received a call from the hospital. He rushed over there. He looked at Bunny and knew the trumpeter hadn't long to live; actually it was a matter of hours.

Another musician of great dimensions, who died shortly before Bunny, was Leon Berry, better known as Chu; he was killed in an automobile accident in 1941, while he was on his way from one

Cab Calloway engagement to another. Chu had joined Cab in the summer of 1937 after working in a series of bands, with all of whom his playing was something close to magnificent. He was, along with Roy Eldridge, one of the stars of the Teddy Hill band, which alternated with Willie Bryant and Chick Webb in 1934 and 1935 at the Savoy Ballroom in Harlem. Earlier Chu had come to New York from West Virginia by way of Chicago, had played with Sammy Stewart at the Savoy and with Benny Carter, his "favorite saxophone player over anybody." Later he moved with Roy into Fletcher Henderson's last important band, the Chicago outfit of 1935 to 1937. With Roy, Chu made four sides for Commodore that rank among the greatest of jazz records, the ten-inch "Sittin' In" and "Forty-six West Fifty-two," and the twelve-inch "Stardust" and "Body and Soul." With Calloway he made a solo record, all his, of "A Ghost of a Chance," which to many people is the definitive example of tenor saxophone playing, a series of beautifully integrated melodic variations on the tune, with that rich tone and steady beat which Chu had in common with Coleman Hawkins and Ben Webster.

There was a kind of somber, dramatic magnificence to the end of the swing era; death achieved it. In 1939 Chick Webb died. In 1941 Chu died. In 1942 Bunny Berigan, Charlie Christian, and Jimmy Blanton died. In 1943 Fats Waller died. The era called "swing" died with them. The United States was at war, and some of its best jazz musicians were in the services. Jazz was going through almost violent changes of idea and execution. With death and destruction a certain perspective was gained. The war years were consecrated to reminiscence and critical evaluation. It was possible as never before in the history of jazz to see and hear where they all fitted in—the singers who were beginning to draw the largest audiences for themselves; the pianists who set so many and reflected as many more of the basic styles; the sidemen who contributed so much, through solos and teamwork; the figures of transition in whose hands the old music was left and the new music was born.

Chapter 18

L PIANISTS

In the development of jazz the solo talents of a few individual instrumentalists have contributed much. The names of some of these men stand for distinct styles and stages in the progress of jazz: trumpeters Louis Armstrong, Roy Eldridge, Dizzy Gillespie; trombonists Lawrence Brown, Tricky Sam, Teagarden, Bill Harris, J. J. Johnson; saxophonists Coleman Hawkins, Benny Carter, Lester Young, Johnny Hodges, Charlie Parker, Lee Konitz; clarinetists Benny Goodman and Buddy DeFranco; drummers Gene Krupa and Sidney Catlett; bassist Jimmy Blanton; guitarist Charlie Christian. But when we come to pianists there is trouble; there is nothing orderly about the development of the pianists as jazz instrumentalists.

For one thing, there are too many of them. The early history of jazz produced only a handful and not too startling a group at that. From New Orleans we had Jelly Roll Morton and some of his contemporaries. Ragtime established James P. Johnson. But nothing especially important musically happened to jazz on the piano until the music got to Chicago and Earl Hines was heard in his proper context, the Louis Armstrong recording bands. This was more like it, and very pleasant to listen to. Then Joe Sullivan, Jess Stacy, and Fats Waller arrived, and, within their bands, Duke Ellington, Fletcher Henderson and his brother Horace, and Count Basie.

Then, an avalanche: Art Tatum, Teddy Wilson, Mary Lou Williams, Nat Cole, Johnny Guarnieri, Joe Bushkin, Mel Powell, Nat Jaffe, Erroll Garner, Dodo Marmarosa, Jimmy Jones, André Previn, Bud Powell, Lennie Tristano, Paul Smith; not to mention the local boys who have stayed local, such as Detroit's brilliant Bobby Stevenson, New Orleans' variously talented Armand Hug, and Chicago's Mel Henke; and not to mention the boogie-woogie pianists.

213

The list is astonishing in its length and, with the exception of the last big group of indefatigable primitives of boogie woogie, in its quality. Analyzing the records of these men carefully, with as little personal prejudice as possible, one can see clearly not merely that jazz is rich in good pianists, pianists of wit and wisdom and experimental audacity, but that it has produced more titans on the piano than traditional music has in this century. Try to make a similar list of really distinguished concert pianists. I don't think it will be half as long. Then play the records of the pianists mentioned in the preceding paragraph, forget the comparisons, and sit back to enjoy a parade of luxurious sound, jazz at its best so far, promising profundity, on its way to full musical maturity.

Earl Hines plays a firm, vigorous piano that has been effectively apostrophized as "trumpet style." It's more accurately described as "trumpet-with-band style" because, while Earl is establishing the trumpet's melodic line with his right hand, he is setting up large ensemble chords with his left, splashes of counterrhythms, flashing tremolos, sometimes suspending the beat with that characteristic ringing pedal tone. He strikes out with full chords far removed from the C-major and C-seventh fundamentals of blues piano. But in all of his career, almost from his first appearance in 1925, at the Club Elite in Chicago, he has been the greatest force in shaping the forms and style of jazz piano and pianists.

It is hard to name a pianist of any importance in jazz, no matter of what school, who hasn't been influenced by Hines. Teddy Wilson, Mary Lou Williams, Art Tatum, Nat Cole, Jess Stacy, Mel Powell have all been more or less under the Father's influence. Fats Waller was a school unto himself, but most of Fats's associates and imitators have been strongly swayed by Hines; their playing constantly reflects his style.

When this most important of jazz piano stylists began his musical studies in Pittsburgh in 1915, he was a trumpeter, then a pianist, but never thought of becoming a dance-band musician. His father was a trumpeter, his mother a pianist and organist. Earl used to play on chairs all around the house, and when his mother could no longer stand the monotony of chair tones she switched him from Duncan Phyfe and Sheraton, sofa style, to a piano, ragtime style.

At nine Earl wanted to be a trumpeter, but his mother saw to it that he was given piano lessons. After four years of private tutoring his keyboard proficiency was such that he was invited to give concerts around town, at schools and small halls.

"They gave me ten dollars and a box of handkerchiefs for a concert," Earl recalls, "and they said, 'He's great.' I had to learn sixty or seventy pages of music for each concert and work like a dog for ten bucks, some linen, and some kind words. It didn't look like a hell of a career, and so, at sixteen, I cut out."

He broke in at a Pittsburgh night club, after school, playing nine months at the Leader House as accompanist for singers, as intermission pianist for the club, which didn't have other entertainment and consequently relied heavily on the inventiveness and imagination of such of its random entertainers as young Hines. After a couple of years of gigging around the Smoky City, Earl left for Chicago and what he hoped would be greener fields. There it was that he really began his career; there he shaped his style and worked in association with most of the great musicians of the time—the late twenties and all the thirties. There he himself became a great jazz musician.

The Club Elite Number Two, at Thirty-fifth and State, one of a chain of night clubs that were more elite in name than in clientele, was his first employer. He opened there with a small Pittsburgh combination, featuring Vernee Robinson, "one of the fine hot fiddlers of the time," Earl says. He stayed for about a year. Of this period Earl recalls most vividly the steady expatriation of distinguished contemporaries.

"An awful lot of good jazzmen went abroad then," he says, "guys who've never been heard from since. A guy like Teddy Weatherford, for example. A fine pianist. He went over to Europe, played all over the Continent, then went to China. He died in India. I certainly wish I could have heard him again."

In 1926 Earl joined Carroll Dickerson at the Entertainers' Club. The Dickerson band played forty-odd weeks on the Pantages vaudeville circuit, hitting as far west as California, then returned to Chicago and went into the Sunset Cafe. That's where Louis joined the band, choosing what Earl calls "the younger set" in preference to King Oliver's New Orleans émigrés, who had made overtures to Armstrong to rejoin them.

When Louis took over the Dickerson band, Earl became its musical director. With musicians like Louis and Earl, Big Green on trombone, Darnell Howard on clarinet, Stumpy Evans ("one of the great tenor players," according to Earl), and Tubby Hall on drums, this was an impressive band. Then Louis, Earl, and Zutty Singleton formed a friendship and musical association that seemed indissoluble. "It got so," Earl says, "that you couldn't hire one of us without the others." The three of them, trumpeter, pianist, and drummer, formed the base for what are clearly the best records Louis ever made, the Okeh series that included "West End Blues," "Skip the Gutter," and "A Monday Date" (Hines' composition); and the series highlighted by "Basin Street Blues," "Beau Koo Jack," "Heah Me Talkin' to Ya," "Tight Like This," and "Weather Bird." The first set was made in June 1928; the second, in December of the same year.

During this time, 1927 to 1929, when Louis had moved up to the Savoy Ballroom (Chicago's, not New York's), Earl moved across the street from the Sunset to the Apex Club to play piano with Jimmy Noone. With that style-setting clarinetist, Earl made the memorable file of 1928 Apex Club Orchestra records for Vocalion, eight sides of which were later reissued in Jimmy Noone's Brunswick Collector's Series album.

After a little less than two years of the Noone band Earl "got tired of the hours and the work. Too hard, man, too hard." The QRS Piano Roll Company was taking a flier in the record business and they invited Earl to record for their new label. He went and did eight sides. And they, "not knowing what it was all about, released all eight at once. Oh, it was a panic!" But the sides were fine, all Hines originals: the inevitable "Monday Date," the brilliant "Blues in Thirds," "Panther Rag," "Chicago High Life," "Chimes in Blues," "Stowaway," "Just Too Soon," and "Off Time Blues."

In 1928 Lucius Venable Millinder, better known as Lucky, was organizing a show for the Grand Terrace, a new Chicago night club. He searched around for a band for the place and could find none with a big enough name and enough talent, so he wired frantically to Hines in New York to come back to Chicago and build him a band. Earl went and stayed twelve years. Whenever he went on the road, from 1928 to 1940, he was always sure of his share of the moneys that were paid other bands at the Grand Terrace, for he became the club's chief attraction and also its over-all booker and musical supervisor.

In a dozen years at the Terrace and several after that, Earl made a sheaf of wonderful records—and some not so good—for Brunswick, Decca, and Bluebird. Such jazz luminaries as trumpeter Walter Fuller, clarinetist and fiddler Darnell Howard, tenor saxophonist Budd Johnson, tenor and arranger Jimmy Mundy, trombonist Trummy Young, drummer Wallace Bishop, trumpeters Freddy Webster, Ray Nance, Pee Wee Jackson, Shorty McConnell, Charlie Allen, and Dizzy Gillespie were, if not all Hines discoveries, at least musicians who seemed to discover themselves when they went with the Father.

The "Father" tag, by the way, was bestowed upon Earl by radio announcer Ted Pearson, a knowing jazz aficionado, who came down to do a broadcast one night at the Grand Terrace. Although older than most of his men, Earl was neither by temperament nor physical constitution the parent of his band musicians in the way that Paul Whiteman, who was known as "Fatho" to most of his regular employees, was. The name was only a presumption of musical paternity which Pearson made for Earl at the time, but one that stuck—and grew more appropriate over the years.

The Father started Herb Jeffries on his singing career; he went to Detroit to get Herb for the Grand Terrace. "Georgia Boy" (Arthur Lee Simpkins) was a Hines discovery, as were Ida James, Valaida Snow, and Ivy Anderson. Earl remembers when Duke was looking for a vocalist and cast about at the Terrace for a girl. Duke sent for somebody, but it was decided among the GTers that this girl wouldn't do, and they told Ivy to go. But Ivy wouldn't. She said she wouldn't audition for anyone, damned if she would. She was finally persuaded to go on stage at the Regal, where Duke was playing that week, to see what the colored audience at the South Side theater would think. She broke it up and was hired on the spot. Ivy played the Oriental Theatre, downtown, the next week, and from then on, of course, was Duke's star singer. Billy Eckstein (as he spelled his name then) and Sara Vaughn (as she spelled hers) were Hines stars before Billy organized his own band. The Palmer Brothers, the delightful male vocal group, are other Hines alumni.

Over the years, Earl says, "I've always had a funny ambition, to do something like Waring and Whiteman along jazz lines. Groups of singers, large bands, every kind of instrumentation and scoring possible." It isn't that he ever actually wanted to give up his regular type of band, a bona fide dance crew spotted with fine brass and reed and rhythm soloists. He simply feels that the size and scope of popular music are broadening enormously all the time and that the future may permit more orchestral experimentation.

Hines has four favorite records out of all that he has recorded. These are late band works. It's not that the Father underestimates the significance of his early recordings; it's just that he is most concerned with present-day problems and thoroughly delighted with the instrumentation and instrumentalists that became available to him. The four Earl Hines sides that really knock Earl Hines out are "Tantalizing a Cuban"; "The Boy with the Wistful Eyes," featuring his vocal quartet of several years ago; Billy Eckstine's "I Got It Bad and That Ain't Good"; and his own brilliant "Boogie Woogie on St. Louis Blues," all on Bluebird—and all but the last scarce as pterodactyl's teeth.

With good bands, and a thoughtful, mature conception of jazz, grounded in such firm traditions as a baby art can have, Earl has done well over the years. Because his authoritative, broad-shouldered, conservatively dressed figure looks like a heavyweight boxer's, because his music is so much in and of our time, Earl Hines' listeners sometimes used to forget that he was one of the pioneer jazzmen who helped start the whole thing. They were reminded of it in the barnstorming concert tours and gala night-club appearances of Louis Armstrong's troupe in 1950, which featured, in addition to Earl, Jack Teagarden and Barney Bigard. Then in 1951, with a Columbia Piano Moods album, came another reminder, that Earl was still a modern pianist, speculative, experimental, fresh. That's as it should be with a man of his equipment and imagination and sharp awareness of his own time and that to come.

Thomas Wright Waller, known to millions for obvious reasons as "Fats," died at the age of thirty-nine. His sudden death stunned musicians and music lovers. The high-spirited, effervescent, boisterously energetic pianist and composer had just completed a four-week personal appearance at the Florentine Gardens in Hollywood. The engagement ended on Saturday; Monday he boarded the Santa Fe Chief for New York; Wednesday, December 15, 1943, he had a sudden heart attack, and when the train pulled into Kansas City he was dead. An autopsy revealed that he had had bronchial pneumonia.

On December 20, at the Abyssinian Baptist Church in Harlem, a vast crowd, including hundreds of prominent representatives of the music world, came to pay homage to Fats. Pallbearers included Count

Basie, Don Redman, Claude Hopkins, Andy Kirk, Andy Razaf, J. C. Johnson, and James P. Johnson. Virtually every prominent pianist in New York who had known Fats was present, including Mary Lou Williams, Willie (the Lion) Smith, Cliff Jackson, as well as the musicians from Fats's regular recording band and others who had made records with him. Mounted police had to clear the way for the cortege through streets thronged with admirers. The following day a memorial program was arranged at Cafe Society Downtown; an hour of it was broadcast, and dozens of Fats's associates and admirers took part in the tribute, proceeds of which went to the New York *Amsterdam News* Children's Fund. James P. Johnson, the pianist whose style had inspired Fats in his formative years, composed a "Blues for Fats" which he played soon afterward at a concert in Town Hall, New York.

Fats was born in New York City. His father was the Reverend Edward Martin Waller of the Abyssinian Baptist Church. Fats studied piano and organ and when still a very small boy often used to play the organ in his father's church for Sunday services. His formal training was under Leopold Godowsky and Carl Bohm. Andy Razaf, lyric writer who collaborated with Fats on most of his outstanding hits, says that Fats "knew Brahms, Liszt, and Beethoven as well as he knew jazz, and often discussed and analyzed their work."

Fats went to De Witt Clinton High School in New York. When he was about fifteen years old he turned up one day in an amateur pianists' contest at the Roosevelt Theatre in Harlem, on the site where the Golden Gate ballroom was later built. He won the prize, playing one of J. P. Johnson's tunes, "Carolina Shout." It wasn't long before he was playing professionally. One of his earliest jobs was as house organist at the old Lincoln Theatre on One Hundred and Thirty-fifth Street. About that time he began writing songs and quickly produced a hit, "Squeeze Me," which he did with Spencer Williams.

While Fats was working at the Lincoln he made a friendship that lasted throughout his life and contributed very happily to his career; he met Andreamentana Razafinkeriefo, who, out of consideration for American tongues, had shortened his name to Andy Razaf. As Andy says, "I used to listen to him there often, and eventually, because everyone knew him and everyone was his friend, I somehow came to meet him." Andy was the son of the Grand Duke of Madagascar,

who had been killed when the French took over that island; Andy
was born in Washington, D.C., just after his mother had escaped to
this country. Forced to leave school in order to earn a living, he
started his songwriting career as an elevator boy in an office building where one of his regular passengers was Irving Berlin. When
Fats met him, he persuaded Andy to take songwriting more seriously.
As Andy tells it, "One of the first things we did as a team was cash
in on a vogue for West Indian songs. As soon as we got broke all we
had to do was grind out two or three West Indian numbers, take
them up to Mills or some Broadway office, and get a nice sum for
them. Around that time there was a heavy demand for cabaret-type
songs with blue lyrics. We did hundreds of those too."

Fats worked with other lyric writers and composers too, including
James P. Johnson, J. C. Johnson, Spencer Williams, and Bud Allen,
"who was Fats's permanent sidekick, helping to keep him on time
for dates, get him home and generally look out for him." But most
of Fats's famous songs were written with Razaf. Together they
wrote the scores of several big musicals, the first of which was
Keep Shufflin' in 1925, which contained the songs "How Can You
Face Me" and "My Little Chocolate Bar."

After this success Connie and George Immerman asked them to
do the score of a Connie's Inn show, and "things really started humming," Andy says. "It was hard to tie Fats down to a job; my mother
used to make all the finest food and special cookies for him just to
keep him out at our home in Asbury Park, New Jersey. We were
working on a show called *Load of Coal* for Connie and had just
done half the chorus of a number when Fats remembered a date and
announced, 'I gotta go!' I finished up the verse and gave it to him
later over the telephone. The tune was 'Honeysuckle Rose.'"

Fats made records in 1929 in what Razaf describes as "amazingly
informal" record sessions. The first time he led a band under his
own name alone, as Fats Waller and His Buddies, the group "was
gotten together only a few hours beforehand, when he suddenly
realized he had to round up some men. Fats arrived on the date
with a rhythm section comprising just himself and Eddie Condon
on banjo, but the records they made ('Harlem Fuss' and 'Minor
Drag') caused quite a stir."

In later years Fats's recording sessions continued to be "amazingly
informal," with a "standard setup at the piano—one bottle on top,

a reserve bottle underneath. Fats would fix up head arrangements, hardly ever bothering with written music for the men." He did have an arranger, however, Ken McComber, whom Andy calls "Fats's closest white friend."

In 1929 Fats and Andy wrote the score for *Hot Chocolates*, a musical which was produced in Harlem so successfully that it was later brought to Broadway. Reminiscing about this show, Andy says, "I remember one day going to Fats's house on One Hundred and Thirty-third Street to finish up a number based on a little strain he'd thought up. The whole show was complete, but they needed an extra number for a theme, and this had to be it. We worked on it for about forty-five minutes, and there it was—'Ain't Misbehavin'.' " In addition to this outstanding song, their score for this review contained "Rhythm Man" and "Black and Blue," the tune which Frankie Laine so successfully revived when he himself was coming into the big time in 1947 and '48.

Fats and Andy turned out many other popular song hits together: "Aintcha Glad," "Blue Turning Gray over You," "Concentratin'," "Gone," "If It Ain't Love," "Keepin' out of Mischief Now," "My Fate Is in Your Hands," and "Zonky." But Waller and Razaf had one ambition that was never realized—they wanted to get "a big break in Hollywood as a team." Despite their many hit tunes, this never happened, although Waller himself did get to Hollywood briefly. He proved himself an unforgettable personality when the movies took full but belated advantage of his miming talents in *Stormy Weather*. He stole scenes with his gaily artful manner and his ad-libbed catchphrases, such as the characteristic "One never knows, *do* one?"

In 1932 Fats went to Europe. He planned to appear as half of a piano-and-vocal team, with Spencer Williams, in London and Paris. But the story goes that one day Spencer couldn't find Fats anywhere; "he'd gotten high and jumped on the first boat back to New York." He didn't return to Europe after that until 1938, when he had a very successful trip, and, Andy says, "he picked up some Scottish dialect in Glasgow, had one long ball in London."

Fats's erratic qualities, probably both cause and effect of his heavy drinking, hurt him more than once. He was drunk at his Carnegie Hall concert in 1939, turning what might have been a triumph into an embarrassing fiasco. About three years before he died he was very ill. A doctor warned him to go on the wagon, which he did for several months. He was ill again in 1942, and again was told to take it easy—in fact, he was warned that he would die in a few months if he didn't. However, as his friend Andy says, "Fats could only take it easy for just so long. Life to him was one long crescendo, and he had to live it fast; but he never consciously hurt anybody but himself. . . . I shall always remember him as a great, happy guy who lived a happy, carefree life that ended much too soon.

"Fats's heart was as big as his body. Money meant nothing to him, and he was a soft touch for everybody; having a good time and looking out for his family were his greatest interests." Fats was married twice; he had one son by his first marriage and two by the second.

And speaking of Fats's musical achievements, Razaf says, "Fats was the most prolific and the fastest writer I ever knew. He could set a melody to any lyric, and he took great pains working on it, getting the exact mood and phrasing until the melody would just pour from his fingers. I used to say he could have set the telephone book to music."

Fats began to record regularly in 1922, both for player-piano rolls and for disks. He accompanied some eight blues singers of varying ability and by 1929, the same year he did the score for *Hot Chocolates*, he was recording his own alternately lovely and lusty compositions. In the year of the Great Crash he recorded such famous original keyboard exercises as "Handful of Keys" and "Numb Fumblin'," such beautiful original melodies as "Ain't Misbehavin' " and "My Fate Is in Your Hands." The next year he recorded his famous piano duets with Bennie Payne, who was later featured with Cab Calloway for many years; the tunes were "St. Louis Blues" and "After You've Gone." The charming tinkles of the two pianos suggested the multifaceted musical personality of Fats; his several sides as an organist, his work accompanying singers and expanding the musicianship of the sides made under the names of the Waller and Morris Hot Babies (the latter was Tom Morris the clarinetist) and the Louisiana Sugar Babes, implemented that impression; his vocals, after he became a star of the Victor label in May 1934, made the impression last. Fats made hundreds of sides for Victor between May 1934 and January 1943, brought at least one first-rate soloist, the guitarist Al Casey, to national attention, and sold millions of records. None of these accomplishments, however, ranks with his contribution to jazz piano.

One inevitably chooses one's own favorite Waller records: the delicate mincemeat his satirical playing and singing make of such a dog tune as "The Bells of San Raquel"; the bumptious delight of his "Jingle Bells"; the gentle trills and exquisite phrasing with which he makes an attractive tune, "Thief in the Night," into something more; the affecting religious feeling of his organ performances of such spirituals as "Deep River," "Go Down, Moses," and "All God's Chillun Got Wings"; his incomparable and surely definitive performances of his own songs. Whichever one chooses of these styles, built out of approaches musical and/or commercial, one chooses unique distinction. In all these styles, at moments or throughout a performance, there is the languorous legato conception of the piano keyboard which Fats brought to jazz. By definition the piano is a staccato instrument, technically a member of the percussion family, and incapable of being slurred or tied together into glissando phrases. Nonetheless, a few remarkable pianists, such as Moritz Rosenthal, Sergei Rachmaninoff, and Fats Waller, have been able to elicit from the hammered strings of the piano a sustained sound which approaches the long bow of the violin, viola, cello, and bass and has the added quality that only a sustained tone on an instrument which does not sustain tone can provide. As further extension of and contrast with this miraculous achievement, Fats offered long rows of delicate trills and evenly articulated arpeggios in his performances, especially of ballads. Sometimes the trills had the effect of a sudden snap or sputter. Count Basie, in his first recording with his full large band in 1937, "Pennies from Heaven," played a seeming parody of these snaps and sputters when he took his piano solo. But while parody of Fats's keyboard devices was possible, as Fats found it possible to parody many others' vocal tricks in his own singing, no pianist ever really succeeded in capturing his grace and limitless flow of tonal beauty. All that was possible was parodying, such as Count Basie's, or admiring mimicry, such as Johnny Guarnieri's. When Nat Jaffe and Earl Hines recorded eight sides as a memorial album for Fats in February 1944, they wisely played within their own styles; however sincere a compliment imitation might have been, they realized that Fats was inimitable.

Fats Waller wasn't imitated so much as he was absorbed, and none absorbed him better than Art Tatum. Though his style was often thought to be derived from Earl Hines', Art himself always acknowledged Fats as his primary source. In one remarkable early morning I spent with Art and Nat Cole and Erroll Garner at an after-hours club on the East Side of Los Angeles, Art played a kind of conversational battle of music with his two distinguished colleagues. The upshot of the evening, full of glittering displays of the techniques and ideas of the three pianists, was a discussion between Art and Nat in which the former put the latter to rights about his derivation. "Fats, man. That's where I come from. And quite a place to come from." And after Art had demonstrated again and again, with astonishing and undeniable Waller detail, Nat was prepared to acknowledge Tatum's acknowledgment and in turn to affirm his own source—Earl Hines, of course. Through all of this Erroll bounced away, with delightful Impressionist asides in the ballads, a little of Hines, a little more of sophisticated ragtime, and still more of Waller, as much the father of Erroll's style as of Tatum's.

From Fats, Art borrowed the left-hand pattern of alternating single notes and chords called "stride" piano. To Fats, Art added the tenth, the bass beat based on the chord of that interval. From Fats, Tatum took touch, soft, sinuous, and classically disciplined. To Fats, Tatum brought bravura execution, deftly inserted arpeggios, appoggiaturas, and other brilliantly interpolated ornament, all performed with an ease that ultimately won him the high praise of Rachmaninoff and Vladimir Horowitz.

From his very first appearance before a large audience, in an amateur program on a radio station in his native Toledo, it was obvious that Art Tatum was something of a keyboard phenomenon. He had switched to the piano from the violin in his middle teens. After that amateur show he was hired as a staff pianist at radio station WSPD. His extraordinary fifteen-minute morning programs on that station were picked up and piped across the country by the Blue Network of the National Broadcasting Company (now the American Broadcasting Company). He was beginning to get a reputation. Adelaide Hall took him out of Toledo to tour with her for a year in 1932, with a long stopover in New York—just time enough to amaze some of the more sensitive natives. After another sojourn in Toledo, during which he considerably enhanced his radio reputation, Art went to Chicago to become a fixture at the Three Deuces. He had recorded for Decca and Brunswick in New York in 1933 and 1934, sides which were snatched up with an almost delirious glow of excitement by collectors around the world. In Chicago he did not record, but when he got to Hollywood for a short appearance in 1937 he picked up a quintet,

most notable for the trumpeting of Lloyd Reese and the clarinet play-
ing of Marshall Royal, and led these capable musicians through four
barrelhouse sides, "Body and Soul," "What Will I Tell My Heart,"
"With Plenty of Money and You," and "I've Got My Love to Keep
Me Warm." These and the four sides he recorded in New York in
November of the same year, shortly before his 1938 tour of Europe,
are properly celebrated by Tatum enthusiasts. The New York sides,
"Gone with the Wind," "Stormy Weather," "Chloe," "The Sheik of
Araby," show Art at his sensitive and gentle best in the first, and at his
most exhibitionistic in the third; the Hollywood sides, on the contrary, show him at his roughest and most roisterous—the beat domi-
nates these performances and for once Art's technique takes a back
seat, although there was no more than a handful of pianists alive at
the time who could have maintained so firm a beat at so fast a tempo.

With the coming of swing came cash and kudos. Art made a Decca
album that sold very well in 1940; his name helped sell Joe Turner
blues records for the same label, and, even more important, he played
some of his most tasteful and titillating piano back of Joe's shouting
on eight sides in 1941. With Tiny Grimes to plop a mighty plunk on
the electric guitar and Slam Stewart to hum a mighty buzz an octave
above his bowed bass line, Art put together a trio in 1943 that, for
two years at least, combined box office and musicianship as they had
rarely been paired before. It was during the several long runs of the
Tatum trio at several of the Fifty-second-Street hot boxes that Art's
several limitations as a pianist and musician became clear, and some
of us who had shouted, "You can't Imitatum!" began to look for
excuses for such an excess of hyperbole. For one thing, there were
the quotations, endless interpolations of the familiar phrases of
Gershwin's "Rhapsody in Blue," perhaps, Sousa's "The Stars and
Stripes Forever," maybe. Occasionally the quote was apposite—when,
for example, Art inserted the melancholy strains of "Good-by Forever," made more poignant in a transposition to a minor key, in his
trio performance of "The Man I Love," there was relevance and sly
wit. But apposition and relevance were rare in Tatum's quotations,
and rarely to be found in those of Tiny Grimes, otherwise an able
swinging guitarist. Then, too, there was the vocal exhibition of
virtuosity: Art was taking himself more seriously than he should have;
he was interrupting conversation that cut, however softly, across his
playing—one of his now legendary interruptions was delivered on his

feet, after an abrupt breaking of an individual measure; he turned to the audience and asked in stentorian tones, "Do I have to perform a major operation in here to get quiet?" Sometimes Art would go uptown to Harlem after a full night's and morning's work on the Street, arriving at an after-hours place at, say, five or five-thirty A.M. He would look around the room eagerly, peering beneath the half-closed lid of his one good eye. He would find somebody to play with, somebody unusually courageous and similarly foolish. For Art played for keeps. These were battles of music, and their winner was always Art Tatum, who slaughtered his opponent with unmatchable keyboard demonstrations.

But Tatum was vulnerable too. The discovery came as a shock to followers, fans and musicians alike, who in their jazz enthusiasms rarely stopped to formulate standards or used such standards as were around. Shortly after the rabid applause had reached a deafening peak, then, came disillusionment, diminishing audiences, declining interest. After a hiatus of a few years, in 1950, Tatum again became an important jazz name, this time properly applauded as he deserved, but no longer worshiped as a piano-playing archangel, a role too big for any man.

Teddy Wilson, born the same year as Art, discovered the tenth-bass independently of Tatum at about the same time. Most directly influenced by Hines, the lineaments of whose style can be felt in one Wilson performance after another, Teddy nonetheless was as original as Art in his elaboration of piano jazz. Even as Art, Teddy tended to ornament, but he added a less frivolous and adventitious decoration. With Goodman, with his own big band in 1939, and thereafter with his several little bands, Teddy played a live, sometimes muscular, sometimes gentle piano. As a soloist he became adept at stringing together ballad phrases with fresh countermelodies and fill-in phrases and a steady moving beat. He submitted himself to traditional keyboard disciplines and later combined his serious piano studies and jazz-playing experience to become one of the finest teachers jazz has ever known, both privately and at such institutions as the Juilliard School of Music and the Manhattan School of Music.

In 1946 he became a member of the staff band at WNEW, the New York radio station that has proved most adventurous in its programming of popular music, both live and recorded. In nightly sessions with the WNEW band and in a long-playing Piano Moods

PIANISTS

record Teddy has shown himself to be not only a fine swing pia̶̶̶̶,
but an able exponent of more modern idiom too.

The capacity for growth which Teddy Wilson exemplifies so well
is in various degrees typical of most of the significant pianists who
followed in the footsteps of Earl Hines, Fats Waller, and Art Tatum.
Nat Jaffe, who died of a vascular ailment at the age of thirty, is a
splendid case in point. A well-trained New York musician, he had
the usual Gotham gigging beginning, then, following the tradition,
put in time with such bands as Charlie Barnet's and Jack Teagarden's.
Finally he became a Fifty-second-Street regular. As an accompanist
he developed an uncanny intuitive feeling for every complication,
every minute melodic and rhythmic variation of which a finger is
capable. Billie Holiday swore by rather than at him and insisted he
double from whatever club he was playing in to whatever club she
was singing in, as her accompanist. His few solo records, made in
1944 and 1945, suggest what he might have become if he had lived
beyond the latter year. On four twelve-inch sides with the guitarist
Remo Palmieri and the bass player Leo Guarnieri, he integrated Debussyan melodic ideas, jazz phrases, and a fresh rhythmic conception,
never losing his continuity; one of these sides, "These Foolish Things,"
is something of a jazz piano classic. In the four sides he made as half
of the Fats Waller memorial album he ran the gamut of his and jazz's
styles; one of these sides, "How Can You Face Me," has a singular
melodic beauty that does credit both to Fats as a composer and to
Nat as interpreter.

Another first-rate accompanist, in his later years perhaps the best
jazz has ever known, is Jimmy Jones. He came to New York to become a Fifty-second-Street regular in Nat's big year, 1944. Jimmy
arrived as one-third of the Stuff Smith trio, plying his strings alongside those of Stuff's violin and John Levy's bass. Like Nat, Jimmy
possesses remarkable intuitive gifts: with John providing an anchoring
beat, he managed to follow every eccentric twist and turn and leap
of Stuff's impetuous fiddling personality. As a stylist he softened the
Tatum line to fit his elegant touch, so soft in its articulations that few
recording engineers have been able to do it justice. Not until his 1950
recordings as Sarah Vaughan's accompanist did Jimmy really sound
on records, although he did make some lovely sides for Wax Records,
notably six of Noel Coward's tunes packaged as an album. Like most
of the first-rate pianists of the last quarter of a century, he also is an

imaginative musician, fully capable of transforming keyboard ideas into band scores. Some of the finest of the records Steve Smith made for his own Hot Record Society label in the middle forties are the product of the Jones imagination, which fits both Tatumesque piano ideas and Ellingtonian orchestral conceptions, and rarely fails in its fitting.

Touch and a mingling of traditions are also the defining elements of the pianists who followed Jess Stacy in his individual departure from the Hines hallmarks. The best example of Jess's individuality on records is that section of the long-playing record of the Benny Goodman 1938 concert devoted to his five "Sing, Sing, Sing" choruses. Here can be heard the curious mixture of Mozartian elegance and honky-tonk brashness that makes up the Stacy style. The trumpet-like phrasing comes from Hines, of course; the sweet, simple, and beautifully apt melodic variations from Stacy himself. A number of pianists, such as Dick Carey and Gene Schroeder, found themselves at ease in this pairing of piano styles. Two pianists in particular, Joe Bushkin and Mel Powell, found the style inspiring, and made much of the inspiration.

Joe is generally associated with the Dixieland musicians congregated around Eddie Condon, Pee Wee Russell, and Bobby Hackett at various times; actually, his most sizable performances were as a band pianist in his long associations, first with Bunny Berigan and then with Tommy Dorsey. In later years his galloping transformations of show tunes, with rhythm or string and rhythm accompaniment, showed him a far more adventurous pianist than any of his performances with the Condon gang had indicated he could be.

Mel Powell is a New York product, a prodigy of sorts, whose considerable talents were nurtured in city grammar and high schools. His precociousness was evidenced in his nursery school years, when he first began to play the piano. He was a good student in every way, under a private teacher at first and then later under the instruction of music teachers at high school, from which he graduated at the age of fourteen. He had his own band when he was twelve, the Dixieland Six, which actually found an engagement for itself; it played for six months at the Palais Royale in Nyack, New York. Still in his teens, Mel played with the musicians of his fancy, Dixielanders and Nicksielanders, such as George Brunies, Jimmy McPartland, Zutty Singleton, Bobby Hackett, and Willie the Lion Smith, who administered further

Dixieland discipline to the youngster. Mel's early style, an intricate lacework pattern threaded with pointed Dixie ornament and particular Stacy embroidery, changed some when he moved from the Muggsy Spanier band to Benny Goodman in 1940. With Benny he was not only a valuable member of the chamber units but also a fine soloist in big band numbers and an excellent arranger. He was a developing musician; with Raymond Scott's radio band and with Glenn Miller's Air Force behemoth he showed more and more versatility, more and more of the ability to play with jazzmen of broader scope than his first associates. After the war, when he made his own sides for Capitol, he enmeshed himself happily in small band arrangements with a texture more suggestive of Arnold Schoenberg than of Pee Wee Russell, Benny Goodman, or Jess Stacy.

Big bands were an aid in the development of Dodo Marmarosa, much as they had been for Joe Bushkin and Mel Powell, but the keyboard style Dodo developed was very different from theirs. Dodo, christened Michael in Pittsburgh in 1926, joined Johnny Scat Davis's orchestra, moved from it to the bands of Gene Krupa, Ted Fio Rito, Charlie Barnet, Tommy Dorsey, and Artie Shaw before settling down in Los Angeles in 1945. There he made a series of records with little bands led by other men and with his own trio for the short-lived Atomic label. All of them displayed a wide range of technique and a felicity of phrase, but his playing eventually settled down in bebop, never again to be revived—at least for public consumption—with the delicacy and variety that made his earlier work sparkle.

Nat Cole, who made his reputation as one of jazz's kings and as an intimate conversational singer, developed rapidly from an able nightclub entertainer and all-around keyboard handyman to a distinguished musical personality who left a firm imprint upon the Hines tradition and upon all pianists after him who were a part of it. His early background included the usual run of one-night and more extended engagements with other bands and his own in Chicago, where his family moved from Montgomery, Alabama, after he was born. Later he toured with the vaudeville unit of the *Shuffle Along* company, and remained in Los Angeles when the revue broke up there. In the movie town he developed a small following, which increased considerably when he organized his trio with Oscar Moore as his guitarist and Wesley Prince as his bass player. Later changes considerably modified the sound of the trio; but in its most important years, Nat's facile fingering and ready thinking combined with Oscar's technically able and richly intuitive guitar to create the best music with which King Cole was ever associated and the peak of his pianistic achievement.

Just as commercial success later narrowed the musical range of Erroll Garner and Johnny Guarnieri, Nat's winning of public esteem constricted his playing and removed him from serious consideration as a jazz artist. The same process gradually debilitated the taste and musicianship of Eddie Heywood, whose broken-chord revitalization of "Begin the Beguine" and other standard tunes ultimately succumbed to inflexible routine in order to maintain an audience—but not before a few delightful records had been made and the charm of Vic Dickenson's lazy, growly trombone had been felt.

Alongside the lure of commercial success, one must place the damaging effect of eclecticism on several jazz musicians. Johnny Guarnieri's consummate ease as a pianist in every known jazz style was first his making and then his undoing as a serious musician. After his preliminary engagements with high school bands, George Hall's orchestra, and Mike Riley's small band, he alternated between Benny Goodman and Artie Shaw for three years, from 1939 to 1942. He played expert piano with both men and later with Jimmy Dorsey, Raymond Scott, and his own trios and small bands; he also played intriguing harpsichord with Artie Shaw's Gramercy 5. He played too well. Johnny's spectacular lack of a musical personality ultimately made him perhaps the best of radio studio pianists; but he lost that individual improvisatory spirit which not only identifies but distinguishes jazz musicians. The decline of young André Previn, from a brilliant executor of Tatumesque and Cole-ish jazz piano at seventeen to a motion-picture virtuoso as arranger, conductor, and pianist at twenty-one, follows a similar pattern. This German-born musician, splendidly trained in Berlin and Los Angeles by his father and others, is both a heartening and disheartening example of what jazz can do to and for a musician. His cocktail piano records for Victor insinuate jazz; they sparkle both because of the remnants of André's early style and because of an undeniable musical wit and wisdom that will always be present in his playing; they are also dulled by a superficial eclecticism that represents nothing more than a concession to record-company and motion-picture standards, with only occasional and subtle reminders of the talent thus conceded. Eclecticism, however, does not necessarily represent decline and fall in jazz; in the music of Mary Lou Williams it has always meant an unparalleled receptivity to new ideas and a captivating catholicity of taste.

Mary Lou Williams started to play the piano professionally at six and she's never stopped since. In the course of her long, intensely active career she has rolled up a record, on and off records, which deserves that much-abused adjective "unique." For Mary has played a vital creative role in each of the three major eras of jazz since its New Orleans beginnings, so important a part indeed that one can almost calculate the quality and the effect of those eras by her contributions to them.

Mary Lou Winn grew up with jazz. "People had to hold me on their laps so I could reach the piano at church affairs and family parties. I would play for an hour and then rest and then come back and play some more." Born in Pittsburgh, she had several private teachers, who taught her the discipline of keyboard performance and the tradition of its literature. Then, at Westinghouse High School, she was taught by the same Mrs. Alexander who soon afterward imparted so much feeling for music and skill in communicating that feeling to Billy Strayhorn and Erroll Garner. In Pittsburgh Mary played the usual number of gigs, listening attentively to Earl Hines' piano when she could, developing under that influence and with the experience of those one-night seats a style very much her own. By 1925 she was ready for a vacation try at the Orpheum circuit, the big vaudeville wheel. She joined up with the Syncopaters of John Williams, whom she later married, accompanying Seymour and Jeanette, the only colored act on the Orpheum boards. Off and on she played with that act until 1928, touring the East and Midwest, getting a thorough schooling in show business. At the tag end of the twenties her saxophonist husband joined Andy Kirk, and she moved with him.

Mary was with Andy Kirk from 1929 to 1942. She says, "I don't know too much about those years. I was too happy to remember." Fortunately that band got around, and its records got further, so its memorable moments are well preserved, particularly those important moments presided over by Mary Lou Williams. She didn't actually join the band until 1931, but while she served Andy as part-time pianist, chauffeur, and arranger she also recorded with him. Her delicate melodic ideas and driving swing bass can be heard in the first versions of "Cloudy" and "Froggy Bottom" made by the band, in

"Mary's Idea" and "Mess-a-Stomp," and in her first piano solos, made in Chicago in December 1930, "Night Life" and "Drag 'Em." Then there is a six-year hiatus during which the band did not record. But Andy was very active in Kansas City in the late Hoover and early Roosevelt years, and Mary was well on her way to a countrywide reputation.

"Jack Teagarden and Paul Whiteman used to drop down to hear me. Glen Gray's musicians never seemed to miss us when they were in town and then, like so many others, made something of a point of getting me to play for them and with them. And what they heard was very different from what you might expect. I know all about 'Kansas City Jazz,' but we didn't play the blues. And Pete Johnson didn't play boogie! Yes, we played them occasionally, but things like the boogie were for very late at night. Musicians would get a kick out of Pete's flashy boogie then, and we used to roll off some of it as a gag, but it wasn't our staple. The things I liked, and played, were things like 'Walkin' and Swingin'' and 'Ghost of Love.' I liked to experiment, of course. But the blues were the easiest for people to hear, and the boogie caught on, and when we came to record for Decca in thirty-six, John Hammond asked us to do those things and so we did more than our share of them."

On Decca the band developed a popular reputation with such extravagances as "Until the Real Thing Comes Along," chortled in coloratura style by Pha Terrell, but musicians and youngsters around the country, responding to the product that was then labeled "swing," listened more carefully to Dick Wilson's tenor and Ted Donnelly's trombone and most attentively to "The Lady Who Swings the Band," as one of the Kirk instrumentals was appropriately called. Mary continued to play and write for Andy right through the big swing years, turning out such intriguing items as "A Mellow Bit of Rhythm," which Red Norvo's band helped make famous; the charming "What's Your Story, Morning Glory," which she also arranged for Jimmie Lunceford, to his morning, noon, and evening glory; and "Little Joe from Chicago," which tacked a story to a boogie line and made "eight-to-the-bar" music as well as monotony.

Boogie woogie stayed very close to Mary after she left the band. As she explains, "Once you get known as a boogie player, you've got to play boogie, boogie all the time." And so she did, at Cafe Society Downtown and Uptown in New York, at night clubs stretched across the country, at concerts and on record sessions. Happily for her sanity, she didn't stick to the same tremolos, the same pedal figures, the same raw routines she had temporarily enlivened for Benny Goodman in "Roll 'Em" and for Andy Kirk in "Little Joe" and "Froggy Bottom." She experimented. She kept moving.

"You can freshen anything. There's no reason to play anything—including Dixie—the way they've been playing it." Mary says this and proves it with her composing and arranging and playing. Listen to her 1936 piano parody, "Corny Rhythm," a take-off so gentle many listeners thought she was playing straight. Listen to her 1944 "You Know, Baby"—on Asch, with Bill Coleman and Al Hall—a witty variation on love songs, that suffered only from inadequate recording. Or listen to what happens to "Star Dust" through two twelve-inch sides of polished and pert writing and playing (by Mary, Vic Dickenson, Dick Vance, Don Byas, Claude Green, and rhythm) made around the same time. Perhaps you heard her dramatic evocation of the signs of the zodiac in the suite for woodwinds, jazz horns, and rhythm which was the centerpiece of her 1945 Town Hall concert, or her two albums of piano performances of the same music. Maybe you heard seventy men of the New York Philharmonic Symphony swing —really swing—their way through three parts of this suite at Carnegie in 1946. In 1946 Mary also invested the drab lines of boogie woogie and the unswinging accents of waltz time with brilliance in her "Waltz Boogie." And then there is "Oobladee," a fairy tale in flatted fifths, which is Mary Lou Williams' fetching freshening of bop.

She doesn't stop because she can't. In Pittsburgh, in 1948, an eighty-year-old man who runs a sixty-voice mixed choir asked her to write for his group. "Do something like that 'Blue Skies' you arranged for Duke," he suggested. Mary got together with Milt Orent, with whom she wrote "Oobladee," and came up with a nine-minute spiritual, "Elijah and the Juniper Tree," setting the words of a New York poet, Monty Carr, to music that employs modern changes and suggests bop in its texture.

"I was trained to play with everyone and to play everything. I grew up around older musicians and I listened to a lot and I learned. I listened to how a pianist pushed, like Count Basie, and I pushed. I broadened, I moved, I experimented. That's what I've always taught the kids who come to me. You've got to keep going. There's only one reason, really, to stop. That's to take account, to

get new sounds, to get the sounds you're not hearing. Today"—this
was in 1949—"Lennie's about the only original pianist around, Lennie
[Tristano] and Bud Powell; you've got to credit Bud. While the other
boys are playing the same runs, the same bop phrases, you've got to
play something fresh and new, even if the form is old. And if the form
is too old, you've got to find new forms. It's difficult for a creative
artist to live; there are all kinds of obstacles. But as long as you keep
your music broad in its scope, fresh in its ideas, and experimental,
you'll make it."

Chapter 19

FIGURES
OF TRANSITION

The structure of modern jazz is not the product of one man or a number of men. It is much more an evolution of forms, sometimes orderly, sometimes disorderly, away from the first catch-as-catch-can attempts of New Orleans musicians, the boisterous phrases of swing, and the intervening music, which was never any one style but was certainly closest to Dixieland. While no single musician or group created modern jazz—although it did evolve from its antecedents— the impact of a few men upon their contemporaries and successors in the decade following the swing period was so strong that, in the jazz sense of the word, it can be said that they "made" modern jazz.

Lester Young, Roy Eldridge, Jimmy Blanton, and Charlie Christian, along with a few lesser figures, can be held accountable, in some such order, for the jazz called modern. It used to be called "progressive," a word which has more philosophical and political significance than musical and isn't very much more precise in those contexts than it is in jazz. The music will, I suppose, continue to be called modern or new, and considerable use of the adjective "cool" will continue to be made to describe the efforts of modern and new jazz musicians; for cool their music surely is insofar as it is relaxed, organized in its lines, and shaped by a soft and consistent sound. And yet the four men who made modern jazz, from whom, in one way or another, most of what is cool derives, are characterized in their playing by an enormous drive, by an unmistakable push and vigor, by qualities that define what used to be called "hot" in jazz.

The epitome of coolness among these distinguished ancestors of modern jazz is Lester Young. But Lester is also a summary example of driving, vigorous tenor saxophone. It is a point not to forget in evaluating the size of his contribution. It is clear that the tone of his instrument was very different from that of other tenormen, though there was perhaps a suggestion of it in the work of a Kansas City contemporary who played the same horn—Dick Wilson of the Andy Kirk band. No one, however, until Lester came along, believed that the sound of the tenor could be other than thick, swollen with vibrato and phrased for plushness—the sound, in sum, of Coleman Hawkins. Lester changed all that. His tone was attenuated, compounded of leanly inflected notes, with a minimum of the furry vibration associated with Hawk and his horde of followers. His phrases were longer than the traditional riff; when at a loss for fresh ideas, he would extend his statements by hanging on to one or two notes in a kind of auto-horn honk that gave his solos a quality of cohesion; his lines hung together, even if suspended precariously from a single note. And how they swung!

It is not entirely true, as the legend of Lester Young seems to insist, that all of his solos with the Count Basie band after 1936, or with various pick-up groups recording under Teddy Wilson and Billie Holiday, remain fresh and stimulating today. Some of his work was as stale and stiff as his competitors', some of it as dulled by riffs, some of it as imitative of Hawkins and as inept as the poorest of the imitations. But the earmarks of a bright style did emerge in Basie's "Taxi War Dance" and "Twelfth Street Rag," in his own "Lester Leaps In," made with a small Basie group, and the coupled "Dickie's Dream." His inventive use of ballad materials is apparent in "You Can Depend on Me" and "I Never Knew"; and even more of the style, which has been used to such engaging effect on ballads by Stan Getz, Allen Eager, Sonny Stitt, Brew Moore, Herb Steward, and Zoot Sims (to mention just a few of the school), can be heard on "Jive at Five." A brief nod in the direction of the clarinet on "Texas Shuffle" and a Kansas City Six date for Commodore indicate that this neglected instrument might have been as richly adapted to cool jazz as the tenor if Lester had been more inclined to follow its humors.

It is fitting that this man, unanimously if unofficially elected president of their numbers by modern tenormen (hence his nickname— "Pres"), should have succeeded Coleman Hawkins in the Fletcher Henderson band when Hawk left for Europe in 1934. The qualities that secured Pres's election were not readily apparent, however, until he joined Count Basie in 1936 and came east with him. Then the New Orleans-born musician (1909) cut all his early ties—which included, besides Henderson, some time with King Oliver and Andy Kirk—

lifted his horn high in the air, and began to *make* modern jazz. It took some years for musicians to spot that horn, raised inches over Pres's head; when they did, right after the Second World War, the panic was on to push vibrato aside, pick up his licks, and produce his sound. After 1945 everybody who was tenor-sax anybody was blowing Lester and getting an audience—except Lester, whose several small bands lived and died in comparative obscurity. But during 1950 it was thought proper—even, one might say, hip—to listen to Lester directly, and he began to catch on a little more as a live figure, still persuasive, still cool, still driving, whatever the limitations of his harmonic and melodic imagination. He is, after all, the Pres.

A similar distinction belongs to Roy Eldridge, but the acknowledgment is less easily forthcoming from young musicians. It is generally understood that Dizzy Gillespie derives from Roy. Most musicians with ears to hear and records to play can distinguish the large change Roy effected on his chosen horn. But while Dizzy moved from Roy's sound to his own, younger trumpeters have been content to borrow from Dizzy directly or simply to carry over Charlie Parker's or Lester's lines to their instruments. The results have not always been salutary. There is always a loss, by definition, when a large step in the history of an art is forgotten or, when remembered, avoided. The consequences in this case have been grievous: bop trumpet was bop all right; it was not always trumpet, and new trumpeters, now that bop is fading as an organized expression, simply are not appearing.

Of the three men who fashioned, in their separate ways, the jazz trumpet as we know it—Louis Armstrong, Roy Eldridge, and Dizzy Gillespie—Roy is the key figure, I think. He marks the transition from New Orleans to bop; under his tutelage the trumpet emerged from a blues bondage and a tonal servitude; as a result of his performances the instrument was extended in range and color and agility. Without Roy, Dizzy would have been impossible and the brass section of the jazz band would never have achieved that full, glowing, vibrant life it has been known to have upon exultant occasion. With the diminutive figure so aptly dubbed "Little Jazz" by that master of nomenclature, Toby Hardwick, jazz was given an additional dimension and the trumpet was brought to maturity.

In a profession that writes off performers almost as quickly as baseball retires its pitchers, Roy Eldridge has been around a long time. He was born in 1911 and he has been playing professionally for close to a quarter of a century. He's been heard with little kid bands around his native Pittsburgh, with a carnival show, with Horace Henderson, the Chocolate Dandies, Speed Webb, Cecil Scott, Elmer Snowden, Charlie Johnson, McKinney's Cotton Pickers, Teddy Hill, Fletcher Henderson, Gene Krupa, Artie Shaw, and his own bands, large and small, American, and recently French. From a peppery little musician who played everything "up," as fast as possible, he developed into a trumpeter who could—and can—do anything anybody else can do on his horn and a number of things nobody else would think of attempting. From the first notes that one can remember hearing Roy blow, there has been that astonishing sound. He describes it best himself.

"I tell you what I love about the trumpet. I love to hear a note cracking. A real snap. It's like a whip when it happens. It hits hard and it's really clean, round and cracked."

Roy is very much aware of the quality of the trumpet which is its own. "When I first came to New York," he says, "I had to play everything fast and double fast. I couldn't stand still. Like a lot of youngsters today, all my ballads had to be double time. I was fresh. I was full of ideas. Augmented chords. Ninths. The cats used to listen to me. 'Well,' they'd say, 'he's nice, but he don't say nothing!' Consequently, I didn't work." There were other things he did. "I was playing fine saxophone on the trumpet. Trying to hold notes longer than they should be held, trying to get a sound which I couldn't and shouldn't get. When I discovered that the trumpet has a sound all its own, and a way of playing all its own, then I began to play."

It's not strange that Roy reached for saxophone lines when he picked up his trumpet. "The two men who have been my favorites ever since I began playing music are Benny Carter and Coleman Hawkins. They really inspired me. I'd listen to them and be stunned, man. I didn't know the right names for anything at first, but I knew what knocked me out. They'd do eight bars and then play what I called a 'turn-around.' Eight and 'turn-around.' Changes, man. I dug." Thus Roy praises these master saxophonists' creative modulations and imaginative alteration of chords and melodies.

Louis too, of course, played his vital part. "I went up to the Lafayette Theatre to try and discover what he was doing. I sat through one show, and nothing happened. I figured this couldn't be it. I sat through another. Then Louis started to build, chorus after chorus; he came to a real climax, an organized climax, right, clean, clear. Man, I stood up with the rest of them. I could see why people were digging him."

What was it about Louis? "It was feeling. It's always feeling when it's right. It's also building, giving your solo shape, going somewhere."

The feeling Roy looks for doesn't occur more than four or five times a year in his own playing, he insists. "When it's there, nothing matters. Range, speed, sound—they just come. It's nothing I use; I can be cold sober. From somewhere, it comes." He describes an intuitive process, in which everything he has ever learned spills over into his music, finding structure and meaning. "Afterward I sit up in my room and try to figure it out. I know I haven't cleaned my horn, but the sound was 'gone'! I know my lip isn't in that good shape, but I made an altissimo C as big and fat as the C two octaves lower. It just doesn't figure." Afterward he is usually sick. "One night recently in Chicago they pushed me up against a bunch of young boppers. Well, maybe I was lucky; I was blowing; it was one of those nights. I got home, and the next day I had pneumonia."

Roy likes much that he has heard of modern jazz. "Man, I don't put anything down that anybody's trying. Naturally I dig Charlie Parker —he's blowing. And I certainly like the long lines when they come off. Chu Berry used to play like that—sometimes two choruses at a stretch. He had a way of breathing in rhythm so he could carry himself all the way without interruption."

He's interested in the possibility of free improvisation. "Clyde Hart and I made a record like that once. We decided in front that there'd be no regular chords, we'd announce no keys, stick to no progressions. Only once I fell into a minor key; the rest was free, just blowing. And, man, it felt good."

But with most of his records, "I just don't seem to make it. I'm not sure I ever made a good record. Usually the tunes are bad, or everybody's in a hurry. Yeah, there is one, anyway. I like the 'Rockin' Chair' I made with Gene. I didn't know what I'd played until Ben Webster played it for me on the Coast. I didn't even know who it was. When I heard the introduction I thought it was Louis. I can truthfully say that I played what I wanted to play on that record. And maybe, too, on the 'Embraceable You' I made with a studio band. Some of the other things—you know. 'After You've Gone' was made to make people applaud. There were some other moments here and there and maybe we got a little bit of the sound of the band I had at the Deuces in Chicago in 1937. 'Heckler's Hop,' maybe; 'Florida Stomp.' That was a crazy band. The most flexible. There was nothing those cats couldn't do. And you never knew what they were coming up with. We could be doing 'Limehouse Blues' way up in tempo, look at the clock, and do a direct segue into the theme."

Those of us who heard Roy and his brother Joe and Scoops Carey on altos, John Collins on guitar, Teddy Cole on piano, Truck Parham on bass, Zutty Singleton on drums in that band, remember very well the suppleness and authority with which it played. It makes us starry-eyed about the mythical Golden Age of jazz when we listen to those Vocalions, even those of us with the most resolute of modern tastes. Perhaps there's a reason and a connection, or maybe a direct sequence of styles and ideas. Roy Eldridge, after all, represents taste and skill, and those are not ephemeral values that fade with the passing of a style, an era, or a movement in jazz. His career reaches into a past that produced jazzmen of solid stature. He came up at a time when it was not possible to achieve full-fledged fame at twenty and extinction at twenty-two. It is true that he played in comparative obscurity for several years, trying unsuccessfully to succeed with his own big band, playing a year with Gene Krupa, during which he received star billing but didn't actually get to play as much as his talents or the billing deserved. Then, in the spring of 1950, he journeyed to Paris to receive the first proper appreciation of his music since his early days with Krupa and Shaw. Paris was Roy's home for a year—almost, it seemed to him, a permanent home; but the standards of music and musicians were not high enough, so in the spring of 1951 Roy came home again to lock horns in battles of music with Dizzy Gillespie at Birdland in New York and to try once again. His taste and skill have not diminished; his time is just as good as it ever was, and some of us sometimes think it was the best; his sound is unimpaired, and those who think it is untouched on trumpet are not so few; his position remains big, perhaps beyond dispute. He has never lost sight or sound of the character of his instrument. Through all the years since 1928 Roy Eldridge has been a brassman with a fondness and a talent for the drama, the passion, and the power which only the trumpet can bring to jazz. Like all the other masters of this music, he has always struggled to get ahead, to make musical as well as economic progress. When bebop came along, Roy was frightened; he found it difficult to understand and didn't see a place for himself in the new music. But after a certain amount of scuffling, a series of disappointing trips with his own band and others, a year abroad, and a return to the United States, he was confident again. He could hear his contribution in other men's playing as well as his own. He had a raft of fresh ideas, nurtured through the bad years and the fine times in Paris. Roy knew once again that the general and the personal struggles were worth making.

Harry Edison, with Count Basie in Lester Young's day and still with him in bebop's, was too shy, too little concerned with his own personal advancement, to battle for his ideas. But all with an ear to hear recognized the advance in trumpet made with his perky triplets, his witty melodic variations and subtle changes of chord structure.

Jimmy Blanton's musical battle was for a line, any line, that could be called his instrument's own. The bass was a thumper when he took over; he left it a jumper. Actually the Blanton battle was a pushover. Duke Ellington, when he heard Jimmy playing with Fate Marable's band in St. Louis, was immediately convinced. Bass players all over America were won with a couple of measures of "Jack the Bear" and "Ko-Ko" and "Sepia Serenade," when they heard the tone and the authority and the beat of the best bassman jazz has ever known. A few of them were fortunate enough to get copies of his duets with Duke, the "Blues," "Plucked Again," "Pitter Panther Patter," "Sophisticated Lady," "Body and Soul," and "Mr. J. B. Blues," all now long out of print. On those exhilarating sides Jimmy demonstrated in 1939 and 1940 that the big violin was, like its small relative, a melodic instrument, that its melodic lines joined those of the brass and reeds in jazz as snugly and imaginatively as a guitar's, and that its rhythmic figures did not have to be limited to so many syncopated beats a bar. Jimmy died of tuberculosis in 1942 in a California sanatorium, having accomplished in the last four of his twenty-three years what few musicians manage in a lifetime. He brought his instrument to maturity, gave it a solo position in jazz, and went much of the way toward revolutionizing the rhythmic patterns which, unchanging, gave every indication of constricting and eventually killing jazz.

It was not only changes in bass playing and writing and thinking that Jimmy Blanton effected in his brief career in the big jazz time. When Jimmy joined Duke in St. Louis in 1939 the Ellington band had lost some of its spirit. It was still making lovely records; there were still occasional experimental scores forthcoming from Duke, such as the 1937 exercise in dynamics and the structure of the blues,

"Crescendo and Diminuendo in Blue"; the small units of the band, led by Barney Bigard, Johnny Hodges, Rex Stewart, and Cootie Williams, had been making charming records and continued to make them until 1941. There was still melodic imagination in songs written to order, such as the downtown Cotton Club Revue pieces, "I Let a Song Go out of My Heart" and "If You Were in My Place"; there were all the swinging vehicles for soloists, such as Lawrence Brown's "Rose of the Rio Grande" and Rex Stewart's "Boy Meets Horn"; Ivy Anderson was as good as ever as she plied the amusing but poignant phrases of "A Lonely Co-ed" and the mood, one of screaming through tears, of "Killin' Myself." In spite of all these happy circumstances, the full measure of the Ellington band's resources at the beginning of World War II was not discovered until Jimmy Blanton joined up. Those resources were epitomized in the members of the organization who were almost as new as Blanton: Ben Webster, who joined just before Jimmy did; and Billy Strayhorn, who preceded Ben by a few months.

Duke knew the work of Ben Webster pretty well by the time he hired him. He knew that Ben had a violent temper which exhibited itself on rare occasions, and to go with it a sweetness of disposition which exhibited itself far more often. He knew that Ben was perhaps the best of all the tenor saxophonists in the Coleman Hawkins tradition—with the exception of Hawk himself—and that he had developed on the Hawkins theme a variation of singular loveliness, articulated in husky tones, occasionally kicked over for a summary blast or two—even as his temperament changed on occasion from a soft affability to erupting ire. Benny, as he was called by his friends, was born in Kansas City in 1909, educated in a local high school and by private music teachers who taught him the violin and piano. Before he went to Wilberforce University he had turned to the tenor, an instrument on which he had received almost no formal instruction. His first professional job was with an Oklahoma band, playing the piano; thereafter he played both the piano and the alto before switching permanently to the tenor in 1929 when he was with the Dean Coy band. Before joining Duke he played with Cab Calloway's sister, Blanche; with the Kansas City bands of Bennie Moten and Andy Kirk; with Fletcher Henderson in 1934; and for almost two years, in 1937 and 1938, with Benny Carter, Willie Bryant, and Cab Calloway, as well as the small bands of Stuff Smith and Roy Eldridge. Although his conception of the jazz phrase and sound was entirely different from Lester Young's, nonetheless his playing with Ellington from 1939 to 1942 had more than a suggestion, in its restraint and careful adjustment of solo lines to orchestral patterns, of the music that was to come in the following decade. In Jimmy Blanton's reorganization of the Ellington band's beat and abrupt modernization of its rhythmic feel, Benny found a sturdy support for his own modern ideas. Their mutual compatibility and dual contribution to the Ellington band in its modern period can be heard in "Conga Brava" and "Cottontail," in "Bojangles," and in most of the other sides they made together from their entry into the band in 1939 and their first recording in February 1940, through the sides made in Hollywood in September 1941.

Billy Strayhorn auditioned for Duke in December 1938 in Pittsburgh, to which his family had moved a few years after his birth in Dayton, Ohio. He played a song called "Lush Life," for which he had written both the words and music. It did not find a large audience until more than ten years later when Nat Cole made it into a big hit with the aid of a lush string orchestra and the musical life that arranger Pete Rugolo was able to give it; but Duke was impressed back in 1938 by this and the other songs Strayhorn played for him backstage at the Stanley Theatre. He told Billy that he liked his songs, said he was sorry Strayhorn couldn't leave copies with him—because they were the only ones Strayhorn had—and suggested Billy look him up when he came to New York. Billy did, the following February; Duke bid for his services, and Strayhorn became a member of the organization. The band recorded Billy's lovely song, "Something to Live For," in which Jean Eldridge—no relation to Roy—made her single but sumptuous singing entry with the band on records. Then Billy was employed as arranger for the small recording units, demonstrated his several scoring talents as arranger and composer, and was welcomed into a position second only to Duke's with the Ellingtonians. It was with Jimmy Blanton playing bass in the rhythm section of the big band and of the small units that Billy's most impressive contributions to jazz were made: the enormously successful middle-tempo tribute to subway life in New York, "Take the A Train," was engineered rhythmically by Jimmy; so were Strayhorn's lovely impressionist pastiches, "After All" and "Chelsea Bridge"; so were his extravagantly lush but wholly successful settings for Johnny Hodges' alto, the small-band "Daydream" and "Passion Flower." The last-named was in a

sense an apt description of Strayhorn's sensuous nature, which led
him early in his professional career to lead a hedonistic life. Perhaps it
would be too much to say that Jimmy Blanton acted as a brake upon
Billy Strayhorn's sentimental musical excesses; nonetheless it is true
that after Blanton's death Strayhorn wrote very little that had the
quality of the compositions and arrangements he scripted when
Jimmy was alive and kicking. The whole band suffered as a result
of Jimmy's death, not only in its loss of an incomparable rhythmic
complement and bass soloist, but also in the consequent sagging in
spirits. It was after Blanton died that Duke composed his monumental
"tone parallel to the history of the American Negro," "Black, Brown,
and Beige." It was after Blanton's death that Duke had his several
Carnegie Hall concert triumphs; and after Jimmy died there were
many fine compositions still to come and still some of the imaginative
solos of such musicians as Ray Nance, Jimmy Hamilton, Taft Jordan, Carney, Hodges, Brown, Tizol, and Tricky Sam. Nonetheless
when Jimmy died the last great solo phase of the Ellington band was
over. Thereafter, however fresh and facile the work of the Ellington
soloists, it was Duke's and Strayhorn's writing for which one listened
to the band; everything else was essentially ornamental. As the writing of extended works in more or less new forms changed the Ellington tradition, so Jimmy transformed the way and the power of these
musicians' playing. His death made performances that came after
necessarily less coordinated and cogent; after him, one had to look to
a whole new generation of jazzmen to find anything comparable in
rhythmic brilliance and melodic ingenuity.

Charlie Christian was just a year older than Jimmy; he was as formidable a solo and rhythmic influence, and a sad parallel in his suc-
cumbing to tuberculosis the same year the brilliant bassist did. Like
Blanton, he joined an important band—Benny Goodman's—in 1939;
like Blanton, he brought his rhythm instrument, the guitar, from
background anonymity to solo splendor; like Blanton, he placed a
hitherto restricted instrument well within the melodic frame of jazz,
raising the guitar line almost to dominating importance in the Goodman sextet. Unlike Blanton, Eldridge, or Young, Charlie Christian has
a direct connection with bebop. He played up at Minton's in Harlem
in those first experimental sessions which yielded, in the early forties,
the altered chords, the fresher melodic lines, the rows of even beats
and contrasting dramatic accents of bop. Some of the participants in

the early after-hours affairs credit Charlie with the name "bebop," citing his humming of phrases as the onomatopoeic origin of the term. All of the musicians who played with him then, as all of us who heard him, insist on his large creative contribution to the music later associated with Parker and Gillespie.

Charlie was born in Texas, bred in Oklahoma; he played in the Southwest and Midwest before joining Benny. His bigtime experience brought him attention and some development of style, but according to all who heard and played with him in his early years, the lines, the drive, and the legato rhythmic feeling were always there. He was a natural musician, whose naturalness presaged the inevitable change in jazz from roar to restraint, from childish blast to mature speculation. Limited by the clatter of riffs in the Goodman groove, his imagination soars free in at least some of his solos on the records made by Benny's sextet; in "Solo Flight" it has most of a record in which to make its impressive point, and there are lovely Christian moments on sides made with Lionel Hampton, Edmond Hall, Eddy Howard, and the Metronome All Star bands of 1940 and 1941.

If one listens to the two sides of the long-playing record that Jerry Newman issued on his Esoteric label, one hears Charlie Christian in all his glory. These sides were originally tape recordings made by Jerry at jam sessions in Minton's Playhouse, the dining room and club that Henry Minton, ex-saxophonist and musicians' union delegate, made out of part of the Hotel Cecil on One Hundred and Eighteenth Street in Harlem. The recording was made in May 1941; it was made because Jerry, like every one of the rest of us who heard Charlie with Benny Goodman or in such sessions, knew he was a musician whose every moment counted. Here, playing with some of the first musicians to make the move from swing to bebop, Charlie plays rhapsodic chorus after chorus, threading his way through such familiar chords and melodic lines as those of "Stompin' at the Savoy" to give shape to a whole new conception of music. The beat never stops; its steady pulsation is elaborated, complicated, simplified. The sound never loses beauty or flourish; the harpsichord-like texture of Charlie's guitar is produced in arpeggios, trills, cascades, clusters, in phrases sometimes of tumultuous power, sometimes of elegant restraint. The recording shows clearly what Charlie did for the electric guitar, which before him was played on jazz records only by Floyd Smith with Andy Kirk's band, in a manner that was engaging but not much beyond the formulations of the blues. Charlie changed the playing technique of the guitar and structured for it a dramatic role in jazz which, for all their imagination and resourcefulness, Eddie Lang, Carl Kress, and Dick McDonough had never dreamed of. He made it possible for guitarists such as Barney Kessel, Chuck Wayne, and Billy Bauer to think and speak musically on a level with trombonists, trumpeters, and saxophonists. So effectively did he transform the guitar from a rhythmic servant into an eloquent master that today very few bands, big or small, can find guitarists good enough for their needs—and after Christian a bad one would be unthinkable.

These are the large figures of transition. Their pioneering is evidence of the inventive brilliance of jazz musicians; without them present-day jazz would not be the provocative music it is, the reflective music, the music of idea and developed statement. Without Charlie Christian and Jimmy Blanton jazz not only misses two vital voices, it lacks any development of the guitar and the bass. Roy Eldridge is still with us, playing with the conviction and the cogency of a vigorous jazzman, but trumpeters are insufficiently aware of him. Lester Young is very much a part of modern jazz, but while the coolness he contributed is unmistakable in his disciples, his drive in most instances seems to elude them. The spirit the Ellington band possessed when Billy Strayhorn, Ben Webster, and Jimmy Blanton were together in it did have a flowering or two after Jimmy's death, but not of equal brilliance. As in the times of migration and depression, new continuity with the past has to be established with each development in jazz. Modern jazz knows where it comes from, but not why. A fresh examination of these men might prove again as suggestive and as stimulating as the first contact with them did, if it digs beneath the surface superficialities of their influence to discover how right, how rich, how inevitable it was that these should have been the men who made modern jazz.

Chapter 20

SINGERS

Singing came in when swinging went out. Off and on a band would do well; regularly a Frank Sinatra or a Perry Como or a Dinah Shore would lead stampedes to the box office, draw screams from an audience and nickels from jukebox patrons, sell millions of their records. A singer, after all, offered not only a voice but a visual manner, not only a face but a calculated grimace. The day of the swooner—for many, more accurately, the return of the seven-year locust—was in many ways a dismal one; it was also a sharp change of focus. The Second World War had as serious an impact upon the American people as the depression of twelve years earlier, although its effect upon their economy was quite the opposite. A kind of papier-mâché romance was used to fabricate the fantasies of the forties.

Earlier the pleasure of the mob, running feverishly to cover from the onslaughts of drought and despair and no work, had elected Russ Columbo, Rudy Vallee, Will Osborne, and Bing Crosby entertainers inordinary. Then, when death had taken one, a change of taste had diminished the stature of two others, and by popular election the last had become a maker and keeper of the American Dream, the public had turned to bands. Bands in turn turned to singers. The leaders of swing had always liked singers; those who had worked with Paul Whiteman had played alongside Bing Crosby and the Rhythm Boys and Mildred Bailey, the first important singer with a band; others, both leaders and sidemen, had accompanied innumerable singers on records, from the royal families of the blues to the passing fancies of the men in charge. When Benny took his band out on the road in 1935 he took Helen Ward with him. Helen was a better singer than most of those who took up valuable time when the swing bands were on the stands and made serious jazz lovers nervous and irritable. Sometimes Helen had a nervous vibrato, which she later conquered

247

in a brief return to music with Hal MacIntyre's band; usually she was capable of tasteful interpretations and an attractive sound. Peg La Centra, who sang with Artie Shaw's first band in 1936, was, like Helen and like Jeanne Burns, who sang with Adrian Rollini's Taproom Gang in 1935, essentially in the Mildred Bailey tradition—warm, languorous in her phrasing, and as delicate as her native gifts permitted. Jeanne, a good musician with an intuitive grasp of the singing line, had a style perhaps a bit more personalized, one which she turned in later years into a considerable songwriting ability. Tommy Dorsey started with Edith Wright and Jack Leonard, the first a showwoman, the second a gentle-voiced crooner who paved the way for Frank Sinatra. Later Tommy featured, along with Frank Sinatra, the Pied Pipers, a well-disciplined vocal group whose proudest boast was Jo Stafford; she became the best jazz singer Tommy ever had, skilled in most of the rhythmic bypaths, but she changed into a straightforward commercial singer when she left the band. Brother Jimmy more than doubled his income as a result of the gimmick he worked out with his two singers, Bob Eberle, to whom was entrusted the first, slow baritone chorus of a tune, and Helen O'Connell, who was given the second, double-time chorus to plunge through. But able as some of these singers were, successful as half of them became, theirs were not the jazz voices; they were with other bands. For a while Artie Shaw had Billie Holiday; Chick Webb had Ella Fitzgerald; Red Norvo had his wife, Mildred Bailey.

Back in 1936 they used to call Mildred Bailey and Red Norvo Mr. and Mrs. Swing. The labels were deserved. Red was the epitome of swing, Mildred the epitome of good swinging and good singing.

Mildred could be counted on to bring the house or the night club or the concert hall down, with songs such as her favorites, "Lover," "Honeysuckle Rose," "Squeeze Me," "More Than You Know," "Don't Take Your Love from Me," and "There'll Be Some Changes Made." Rehearing her old concerts and personal performances on records confirms the original impression she used to make: Mildred was an audience spellbinder, with her exquisite phrasing, the intrinsic loveliness of her voice, and her fine rocking beat. The song most closely and permanently identified with her, of course, was "Rockin' Chair." This and other pieces written especially for her, like the witty Sonny Burke–Bill Engvick–Hughie Prince "Scrap Your Fat," and other beautiful Baileyana such as "From the Land of the Sky-blue

Water," the familiar Indian plaint in swing tempo, Mildred sang warmly, wonderfully, singing her heart out, singing with delicacy and grace. She was a feelingful and affecting singer and, when necessary, a funny one. She was almost a tradition in herself.

Mildred Bailey was born in Tekoa, Washington, in 1903. Her mother, who was part Indian, used to run through Indian songs and rites with her and, when the family moved to Spokane, often took her over to the near-by Coeur d'Alene Reservation. Mildred said of her Indian repertory, "I don't know whether this music compares with jazz or the classics, but I do know that it offers a young singer a remarkable background and training. It takes a squeaky soprano and straightens out the clinkers that make it squeak; it removes the bass boom from the contralto's voice, this Indian singing does, because you have to sing a lot of notes to get by, and you've got to cover an awful range." As a child, the one girl in the Rinker family, Mildred covered many musical ranges—with her three brothers, all of whom ended up in the music business; with Bing Crosby, who was a neighbor; and with all the other jazz fans in their part of town who sang or hummed or played. Mildred was married at an early age and moved to Los Angeles. There she was divorced; there she sang some and listened more—to men who were making "the West Coast kick in the late twenties." In late 1929 Paul Whiteman was in California and looking hard for a girl singer. Until that time no girl had sung regularly with a jazz band, and Paul wanted to be the first in this, as he had been in so many other things. Musing one night at a party about his troubles in finding a girl, Whiteman ran into the family patriotism of Mildred's brother Al and Bing Crosby, two-thirds of his own Rhythm Boys, whose high praise of Mildred sparked Paul's interest. They called Mildred, and she ran right over to audition for him—and that, of course, was enough; she was hired on the spot. She didn't record with Paul Whiteman, but she made many sides with musicians from his orchestra: with Eddie Lang she sang Hoagy Carmichael's arrangement of "What Kind o' Man Is You"; with Mattie Malneck and many of the Whiteman musicians she made Carmichael's "Georgia on My Mind" and, among nine other sides, "Rockin' Chair." Mildred became inseparably associated with the ditty of pity for dear old Aunt Harriet. The year she made her first sides with Malneck—1931—she met and fell in love with Red Norvo, who joined Whiteman in Chicago at the end of the year.

Just after she and Red left Whiteman, in the winter of 1933, they
were married. Mildred recorded with pick-up bands led by Benny
Goodman and the Dorsey Brothers, with the Casa Loma band, and
with several of her own date outfits; Red did some gigging around
town and some recording too, but the two years after Whiteman
were lean. The leanness left them when Kenneth, as Mildred always
called Red, turned his little band into a big one and made Mildred
his co-leader. While that band was abuilding the Norvos threw a
party that had a lasting effect of which they hadn't dreamed. Benny
Goodman and Teddy Wilson were guests at the party, and so was a
young cousin of Mildred's who played a little drums. As musicians
like to do, they organized an informal session, following Mildred's
suggestion that Benny and Teddy should play with her drummer-
cousin. The musicians liked the combination of instruments so much
that soon after they substituted Gene Krupa for Mildred's cousin and
became the Benny Goodman trio.

There was, unfortunately, much more to bandleading, even when
the duties could be split in half, than the pleasures of parties and
pleased and pleasing audiences. With all the good music, Mildred
said, there were plenty of headaches. "It's no fun to have to worry
about making trains on time and whether this or that booking is
better for the band, shall Mr. Eddie or Mr. Charlie do the arrangement on this new pop, and will I take one or three choruses on this
old standard. Many's the morning we stumbled into a town, half
dead from sleeplessness and worried over a missing trunk or make-up
kit, only to find that we had a record date, band or me, for that
early afternoon. Sometimes that meant hunting up good musicians
for an improvised date, sometimes that meant taking our band and
rehearsing them in a new number they'd never seen before—all in
one or two or three hours. It was these headaches that finally drove
me out of the band business."

Mildred never did really get out of the band business; she always
found the musicians she needed for her record dates, usually the best
musicians available in jazz. She recorded with Bunny Berigan, Johnny
Hodges, and Teddy Wilson in one memorable date; with Ziggy
Elman, Artie Shaw, Teddy, Dave Barbour, John Kirby, and Cozy
Cole in another. With the band she and Red led, she made several
dozen sides; with Mary Lou Williams in charge of a band, she made
half a dozen of her loveliest recordings; with Alec Wilder providing

manuscript fit for her voice and an intriguing combination of wood-winds, rhythm, Roy Eldridge, and Teddy Wilson, she made eleven of the really great vocal records of jazz. A fair sampling of her various backgrounds, technical efficiencies, and inspired transformations of good songs can be heard in her long-playing record, *A Mildred Bailey Serenade,* issued in 1950 when she was first hospitalized with her fatal illness. There, in eight performances, as in every one of her other sides, sound her sumptuous middle register, her exquisite upper register, her subtle nuances. Jazz was well provided with its first band singer until December 1951, when Mildred died.

One winter night at the end of 1935 Mildred Bailey journeyed up to the Savoy Ballroom in Harlem to sing her bit in a Scottsboro Boys benefit. In a long night of superb performances by the foremost musicians and singers of jazz, Mildred's singing stood out. So did Bessie Smith's and that of Chick Webb's vocalist, Ella Fitzgerald. Ella had joined Chick only a few months before. Just a seventeen-year-old girl from Virginia, she moved simply to a microphone, opened her lips, and sang—sang with a natural ease and a musician-ship which, though untutored, needed very little assistance from Chick or his musicians. Ella was and is the prime example of an intuitive singer in jazz. From her first recording with Chick, "Sing Me a Swing Song," to one of her latest solo albums, devoted to songs by George and Ira Gershwin, she has always found the right tempo, and right interpretive nuance, the right melodic variation. She was an added soloist for the Chick Webb band, the most distin-guished of a group of distinguished musicians; it was undoubtedly her presence with the band, in person and on records after the spring of 1936, that catapulted it to sudden, unexpected but thoroughly deserved success. In November of the same year Ella became a re-cording name in her own right, when she made four sides for Chick's home label, Decca, with her "Savoy Eight," made up of Chick's best musicians, including Chick himself, of course. The next year she did a date with the Mills Brothers and two others with the Savoy Eight. She continued to record under her own name, and with Chick she made one of the best-selling records of all time, "A-Tisket, A-Tasket," later followed by a fairly successful sequel, "I Found My Yellow Basket." Her great skill in these years and in those to come, after Chick's death, was a versatility that permitted her to sing material that was nothing less than nauseating in other perform-

252   A HISTORY OF JAZZ IN AMERICA

ances, but something more than tolerable in hers. There were not
only the contrived nursery rhymes and the clumsy novelties—songs
of short duration in people's memories—but also soft and insinuating
ballads, such as "My Last Affair," or driving instrumentals to which
words were added because Ella's voice made her vocals valid parts
of improvised band performances.

When Chick died Ella was his logical successor. She led the band
—which was renamed, with some justification, Ella Fitzgerald and
Her Famous Orchestra—until early 1942, when the same strain which
had told on Mildred began to wreak havoc in her personal life and her
singing. Then came her felicitous collaborations with such likely
associates as Louis Armstrong, the Delta Rhythm Boys, and Eddie
Heywood and with such unlikely ones as the Ink Spots. With all
of them her sinuous imagination was given full play. No matter the
arch mannerisms and distorted falsetto sounds of the Ink Spots; Ella
felt the glow of Duke Ellington's song "I'm Beginning to See the
Light" and transformed it into exquisite sound; no matter the un-
familiar calypso inflections of "Stone Cold Dead in the Market" and
the raucous personality of Louis Jordan, Ella turned both song
and singer into rich duo comedy. In 1946 and the next year, with
able studio bands led by Vic Schoen and Bob Haggart, she pressed
the full impact of her scat-singing personality into record grooves;
through "Flying Home" and "Lady Be Good" Ella effused, singing
bebop figures and swing phrases, finding the verbal equivalents for
trumpet, trombone, and saxophone sounds. In 1939, in her recording
of " 'Taint What You Do, It's the Way that You Do It," she
scatted around the engaging tune and ended one of her phrases
with the word "rebop," undoubtedly the first appearance of the
first accredited name for Dizzy Gillespie's and Charlie Parker's music.
In 1946 she coined the whole new scatting vocabulary. Three years
later she exhibited another of the facets of her singing personality
when she did a perfect imitation of Louis Armstrong's guttural
style in her recording of "Basin Street Blues." Here, and in her duets
with Louis, she demonstrated that catholicity of taste and talent
which has always been her hallmark. She says of both Louis and
Dizzy, "I like him just the way he is." She says of Les Brown's
band that it is among her pets "because it plays a variety and sounds
like bands used to sound." Her attempts at songwriting, usually successful both musically and commercially, show the same breadth of

interest: they range from the swingy phrases of "You Showed Me the Way" and "Oh, But I Do" to the handsomely coordinated lyrics she wrote for "Robbins' Nest." At times in recent years her versatility has betrayed her: her phrases and intonation never falter, but they do sometimes take on a mechanical edge. She works hard, she works often; she is or has been the favorite singer of most of America's favorite singers, drawing such plaudits as Bing Crosby's enthusiastic summation of her position: "Man, woman, or child, the greatest singer of them all is Ella Fitzgerald." The penalty of so much singing may be a hard sound and a cold inflection; it can never be so severe, however, that jazz, jazz musicians, and jazz singers will forget the size of her contribution and the electricity her name has always carried.

For six weeks in the worst heat of July and August in 1948 another jazz singer who has contributed greatly to modern jazz acknowledged the applause of large audiences at the Strand Theatre in New York City—the largest audiences that theater had seen in many years. The movie, *Key Largo*, pulled in a large part of the audience; Count Basie and his orchestra drew some of it; but there had been big movies before, and Count Basie had appeared at New York theaters before. The main draw was Billie Holiday.

Like very few singers in our time, like no other uncompromising jazz singer in our time, Billie was a big box-office attraction. She had her own bitter explanation of her popularity. "They come to see me get all fouled up. They're just waiting for that moment. Just waiting. But they're not going to get it. I'm not going to get all fouled up. I'm not! I'm not. . . ."

Billie had—and has—many friends and admirers, many fans. Some of the enormous number of people who came to see her came because of her voice. Most of them, Billie felt sure, came to see the great "Lady Day" fall flat on her beautiful face.

"I'm tired of fighting," Billie said. "All my life it's been fighting. I'm tired of fighting."

It had been hard to have to quit school in the fifth grade. She had had to quit, to help with the groceries and the rent. There were no child-labor laws in Baltimore when Billie was eleven. And even if there had been, the Holidays needed groceries and, once a month, the rent. So, at the age of eleven, Billie went to work, washing down Baltimore's famous white stoops.

At fifteen she was singing at Jerry Preston's in Harlem. Life came fast uptown, with no holds barred, no experiences withheld. If Billie had talent to begin with, she had maturity almost as soon— maturity of a sort. When most girls were just emerging from their stiff organdy party dresses and just beginning to worry about dates and kisses, Billie was singing for all-night parties in after-hours joints. Before she was out of her teens she was on the road with bands, and she reached her majority plunking two bass notes with her left hand for Artie Shaw, while the intellectual clarinetist wove the melody of "Nightmare" out of the early morning hours and called for more of her exquisite singing.

Her singing won plaudits and received all sorts of audience and critical appreciation. Then came a Paul Whiteman recording session for Capitol in 1944, in which she sang "Travelin' Light"; and with that notable side Billie was really recognized as a uniquely distinguished jazz singer, as a uniquely fascinating personality whose private perceptions were articulated in original and delicate vocal patterns.

In 1947 Lady Day was sent to prison. Although there was this record—and there were other records to remind us of her great talent—and many newspaper stories to apprise us of her wrongdoing, and many, many friends to echo her suffering and her sorrow, only Billie herself could sing Billie's blues. It was not until she returned from jail that we could understand exactly what she had been through, what she looked forward to and what not, and why it was and is so important to her to affirm the true, the real, and undeniable, and the unanswerable.

"Easy Living." "Travelin' Light." If you want to be corny you can tell Lady Day's story through the songs on her records, making sure that you interrupt the narrative of light life and debauchery with the tender "God Bless the Child" and the angry sorrow of "Strange Fruit." Anybody who has watched Billie sing "Strange Fruit" knows what the singing of that song does to her; anybody who really knows her knows that her tears over the victims of lynch mobs stop only when she wrenches herself violently away from the facts of Negro life. Even the casual listener to her most poignant record, "Porgy," knows how real a struggle against temptation and weakness hers has been.

They threw her into a cell, and a nightgown and a mattress and a bed after her, and she was on her own. No coddling, no cozening, no letdown, no matter how difficult; and the descent from the illusory heights of dope is generally acknowledged to be of the nature of the journey from the first circle to the icy center of the ninth of Dante's Hell. Billie gritted her teeth and held on to her mind and came out many months older, cleaner, closer to herself and the truth.

"When I was on it," she says, "I was *on* it! I wouldn't stop for anybody, anywhere, ever. Now I'm off it and I don't want it and I won't have it, and that's the end of it."

She went to her doctor's to get a very careful general check-up, which showed her supremely well, healthier than she had been in years. But she knew she was frantically tired and uncertain of herself. She also knew she would sing, and while in those bad years before she had buoyed her sagging spirits and propped her weary body with narcotics, now she was on her own. She went on singing, of course. She sang, of course, as beautifully as ever, perhaps more beautifully. And then she wasn't entirely on her own. There were friends and admirers, friends like Bobby Tucker and his wife and his father and mother, who had kept their Christmas tree going until March 16, when she got out, and admirers like the concert audiences and Broadway theatergoers who went to her first appearances in March and April and cheered themselves into late winter colds, welcoming her home.

In March 1949 Billie Holiday once more stood accused. Once more the sights of a million scandalmongers' guns were trained at her not insignificant figure. As before, she was accused of breaking the strict laws of the land, which specifically forbid the indulgence of those peculiar appetites that call for a drug here, a charged cigarette there, a dose of opium or hemp or any of the other short ways around to an illusory Nirvana. Billie said she was framed. She was tried and found innocent and released.

It makes big newspaper headlines to catch a movie star or a jazz singer redhanded and heavyhanded with the hot stuff; but their guilt is small compared with that of the gangsters who run the dope and the rope into the country and peddle it from dressing-room to dressing-room, from night-club entrance to night-club exit, from alley to alley. Government agents are busy trying to run down the gangsters and the middlemen called "connections," but these efforts never seem to make the headlines or even the small print of the back-page continuations of the page-one stories. The only way to end the terror and threat of drugs is to stop the flow at its source, to start directing the publicity as well as the undercover activity toward that end, and to turn our healthy indignation on the promoters rather than the victims of the racket. The opposite procedure is too much like putting a beer-drinker in jail for Al Capone's crimes.

All of this left Billie with a gnawing fear. She continues to sing well, but she is never sure that she is received by audiences as a singer. Is she stared at as a scarlet lady? As an ex-convict? Or simply as a magnificently constructed woman? The inner disturbance is dreadful, but the outer calm remains, and along with it perhaps the most brilliant and inspired singing in jazz.

Most women wouldn't worry about being too pretty, but Lena Horne worried long and hard about it. She worried that people liked her for her looks and not for her singing, much as Billie Holiday worries; she worried so much about it that, in the beginning of her career, her singing suffered as a result.

After a brilliant debut at Benny Goodman's Carnegie Hall concert in 1942, Lena skyrocketed to fame. She made a much-appreciated appearance at Cafe Society Downtown, and then was grabbed by the movies. For almost five years she was a motion-picture singer, making occasional sorties into the recording studios to relieve the monotony of specialty bits in Metro-Goldwyn-Mayer musicals, and winning two starring roles in the ill-starred all-Negro movies, *Cabin in the Sky* and *Stormy Weather*. She continued to command attention because of her astonishing loveliness, and a considerable coterie of Horne fans continued to clamor for more of her voice; when Lena's faith in her singing wavered, theirs didn't budge. One of the most firm and unyielding in his admiration for her singing was Lennie Hayton, arranger and musical director for MGM, whom she later married. He badgered her; he worked with her; he read her lessons out of the musical copybooks which he himself had long ago mastered. The result, if I may borrow a limp line from the collected works of the press agents of our time, was a new and greater Lena Horne. Her musical tastes did not merely advance; she became part of what can properly be called the vital vanguard, those hardy souls who have clearly formulated ideas in the generally abstruse field of music, who can articulate their ideas and do. She studied Stravinsky's *Sacre de Printemps*—"It took me two years to connect with that." She resisted Stravinsky's dissonances at first, but under the insistent tutelage of Billy Strayhorn she came to understand and enjoy what had at first seemed like nebulous noises. And under Lennie Hayton's tutelage she studied Hindemith. She began to approach modern music in general with urgency and expectancy.

The true scope of Lena's talents has been only suggested, I think. She can portray anguish and terror in a song. She feels what she sings and articulates her feeling with just enough restraint to keep it within the bounds of good taste, with just enough dramatic impact to reach below her listeners' heads and above their glands for their hearts. In addition, she has that necessary incidental, a fine natural voice, a husky organ of great conviction.

There are some people who think that all instrumental music is written or played in imitation of the human voice. When you listen to a singer like Mary Ann McCall you can understand such thinking. For, without the range and volume of Kirsten Flagstad, with only a modicum of the musicianship of Elisabeth Schwarzkopf, she has much of what they have and something else besides. Her voice is at once that of a voluptuary and a vestal; simultaneously she crosses herself and opens up her arms wide. She expresses the extraordinary paradoxes contained in all the successful sounds of jazzmen; in her music Mary is at the same time wonderfully naïve and sophisticated. And here, in this voice, is what jazz is all about.

Mary Ann McCall sang with Woody Herman off and on for a decade, with Charlie Barnet, with Teddy Powell, for a couple of weeks with Tommy Dorsey, and, in San Diego between 1942 and 1946, with numerous small bands. She always demonstrated more than a passing skill in rhythmic novelties and had a pleasant ease in burning ballads, but not until she rejoined Woody in 1946 did anyone realize that she was a really outstanding singer. During her early years with Woody there wasn't much opportunity to hear her curl herself around a song, but in "Wrap Your Troubles in Dreams" and "Romance in the Dark" there was no mistaking the dimensions of her talents. When she joined the reorganized Herman band in late 1947, her singing hit some musicians and other discerning people with an impact that isolated her. They listened to those intriguing conflicts again, to passion unabashed and unashamed, and to something like schoolgirl wonder at the order and disorder of the world, all articulated with an uncommon skill. Can you really hear all of this in the voice of a girl singer with a jazz band? Passion is not rare in girl singers, but this sort of sensuousness is. Schoolgirl wonder is not rare in schoolgirls; it is to be found in only one other girl's singing, however—Ella Fitzgerald's, of course.

It doesn't come as any surprise, then, to hear Mary Ann McCall say, "Ella is my idol, always has been." Mary's skill is like Ella's; she attacks her notes with that forthrightness, with that rhythmic precision we expect only in the most finished musicians. Mary's understanding is like Ella's; she wraps herself around songs, enlarging and diminishing her volume to fit the demands first of the melody and then of the lyric, setting up her own variations on the melody when it lacks continuity, her beat always right, never stopping. She is rhythmically knowing and melodically secure; her performances have continuity. And they have sound. She is blessed with that husky voice that is best adapted to the rigors of improvisation in jazz, with three, ten, or twenty men whispering or blasting behind her.

If one knows or believes these things to be true of Mary's voice, it is strange to learn that she didn't start out to be a singer but a dancer. She never had any music lessons, "just dancing school." Why dancing school? "I had rickets. Not just rickets—I was crippled. They wanted to break my legs. Try to reset them. We wouldn't let the doctor do that, so massages were prescribed, acrobatics, and dancing school." She got a job as a dancer at Frank Palumbo's in her native Philadelphia—sixteen-year-old Marie Miller, who had beaten the bow in her legs. It's unfortunate that so many bad movie musicals have made such a remarkable story as Mary-Marie's commonplace, filtering out of the narrative all its real heroism and suspense. The next step in her life was in the movie tradition—but remember that it can happen this way, and forget for the moment Joan Crawford and Dorothy Lamour and Doris Day who have been reduced so often in their time to fleshless, bloodless heroines reliving what happened to them in much the same way as Mary's career happened to her. Sure enough, the girl singer at Palumbo's got sick; Mary sang with the band, and that was it. She worked with Tommy Dorsey very briefly, with Charlie Barnet for quite a while, with the Band that Played the Blues ("we struggled—fifteen dollars a week, they told me, and room and board"), with Charlie again, and with Teddy Powell. Then she got married. She had a baby boy and stayed home for a year, and then worked around San Diego for four years as well as with Freddy Slack before going back with Woody and a very different sort of music from that which she first sang with his band.

It's fun to listen to Mary's old records with Barnet, to hear the seeds of her later style, but it is much more than casual entertainment to hear her several sides with Woody after 1946. "Wrap Your Troubles in Dreams" was recorded without rehearsal, its arrangement sketched between band numbers by arranger Ralph Burns. "Romance in the Dark" had to be cleaned up, sixteen bars of blue lyrics rewritten at the last moment on the date. "P.S. I Love You," "I Got it Bad and That Ain't Good," and "Detour Ahead" went off without a hitch, and other dates for the Discovery and Roost labels were untroubled. But Mary had trouble in the next few years, trying to find the large audience that her talents deserve. She has worked all sorts of night clubs, especially those that work a performer until far, far into the morning; she has always elicited an enthusiastic response in these clubs. She has also made some pleasant record sides for Jack Hook's Roost label. But she is not by any means the great success that Dinah Shore continues to be, that Peggy Lee, Jo Stafford, Margaret Whiting, Kay Starr, and Doris Day, Fran Warren, and Toni Arden are. It is as if the converse of the Tolstoyan aesthetic, in its perverse way almost a fixed law in jazz, has worked steadily against her: if your quality as a jazz performer is high, the quantity of your supporters must be small.

Lee Wiley has been praised in the public prints as often as any of her more famous singing sisters; her picture has appeared along with rapturous critical comment in the fashion magazines and in *Time* and *The New Yorker*. She has made her sumptuous sound known in recordings with the best of the Dixieland musicians of the thirties, forties, and fifties. She has revitalized lovely but forgotten Gershwin, Porter, Harold Arlen, and Rodgers-and-Hart songs. But her style, barrelhouse and torchy as it is, has been too high for mass appeal; her records become collectors' items within months of appearance and her plaintive vibrato has even more cause to be.

Dinah, Jo, Maggie Whiting, and their associates at the top of the best-seller lists have never lacked for an audience. Each was almost an immediate success when she reached records; none of them, except for an occasional collaboration with large or small jazz bands, is to be found in the Hot Discographies. But let it be said that all these singers were molded by the disciplines of jazz, and each has to some extent preserved her original musical influence. Dinah, in her first radio programs and early Bluebird records, showed jazz feeling and a softness of voice and Southern accent that fitted naturally into the settings provided by her accompanying orchestras, usually made up of able jazzmen. Peggy Lee sang a blues with Benny Goodman in imitation of a jukebox favorite, Lil Green ("Why Don't You Do Right?"), became a fair stylized singer when she left Benny ("You Was Right, Baby"), turned a husky voice and whispered inflections into a caricature of herself when she became famous ("Don't Smoke in Bed"). Jo not only sang some viable jazz with Tommy Dorsey but also continued from time to time to get the all-important beat in her voice and to turn a phrase with jazz accent. Fran's passionate outpourings with Claude Thornhill raised her from a fair vocalist with Charlie Barnet to a touching sentimentalist; unfortunately, when she stepped out on her own, the passion became purple and, with few exceptions, the sentiment excessive. Maggie, musicianly daughter of a musicianly songwriter, Richard Whiting, has always avoided the unctuous and concentrated on the song at hand; with a better than average vocal organ and excellent taste, she has always been pleasant to listen to, but the amount of jazz in her voice depends entirely on the amount of jazz played behind her, and that often isn't very much. Toni Arden is closer to Fran in her conceptions than anybody else—the old Fran, moved and moving, but only rarely maudlin. Kay Starr, like Anita O'Day and June Christy, is a natural jazz singer, with rhythmic imagination and a larynx that is at least a second cousin to Bessie Smith's. But Kay has had to yield to the importunities of recording executives and a mass audience, and she doesn't often achieve the contagious power of such of her performances with the Charlie Barnet band as "Sharecropping Blues." In the same way, Pearl Bailey's once expressive hands and amusing laconic delivery have hardened into the facets of a commercial rather than a jazz style.

Anita O'Day is an example of the minor intuitive singer who might have been major. Essentially self-instructed, she broke in with Max Miller's small band in Chicago, joined Gene Krupa there in 1941, and then, three years later, after a brief retirement, put in a year with Stan Kenton. She has always been, as one of her musician admirers put it, "a blowing chick." Her singing with Krupa, alone and in duet with Roy Eldridge, had a brashness about it and an inventiveness that always brought to mind a first-rate jazz soloist. There was some of the same jazz quality about her work with Kenton. The sameness, however, was after a while a considerable deterrent, and although her singing has not often been less than able, the constant hoarseness of voice and hotness of phrase have not worn too well. One would have to say the same for most of June Christy's work with Stan Kenton; she replaced Anita and followed carefully, too carefully, in Anita's vocal steps. But June later emerged as a more technically controlled and more broadly imaginative singer, to become a part of the most recent expansion of jazz style and idea. Doris Day was for a while, in her second and longer stay with the Les Brown band, identifiable by the elements of O'Day in her style. Her voice was never as husky or as voluminous as Anita's; she always managed some injection of personalized interpretation. Like Bing Crosby, when she became a movie star (in 1949) she retained her ability to inject jazz feeling where it belonged, whether on a film sound track or a recording disk. Her charm made a movie contract and accompanying success inevitable; her continued taste and talent for and support of jazz were not so easily to be foreseen. In her present glamorous career jazz plays an uncommonly salutary role.

In the swooning and crooning and baritone bellows of the leading male singers of our time, jazz has also been very important, if not always so obvious as in the case of the girls. Dick Haymes sang some with Tommy Dorsey before he became a movie star, and continues to make records suggestive of Tommy's commercial concerns. In 1940 and 1941, however, singing with Harry James, Dick was more than a conventional romantic baritone. For one thing, he exploited the luxurious lower reaches of his voice far more than he has since. For another, he sang with a delicacy and deftness that came only from jazz, the brisk jazz the James band was playing in those years. He made lovely records of "I'll Get By," "Minka," "You've Changed," and "You Don't Know What Love Is," giving good songs additional distinction by the strength of his feeling and the uninterrupted length of his phrases. "Ol' Man River" was lifted above its basically lugubrious caricature of Negro plaints by Dick's delightful understatement and Harry's fresh conversion of the tune into an uptempo jazz piece. A similar authority and wit distinguished Perry

Como's singing with the Ted Weems band before and during the swing era. Many of us found it possible to sustain an evening of ordinary dance music and novelties in order to hear Perry with that band. When he struck out on his own in the early forties, he retained those qualities and added to them a canny appraisal of audience tastes, which has served him well in radio and television, in both of which he has become a major figure. The jazz in Perry's singing has always been a skillful compound of the Crosby-Columbo style and the later ministrations of band singers. That compound has made his hundreds of record sides devoted to second- and third- and fourth-rate songs endurable, and made his broadcasts and telecasts and theater appearances musically interesting. Perry's sunny disposition and gentle visual and verbal wit have also been sizable adjuncts of his singing personality. He is an outstanding family man, one of the few in his profession, who never forgets his beginnings as a barber and never lets his audiences forget that he is one of them. Unfortunately none of this can altogether offset the tawdry substance of the songs to which he gives his almost undivided attention. One must wait wearily for that rare spark, the sudden catching fire of singer and song which makes Perry Como still a part of jazz.

The most popular of these popular singers with jazzmen is Frank Sinatra. His 1939 appearances and recordings with Harry James caught the attention not only of his colleagues but of most band musicians around the United States. When, in 1940, he made such sides with Tommy Dorsey as "I'll Be Seeing You," "I'll Never Smile Again," and "Trade Winds," he was followed almost as avidly by jazzmen as by bobby-soxers. Through the next few years with Tommy, and through most of the remaining forties as a recording artist and movie and theater singer, Frankie was everybody's idea of the perfect juggler, who could manage at one and the same time to bring the kids to their saddle-shoed feet and maintain a meaningful vocal musicianship. In the woeful days of the musicians' union ban on recording activity, from the fall of 1942 to the fall of 1944, such recording activity as there was in the United States was confined to singers accompanied by singers, soloists with choral backgrounds. Frank made his Columbia debut—after having made a few sides with real live musicians for Victor—with such a choral background. Singing the songs so insistently popular in and out of the Rodgers and Hammerstein operetta *Oklahoma*, Frank showed the same firmness of tone and freshness of phrase that had made his records with James and Dorsey successful among musicians. Through the middle of 1948 Frank remained on his unique pedestal, lovingly erected by press agents and children, lastingly maintained by musicians. Then the years of bad publicity—publicity that his indefatigable press agent and manager, the late George Evans, did his best to balance— had their effect. He had appeared at the "wrong" political rallies in Hollywood, making speeches in ballrooms and ballparks, collecting funds for people unable to help themselves. Unknown to him, in some of these activities, seemingly so worthy, the fine Russian hand of the Communist party was present. With the best motives in the world, Frank found himself tricked first by the Communists, then by the Hearst papers, which made lurid headlines of his political speeches and later turned his words into a public confession of wrongdoing. In 1947 Robert Ruark, a Scripps-Howard columnist who had replaced Westbrook Pegler as the star of the syndicate, reported that he had watched Frank shake hands with Lucky Luciano in Havana. Thus started a one-week newspaper sensation that boosted some newspaper circulation sky-high but did nothing to boost Frank's reputation. What had earlier been good-natured humor about Frank's slight figure and swooning stance became heavy-handed disparagement of the "caverns in his cheeks," of his "English droop figure," of his "dying swan deportment." The coup de grâce was administered when newspapermen found a romantic scandal with which to sock the Voice. Not one such headline, but several, and finally the divorce of his wife, Nancy, made Frank, a scandalous newspaper figure. In 1947 there was Lana Turner; in 1950 there was Ava Gardner—and a Spanish bullfighter competing with Frank for her affections. On top of all this, the musicians' union instituted another record ban, beginning the first of January, 1948. In preparation for months of inactivity, Frank made one record after another, day and night, until his voice began to crack. Although he continued to sing ballads, continued to make some records requiring long sustained notes and the delicate scoops of pitch that had made brilliant moments on some of his earlier sides, he doubled the number of middle-tempo and up-tempo songs he did. Frank became much more of a jazz singer; rhythmic twists of phrase became much more a part of his style. As he had in the past, he continued to use such jazz soloists as Bobby Hackett behind him and between his choruses, and his accompaniments perked up a bit to match the change in singing style. It is not certain that Frank will make as much of a mark in jazz with his more jazzlike singing of late as he did with his lovely transformations of ballads in the early years of his career. It is clear that such singing as can be found in his first album (now on long-playing records) will remain an important part of that popular music which achieved its distinction through the employment of jazz devices. Singing with woodwinds, a string quartet, and rhythm section, Frank made perhaps the definitive recordings of "Try a Little Tenderness," "Why Shouldn't I?" and "Paradise," and did as much for Cole Porter's "I Concentrate on You" in his second album. For his delicacy of accent and phrase and for his articulate appreciation of the musical possibilities of the romantic ballad, Frank Sinatra's singing will remain a standard for vocal style and achievement. Whatever his faults, he is already a tradition, a maker of popular singing patterns based upon jazz procedures.

For too long Herb Jeffries has suffered under the cheerfully meant but cheerlessly understood appellation of "the singers' singer." The well-meaning friends, critics, press agents, and singers who have so called him haven't realized, perhaps, that there are few more forbidding descriptions than "musicians' musician" or "writers' writer" or "singers' singer." The public, for whom all musicians make music, writers write, and singers sing, immediately thinks of a technician when such terms are employed, somebody with extraordinary polish or finish but very little of the magic they can understand. And though no artist in any art can produce anything of distinction so long as his single goal is public acceptance, neither can he entirely forget that amorphous collection of heads and hearts and souls. It has been particularly unfortunate to suggest that Herb Jeffries sings without concern for the man in the street, at the other end of the loudspeaker, or in the theater seat, for if ever there was a singer for the masses, it is this "singers' singer."

Everything about Herb Jeffries' life springs from the acid soil in which the common man grows. His father was part Negro, his mother white. As a kid, Herb literally hoboed around Detroit (where he was born), New York, and Chicago. It was in the last of these cities that he made his first important appearances, with Erskine Tate's huge orchestra in 1930. Earl Hines heard him, signed him for the Grand Terrace revue, and later took him on as regular singer with his band. Herb sang with Earl for three years and then had a short term with Blanche Calloway's band, then left Cab's sister in Hollywood to do a few amusing stints as a cowboy star in all-Negro Western films. Duke Ellington, who remembered Herb from his Grand Terrace days, insisted that he drop the boots and saddle for the shawl collar and cummerbund of a boy singer again, and in mid-1940 Herb moved into his most important job, as a singer with Duke Ellington.

With Duke, Herb fastened his mellifluous tones forever to Ted Grouya's and Edmund Anderson's "Flamingo," making that song his from the opening bass scoops to the falsetto coda. With Duke he demonstrated an ease with slight pops ("You, You Darlin'") and serious songs ("I Don't Know What Kind of Blues I've Got") alike. With Duke he made a striking appearance, all six feet three inches of him, in the revue *Jump for Joy*, sauntering through the delicate sentiments of "A Brownskin Gal in a Calico Gown," jumping through the defiant lines of the title tune, afterward as indissolubly associated with his name as the saga of the tropical bird, "Flamingo."

After leaving Ellington, Herb settled in Los Angeles. He made a successful foray into the night-club business with an after-hours spot called the Black Flamingo, moved around LA's other clubs, East Side, West Side, all around town, and finally wound up, in 1945, with a contract with Exclusive Records, very much to the mutual advantage of record company and recording artist. Songwriter Leon Rene's independent company was as rugged and honest in its race relations as Herb; its Negro ownership consistently practiced fair employment. For Exclusive, Herb recorded the memorable six sides that make up the *Magenta Moods* album, and such singles as "Body and Soul," "What's the Score," and "My Blue Heaven," in all of them joining lush voice to Buddy Baker's choice Impressionist scoring.

Herb's career as a singer has been a little uncertain commercially. He has always had an audience of singers, musicians, critics, and that body of fans who are not frightened by his technical prowess or the swooping and whooping sound effects fashioned for him by conductor Mitch Miller in Herb's brief sojourn with him at Columbia. Herb has shifted now to Coral, the subsidiary of Decca records, and has been promised treatment more sympathetic to his basic qualities. However, he is recording songs already in the hit classification or being groomed and plugged for it, and that means he is subject not only to the whims and fancies of song publishers and recording executives in this dubious enterprise, but also to the fickle fancies of the mass audience. His may be one more depressing example of the talent ripened by jazz and spoiled by too much contact with the world of commerce. He has not had—and may never have—the luck of Billy Eckstine, who found his huge audience as a direct result of his jazz singing. He may not have the fortitude of Sarah Vaughan, who refused to compromise her musicianship and nonetheless was given popular support after a long struggle. The masses may never discover how much their kind of singer Herb Jeffries is; their loss will not be small.

Chapter 21

BOP

It wasn't so many years ago that Billy Eckstine was just an eccentric band vocalist, a gravel-throated young man who used to shuffle on stage or floor toward the end of an Earl Hines set, walking with deliberate relaxation, very, very slowly, toward the microphone, his hands in as often as out of his jacket pockets, his jacket as far off his body as it could be and still hang from his shoulders. His voice? It was the sound of caverns in which somebody had let loose the bloodcurdling cry, "Jelly, jelly!"—sexual euphemism and title of Billy's most successful blues—to echo endlessly through the stalagmites and stalactites. It was a series of tremulous hotblasts, often capped by metallic bursts from a suddenly animated trumpet section, designed to make the second balcony jump.

Billy still walks out on a stage slowly, but the pace is less contrived. Now his relaxation doesn't seem so planned. His hands are still in his pockets as often as not, but they belong there; they're not so much part of an organized effort to impress an audience. His clothes fit him today, either because his figure has filled out or because he has a better tailor or because the fashionable drape is a little closer to a man's shape. His voice? It still suggests echoes, but they have come up for air and sunlight; the jelly has been preserved and bottled as a historical oddity, and the blasts are much cooler and tremble far less.

Mr. B., as the erstwhile eccentric is best known to his ardent fans, has come all the way from subterranean depths to box-office heights, and while he has lost some of his bottom notes and almost all the gravel en route, the trip has been a good one. Billy Eckstine is not just a good singer; he is enough better than that so that one is tempted to call him great—and would administer the adjective gladly if it were not necessary to remember earlier disappointments and to keep firmly in mind the limitations under which any singer who gains large approval must work.

His voice is almost always a thing of beauty, if not with any certainty a joy forever. Because of its masculine strength, it moves from note to note with vigor and never falls into the whispering faint that makes listening to the swooners and crooners so disturbing. Because its master, Mr. B., is a natural musician, whose barely tutored trumpet and trombone performances were as provocative as they were unlettered, the voice is in tune and makes its cadences with musicianly effect, occasionally lengthening a melodic line beyond its written limits into a statement that has the quality as well as the quantity of a first-rate instrumental jazz solo.

As a matter of fact, Billy's only teacher was Maurice Grupp, a columnist in *Metronome* of an earlier epoch, who gave him a few trumpet lessons and more than a few pointers about breath control. Billy's testimonial to Grupp is warm—and well it might be, judging from the change in his breathing since his jelly days, all for the better. There have been other changes made too, however, and these have not been so salubrious. Perhaps it isn't fair to blame Billy for them, but they exist. I am speaking about the material with which MGM has loaded him and the changes in phrasing and sound this material has wrought.

When MGM awoke to the size of its new singing star early in 1949, it awoke with more than a casual ringing of the alarm. It made a momentous announcement: hereafter, said the record company, Billy Eckstine would be assigned number-one plug tunes. This was flattering recognition of Billy's achievement; it was exceedingly pleasant to note such appreciation of a singer who was distinctly in the jazz tradition; it was gratifying to watch the color line break before a powerful voice. The change was all that; but it was more. It produced such unpleasant exhibits as "Roses" and "Baby, Won't You Say You Love Me," songs so feeble that not all of Mr. B.'s considerable equipment could redeem them. It also produced a lessening of Eckstine's tension, which can most readily be identified by the gravelly sounds that liven much of the otherwise unimpressive singing on the earlier National records. It produced a new smoothness that doesn't sit well with the Eckstine voice, a softening of fiber and sweetening of texture, which may suit the color and fragrance of rose blossoms and the nature of wheedling love plaints, but which certainly do not fit the quality of Mr. B.'s voice.

Billy reached his peak in 1950. The public was even more generous in its recognition and appreciation than MGM. He was crowded, getting on and off a night-club stage, by hordes of bobby-soxers, as resolute in their attentions as the screaming kids who surrounded the other Voice in its most palmy days; he attracted a secondary ring of older fans, who were devoted and intelligent listeners without the clangor and clamor of their youthful associates. He was the subject of stirring racial controversy in the letter pages of *Life* magazine as the result of a picture story which, without calling specific attention to the size of his white audience, made the proper point that Billy was not simply a successful Negro entertainer but the country's biggest male popular singer.

It is possible that Billy Eckstine's most lasting achievement will turn out to be his short-lived band rather than his enormous success as a singer. His band sprang from the Earl Hines orchestra, with which he was in 1943 the major attraction. In the Hines band Little Benny Harris was the musical sparkplug; his skill on the trumpet was second, actually, to his shrewd musical taste. Charlie Parker was in the Hines band in early 1943, and Little Benny was much aware of his presence. He was intrigued with everything Charlie had ever done and went so far as to copy out Charlie's alto solo on the Jay McShann band recording of "Sepian Bounce." When he played it on his trumpet one night, Dizzy Gillespie, who had just joined the band, looked up with interest. Benny identified the source, and Dizzy was on the spot on his way into Parker's pastures. The Hines band, featuring Little Benny, Dizzy, Parker, Eckstine, and Sarah Vaughan, was not only the incubator of bebop but a formidable musical organization in its own right. Then Billy left the band to work as a solo singer, and the great days of the Hines organization were over. Earl added a string section to his band, with girls plying the bows; he mixed the sounds of his musicians and the quality and quantity of his jazz with lush and somewhat soupy arrangements.

The first of the bop bands did not have Charlie Parker in it. In early 1944 Oscar Pettiford, a brilliant technician on the bass and an affable front man, combined with Dizzy to organize a jumping little outfit with Don Byas on tenor, George Wallington on piano, and Max

Roach on drums. It was with this band that Dizzy sang his octave-
jump phrase, "Salt Peanuts! Salt Peanuts!" a triplet in which the first
and third notes were an octave below the second. It was with this
band that the same sort of triplet became famous for its last two notes,
articulated with staccato emphasis that could be verbalized, as it sometimes was, "Bu-dee-daht!" This just as often became "Bu-re-bop!"
Because the emphasis was on the last two notes of the triplet, the tag
was best remembered, for humming or other descriptive purposes, as
"rebop." And because man's taste for the poetic, whether he so identifies it or not, leads him again and again to alliteration, "rebop" became "bebop." Enthusiasts for the new music began to describe it as
rebop or bebop. One of these enthusiasts was Coleman Hawkins, then
leading a little band at Kelly's Stable on the second and lesser of the
two blocks that made Fifty-second Street Swing Street—between
Sixth and Seventh Avenues. Dizzy organized the music for a two-
night session that Hawk led for Apollo. Dizzy's lovely melody,
"Woodyn' You," was recorded, along with several other sides, including a blues instrumental, "Disorder at the Border," "Rainbow
Mist," which was a set of variations on Hawk's variations on "Body
and Soul," his phenomenally successful 1939 record for Bluebird, and
"Bu-dee-daht," Budd Johnson's tribute to the new music.

Budd joined Oscar and Dizzy at the Onyx Club when Don Byas
left for a job with Duke Ellington that never panned out. Intrigued
by the sound of Dizzy's music, Budd had Dizzy write out some of his
ideas so that they could play them in unison, and the resultant tenor
and trumpet lines became the base for many instrumentals, big band
and small, acknowledging Dizzy as their source or not. Then Oscar
and Dizzy split up, Dizzy going into the Yacht Club with Budd and
Max Roach, Oscar remaining at the Onyx for four more months, with
Joe Guy on trumpet, Johnny Hartzfield on tenor, Joe Springer on
piano, and Hal West on drums—the style remaining with him too.
It was clearly a new era in jazz; the musicians knew it, the habitues
of the Street knew it; Billy Eckstine, organizing a band with which
he hoped to snare larger and more understanding audiences than he
had found on the Street, knew it.

Billy's band had to be a bop band; he himself played just enough
trumpet and trombone to have a feeling for the lines the new musicians were putting down, and he had enough idealism as a leader to
feel that only the freshest and most significant jazz had a place in his

band. As a result he convinced his manager, Billy Shaw, that Dizzy was the only logical musical director for him; that Charlie Parker, then playing with Carroll Dickerson's band at the Rhumboogie in Chicago, was the inevitable lead alto man for him; that he had to get other bop musicians to fill out his personnel. The personnel did not stay the same during the band's several years of chaotic but money-making existence. It was recorded so badly that not one of its DeLuxe sides can be pointed to as more than an indication of the way it sounded on a stage or in a club. But in person, in spite of the ragged-ness of section performance that was inevitable with such constant changes of personnel, such soloists as Dizzy or Fats Navarro, Leo Parker on baritone or Lucky Thompson on tenor, J. J. Johnson or even Billy himself on trombone, gave the developing art a structure that the many Fifty-second-Street outfits playing the music did not have, and made for Billy Eckstine a permanent niche in jazz history.

The best of the many Fifty-second-Street bands that played bop at one time or another was, of course, the outfit Dizzy led in early 1945 at the Three Deuces, with Charlie Parker, Al Haig on piano, Curly Russell on bass, and Stan Levey on drums. With Sid Catlett replacing Stan, this outfit recorded four of the classics of bebop for Guild, in May 1945—"Shaw 'Nuff," in tribute to Dizzy's new man-ager, Billy Shaw; "Salt Peanuts"; "Hot House," which was Tadd Dameron's bop revitalization of Cole Porter's "What Is This Thing Called Love?"; and "Lover Man," which featured Dizzy's old Earl Hines colleague, Sarah Vaughan, as singer. A few months earlier Dizzy had recorded "Blue 'n' Boogie" with Dexter Gordon on tenor saxo-phone and a curious rhythm section, made up of Frank Paparelli on piano, Chuck Wayne on guitar, Murray Shipinsky on bass, and Shelly Manne on drums. Then he had done three sides with Charlie Parker, Clyde Hart on piano, Remo Palmieri, one of Red Norvo's fine discoveries, on guitar, Slam Stewart on bass, and Cozy Cole on drums—"Groovin' High," a translation of the venerable favorite, "Whispering," into bop language; "Dizzy Atmosphere," and "All the Things You Are," these last two not issued until a year later when Musicraft took over the Guild sides. There were in all of these trans-formations, as in the work of the Gillespie-Parker band on the Street, an entrancing set of new ideas and the conviction of the performers that the ideas were right. In another two years bebop, or bop, as it came to be called among musicians and followers, would be making newspaper headlines, usually derogatory in nature, filling out space in *Time* and *Life*, and frightening jazz veterans who either couldn't or wouldn't understand bop and saw no reason to make the intense effort necessary to understand it and then to play it.

Louis Armstrong, who at first had blessed the new music, then decided he didn't like it and dismissed bop this way: "I play what I feel, what's inside of me. I don't expect to please everybody. You know a lot of the new cats say, 'Armstrong, he plays too many long notes.' They want me to change, but why should I go ahead and change just to please a lot o' cats who are way ahead of themselves anyway? I listen to what I play, and if it pleases me it's good. That's the only way to judge what you're doin'. I'm my own best audience. I'd never play this bebop because I don't like it. Don't get me wrong; I think some of them cats who play it play real good, like Dizzy, especially. But bebop is the easy way out. Instead of holding notes the way they should be held, they just play a lot of little notes. They sorta fake out of it. You won't find many of them cats who can blow a straight lead. They never learned right. It's all just flash. It doesn't come from the heart the way real music should."

Certainly much that wasn't bop was masquerading as the new music. "Bebop" and "bop" were catchy terms; they were used, as "swing" had been, to describe everything from eccentric singers and dancers to the real thing. But there were better headlines to be made if the false music was called bebop and damned as such for something else entirely. In March 1946 radio station KMPC in Los Angeles banned bebop. The week after bebop was banned *Time* explained: "What bebop amounts to is hot jazz overheated, with overdone lyrics full of bawdiness, references to narcotics, and doubletalk." They might just as well have banned the diatonic scale or the Dorian mode as ban an eighth-note rhythmic pattern, which is all that bebop is. As for its "overdone lyrics, full of bawdiness, references to narcotics," etc., the only lyrics Dizzy, Charlie, or any of the other genuine beboppers ever sang were "suggestive" odes such as "Salt Peanuts." The words? "Salt Peanuts, Salt Peanuts." That's all. Read what you will into that phrase—bawdiness, a reference to marijuana, or maybe sinister doubletalk instead of just three syllables with the right meter for the phrase it verbalizes.

KMPC and *Time* both confused the frantic antics of Harry the Hipster Gibson and Slim Gaillard with the intense but very different blowing of Gillespie, Parker, and their cohorts. Gibson and Gaillard were not merely doubletalk experts; their songs were thick with reefer smoke and bedroom innuendo. Their mixture of this with jazz lingo did all jazz musicians a disservice. Radio has long functioned by a prude's code in which words stronger than "darn" and the mere suggestion of an antipode to Heaven in somebody's theology are sufficient to assure banning from the pure air.

It wasn't easy to take bop out of the category of flagpole sitting, marathon dancing, and pyramid clubs into which it was so carefully put by the magazine and newspaper editors of America. Bebop is not and was not a game, a schoolboy passion, or a neurosis in rhythm, but a serious form of music. The music editor of *Time* so little understood bebop that he managed, over some one thousand words, to convince himself that it was made up chiefly of bawdy lyrics; but the lyrics of bop, like the associated goatees, hornrimmed glasses, and berets, were simply surface symptoms of a difficult operation that had been performed upon jazz. Such singing syllables as "Oo-pappa-da" or "Oolya-koo" or "Oo-bop-sh-bam" were simply convenient ways of turning the singer's function from the relaying of synthetic passion into the improvising of musical ideas. In a picture story the editors of *Life* reduced bebop to a way of greeting people that seems to have come from some old and unsuccessful vaudeville act and a curious perversion of the Mohammedan religion, as well as a way of wearing eyeglasses and goatees. But we can cut through such nonsense to get at the meat of bop, which upon careful examination turns out to be a very tasty viand.

It has been the fortune of jazz to elude any and all attempts to tie it down, even to words. For better or for worse, in sickness and in health, the very name of this music has resisted any really satisfactory explanation. Often, when the whole cannot be defined, it is possible to make some sense out of it by summing up its parts. But when a part grows so big that it almost eclipses the whole—as bebop spurted beyond the confines of jazz—simple definition becomes utterly impossible, and complex description must take its place. In reporting the effect of the bop musicians, one must reflect upon the accidental nature of jazz, wondering whether or not the ultimate arrival of bebop would have been merely delayed without Lester Young's and Charlie Christian's lines or swept altogether aside for an even louder, more raw effusion of blues riffs and pseudo-classical productions than we suffered in the years just after swing. The really staggering fact is that jazz did escape from two-bar statement and the swinging void. Whatever its limitations, Young and Christian more or less unconsciously, and Dizzy and Parker more deliberately, took the old beat and refurbished it and set it to new tunes, and the new tunes took over.

Technically one must first point to the weakening of the riff under the impact of bop, and the broad invention with which bop musicians have treated the twelve-bar form, departing from the constricting tonic-subdominant-dominant roundelay which has worn so many ears to a frazzle, carrying the melody from the first through the last bar, punctuating both the melody and its harmonic underpinning with bright and fresh interjections. The same sort of imagination has been at work upon those most venerable of chordal undergrounds, "I Got Rhythm," "Back Home in Indiana," "How High the Moon," and a half-dozen other tunes notable for their key changes. Next in order are the up-beat accents of bop, the double-time penchant of such soloists as Dizzy, and the vigorous change that has overtaken drumming under the ministrations of Kenny Clarke, Max Roach, and their followers, the bass drum replaced by the top cymbal as custodian of the beat, and a multitude of irregular accents and sounds introduced on the remaining paraphernalia of the drummer. Finally, in the key section of any analysis of bop, one comes to the use of unusual intervals, of passing notes and passing chords in the construction of bop lines and their supports, ending with that celebrated identifying note of the medium, the flatted fifth, with which almost every bop performance comes to a close, which salts and peppers almost all solos from that of the most sensitive gourmet of this music to that of the mealiest feeder on crumbs.

This new way of thinking shaped musicians, pushed crude entertainment aside for imaginative ideas, and at least suggested the disciplined creative potential of the young music. Lennie Tristano pointed out some of the limitations of the new school when it was at the zenith of its popularity, in 1947. In an article entitled "What's Wrong with the Beboppers" in *Metronome* magazine, Lennie suggested limitations:

Artistically the situation is . . . deplorable. These little monkey-men of music steal note for note the phrases of the master of the new idiom, John Birks "Dizzy" Gillespie. Their endless repetition of these phrases makes living in their midst like fighting one's way through a nightmare in which bebop pours out of the walls, the heavens, and the coffeepot. Most boppers contribute nothing to the idiom. Whether they play drums, saxophone, piano, trombone, or glockenspiel, it still comes out Gillespie. Dizzy probably thinks he's in a house of mirrors; but, in spite of this barrage of dead echoes, he still sounds great. They manage to steal some of his notes, but his soul stays on the record.

Lennie also pointed out some of the achievements of bebop, in this article and in a sequel to it called "What's Right with the Beboppers." In doing so, he also indicated some of his own concerns, the concerns that were shaping and were going to shape his own music:

It must be understood that bebop is diametrically opposed to the jazz that preceded it (swing as applied to large groups, and Dixieland as applied to small ones). Swing was hot, heavy, and loud. Bebop is cool, light, and soft. The former bumped and chugged along like a beat locomotive; this was known in some quarters as drive. The latter has a more subtle beat which becomes more pronounced by implication. At this low volume level many interesting and complex accents may be introduced effectively. The phraseology is next in importance because every note is governed by the underlying beat. This was not true of swing; for example, the long arpeggios which were executed with no sense of time, the prolonged tremolos, and the sustained scream notes. . .

Though Dixieland presents a single and crude form of counterpoint, its contrapuntal development ends in a blind alley. Each line is governed by the end result, which is collective improvisation. Collective improvisation is limited by a small number of chords, perhaps six or seven. A good melodic line is sacrificed completely. . . .

The boppers discarded collective improvisation and placed all emphasis on the single line. This is not unfortunate, since the highest development of both would probably not occur simultaneously. Perhaps the next step after bebop will be collective improvisation on a much higher plane because the individual lines will be more complex.

→ Bebop has made several contributions to the evolution of the single line. The arpeggio has ceased to be important; the line is primarily diatonic. The procedure is not up one chord and down another, nor is it up one scale and down another; the use of skips of more than a third precludes this seesaw motion. The skillful use of scales fosters the evolution of many more ideas than does the use of arpeggios, since an arpeggio merely restates the chord. Instead of a rhythm section pounding out each chord, four beats to a bar, so that three or four soloists can blow the same chord in arpeggio form in a blast of excremental vibrations, the bebop rhythm section uses a system of chordal punctuation. By this means, the soloist is able to hear the chord without having it shoved down his throat. He can think as he plays. A chorus of bebop may consist of any number of phrases which vary in length. A phrase may consist of two bars or twelve bars. It may contain one or several ideas. The music is thoughtful as opposed to the kind of music which is no more than an endless series of notes, sometimes bent.

Trumpeters did it, tenormen did it, trombonists and pianists did it, alto-men of course—they all imitated Bird; even Dizzy did. As bebop made its intricate way among the jazz bands of America, the ideas of Charlie Parker circulated among the soloists.

The musician they call Yardbird has had a long journey, starting on the road at seventeen, winning some recognition with Jay McShann, some more in jam sessions around Chicago and New York in the early forties, fighting illness, despair, and wavering audience interest, but always, invariably, gathering larger and larger support among musicians. Finally his ideas obtained; his following increased to the point where youngsters coming up were imitating imitations of imitations of Charlie; his reputation catapulted him to the top of the alto heap.

Bird was born in Kansas City on August 29, 1920. Before joining Jay, the boogie-woogie pianist with the jumping Kansas City band, Bird flew through school, stopping halfway through the secondary grades, blew some baritone horn with the school band, gigged around and played with Lawrence Keyes and Harlan Leonard, two local bands—the second of which gained some national attention, though not when Bird was in it. McShann showed up in Kansas City in 1937, and Charlie moved in. With Jay he came to New York in 1942 and moved a few people to superlatives. The band had a good beat, a good blues singer (Walter Brown), a good balladeer (Al Hibbler), and a brilliant alto saxophonist. Bird stayed with the band until Detroit, then picked up horn and reeds and flew back to New York. There he became an uptown mainstay, sitting in at the Minton's sessions, helping to evolve the new ideas, those which became bebop when formalized. He was part of the fine little band at the Uptown House, associated with drummer Kenny Clarke, and put in a nine-month stretch with Noble Sissle, doubling on clarinet; then, in 1943, he joined Earl Hines. With the Father, Charlie played tenor, Budd Johnson's chair being the only vacancy. There was a year with Hines, then brief stints with Cootie Williams and Andy Kirk before Bird joined the Billy Eckstine band of 1944. Thereafter Bird was a small bandsman; he joined Ben Webster on Fifty-second Street; then Dizzy; then he took out his own band—Miles Davis made his first auspicious appearance with Bird at the Three Deuces. Shortly after, in late 1945, Bird rejoined Dizzy for the ill-fated California jaunt which left Bird a sick man in a sanitarium near Los Angeles. In early 1947 there was sad talk about Charlie. The word from California was that he was through; he was recovering from a series of bad breaks there. A short story published in a major magazine made bitter fun of those who tried to capture Bird's last notes before he succumbed to sickness and melancholy; the central character was thinly disguised as "Sparrow." But Charlie Parker wasn't through. He came back to New York and played better than ever. He elicited more enthusiasm and more imitation than before. He took over as the major influence in jazz.

Perhaps the greatest compliment that can be paid this imposing musician is an accurate description of his talent. Where other purveyors of bop stick closely to the cadences, changes, and rhythmic devices that identify their formularized expression, Charlie goes further and further afield. If any man can be said to have matured bop, Charlie Parker did it. If any bebopper could break away from the strictures of his style, utilizing its advances and advancing beyond them, Charlie Parker could do it.

Another musician who helped expand the resources and mature the performances of bop was the man called the Disciple. Maybe "the Mentor" would be a better name for Tadd Dameron, since so many of the young beboppers crowded around him, demanding and getting opinions and advice. He had no formal musical education; he wrote music before he could read it. He regarded bop as just a steppingstone to a larger musical expression. Yet no one who gives bebop serious consideration can omit Tadd from the list of prime exponents and wise deponents of this modern jazz expression.

You know his work if you have heard Dizzy Gillespie's "Hot House," Tadd's own construction based on the chords of "What Is This Thing Called Love?" Perhaps you have heard Dizzy's "Good Bait," "I Can't Get Started," or "Our Delight." Or Georgie Auld's "Air Mail Special," "Just You, Just Me," or "A Hundred Years from Today." Or Billy Eckstine's "Don't Take Your Love from Me." Or Sarah Vaughan's exquisite "If You Could See Me Now," "You're Not the Kind," and the two other sides made at that same memorable date, using strings, Freddy Webster on trumpet, Leo Parker on baritone, and a fine rhythm section built around Kenny Clarke on drums. They are all Tadd Dameron's and all of more than casual interest, but not for Tadd. "All turkeys!" he insists. "I've never been well represented on records."

Tadd has never been well satisfied with anything he's done. He was all set to become a doctor, had finished some years of his medical education when the sight of an arm severed from the body of a man decided him firmly against that profession. "There's enough ugliness in the world," Tadd decided. "I'm interested in beauty." He had listened to his mother and father play piano, had picked up the rudiments of the instrument by himself and learned something of jazz from his brother Caesar, a well-known alto saxist around their home town, Cleveland, Ohio. It remained for Freddy Webster, the brilliant trumpeter who died in early 1947, to get Tadd really interested in music. Freddy never found much of an audience for his huge tone and moving ideas; he was heard most in his brief sojourn with Lucky Millinder. But the boppers heard him at Minton's—and he heard Tadd and persuaded him to join his band. In 1938, when Tadd had just attained his majority, he left medicine well behind him for the happiness and misery of life in the clinics of jazz.

After a year with Freddy and a couple more with Zack White and Blanche Calloway, Tadd emerged at the surgical end of jazz, learning about the morphology of band arrangements, appreciating—with the help of a Cleveland friend, Louis Bolton—the devious devices employed in altering chords, especially fascinated with stretching the wretched notes. By 1940, after some time in Chicago, he was a recognized arranger; he left town with Vido Musso. Vido's short-lived band folded at Brooklyn's Roseland and sent Tadd to Kansas City with Harlan Leonard. A year of the latter, and he went to work in a defense plant. A year of that, and he was free to arrange for Lunceford and Basie and Eckstine and Auld; this work carried him from 1942 to 1945 and Dizzy's waiting arms.

With Dizzy, Tadd found himself. His arrangements for Dizzy's big band went beyond the formulations of the bebop pioneers, though he retained their most vigorous advances—the long phrases, the powerful upbeat rhythms, the chord changes. As long as Dizzy had a big band to write for, Tadd had work. But Tadd began to write for other bands and to lead his own bands at the Royal Roost on Broadway, where bop was ensconced in 1948 and 1949, finally to become a full-time arranger with only occasional sorties into the recording studio as pianist and leader.

Until almost half of 1947 was over Dizzy Gillespie was a man without a regular band. He had bands, many of them, large and small, good and bad, important and frighteningly unimportant. From his earliest collaborations with Charlie Parker, Slam Stewart, and Oscar Pettiford, he had indicated his ability to lead a fine musical organization. But never until the summer of 1947 did he show that he could whip a band into shape, hold on to it, fight with it, win with it, lose with it.

The way of a colored band is never easy. That axiom has been too often demonstrated to need detailing here. In Dizzy's case the difficulties were doubled. He was trying to sell a new music, one that seemed patently uncommercial, beyond the ears of the people who would have to pay to see and hear it, who would ultimately have to underwrite it. But a lot of people had faith in Dizzy as a musician and leader, as a showman and trumpeter, as a composer, arranger, and musical personality. He would, they insisted, demonstrate such unmistakable individuality that he would have to be accepted. For as soon as more than a passing technical competence is achieved, the major hurdle for a jazz musician in the race for public acceptance is the establishment of his individual sound. In this problem he is no different from the strictly commercial musician, who must create such an undeniable identity that a million record buyers, several million more radio listeners and theatergoers, all who go to hear and see bands, will know it's he as soon as they hear a couple of choruses of his outfit. This Dizzy had done for himself as a soloist. Could he do it for his band? He could. He did.

Dizzy sought his individuality in manifold ways. He didn't stop at the forms and formulas of bebop, clear as they were, associated with him as they were. He went on to develop a visual personality— little bowing motions and big, characteristic wearing apparel, such as his visored beret, characteristic heavy eyeglasses, characteristic goatee. All over America young boppers who had never worn hats donned the Dizzy cap; young boppers who had never been able to raise sufficient hirsute covering to prove their age struggled with chin fuzz in an attempt to build the Gillespie goatee; young boppers with their own little bands began to lead from the waist and the rump; some, with perfectly good eyesight, affected the heavy spectacles. Dizzy was a character; he had a personality to go with his music; he was well on his way to national importance, although more saluted for the accessories of his music than for the music itself.

All of this was impressive. The interest in Gillespie was large, but the box-office returns the young boppers could contribute were not sufficient to make Diz a major draw. Something more was indicated. The time was, as the fruitgrowers call it, ripe. In came a professional bandgrower.

Billy Shaw was once a musician, a working musician. He had booked all kinds of bands in his successful managerial career at MCA and William Morris, but the bands he really enjoyed booking and building were the musical bands. He was one of the group with faith in Dizzy. He went out and worked. He negotiated a contract with Victor records, placing Dizzy's product within reach of the squarest disk jockey, the most rectangular jukebox, the dimmest listener. He helped organize a Carnegie Hall concert under Leonard Feather's eager auspices. And when Dizzy drew standees at Carnegie, Billy seized the opportunity. He laid out a concert series around the country for the Gillespie band. That wasn't enough. There were offers from Europe, where bebop was proving a postwar sensation. Billy signed Dizzy, at a handsome figure, for a month's tour of Scandinavia, the Low Countries, and France. He augmented this strong chain of paying dates with steady publicity. From the Gale office, where Shaw vice-presides, streamed reprints of articles about Diz, a steady diet of Gillespie food for editors, columnists, and jockeys. Stones were not to be left unturned; they were to be bulldozed out of the way. By the end of 1947 Dizzy and Billy and the men who played Dizzy's music could breathe more easily, could smile expectantly, could look forward to more folding money. Maybe Dizzy wasn't a threat to Sammy Kaye or Stan Kenton, but he was moving ahead, he was beginning to crowd the top men, he was proving that a colored band with a difficult music could make enough sense to enough people to pay off.

Certainly the Gillespie band did not prove in 1947 that it was the musical equal of the handful of top bands of the past. It was too young; it was too rough; its personnel shifted too often. But it did show astonishing progress. Trace the band's sound from its first Musicraft records to the two sides which marked its Victor debut, "Ow!" and "Oopapada." By the last of these it had achieved smoothness, playing ease, the beginnings, at least, of the polish that is necessary for top rank in the band business.

The smoothness and ease and beginnings of polish did not last for Dizzy. Some of the chaos and uncertainty that afflicted the Billy Eckstine band began to disrupt performances of Dizzy's large outfit. There were personnel changes and changes of musical policy. Eventually Dizzy's clowning proclivities obtained; by conscious reasoning process or by intuition, audiences of all kinds, general and indifferent to jazz or particular and sympathetic to bop, took an aversion to Dizzy and his music. There were several editions of the big band, then several little bands of short life. Dizzy's recordings and public performances with small bands in 1951 were of a higher order, however; although not yet back at the extraordinary level of the Guild records of the Fifty-second-Street bands of 1945, he seemed at last, perhaps because there was no commercial alternative, to be concerned again with the making of music. What had been a long reign, as jazz dynasties go, had been over for several years. Fats Navarro, who in the last years of his life had interested serious musicians and followers of jazz more than Dizzy, was dead, but Miles Davis and the music associated with him were still very much alive.

In the short history of jazz there have been two substantial musicians nicknamed Fats, men of substance both physically and musically: first Fats Waller, then Fats Navarro. Theodore Fats Navarro, a behemoth of a man, was not as large physically as his famous nomenclative predecessor; musically he gave promise of becoming as large a man—but he died before he could fulfill his promise.

Fats was a trumpeter of size all right. His tone was more compelling than that of anyone since Roy Eldridge—warm, supple, pulsating. He had a drive like Little Jazz too, with the style and imagination of Dizzy Gillespie, whom he replaced in the Billy Eckstine band in 1945. He was the most consistent of the so-called beboppers in his rides down the chords, making his notes, phrasing them consciously rather than capriciously, an astonishing technician.

Fats didn't like the name "bebop." "It's just modern music," he said. "It just needs to be explained right. What they call bebop is really a series of chord progressions." He protested further. "None of us play this so-called bebop the way we want to yet. I'd like to just play a perfect melody of my own, all the chord progressions right, the melody original and fresh—my own." In 1947 he thought he knew

the major limitation of musicians, young or old, beboppers or not.
"They don't know the chord progressions. When they know them a
lot better, when they become really familiar with them—then maybe
we'll have a real modern jazz."

Fats was indefatigable in his work, spending hours at home during
the day practicing his horn, and half his spare evenings blowing with
the boys. He was what his bop colleagues called a "serious musician"
and had been for half of his twenty-seven years. He had been attached.
to music ever since he began to study the trumpet at thirteen in his
native Key West, Florida. He had taken some piano lessons when he
was six, but, as is so much the way with piano lessons at six, he "didn't
learn anything." Well-schooled in jazz fundamentals, Fats left Key
West in 1941, after high school. "I didn't like Key West at all," he
said firmly. He joined Sol Allbright's band in Orlando, Florida, came
up to Cincinnati with it, and soon after left to join Snookum Russell
in Indianapolis—but not until he had had a chance to work with
another teacher in the Ohio town. He was with Russell for two years
and then, in 1943, joined Andy Kirk for a two-and-a-half-year tour
of duty, a most vital one in Fats's development. Howard McGhee was
one of his section-mates. "He was the influence," Fats said. "I used
to go and jam with him all the time." And through McGhee, Fats
made the acquaintance of Dizzy Gillespie's ideas and of their origi-
nator. When, in 1945, Dizzy left Billy Eckstine's band, the organization he had helped stock and stylize, whose musical director he had
been, he recommended Fats as his logical successor. Dizzy has never
shown better judgment.

After leaving Eckstine himself, in June of 1946, Fats gigged around,
played short jobs in and out of New York, made a few records, and
caught fire with those musicians and aficionados fortunate enough to
have heard him at Minton's in Harlem, at various cafes on the Street,
or in his brief but noteworthy appearance on WNEW's Swing Sessions in 1946. On records he teamed up with Coleman Hawkins for
Sonora, making "Bean and the Bop" and "I Mean You" with the man
he regarded as "one of the peaks of jazz" because of an ability to keep
up with changes in jazz. "Whatever happens, he knows." While he
was with Eckstine, Fats made two sides on which he can be heard
between National's surface scratches—"Tell Me, Pretty Baby" and
"Long, Long Journey." With Eddie Davis on Savoy he did "Hollerin'
and Screamin'," "Maternity," and "Stealin' Trash." Under his own

name, on the same label, he made "Eb-Pob" (bebop spelled backwards) and he appeared on eight sides of Savoy's bebop album as trumpet soloist with the Bebop Boys.

Fats intended to make more and more progress. He listened to and enjoyed Bach and Beethoven, expanded his knowledge of chord progressions, made his lip more limber, his fingers more flexible. He seemed to be broadening his resources beyond the bounds of bebop. Fats was, however, a split personality, whether or not a psychiatrist would so have diagnosed him. On his instrument he was almost always calm, cool, reserved, collected, and controlled. Away from his instrument, he didn't increase the volume of his voice or the pace of his step, but he did raise the temperature of his living to a point at which human beings cannot survive. In spite of the warm reception accorded bop by musicians and camp followers, and despite all the publicity it received in the newspapers—more bad than good, but very much of it—work was infrequent for bop musicians, even for so pre-eminent a one as Fats. Practice could occupy only so much of his time. What was left? When the world seemingly rejected his gifts, he turned to drugs to narcotize the hurt. In July 1950, wasted away to one-fourth of his normal size, Fats Navarro died of tuberculosis. The tributes at his funeral were beautiful, the shakings of heads intense, the tears genuine. But Fats was dead, and so was bop.

Bop musicians continued to play, some better than others, a few with continuing distinction, one or two with the individuality of idea and the structured development which go beyond the limitations of school and formula. Charlie Parker is the outstanding example of the latter kind of musical personality. Momentarily captivated by the siren sweetness of violins, violas, and cellos, he has been able in a recording session with strings to emerge above their conventional inflections in his most cogent solo on records, "Just Friends"; listening to him at a night club, one feels that, like its bodily housing, his creative spirit is indestructible and that he still has far to go. As much may be said for Miles Davis, under whose aegis one of the significant developments of cool jazz was made.

Miles, born in Alton, Illinois, in 1926, played the trumpet in his high school band in East St. Louis, worked with a St. Louis band, studied briefly at the Juilliard School of Music in 1945, and then put in several years on Fifty-second Street, in sessions at Minton's, and five months with the Eckstine band, before fronting his own outfit at the

Royal Roost in the fall of 1948. He and Fats and Howard McGhee were the trumpet stalwarts of bop, following Dizzy's pioneering. McGhee, the oldest of the group, is a Tulsa, Oklahoma, boy, born in 1918, who grew up in Detroit, played clarinet in his high school band there, switched to trumpet while still in his teens, and led a twelve-piece band at the Club Congo in Detroit before joining Lionel Hampton in 1941. He made his reputation with Andy Kirk, Charlie Barnet, and a couple of small bands led by Coleman Hawkins. Always a forthright, well-organized trumpeter in the middle register, he extended his thinking range when Dizzy's conception became his in 1944. His chief variation on bop themes is a slowing down of the rapid-fire figures of bop so that the augmented chords and whole-tone melodies reveal their Debussyan source more clearly. While only rarely successful in his Impressionist meanderings, he is still capable of a fresh twist or turn of phrase, especially if playing in the register he has made his own, the middle.

The best of bop trombonists was J. J. Johnson, an Indianapolis youngster who graduated to the big jazz time with Benny Carter, with whom he made an indelible impression from 1942 to 1945, demonstrating an almost incomparable knowledge of his instrument's resources and a fresh set of ideas. These ideas moved handily into bop when Johnson made the transition to small Fifty-second-Street bands with the Count Basie orchestra in late 1945 and '46, when there were other exponents of the new music with Count too. There are few more exhilarating moments in jazz than J. J.'s spectacular maneuverings of his trombone's slide at the fastest of playing tempos. Beside his best work, that of other modern jazz trombonists—even of such skillful musicians as Kai Winding—seems of little significance. His limitations are those of bop—inconsistency of performance and a weakening dependence upon formula.

These are also the limitations of bop's tenor saxophonists. Gene Ammons, son of the famous boogie-woogie pianist Albert Ammons, promised much when he was with the Eckstine band, delivered some, but also lost some along the way in his battles of music with, first, Dexter Gordon, then Sonny Stitt. Dexter Gordon lost most of the reputation he made in his several years with Lionel Hampton when, in the late forties, he began to rely either upon the stereotyped patterns of the Lester Young imitators or on musical honkings and ascents and descents of scales. Sonny Stitt was just one more imitator of Charlie

Parker's alto until 1949, when his switch to tenor showed him more resourceful than most boppers on this instrument, and closer to the formulations of the cool jazz musicians than to the boppers. The best of Bird's imitators on his own instrument, the alto, was Sonny Criss, a Memphis musician who progressed from Los Angeles bands, through outfits led by Howard McGhee and Al Killian, to the Billy Eckstine band when it was in California; he ended up as a sufficient star on his instrument to be made, at least temporarily, a part of Norman Granz's touring "Jazz at the Philharmonic" troupe.

Bop has also had its baritone saxophonists, its pianists, bass players, and drummers. Leo Parker, a Washington baritone saxist who broke in with Eckstine, played with Benny Carter and various outfits in Harlem, including some in Minton's, and corrupted his fresh style to match the honkings and caterwauls of Illinois Jacquet when he joined that high-flying, financially successful but musically disastrous little band. Serge Chaloff offends some people with the large and sometimes raucous tone he developed in the Georgie Auld and 1947 Woody Herman bands; others, recognizing Chaloff's pioneering as a baritone bopper and his considerable control of his instrument, admire the facility with which he gets around his horn, the fluency of phrase that, before him, was unknown on the baritone saxophone.

The piano was used in bop chiefly as an accompanying instrument; it had little place in a music that was essentially a one-line form of expression, played by a single-line solo instrument or by several in unison. Tadd Dameron, John Lewis, and George Wallington play what musicians call "arrangers' piano." The pleasure one receives in listening to them is chiefly from the introduction of a deft variation here, a dextrous departure there; they are fitted by neither technique nor interest for much more than that. Al Haig, however, has always been capable of something more; though chiefly employed by the boppers as rhythm-section accompanist, he made enough of his occasional solos to warrant serious consideration as a pianist, and made enough more of them when he joined forces with Stan Getz to show himself a fleet-fingered performer with delicacy of taste and of expression. The late Clyde Hart gave bop piano a start, but he was more distinguished as a creator of melodic lines for the new music than as a piano adapter of them. Bud Powell made the piano an integral part of bop. Born in New York in 1924, Bud comes from a musical family and has devoted most of his life to music. He left school at fifteen to begin a gigging life that has taken him all over Greater New York, from Coney Island to the upper reaches of the Bronx. He was to be found either playing or listening at Minton's during the famous formative sessions. He played some dazzling piano with Cootie Williams' band in 1944 and 1945, piano which sprang almost entirely from bop ideas—long lines impeccably articulated by the right hand, with rhythmic accents and chordal elaborations contributed by the left. Bud's piano wanderings sometimes suggest his own career—the large number of his short-lived appearances with Fifty-second-Street, Minton's, Royal Roost, and Birdland bands; his 1948 nervous breakdown; his aimless approaches to the bandstand and departures therefrom. He will set up an intriguing pattern of ideas, aptly constructed, brightly developed, and then suddenly will break the structure and the development to repeat one or two of his phrases in seemingly endless and senseless reiteration. His solos sometimes have a nagging, fragmentary quality, like a series of boxes piled precariously on top of one another, without point or purpose. But then there are the solos that swing furiously from the first to the last bar, that add lines in a constant enrichment of idea, that give bop its only real piano voice.

Erroll Garner has often been called a bop pianist because he has been linked with bop musicians in most of his recording and public performances. Actually, his Impressionist meanderings in and around middle-tempo jazz and very slow ballads are only incidentally modern. An unlettered pianist who grew up in Pittsburgh (where he was born in 1921) and matured in New York (where he settled in 1944), Erroll has an intuitive gift for the music that charms, whether it is ragtime, Waller, Debussy, or bop in origin. His cheerful bounces proceed from the first two, his languid ballads from the second pair. The pleasure he gives can be measured against one's taste for lushness for lushness's sake. His playing, adored by bop musicians, serves also as a measure of the taste of the men who played bop and of the sound they would have had if they had been slowed down from a gallop to a walk and had been more concerned with sound and less with idea.

If Oscar Pettiford can be called a bop bassist, because of his early association with the music, then bebop has had a distinguished bass player; but Oscar is closer to Jimmy Blanton and to the tradition in which solos are assigned his instrument than he is to bop, in which solos are not given the bass. No Blanton, but a superb technician, Oscar recasts Jimmy's ideas with ease and a huge tone, both of which served him well when he shifted bow and fingers to the cello. For the rest, there are Ella Fitzgerald's husband, Ray Brown, veteran of Dizzy's bands, able but hardly inspired; Al McKibbon, a well-schooled musician, probably the best of the big-band bop bass players; Curly Russell, another jazz and bop veteran, another able bass player; and Tommy Potter, probably the best of the small-band bop bass players.

Kenny Clarke was one of the founding fathers of bop and, at his best, its incomparable drummer. Born in Pittsburgh in 1914, into a musical family—his father played the trombone, his brothers the drums and bass—he himself played piano, trombone, drums, and vibraphone and studied musical theory in high school. He played with Roy Eldridge in 1935, then with one of the several unacknowledged territory bands of jazz, the swinging Jeter-Pilar orchestra in St. Louis, before joining the pianist Edgar Hayes for a tour of Scandinavian countries in 1937 and 1938. When he got back he played with Claude Hopkins and was Teddy Hill's regular drummer until Teddy disbanded. Kenny was with Teddy when Dizzy was part of the band, and he took several of the Hill musicians into Minton's, where Teddy himself was manager. There, at various times between jobs with Louis Armstrong, Ella Fitzgerald, Benny Carter, Red Allen, and Coleman Hawkins, he played a formidable part in the rhythmic structuring of bop. Teddy Hill reports that when Kenny was playing "those offbeats and little rhythmic tricks on the bass drums," he used to ask, "what is that kloop-mop stuff?" "That's what it sounded like, kloop-mop! And that's what we called the music they were playing. Later on we called it bebop." Kenny's nickname is Kloop or Klook, celebrating the part he played in the building of bebop. He was in Europe with the Army for three years, from 1943 to 1946, and he returned to the United States to play with Dizzy and Tadd Dameron. He went back to Europe with Dizzy in 1948, to stay, to become one of the highly respected American jazzmen in France, where American jazz is so highly respected.

The great change wrought by bop drummers was in their organization of a one-one-one-one-one-one-one-one beat, as against the syncopations of swing and Dixieland drummers; they reserved the bass drum for accenting—accenting beats as individually as they could, and deliberately divorcing them from regular patterns. They kept the basic beat going on the top cymbal, annoying many listeners and some musicians with the clatter they thus set up, but giving boppers a

rhythmic push like none they had ever felt before. The most popular
of bop's pushers was Max Roach. Ten years younger than Kenny, he
learned from him most of what he knew when he first broke into the
business. He was with Dizzy from the beginning, the rhythmic bul-
wark of Benny Carter's fine 1944 West Coast band, and the solid support of dozens of Fifty-second-Street bands and recordings made by
such units. As he demonstrated in his performance with the 1951
Metronome All Stars on record, dueting with Kai Winding, Max is
a rhythmic thinker; his solos are not like swing drummers', not dependent upon sheer noise and intensity to make their point; his interest is in setting up drumming phrases that, without melody or
harmony to buttress them, have nonetheless the shape and structure
and integrated meaning of a solo by Charlie Parker. His solos and his
work behind soloists sometimes have such quality, when the men he
is working with are boppers or can adjust themselves to bop accenting; with others, more or less modern but different in jazz conception,
Max's drumming, even as other boppers' trumpeting or saxophoning,
just doesn't fit. With the exception of Bird and Miles, bop conditioned
its musicians too well.

Bop is and isn't dead. Its decay as a formularized expression set in
long before its reign was officially over. Its impact as the inevitable
development of jazz that it was will always be felt. Bop lengthened
melodic lines, weakened the grip of the two- and four-bar riff, gave
jazz a rhythmic lift and fresh melodic and harmonic inspiration. Freshness was the key element in bop; when bop musicians could no longer
recognize staleness and themselves became susceptible to stereotypes
and clichés, they were finished as a cohesive group. The music itself,
however, was not finished: its influence on cool jazz was indirect; on
two important singing voices, Billy Eckstine's and Sarah Vaughan's,
unmistakably direct. And it was these singers, after all, who brought
bop to the millions and made them like it. Although the millions
didn't know that there was any bop in what they liked of Billy's and
Sarah's singing, they were aware that this was a different, a fresher, a
more experimental kind of singing than any they had heard before,
and they were perfectly content to accept it as such.

When Sarah Vaughan made her first records for Musicraft in 1946,
an impatient man stood on the sidelines. He was one of the vice-
presidents of that executive-heavy organization. Lifting his head

angrily, he looked in the direction of the singer and turned to the recording director.

"Good God," he said, "she can't do that. Tell her to sing it straight. That stuff will never get anywhere. We'll lose our shirt."

Musicraft subsequently lost its shirt, but not on Sarah. She could do "that"; she did do "that"; "that stuff" got very far. In its last moments the record company represented by the impatient vice-president stuck grimly to its business; the glue was provided by Sarah, whose records were among the few large assets Musicraft had at the end.

Actually, outside of those few combative moments with the V.P. and a couple of periods of deep freeze from the bookers and the club owners of the music industry, Sarah Vaughan has not had a notably difficult career. Not without hardship, but certainly without hysteria or dramatic highlight of any sort, her story is pitched in a middle key, the comfortable tonality recognized by most of us as human. It's a simple story, and one has to look hard to find the ingredients not so much of Sarah's success but of her very large musical accomplishment. She was born in Newark, New Jersey, that somewhat faded carbon copy of New York, in 1924, and she still lives there. For eight years, from the age of seven until she was fifteen, she studied the piano, and then she moved to the organ for a couple of years. She pulled stops and ranged the manuals in school and at church, and sang in the Mount Zion Baptist choir alongside her mother, who still sings Sunday service with the group. There is music in her father, too; a carpenter, he finds rest and relaxation on the guitar. But Mamma was the moving musical force; she wanted Sarah to become a concert pianist and continued to look hopefully at Carnegie after her daughter stepped into the jazz world, never dreaming for a moment that Sarah would make the great concert hall on the strength of her voice and not of her fingers.

In October 1942 Sarah made the step. She walked onto the stage of the Apollo Theatre in Harlem a little after midnight on a Wednesday, to appear in one of those amateur hours that have uncovered a high percentage of talent. The headliner on the regular bill was Ella Fitzgerald. Like Ella, Sarah fractured the audience. Like Ella years before, she won that night's competition. Like Ella, she got a handsome career under way as the Apollo Amateur Hour winner. She did a week at the theater as a reward for winning and was heard by Billy

Eckstine. Billy, then singing with Earl Hines' band, told Earl about her, and a few weeks later she joined the band for a one-nighter at the Manhattan Center.

"There it was," she says, "my first job. Period."

Sarah stayed with Earl for a year, part of a mammoth organization which featured, in addition to Billy and herself, Madeleine Green and a variety of girl instrumentalists. In those days she sounded much like Ella, although without any conscious imitative effort. Her voice was warm, supple, under control.

In November 1943 Sarah cut out. In the summer of 1944 she joined Billy's brilliant bop band. In between? "Nothing. Just starving." With Billy, with food regular again, she sang her head off, but again with little permanent effect. She made just one record with that band, "I'll Wait and Pray." It is still pleasant to listen to, but something less than an accurate index of the growing musicianship she was demonstrating. Sarah stayed with Billy a little more than a half-year, then began the curious shuttling back and forth which is basic to all building singers: records for H.R.S., Guild, Crown; a few weeks at the Copacabana Lounge with John Kirby, stretching from the end of 1945 just past the New Year's celebration that ushered in 1946; six months or so at Cafe Society Downtown; records with Teddy Wilson for Musicraft —a good omen, since it was with Teddy on Brunswick that Billie Holiday made her significant early appearances. The big break was Fifty-second Street, appearing at the Onyx and Downbeat. She was paid seventy-five dollars for her Street debut at the first-named; when she returned a year later her weekly ante was nine hundred dollars; when she came back to New York a year after that no such club could pay the money she was worth.

She was married on September 17, 1946, to trumpeter George Treadwell, and her life seemed balanced, burgeoning, brightly burdened. The seeming wasn't dreaming; from then on Sarah moved. She moved from coast to coast, from the Street to the Blue Angel to the Rhumboogie and Sherman in Chicago to the Bocage in Hollywood. Musicraft recorded her with Georgie Auld ("You're Blasé") and Tadd Dameron ("If You Could See Me Now"), and musicians lifted their ears. She did another trip around the country's night-club and theater wheel. Musicraft recorded her with her husband and studio combinations ("Body and Soul," "Don't Blame Me," "Ghost of a Chance," "Tenderly," "I Cover the Waterfront," "Everything I

Have Is Yours"), and the public lifted its ears. Disk-jockey-concert-promoters like Dave Garroway made her singing their special concern, and she made something special of "It's Magic," a record that got just as big as the rapidly failing Musicraft concern permitted it to get. When she returned to Los Angeles late in 1949, to do three weeks at Ciro's and four at the Casbah, she had reached the $3250-a-week class and was still soaring. When she made her first Columbia records, in January 1949, after suing the defunct Musicraft company and thus emerging from contracted inactivity, she reached the musical heights that "If You Could See Me Now" and some of the early records had suggested.

Those are the facts. A pleasant history with few downs, more ups, and an almost straight line to the top billing, following a pattern that almost seems lifted from her singing. As all of listening America knows by now, Sarah's style is compounded of a few downs, more ups, and a great drive to the top of a bar, a phrase, a song. Her filling of intervals, her breaking of half-notes into eighths, of quarters into sixteenths, her careening melodic variations, have been imitated since 1946 by every singer of consequence with ears to hear and voice to sing. Sarah says she's had only one influence—"Eckstine, of course." The smile that accompanies this admission betrays as much of her retiring personality as she generally permits non-singing expression. Of course the influence was mutual. Of course Billy bursts explaining the strength of Sarah Vaughan's influence upon his singing. Whichever way you cut it, she is certainly Billy's running-mate, one-half of a pair of singers who have broken every commercial tradition, every bigoted bar, as they have made America accept musicianship, a degree of detachment, and a governing jazz sound that springs from bop and courses beyond.

Chapter 22

THE PROGRESSIVES

After years of struggling, some better than others but none filled with fame or fortune, Woody Herman finally emerged as the major band-leader of his time in 1945. The particular pleasure afforded his friends then was the realization that he had "made it," as the ambiguous colloquialism goes, with the best band he had ever had and one of the very best ever. Only once before had a band of such unequivocal standards and evenness of musicianship been organized. It looked in 1945 as if at least one promise of the millennium had been fulfilled: good jazz was making money. Then came the end of the war; a much greater promise was fulfilled. The cessation of hostilities also brought the close of another great battle, the one waged to make jazz acceptable to the multitude. Both victories were, of course, short lived. Because jazz was without an UNRRA or a Marshall Plan, its conquests were quickly dissipated. With postwar inflation, bands became too expensive for their leaders, the public shifted its taste just enough to make the shakier leaders quicken a bit and then give way more; heads fell, bands broke up.

The demise of the great Herman band in late 1946 was not altogether unexpected. There had been dissension and corollary difficulties in the band. Woody was a remarkable leader who had had several significant bands, though none as good as this one, but he was also a human being. The taut and precarious tightrope he had had to walk with this greatest of his bands eventually gave way. Family problems piled up, and Woody was devoted to his wife and child; band problems accrued, and Woody was devoted to music and to his musicians. He was no longer able to assuage with the pride of achievement the feelings of frustration and incompleteness that attack such a man so far away from home so much of the time. He could no longer convince himself that the enormous success of his band would ultimately give his personal life a perfect balance. He quit, and the best band that jazz had ever known—apart from Ellington's—broke up. During 1947, Woody's year away from bandleading, many tears, salt and crocodile and very real also, were shed over the loss of the band, and a certain perspective about it was achieved. Looked at, even from that short distance, the real contribution of his band could be assayed, and for the first time, perhaps, Woody's leading and defining role in its performances could be properly seen.

It was not until the advent of the band that seemed in 1947 to be Woody's glorious farewell to his profession that he was overshadowed by his musicians. Until 1944, at least, Woody Herman was always the star. He was a singer and dancer who stopped shows before he was nine, working with his father, a onetime member of a vocal quartet known as the White City Four. When he was nine he bought a saxophone out of his own earnings, and after three months introduced it into his act. For two years he studied the saxophone with a teacher in Milwaukee, his home town; when he was eleven he picked up the clarinet; when he was fourteen he left the stage to join the Myron Stewart band at the Blue Heaven, a road house just outside Milwaukee. Featured as a singer and instrumentalist, he played with Stewart for six months and then began to work around town with a series of local outfits. He was heard and hired by Joe Lichter, a Milwaukee violinist with a good jazz ear and some Chicago musicians to implement it. With Lichter, Woody was brought close to the central jazz tradition, both as a record listener and performer. That did it for him, and thereafter he was fully committed to the music in which he became in time a formidable name.

After working on the road with Lichter, Woody finished up his high school work in Milwaukee, studied music for one term at Marquette University there, and gigged around town. Tom Gerun, leader of a dance band of large reputation and some musical quality, brought his musicians into the Schroeder Hotel to play and to look for a few new men, if they were available in Milwaukee. Hearing about Woody, he sent for him, auditioned him, and hired him. Woody had arrived in the big time; he was featured vocalist alongside Al Morris—who played tenor and baritone sax and sang so well he was able later, under the name of Tony Martin, to make himself a major figure in American show business—and an attractive young girl named Virginia Simms, later to become Kay Kyser's great attraction. Woody stayed with Gerun for four years, singing and playing tenor saxophone solos, on which he sounded, he says with his usual self-deprecating air, "like Bud Freeman with his hands chopped off." He left Gerun to join Harry Sosnik's band at the Palomar Ballroom in Hollywood. He remained eight months with Sosnik, who had a fair band—made easier to look at by the face and figure of Adele Girard, who sang and played the harp, easier to listen to by the jazz arranger for the band, Dave Rose. After eight months with Sosnik and two singing but not playing in theaters with Gus Arnheim, Woody met three old friends of his who were all playing with the Isham Jones band—Walt Yoder, Pee Wee Erwin, and Jack Jenney. This, the old friends decided, was their man. They talked Isham into hiring Woody and having him join them early in 1934 in Denver.

The Jones band was distinguished for the original tunes of its leader, one of the more gifted popular songwriters of his time, and for the occasional solos of its jazz musicians. It was a fairly important band for the new recording company, Decca, and it wasn't difficult to persuade Jack Kapp, whose child Decca was, to record the small band the jazz musicians had formed within the larger organization. The Isham Jones Juniors, as they called themselves, made two dates for Decca in March 1936—six sides, the only one of which to feature Woody as a singer was "Fan It," the only side to endure. The musicians who worked with Woody here were to become the nucleus of the Herman band. That band, a cooperative organization, was formed by the Jones musicians when Isham gave them notice early in 1936 that he had tired of the profession and would break up a month later in Tennessee.

Walt Yoder went to New York and convinced some of the executives at the important Rockwell-O'Keefe booking agency that the Jones jazzmen were ripe for success in swing-crazy America. Woody got some arrangers together, gathered his musicians at the Capitol Hotel in New York, and started rehearsing them in the free space the hotel gave them. Six weeks later the band made its debut at Brooklyn's Roseland Ballroom and after a short stay there moved into the Manhattan Roseland, the most important ballroom in New York. Working the arduous routine of waltzes, rhumbas, and its own brand of music—jazz—the band managed to satisfy Roseland patrons —sailors, shopgirls, and the rest of that hard-dancing fraternity—

and also to expand its repertory beyond a meager twelve scores, including its theme, "Blue Prelude." There were some impressive Dixieland soloists in the cooperative group: Joe Bishop played a pretty ballad with overtones of Beiderbecke on his fluegelhorn; Neal Reid doubled as road manager and barrelhouse trombonist; Walt Yoder and Frankie Carlson, on bass and drums respectively, kept the two-beat judiciously syncopated. Woody's taste and that of his musicians was best expressed by the blues, and the blues the band played, even when bookers, ballroom and night-club managers, and recording executives explained that a steady radio, record, and bandstand diet of the blues would be too heady for the average audience. One night when they were playing at a major hotel in Houston, Texas, Woody received a note from the manager: "You will kindly stop singing and playing those nigger blues." They received short shrift at the hands of a hotel manager whose taste ran to Viennese waltzes, and shorter at other places which expected the band to work under union scale and the music to be as simple as the C-major scale. In April 1939 Woody recorded an instrumental named after the small band within the band, "Woodchoppers' Ball," and almost overnight the years of scuffling for food and with managers were over. An album of the band's better blues sides, *Blues on Parade*, was a success and, with Mary Ann McCall singing well and the band playing better, Woody was a success in the cubbyhole called a night club, the Famous Door, on Fifty-second Street.

The draft removed most of the members of the cooperative corporation and, with the help of its new managers, lawyers Chubby Goldfarb and Mike Vallon, its form was reorganized along more conventional lines with Woody as the proprietor of a gradually improving band. Cappy Lewis joined at the end of 1939 and gave the trumpet section a sizable growling soloist. Hy White, who came in at about the same time, added a significant guitar voice. Such soloists as trumpeters Ray Lynn and Chuck Peterson, tenor saxophonists Pete Mondello and Dave Matthews, played with the band from time to time and considerably modernized its outlook, Dave adding manuscript with an Ellington flavor as well as solos similarly constructed. At the end of 1943 the personnel was almost completely changed. Chubby Jackson became the band's official bass player and unofficial cheerleader, Ralph Burns its pianist and arranger, and Frances Wayne its featured vocalist. It seemed reasonable to ask such a musician as

Ben Webster to record with the band, and he did in November 1943. It seemed fair to ask the best trumpeters and saxophonists and trombonists around to join up, and they did in 1943 and 1944, until at the end of the second year a more or less fixed personnel had greatness thrust upon it.

The first records the band made for Columbia in February 1945 caught its quality, and every side it made until December 1946, just before it broke up, had the same exultant collective spirit and endless individual inspiration. The first sides issued were "Laura" and "I Wonder," and they were, as they should have been, Woody's—exhibitions of his sensitivity and warmth as a singer, of an individual style best in ballads, as its progenitor's, Red McKenzie's, had been. Then came "Caledonia," a transformation of a Louis Jordan jazz novelty, with jubilant Herman singing and an extraordinary five-trumpet unison chorus built on bop lines but unplayable by any bop trumpet section before Woody's. Coupled with it was Frances Wayne's exquisite "Happiness Is a Thing Called Joe," in which her controlled anguish was given jazz emphasis by her own phrasing and the almost violent eruptions of the band behind her. Then came the driving instrumentals—"Apple Honey," "Northwest Passage," "The Good Earth," "Your Father's Mustache," "Wild Root," "Blowin' up a Storm"—driving but, like Frances's anguish, controlled; powerful in their brass flourishes but also subdued and delicate in individual solos. In between the blasts and the bellows there was time not only for a solo or two, but also for whole numbers of a different volume, mood, and musical intensity. "Bijou," Ralph Burns' "rhumba à la jazz," was the side that caught Igor Stravinsky's attention and moved him to write his "Ebony Concerto" for the band's Carnegie Hall concert in 1946. Its rhythmic accents and organization of brass and reed sounds were at least suggestive of his own work; its infectious figures were played by the band as a whole and by Bill Harris as trombone soloist with a finish and a freedom at the same time that were like nothing else that Stravinsky, or anybody else, had ever heard. A group of able musicians were so fired by each other and by the collective sound they managed together that an entirely new kind of jazz eloquence and playing decorum was instituted. The Herman musicians were individually impressive; as a band, they were incomparable.

Chubby Jackson was responsible more than any other single musician with Woody for the quality of the band. It was not only his playing and talking enthusiasm; he was also, as the Jones jazzmen had been earlier, the indefatigable supporter of the talents of musicians he thought belonged with the Herman band. He was a searcher, and just as his searches had never succeeded in the days before Woody, they struck fire every time he went looking for musicians after he joined the band. Show business was an integral part of his life; his mother, the former Dorothy Wahl, had been a vaudeville and musical-comedy singer. Known to all of Chubby's friends as "Mom," she has long presided over the house in Freeport, Long Island, that Chubby bought, providing meals and roaring enthusiasm for a group of sometimes stray but always talented musicians. Chubby switched to the bass in high school, inspired by Arnold Fishkin, who sold him his first bass for three dollars. Chubby played it some while he was in high school and some more at Ohio State University, where he completed his freshman year and broke seriously into the dance business with small bands around Columbus. Back in New York the next year, he played with Mike Riley at Nick's, studied his instrument with a member of the New York Philharmonic Symphony, and became a notable of the swing era as an entertainer and personality. He played with Johnny Messner, Raymond Scott, Jan Savitt, Terry Shand, and Henry Busse before he found the opportunity to demonstrate his enlarged musicianship and diminished dimension. With Charlie Barnet for almost two years, he participated in the stimulating performances that musicians like the trumpeters Al Killian, Howard McGhee, and Peanuts Holland, the clarinetist Buddy De-Franco, the guitarist Turk Van Lake, and the trombonist Eddie Burke provided. When Chubby joined Woody, in late 1943, he brought with him Jimmy Blanton's bass conceptions and his own brand of enthusiasm. His effervescent personality bounced through the rhythm section, inspiring comparative youngsters in the band, and reinspiring such veterans as Dave Tough. His loudly encouraging "Go! Go! Go!" sailed over the band, moving both musicians and audiences. His constant experimentation involved, first, the hiring of new men, and second, a variety of rhythmic tricks, the most exciting of which, replete with doublings of doubled tempos and halvings of halved times, can be found in the Woodchopper album made in 1946, on the side called, in description of the beat and the number of musicians attacking it, "Four Men on a Horse."

Dave Tough had played all the Dixieland he wanted to when he joined Woody in 1944. He was proud of his pivotal position in the growth of jazz in Chicago, as the steadiest, the most gifted, and the most inspiring of the drummers who kept time for Frank Teschemacher, the McPartlands, and their various and sundry associates. He had enjoyed himself in his two outings with the Tommy Dorsey bands, with Bunny Berigan, Benny Goodman, Jack Teagarden, Artie Shaw, and in an earlier, brief appearance with Woody in 1942. But two events stayed with him always in his short life: his two and a half years with Danny Polo and other musicians in Europe, from 1928 to 1931, and his year and a half with the Artie Shaw Rangers, the Navy band with which he played from 1942 to 1944. The one introduced his eager and receptive mind to the vast delights of European culture; he never tired of describing the titillating pleasures of such appeals to mind and body as he found in reading Baudelaire on the beach at Deauville. The other confirmed his low opinion of the human species; he came back from the war bitter and discouraged and certain that the affront to his and others' dignity was of the nature of things and that no amount of struggling against it would avail. The sense of humor he had displayed in his drum articles for *Metronome* changed; he was no longer capable of such charming explorations of drum styles as the passage from a 1937 column in which he explained that George Simon "is working out a formula of musical criticism. . . . Postulating that:

$$\frac{(6 \text{ saxophones }^2 \times \text{Ray Bauduc }^6)}{(\text{Pi plus Ray McKinley }^6)} = \frac{(2 \text{ tom toms} \times \text{Chick Webb }^3)}{(\text{Big Sidney plus Zutty})}$$

he has a tentative three-dimensional equation that will set the musical cognoscenti back on its heels."

The new Tough justified his surname. His gentle nature, notwithstanding the postwar discouragement, did take over for a while. With Woody for almost a year, from late 1944 to late 1945, he took authoritative charge of the rhythm section, complementing Chubby's rhythmic fancies with his unyielding beat and inspiring variations thereon. He didn't last; his body was not up to the anodynes with which he attempted to prop his failing spirits. He left Woody to spend almost five years in sulking, sodden deterioration, which came to a tragic close in Newark in December 1948, where he died of complete exhaustion.

Dave was replaced by Don Lamond, son of an Oklahoma City lawyer, who had moved with his father to Washington, D.C., when Don was very young. Don was one of the Washington School, a group of District of Columbia musicians who found a meeting of minds and styles in each other and kept both intact in bands around Washington from 1940 to '42 or '43, then with Boyd Raeburn's band from '43 to '44, then back in Washington again when Don led a group of them at the Kavakos Club. When Dave Tough became too ill to play Don was sent for on the recommendation of Sonny Berman. Sonny was enthusiastic—but not enthusiastic enough. Not since Dave himself had come up in Chicago had so facile and shrewdly intuitive a big-band drummer emerged. He took up where Dave left off, maintaining the steady beat, driving the rhythm section and the rest of the band, putting down that difficult row of even beats which the bop formulations of these musicians required. Although few musicians afterward, including, perhaps, Don himself, were able to keep such a demanding and subtle conception of rhythm going with such contagious lightness, he did set a pattern which jazz drummers will be shooting at for decades to come.

Billy Bauer had had an ordinary playing career when he joined Woody—keeping the beat steady with Carl Hoff, Dick Stabile, Abe Lyman, Louis Prima, and numerous little bands around New York. Chubby brought him into the Herman band, and the band perked up that much more when Billy's guitar artistry was made a part of it. His solidity of performance was such that by comparison no other rhythm-section guitarist after him seemed quite professional; but his full impact was not felt until he joined Lennie Tristano in 1946. Tommy Aless, who replaced Ralph Burns on piano after the Herman band took a layoff in Detroit in June 1945, was essentially a rhythm pianist with Woody; his major duty was to combine with Don, Chubby, and Billy, to keep feeding the saxophone and brass sections the necessary beat, which he did very well.

Ralph Burns was clearly the best pianist and the best arranger Woody ever had. He was essentially a band pianist, who could, like his Herman confreres, manage a very good beat, and a soloist who, with an arranger's mind, always made his solos a part of the larger texture of the performance. As an arranger, he always had Duke Ellington's kind of ear; he always adapted his arranging and composing ideas to the sounds and conceptions of the musicians making up the bands for which he was writing. Ralph came by his several skills at an early age. He sums up his first years in one breathless statement: "We always had a piano in the house and my sister and I took lessons for about five years with private teachers and then I went to the New England Conservatory of Music for four months and then I went to work at a little beer and pizza joint at Revere Beach and that's where I started arranging and wrote 'Goodmania' and that's how I became a musician." Ralph comes from a big Boston Irish family; he was born on June 9, 1922, one of what was eventually to be a family of twelve. He played around his native Newton, a Boston suburb, with Bob Adams' orchestra before joining the band led by Frances Wayne's brother, Nick Jerrett. His arranging began with "Goodmania," which, he says, "was a lot of 'Sing, Sing, Sing' and 'Don't Be That Way.' I copied the records. Oh, it was horrible too. I loved the Goodman band. And Bunny Berigan's band —loved it. Boston's Bunny Berigan, Cushing Bean, was in the Bob Adams band. He was so blind he couldn't read music, even with special glasses—but how he blew!"

Curiously, for an arranger whose thinking has been so much like Duke's, Ralph didn't like Ellington's work when he first started arranging. "But he came into Boston to play the Ritz roof in 1939 and I went in there all the time to hear him, and tried to understand why I didn't like him. And I got to know and love his music. Sure was great." Ralph came to New York with the Jerrett band in 1941, to play at Kelly's Stable on Fifty-second Street, with Frances Wayne singing with the band. Charlie Barnet came in often to hear Frances, and heard Ralph as well and hired him. Ralph did some arranging for Charlie, Duke's "Cottontail" and "Caravan" as a kind of penance for his original attitude toward Ellington, and also "Happiness Is a Thing Called Joe," which he brought with him when he joined Woody at Christmas time in 1943. Before joining Woody, he played with Red Norvo's overseas band in the spring of '43—the band, as Ralph says, "that never got across the East River. But what a wonderful ball that was!" It was also the first time Ralph's keyboard facility and felicity of phrase became audible on records, in the excellent series of V-disks Red made with that band for the Army.

When Ralph Burns joined Woody Herman it was almost certain that after a year or two he would leave the piano to spend full time with pen and score. At the age of twenty-one he had reached the maturity as arranger and composer that no other scripters with bands except possibly Duke Ellington and Billy Strayhorn could match. With a taste and ear for both the orchestral formulations of Stravinsky and the jazz ideas of Ellington, he was able to mass sections in three-minute tone poems that had some of the eloquence of both his major influences, and to balance the mass of sound of his ensemble writing with solo passages of notably restrained and soft invention. In the Herman band he found sections and soloists to give that balance proper articulation.

The Herman saxes achieved their quality not so much from the work of their most famous member, the tenor saxophonist Flip Phillips, as from the team sound they achieved under the leadership of Sam Marowitz. Sam, talented member of a Middletown, New York, musical family, started his career on the C-melody saxophone when he was ten; by the time he was twelve he had started jobbing with local bands, playing in Catskill resort places. When he was nineteen his family moved to New York; he started auditioning and got his first name-band job shortly afterward, with Harry James, when he was just twenty. He stayed with James almost four years, playing on many of the band's records, but with no solos except for a few odd bars on "Trumpet Blues" and a few others and on a transcription of, "Let's Go Home." With Woody, his main concern was to keep the section in order, leading it with a tone suggestive of his own alto favorites, Benny Carter and Johnny Hodges. He was also lucky to have under him so facile a musician as John LaPorta, a fine arranger who did a couple of originals for the Bob Chester band, with whom he played before Woody, and for Woody too. Mickey Folus, like Sam an upstate New Yorker, played with Woody several times in 1937, 1938, 1941, and 1942, and rejoined him in 1945 after being discharged from the Coast Guard; he had little opportunity to solo in the great Herman outfit, but his warm and large tenor tone was a considerable asset in the saxophone section. The same can be said for the baritone playing of another prewar Herman saxophonist, Sammy Rubinwitch; molding his work on that of Harry Carney, Sammy managed to sustain the anchor end of the section with a friendly bleat. Joseph Edward Phillips, best known as Flip and a soloist, also upheld his section end very well, having developed from a jumping Fifty-second-Street tenor saxophonist who would take on all comers (whence his name, Flip, from one of the synonyms for going wild, or snapping one's cap, blowing one's top, or flipping one's lid) and could not read music very well, into an able team-mate. Most of the saxophone solos with Woody were his, and he was capable of playing them with softness of tone, celerity of finger-ing, and subtlety of phrase. His ballad meanderings were always more impressive than his self-conscious frantic jazz, but it is the latter facet of his playing style that has made him a big name in recent years, as a soloist in "Jazz at the Philharmonic" concerts.

Solos for a while were almost evenly distributed between Flip and Bill Harris. Bill, who was born in Philadelphia in 1916, started as a versatile musician, playing trumpet, tenor, drums, almost any-thing he could get his hands on, when he was a youngster. "I found it didn't pay too well to be a musician, and that I had to take a lot of other jobs. What kind of jobs? Well, let's see—I was a truck driver awhile; I worked in a warehouse; I read electric meters. All kinds of things, playing club dates on the side." On those dates he played with two other distinguished Philadelphia musicians, Charlie Ventura and Buddy DeFranco. Charlie kept them working at Italian wed-dings. Then Bill's father sent him out as an able-bodied seaman in the Merchant Marine. He was nineteen when that happened; when he got back, two years later, he married and settled down in Phila-delphia. In 1938 Charlie Ventura sent for him to join Gene Krupa's band. But Bill couldn't read nearly fast enough in those days and, in his own words, he "laid an egg." The job lasted one week. Back home again, operating a machine in a defense plant, Bill "got real mad" about the Krupa incident and studied hard to overcome his handicap of poor reading. Nonetheless, he laid another egg with Ray McKinley, trying to play first trombone parts; "so I went back in the cellar and studied some more." He was more successful with Buddy Williams' band and still more successful with Bob Chester's. When Benny Goodman heard the Chester outfit over the air he sent for Bill. Bill was a great success with Benny, only suggesting the kind of imaginative modern reworking of Dixieland procedures which he made into the most popular trombone style of his time after he joined Woody. After Benny disbanded Bill put in some time on the Coast, and then with his own little band at Cafe Society in New York. He joined Woody in August 1944, in Detroit, after playing with Chester again for a few weeks. "Bijou," if it is anybody's achievement besides Ralph Burns', is Bill Harris's: the slight burr in

THE PROGRESSIVES 303

his tone, the long extension of his trombone slide across acres of skipping notes, his identifying vibrato—all these things made an impression upon jazz in general and jazz trombonists in particular unequaled since the early days of Jack Teagarden. The contagion of Bill's style extended through all the bands that played or pretended to play jazz in the late forties, not excepting Woody's. Ed Kiefer and Ralph Pfiffner played almost as much in the Harris idiom as Bill, when they were joined to him in section performance. Both skilled and broadly experienced, both quiet and unassuming, they were keenly aware of their individual responsibilities, which they discharged with distinction.

No trumpet section in jazz was more distinguished than Woody's. At its 1945 peak it scaled the heights of human sonorities in the playing of Pete Candoli, whose physical prowess as a trumpeter was matched by his swimming and weight-lifting attainments; he could always be counted upon to bring a playing performance to an exultant climax with his altissimo notes, or a stage show to a hilarious ending with his impersonation of Superman at the end of the driving, screaming "Apple Honey." Neal Hefti composed two of the band's finest instrumentals, "Wild Root" and "The Good Earth," and contributed to the band a refinement of bop trumpet style that reflected his experience with Bobby Byrne, Charlie Barnet, and Charlie Spivak, as well as an unusually imaginative mind, essentially restless on the trumpet, but beautifully grounded on manuscript paper. Irv Lewis was one of the leading actors in the band's troupe of Jewish comedians, fitting neatly into histrionic place beside Chubby Jackson, Sam Marowitz, and Sonny Berman. He was also a splendidly versatile trumpeter, veteran of Detroit club dates and radio work, of the Henry Busse band when Chubby Jackson was with it, and of innumerable recording dates. He was replaced by the most brilliantly gifted lead trumpeter in jazz, Conrad Gozzo, at the same time that another of the able musicians of the Washington school, Irving Markowitz, replaced Neal Hefti. Goz and Marky carried on the Herman trumpet tradition with all the skill and addiction to playing duties which marked their new associates. The same was true of Shorty Rogers, born Milton, in Great Barrington, Massachusetts— a difficult nativity to believe when one hears his musician's Southern accent. Shorty, when he joined the band in 1945, brought into it a delicacy of style and subtlety of idea that had been tutored by Red

Norvo when Shorty played with his small band in 1942. A product of Fiorello La Guardia's pride and joy, the New York City High School of Music and Art, Shorty was well trained in the classical tradition and, as a result, never at a loss in composing and arranging, first for the Herman band and later for Stan Kenton.

All of these men contributed to the band its extraordinary flash and power and contrasting accents; none of them was quite the equal, as a soloist, of Sonny Berman. Sonny played with seven bands in his six years in the jazz business, but not until he joined Woody Herman in late 1944 did his unusual skill and taste become widely apparent. At first, with Woody, he was end man in the trumpet section, a funny kid whose square countenance looked so much like the front of a subway car that it earned him the extraordinary sobriquet of "BMT-face." Then came the famous vitalization of Woody's band, and Berman became to Herman what Chubby Jackson and Bill Harris and Flip Phillips and later Red Norvo did—a sparkplug in the band's celebrated drive to the top of jazz. He was never too well featured with the band on records—you can hear him at his best on "Sidewalks of Cuba"—and it remained for a set of Woodchopper disks, a couple of V-disks, and one side in Dial's bebop album ("Curbstone Scuffle") to carve his groove in eternity. But anyone who heard the Herman band in person will remember Sonny's solos, those long cadences and flattened notes piercing the wildest up-tempo jazz with such lovely poignancy. There was always something poignant about Sonny, no matter what he was playing or saying, in his role as Yiddish dialectician and storyteller or as a slapstick comedian knocking everything down before him in his determined pratfalls. Sonny was funny with a touch of sadness—sad with a meaning, sorrowful on his horn, touching as a person when you got to know him and got beyond the frantic exterior. This boy was well on his way to a mark in jazz beside the handful of titans on his instrument, until the ways of the jazz world caught up with him. His was one of the few fresh new trumpet sounds after Dizzy's, Fats's, and Miles'; he was a musician potentially of the stature of Louis Armstrong, Cootie Williams, and Roy Eldridge. But the grim fact is that, at the age of twenty-one, Sonny Berman died of a heart attack, brought on by events at a wild party.

In 1942 a Charlie Barnet record started people talking about a singer with overtones of Billie Holiday in her voice and style—

Frances Wayne. That record was "Black Magic." In 1945 a Woody Herman record started the same people and a lot of others talking about Frances Wayne all over again. That record was "Happiness Is a Thing Called Joe."

Frances was a good singer when she made "Black Magic." She was an excellent singer through her three years with Woody. But "Happiness" struck the right chord—a brilliant ensemble chord scored by Ralph Burns—and tempo—slow—for her voice and temperament. She is essentially a moody, torchy singer, a more modern, handkerchiefless Ethel Waters. She sings with Italian operatic intensity of feeling in a jazz frame. The intensity reminiscent of Verdi and Puccini and Donizetti comes from her Italian family background. The jazz feeling springs from similar sources: her brother, clarinetist Nick Jerrett, led one of the good little jump bands around Boston and New York and Syracuse until 1943. Frances sang with Nick off and on, between single turns, stretches with Sam Donahue and Charlie Barnet, and a layoff to recover from the ravages of a strep throat.

Frances was born Chiarina Francesca Bertocci. She spoke better Italian than English until she was eight years old. A native Bostonian with a father from Tuscany and mother from Naples, she spent three years of her childhood in their native land, went to a convent school in Naples, and visited the opera house in Rome on weekend jaunts with her father. Frances finished her schooling in Boston, didn't sing until she was twenty, only had four months' formal teaching. She had always had musical-comedy ambitions, but her family didn't approve of them. She starred at the Hi-Hat in Boston for nine months with a small band of which Hy White was also a member, and then worked in other night clubs before joining her brother, Nick, who was studying at the New England Conservatory, where he formed his small band with Ralph Burns. Later they all came to New York and played at Kelly's Stable. Eventually the whole band except Nick and Ralph was drafted. Frances took a job with Charlie Barnet, stayed eight months, and waxed the above-mentioned "Black Magic" for Decca. For eight months after that she was ill and didn't sing a note. Then she worked locally as a single again. One night Woody Herman heard her, and she joined him two days later.

Frances Wayne was welcomed to the inner circle of jazz singers, that very small number of distinguished men and women who sense

the great heart and soul of popular singing at its best, who are aware
of its philosophical tractability, and are able to communicate all of
these things with a beat.

Besides his own and Frances's singing and the soloists on the conventional jazz instruments, Woody offered first Marjorie Hyams
and then Red Norvo on vibraphone, flavoring the sound of the band
with a seasoning only a handful of musicians have been able to
manage. Marjorie's alternation of bland countenance and electric
smile paralleled her playing with Woody. Sometimes she was only
a plunk or a series of amplified sounds to sharpen the texture of the
band's performance; occasionally, granted a solo, she expanded the
melodic fragment handed her by the previous soloist or the band as
a whole into soft, simple, and beguiling elaborations. Red, of course,
had invented and defined most of the possibilities of xylophone or
vibraphone mallets before he joined Woody at the beginning of
1946. With the Herman band his was not so much technical practice
as a demonstration of the breadth and depth of vibes in modern jazz.
Most of the musicians with whom he played were old friends, personally and musically, and he played beside them as if he had been
with them from the band's beginnings. Such alterations as were required Red accomplished with a minimum of show and a maximum
of taste. The size and value of his adjustment can be heard in his
performance of one of his most famous solos, "I Surrender, Dear"
in the Woodchoppers' album.

Red's contribution to the Carnegie Hall concert of the band was
on his own high level, which was matched, note for note, bar for bar,
inspiration for inspiration, by all the musicians in the band that evening. With the addition of French horns and harp, the slightly
changed personnel of the Herman band moved through Stravinsky's
"Ebony Concerto" as if his dry accents and fragmentary phrases
were ancient conquests. They played their ragtimey work, with its
wry overtones of a German band, with a finish and polish that Virgil
Thomson, who did not like the band's jazz, admitted was without
equal as a performance of Stravinsky. "Ebony Concerto" was the
succès d'estime of the evening; Ralph Burns' "Summer Sequence"
was the major musical achievement. In its four parts, evocative but
not programmatic distillations of four summers spent in different
parts of the country, the power of the band ensemble, the sweetness of such soloists as Bill Harris and Flip Phillips, and the pianistic

imagination of Ralph were given full display. One of its most felicitous phrases, in repetition and variation, was built out of Beethoven's familiar piano-practice piece, "Für Elise," and assigned to piano (Ralph), guitar (Chuck Wayne), bass (Chubby). A similar invention was to be heard in "Lady MacGowan's Dream," one of the last of the band's recordings, not issued until after it had long broken up—as was true of "Summer Sequence" too.

Woody's success was contagious. Following the spectacular changes effected in jazz by the boppers, it suggested to many that a new era had begun, one in which the technical inefficiencies and the clichés of Dixieland and swing would be replaced by a more skillful and imaginative organization of jazz resources. Suggestion became conviction, and conviction became cult. With startling rapidity lines were drawn, barricades built, and war declared. It was an old war in jazz; it had not been declared by the swingsters or the boppers. With the rise of swing, a generation of early jazz enthusiasts took root and found newspapers and magazines and beer parlors across the country in which to blossom. Assuming a false parallel between successful swing bands and successful tinsel—movies, magazines, the writings of such as Faith Baldwin and Kathleen Norris and Kathleen Winsor—these enthusiasts pummeled Benny Goodman and Art Tatum and even found Duke Ellington wanting—he had succeeded commercially, ergo he had failed musically. When bop came along the tools were sharpened, the adjectives were bared, and adherents of the new music were damned as specious entries in a sacred tradition, which, it was said, decayed a little more with each of their ministrations. Besides, it was a complicated music, and nobody understood it, and wasn't it that most noxious of qualities, intellectual?

If these arguments had come only from one obvious source, the philistine newspaper columnist, it is unlikely that the battle would have raged so furiously. But these were the attacks of generally sensitive and knowing people, those who had grown up with jazz in the twenties and those who were growing up with it in the thirties and forties. On college campuses around the country the vote was better than two to one for the old jazz; it was infradig to support modern jazz at any of the Ivy League colleges, and maybe a little subversive too. A whole network of little magazines devoted to the "art" of Dixieland, New Orleans and Chicago versions, in contradistinction to the "commerce" of swing and bop, took shape and called names. One of the favorite debating points of this cult, both in conversation and in print, was the argument from analogy: the failure to recognize the incomparable size of the unique contribution of the Dixielanders was akin to calling Bach and Handel, or perhaps (if the arguer was better equipped and knew his musical history better) di Lasso and Palestrina, corny. When the cudgels of the Communists were joined to the battering rams of the Dixieland lovers in support of "the people's music," the modernists saw blood. Infuriated, frustrated by the non sequiturs and nimble evasions of their opponents, admirers of the new jazz reduced themselves to the level of name-calling and the construction of questionable analogy.

In 1945 *Metronome* published an article which, employing the coinage of a sailor, Sam Platt, who had written a letter to *Esquire*, made a label for the bigoted Dixieland devotee stick. Platt's letter was a protest against what he called the "Moldy Fig" genre of jazz lovers. The article pointed out that the musicians who were beloved of the Moldy Fig pointedly disagreed with the bigoted view, and quoted several of them side by side with Fig detractions to prove it. In a magazine called *The Jazz Session*, representative of the Fig position, Benny Goodman was summed up as "without doubt, probably the poorest musician in America. An uncreative riffster trying desperately to copy even the poorest of Negro musicians, and failing miserably." In answer, Edmond Hall, a New Orleans clarinetist in high favor with the Figs, was quoted: "They don't come any better than Benny. . . . Benny's always been my favorite jazz musician. I've never heard a bad performance by him. If I buy a Goodman record, big band or small band, I always know it's going to be great." Another of these magazines, *Jazz Quarterly*, disposed of Art Tatum by comparing him to a hillbilly bandleader and singer who had had fantastic success with one record, "Pistol-packin' Mama." Art, the *Quarterly* opined, "knows about as much about jazz as Al Dexter." But Mary Lou Williams, enormously popular among Figs because of her occasional forays into the venerable precincts of boogie woogie, could be quoted too; for her, "Tatum is the greatest jazz musician I have ever heard."

If the Modernists had remained content with musical analysis and the comparison of fanatic fans' views with measured musicians' judgments, the controversy would clearly have been one-sided, and a degree of dignity could have been maintained. The challenge was incendiary, however, and intelligence was affronted. Into the fray went critics and amateur crusaders. Dixielanders were labeled "reactionaries" when the air was cool and the offense mild, "musical fascists" when the temperature and the blood rose to a serious occasion. As the Figs refused to listen with any attention—if at all—to any jazz later than 1929 in style and idea, so the Modernists turned from jazz earlier than 1935 in origin—except perhaps for an occasional Duke Ellington record. The full fury of political differences between Right and Left was vented upon these arguments. Finally, as "commercial" carried all the calumniatory opprobrium of the Fig with it, "progressive" was weighed down with all the venerating approbation of the Modernist.

Woody Herman's 1944–1946 band was the first vehicle of "progress" for the outspoken supporters of such in jazz, and with it bebop and singers like Billy Eckstine and Sarah Vaughan. The second recipient of the honors of progress, first class, was Boyd Raeburn. Boyd, who had made money and something of a name for himself as leader of a commercial band in Chicago, did his best to carry the torch. In 1944 he brought a band into the Lincoln Hotel in New York that featured Johnny Bothwell and supported that alto saxophonist's Hodges-like musings and wanderings with the Washington School of Jazz musicians—Earl Swope on trombone, Emmett Carls on tenor, Mert Oliver on bass, and Don Lamond on drums. The next year Boyd's books carried a heavy load of bebop, and the band recorded with such significant boppers as Dizzy Gillespie, Benny Harris, Serge Chaloff, and Oscar Pettiford. These sides and four others featuring Trummy Young were recorded for Guild, bop's home label in 1945. The real force of Boyd's band was not felt until it settled down to starve and fight as best it could on an empty stomach in California in 1945 and the next year.

The band Boyd led at the Palace Hotel in San Francisco in August 1946 was distinguished by any jazz standards. It was well rehearsed; its ensemble sound was handsome and its own. It had a fresh alto soloist in Hal McKusick and a tenorman with a provocative set of new ideas in Frankie Socolow. Johnny Mandell played his own set of trombone variations on Bill Harris's ideas and wrote arrangements that were fresher still. George Handy played piano and wrote scores that showed an astonishing growth beyond what he had been doing for the band in New York a year earlier. He had begun to write in earnest, utilizing his playing experience in his native city, New York, and his intensive pursuit of modern musical ideologies at New York University, the Juilliard School of Music, and in private lessons with Aaron Copland. The ideologies were omnipresent: there were echoes of Bartok and Stravinsky, rolled into captivating hollers, in his ar- rangements of "There's No You" and "Out of This World"; there were obvious traces of the same influences in his collaborations with McKusick, "Yerxa" (the name of a Los Angeles columnist that intrigued George) and "Tonsilectomy" (sic); they were unabashed in "Boyd Meets Stravinsky." Nonetheless, in such original composi- tions as "Dalvatore Sally" and "Bloos," which he wrote for Norman Granz's experimental album, *The Jazz Scene*, he was emerging as a jazz thinker of striking originality. There was more than a play on the name of a Surrealist painter in "Dalvatore Sally"; there were too a nimble handling of changes of tempo, polytonality, and a lovely overlying melody. The "Bloos" reached entertainingly after twelve- bar chorus clichés and the combined resources of strings, wood- winds, and jazz sections. "Stocking Horse," the musical story of a horse born with silver stockings on its hoofs, which George wrote for Alvino Rey, changed time piquantly, as its subject demanded, shuttling back and forth between four/four and five/four time and other multiples of the quarter-note that permitted the rhythm section to maintain its basic beat.

After 1946 George disappeared from the jazz scene, and so did the Raeburn band, with the exception of a few well-managed record performances of Johnny Richards' excursions into Debussyan and Ravelian pasture, and occasional theater and club appearances with personnels very different from the California organization. George succumbed finally, although not forever, one hopes, to his calculated unorthodoxies. As others suit deed to word, George's actions fol- lowed his music. His nonconformist practices ranged from the mild eccentricity of lapel-less jackets to the more out-of-the-way habit of wearing a beard (before and after the boppers made the hirsute adornment de rigeur) to the highly irregular procedure of dyeing his hair red, in which he was imitated by many adoring young musicians. Such behavior patterns and their enlargement into a life dominated by the lust for gratuitous pleasures have taken their toll of many more jazzmen than George and his aping attendants; they have rarely debilitated a better musician.

Stan Kenton tried hard a few years later to fit George Handy into his concert plans. At one time or another he has tried to make every serious jazz musician a part of his plans. He has been called "the savior of American music" and "an empty noise." He has accomplished things with strings that no symphony orchestra in the world can equal, and he has also produced some of the most revolting sound ever to come from a group of musicians ostensibly playing together. He, more than any other, gave meaning to the term "progressive jazz"; more than any other he helped make the term ridiculous. But up or down, good or bad, he has been a force of very real importance in music. In 1949 and 1950, almost singlehandedly, he made audiences listen to, learn about, and even enjoy the avant-garde formulations of jazz and classical music. Without the jazz splendor, either of band or soloists, of the Woody Herman organization of 1944 to 1946, he has polished an orchestral instrument to the disciplined point at which nothing fazes it. If only because he has made the playing potentialities of jazz musicians into actualities, Stan Kenton has made a significant contribution to jazz.

Stan comes from Wichita, Kansas, where he was born on February 19, 1912, but his six and a half feet and rugged countenance have always convinced people that he was a Texan or a Californian. He did grow up in California, in the Los Angeles suburb of Bell. His mother tried to make him into a pianist when his major interest was playing baseball. When two cousins of his, both musicians, stayed at his family's house for a few weeks and began to play jazz, Stan was convinced. He studied some with his mother and some more with an organist. He used to play jobs at Bell High School and increase his income some by working in a hamburger joint. In 1930 he was earning thirty dollars a week in San Diego on a summer job. "But I got homesick and I kept hoping the job would blow up so I could go back home. It did. I went home." In 1934 Stan played the piano and wrote arrangements for Everett Hoagland, then "a big man at the Rendezvous Ballroom at Balboa Beach." At the same ballroom, a few years later, Stan led his own band, the first of many editions of an organization that was changed again and again and usually for the better. In 1942 Stan brought the band East, to play ballrooms and theaters and hope for the best and almost always get the worst.

The band that Stan brought East was essentially on a Lunceford

two-beat kick; if anything, it hit those syncopations with a blasting
insistence that was stronger and more obvious than the playing of
the originators of the style. Stan knew what was wrong, knew it
with the kind of electrifying intuition he has always depended upon.
"I realized that my style had become antiquated. There was nothing
really new, no new sounds, just a lot of rhythmic accenting. Today
all styles that are concentrated on accenting beats are through. Now
it's the manner in which you phrase. Every tone must have a pulse.
Anything stiff has got to go today. That's what was wrong with
my band; it was much too stiff. I have learned, I have felt, that music
today is a natural, human, pulsating sound. It's no longer mechanical."

Stan's realization of the limitations of his first style has been
packed away in recording after recording since 1944, when the first
important changes in his style were effected. Those changes, to begin
with, were in the direction of a looser, more modern jazz, with Anita
O'Day and then June Christy to give the jazz vocal articulation, and
such arrangements as "Just A-Sittin' and A-Rockin'" and "Painted
Rhythm" to demonstrate the instrumental capacity of the band. In
1946, with the band's first album, came some of the first successful
experiments, of which the presentations of drummer Shelly Manne
in "Artistry in Percussion" and of bassist Eddie Safranski in the
piece named after his last name were the most successful. In 1947
the band went through its Cuban period, from which it has never
fully recovered, but which it has relaxed some, following the general
decline of bongos and Latin American accents, which threatened for
a while to engulf jazz. As Stan said, "All styles that concentrate on
accenting beats are through."

Later albums emphasized the experimental nature of Stan's ideas.
Again there were pieces built around soloists, this time some better
soloists, such as the constantly improving alto saxophonist Art Pepper.
For the first time, in his *1950 Innovations* album, recorded to demonstrate the music played across the country by his first concert orchestra, Stan gave Pete Rugolo a satisfactory opportunity as a composer.
Basically a composer in the modern classical idiom, Pete showed himself more at home in occasional quarter-tone flights than in the
deft but undistinguished jazz instrumentals he has spent most of his
professional time in writing. In his next album Stan presented Bob
Graettinger's "House of Strings," a work steeped in the adventurous
patterns of atonality, with reminiscences of Schoenberg and Alban

Berg, but reminiscences more in the listener's head than in the composer's, since Bob has never knowingly heard their music. The writing is unusually skillful; the playing is impeccable, a definitive example of the fluency, precision, and masterful attack of which musicians—even violinists, violists, and cellists trained in a foreign idiom—are capable when they have been disciplined by their work in jazz and under a leader of Stan's caliber.

Soloists have never meant as much in the Kenton band as they have in other jazz orchestras. Rather the section work of such trumpeters as Buddy Childers and Ray Wetzel, of such trombonists as Bart Varsalona, of such a drummer as Shelly Manne has been important. Vido Musso was once a featured soloist, but he was more successful because of his earlier performances with Benny Goodman than because of his playing with Stan. Eddie Safranski built a reputation as a bass player with Stan that only Oscar Pettiford has challenged in recent years; essentially a technician with a catholicity of musical interests that includes both jazz and classical music, he has found proper recognition as an NBC studio musician, playing in jazz trios with Billy Bauer and in the NBC Symphony under Arturo Toscanini. In 1951 the band had some able saxophone soloists in the altoist Art Pepper and the tenorman Bob Cooper, both close to the cool sound of Lee Konitz and Stan Getz. It had, in Shorty Rogers, the best of the trumpeters influenced by Miles Davis; in Milt Bernhart, a trombonist who has lifted the Harris style far beyond its Dixieland base. Most of all, the band still had Stan Kenton, and Stan makes more sense today than he did in 1940, 1945, or 1948—more musical sense, though he has had to divide his audience in two. For one part of his audience Stan plays jazz, occasionally lets loose the atomic blasts that first won him his reputation, and just as often softens them with the languid movie music that helped him keep it. For the other half he plays his concert music. For both halves he has more measured and more meaningful words. Until about 1949 Stan ran for election every time he opened his mouth to engulf a microphone in a disk jockey's studio or on stage. He made sense, but a sense that was often garbled by his intensity. In 1946 he talked about progressive music in this fashion:

Jazz is progressing rapidly; much faster than most people think. Soon there'll be no more "in the middle" bands, no more of those that try to play something new for a few minutes and then settle back into the old way because it's more commercial. The pace is much too fast for that sort of thing. Duke and Woody are putting themselves in a class by themselves. That's the kind of music that's going to be *it* from now on. The rest of the bands will have to make up their minds whether they want to be plain, commercial dance bands or whether they want to be progressive, musical bands. Quite frankly, I think that if the commercial bands try to compete with the more modern type of bands, they'll wind up making asses of themselves.

What are we trying to do? We are trying to present a progressive form of jazz. We've got that common pulse now, we know what we want, we know what we are going to do and we know how to do it. We want to make our contribution to real music and we want to make it a really worth while contribution. So, my friends, this is it, and you can take it or leave it, because from now on in we're not going to change, we're not going to listen to anybody else. We've found what we've wanted, what we believe in. For we've found that common pulse at last!

In 1950 he recognized that his was not the only jazz and that the music his band played, like all jazz, had roots:

I'm clear beyond the stage where I start arguing the merits of progressive jazz against swing and swing against Dixieland. We just have to accept all the different phases and let the thing go. I think Dixieland is the basis for all of our jazz. And these fellows got brave and ran out in front, but oops! they got afraid; they had learned a little bit about music, so it was pretty hard for them to be basic and simple as they used to be.

He hesitated a bit about 1950 jazz:

In modern and progressive jazz and bebop there is such an urge today for new harmonic sounds—everyone is in the throes of creating new harmonic excitement—that the music has suffered greatly by the lack of rhythmic assertion and the lack of real emotional character. Charlie Parker is about the only example today of someone who has progressed harmonically while at the same time maintaining a jazz character. The young jazz player should listen to Charlie not just for the technical and harmonic part of his creativeness—but to see how honest and free his projection is.

But Stan wasn't going to turn his back on jazz as he had done twice before, when he had disbanded for short periods, under the impression that he was finished with jazz and that jazz was finished with him—when "I felt I didn't have it, musically speaking, to reach the top. Our music seemed out of tune with the people; we just had no common pulse. I guess I just had the wrong goddamned feel for music.

Yes, some people with lots of nervous energy could feel what we were doing, but nobody else could." In 1951, with full respect for what had gone before him, he summed up the past and confronted the future:

> The thirty-five or forty years of jazz are finished as an era. We might as well close the door on it. Maybe it should have been closed three or four years ago. Maybe we're going to go back to the minuet or the Viennese waltz. Wherever we go, we're certainly not going to jitterbug again. The future is broad and inspiring. Modern musicians will use every conceivable method, no matter what it is. My band has gone beyond my own technical knowledge in its use of the complexities of modern orchestration.

The tribute he pays his musicians is not false modesty on Stan's part. The compliment works both ways: in jazz, as in the other arts in which collective performance is involved, there is no clearer sign of maturity or strength of leadership than this one. In acknowledging the high achievement of his musicians, Stan indicates his own.

Chapter 23

COOL JAZZ

The making of the modern tenor saxophonist in the image of Stanley Getz was accomplished by one record—maybe two. The one record is "Early Autumn"; the "maybe" is occasioned by the last side of Ralph Burns' other seasonal salute, "Summer Sequence." For there is little doubt among devotees of modern jazz that the tenor is properly sounded by Stan and those who follow in his tonal tradition.

"Cool" is the adjective that best describes that sound—"cool," inevitably overworked because it seems such a precise description of the almost indescribable. One of the great changes effected in jazz in the late forties was a revolution in thermodynamics, a new conception of the relation between heat and the mechanics of making music. The change, the new conception, the revolution, all are best illustrated by the playing of Stan Getz.

When we were first confronted with the look as well as the sound of cool jazz, some of us were dubious about its qualities. The component parts of the look were a relaxation of the body to accompany the restraint of tone, and an indifferent facial expression amounting to apathy. The phlegmatic personalities of the Woody Herman band of 1948 suggested that the coolness would soon become frigidity, so blasé did these musicians seem as they moved, or rather mooched, about the completion of their appointed tasks. But from the icy stare and the immobile mien something good and positive and musicianly did emerge. A four-tenor voicing that Stan suggested, and he and three of his associates developed, relieved the monotony of saxophone writing and playing in big bands; with a baritone substituted for one of the tenors, it was immediately compelling as heard in Woody's "Four Brothers" and "Early Autumn." A tenor voice of substance and size leaped forward, developed from the suggestive performances of several musicians, notably Herbie Steward. Stan's polished authority on his instrument became the highly attractive center of cool jazz.

At twenty-four, Stan could look back on nearly a decade of big and small band blowing of all kinds, with every variety of music and musician in jazz—playing experience that had to make him either a hopeless eclectic, with a little of everybody's sound and none of his own, or a distinct personality immediately identifiable as himself. He was born in Philadelphia and grew up in the Bronx. He played the bass fiddle in his junior high school orchestra and switched to bassoon in high school in order to get into the main school orchestra. He played with the All City Orchestra, made up of New York's best high school musicians; picked up the harmonica when Borrah Minnevitch's advertising promotion brought the mouth-organ to the attention of his school orchestra; and then, when he was fifteen, dropped out of school to join Dick Rogers' band. A truant officer dropped him right back in school, and he dropped out again quickly to join Jack Teagarden. The school authorities pursued Teagarden all over the country because of Stan, until Jack signed guardianship papers to keep the kid with him. Stan stayed with Jack for nine months, a period that he remembers affectionately. "I can appreciate all Dixielanders," he says, recalling the period with Big Gate. "Not their jazz ideas—that's out of the question, of course. But I've never heard any modern trombone player get the sound Jack gets. His way of playing a sweet solo is crazy. A friend of mine and I got our union cards in New York the same day; I thought he was getting the better break—he went right out with a four-beat band, Hal McIntyre's; I went out with Teagarden. Now I think I got the better break. Dixie is a foundation. It's simple enough; you know what you're doing all the time. It's a good way to get started, or at least it was good for me."

The job with Teagarden spanned the country, leaving Stan finally in Los Angeles. He took a job there in a men's clothing store, while he worked out his union card, which, in Los Angeles as in other big cities, couldn't be his until he'd played a prescribed number of short-term jobs for a prescribed number of months. Then he joined Bob Chester for a month at the Trianon Ballroom. After an uneventful thirty days, he became part of a six-piece Dixie group led by Dale Jones, who had written "Between Eighteenth and Nineteenth on Chestnut Street" with Stan's first employer, Dick Rogers. "I was happy, though I didn't realize it then. I didn't know anything and wasn't aware of it—that's when you're happiest, maybe."

After six months with Jones, he played the last fifteen broadcasts of the Bob Hope show with Stan Kenton, joined Jimmy Dorsey for a month, and then Benny Goodman for six. "With Benny I had to push, to get that hard sound he likes from his saxes, but I was beginning to dig Lester." His digging is only barely evident in his recorded solos with Benny on "Swing Angel," "Give Me the Simple Life," and "Rattle and Roll"; it's much more apparent on the small-band sides he made with Kai Winding at the same time—notably, "Always."

Singer Buddy Stewart's sister, Beverly Byrne, was working with Randy Brooks then, and Stan and Beverly were close. She got him into the band; he married her. There followed short engagements with Buddy Morrow's motley of sounds and styles, with Herbie Fields, and then Hollywood again, where he worked with Butch Stone in a remarkable group made up of Herb Steward, Shorty Rogers, Butch, Arnold Fishkin, Don Lamond, and himself. Then the original Four Brothers—Stan, Herb, Jimmy Giuffres, and Zoot Sims—worked a Spanish ballroom, Pontrelli's, in Los Angeles, with Beverly singing. The quartet of tenors moved bodily into the Herman band formed in Hollywood in September 1947.

"It sure makes you want to blow when you've got those cats with you," Stan said. "You hear the right sounds all night; finally the right sounds come out of you."

When Stan stepped out of the Herman band in 1949, it was to gig around New York, lead some of his own groups, make small-band records, of which he likes "Long Island Sound," "Lady in Red," and "Indian Summer" best. The records he made with Woody caught on, his own began to move, and his identification with the soft, clean, clear air of the new sound was complete.

Stan has always had a photographic memory for music. There are few musicians who know as many tunes as he does, as anybody who has worked with him can attest. He used to memorize the library of each band he was with; he knew his book cold—and cool. Ballads have been his big attraction, as he is most attractive in ballads. "Fast tempos seem unnatural to me. The fastest I like to get is 'Lady in Red.' Faster, I don't feel it's relaxed; I have to stop and think about the chords, my time goes, I lose my ideas. When you go slow you can create. I like to play simply, to hold back some of my ideas. Listen to Bird; you know he's holding back, that he's always got something in reserve. You can't play everything you know."

Sometimes Stan plays too simply, too close to the melody, and is too anxious to make the public know it. That's when his phrases shorten, his naturally long line and even-flowing time get choppy, and some of the loose stride disappears. But Stan is a serious, thoughtful musician. He dreads becoming caught in a rut he may have mistaken for a groove, and no matter what the commercial allure, he is not, consciously at least, going to sacrifice his talent for security, much as he wants to know his wife and child are well cared for. He knows that relaxation can be carried too far. He will fight for an orderly development of his gifts.

The great struggle among the adherents and practitioners of cool jazz was for order and development. They emerged from bop and from the big bands that built upon bop with an inevitable background chaos in their work. This chaos sometimes sidetracked performers like Stan Getz. Only one man of this group remained unaffected. Lennie Tristano's whole life has been the wresting of order from chaos, development from immobility.

Lennie Tristano was born in 1919, at the height of the paralyzing flu epidemic that followed the First World War. He was the second son of four in a second-generation Italian family solidly ensconced in the great Italian section of Chicago. True to Italian family form, he went to a parochial school at the age of four. He spent a year and a half in the first grade, after the nominal kindergarten period. "They just didn't think I learned easily. And I just didn't think I wanted to stay in the first grade forever. So I moved to another school." For three or four years he went from school to school, his progress marked by increasing physical difficulty and growing mental ease. At six he suffered a serious attack of the measles. His eyesight, weakened at birth by influenza, grew dimmer. When he landed in his last public school in Chicago, at eight, he was placed in a class for handicapped children—one room holding children with all forms of disability, in all grades from the first of elementary school to the last of high. At ten Lennie's sight was just about gone, but any difficulty that his long term in the first grade might have suggested was gone too. He was able to do long and complicated mathematical problems in his head. He was, as a matter of fact, quite a boy. Since his fourth year he had been able to sit down at the piano and work out simple tunes, such enduring items as "The Stars and Stripes Forever." By his tenth year, after a brief and not very satisfying foray with a private piano teacher,

Lennie had become very adept in the ways and wiles of popular songs. He became, with mixed tricks and an appealing young personality, a pert parlor performer.

In 1928, acknowledging his blindness, his parents sent Lennie away for the pivotal ten years of his life—from nine to nineteen—to a state institution for the sightless in a little Illinois town some considerable distance away from Chicago. "The place," says Lennie, "does one of two things to a student—either it makes an idiot out of him, or a person. I was lucky enough to fall into the second group." In the first were all manner of blind children, babblers, the feeble-minded, the imbecilic and idiotic. The only qualification for entrance was blindness, and the result was a shambles of a school population, rigorously disciplined in its conduct, girls strictly separated from boys for all activities except an occasional heavily chaperoned party. Sexual tensions developing in adolescent boys were treated as monstrous growths to be shunned, somehow to be shaken off. The surroundings were prison-like, the education sparse. The brighter boys were treated like well-esteemed trustees. And yet Lennie flourished. He studied piano, saxophone, clarinet, and cello. He led his own bands from his second year at the institution. His groups played occasional dates at local taverns. Some of the intellectual disciplines were well taught, and he became a skilled mathematician, a highly facile student. There were opportunities to play most of the team sports, and these he engaged in with distinction. By the time he was ready for college, his musical talent was sufficiently obvious that his music teacher took him to the American Conservatory in Chicago and warned the school to "pay particular attention to this boy, because he's going to do everything faster than you're used to."

Lennie sped through the conservatory. If they had permitted him to maintain his own rate of development, he might have completed the four-year course in less than two; as it was, with every possible restriction, he got his Bachelor of Music degree in three, and had completed all the requirements for an M.A. except for final exams, when he decided to skip the five hundred dollars or so necessary to sign up for the graduate degree, and to make his way as at least a part-time jazz musician. At the conservatory he had run through a huge selection of the orthodox repertory, had composed in all the required forms, and had had a string quartet performed at one of the school's concerts. "It was a jazzy piece, but jazz was so far from that faculty's experience that they didn't hear it in the quartet. They simply thought it sounded fresh."

Lennie gigged around Chicago more seriously than he had in his school years. He played the leading role in a small rhumba band, played it so successfully that the band's leader took him aside and offered to make him "the King of the Rhumba." With very little effort, Lennie was able to refuse the gracious offer and to get on with the piano he had begun to take seriously after playing most of his jobs on tenor sax. As a tenorman, Lennie says, "I was somewhat influenced by Chu Berry but didn't imitate him. As a pianist, in 1944, I had reached the point where I could rifle off anything of Tatum's— and with scandalous efficiency."

The remaining Chicago years were lightened for Lennie by his meeting with Judy Moore, a beautiful product of Racine, Wisconsin, who sang with him at the Zanzibar for several months in 1945, and whom he married that July. The years were made heavy by infrequent work and by the increasing puzzlement with which his music was greeted as he shook off influences and conventions and shaped his own striking style. On one date, which was scheduled to run three days, the manager came up to him after his little band had played for a couple of hours and said, "I don't want you to think this is anything personal, but everybody in the place thinks you stink. So I'll be glad to pay you for the three days now, if you'll quit immediately." He says he drove another manager to a nervous breakdown. "He just got out on the middle of the floor, pulled some hair out and screamed when he heard us play some things in three keys at once." A couple of other places at which he played went into bankruptcy—"voluntary, I'm sure, after hearing us," Lennie muses.

Chubby Jackson thought differently from the Chicago club managers. He was planning a "monster" tour when he stopped off with the Woody Herman band in Chicago in the late spring of 1946, and prevailed on Lennie to come East that summer to join him. The tour never materialized, but a job in Freeport with Arnold Fishkin and Billy Bauer did. Another brief spot on Fifty-second Street followed. Lennie became a New York fixture, setting up shop as the brightest of the new jazz musicians, playing occasional engagements with his own groups, taking on an imposing list of pupils—Lee Konitz (who had worked with him earlier in Chicago), Warne Marsh, John LaPorta, Bud Freeman, Billy Bauer, Arnold Fishkin (who left Cali-

fornia to rejoin Lennie in late 1947), and lots of youngsters interested in the future of significant jazz.

Lennie's is not only an inquiring mind but an instructed one; in
the realms of literature and philosophy, as in music, he is not content
merely to feel something; he has to explore ideas, to experience them,
to think them through carefully, thoroughly, until he can fully grasp
them and then hold on to them. He takes possession of such a book
as Tolstoi's *War and Peace* or Dante's *Divine Comedy* as delightedly
as a child seizes a new toy; he takes them apart as eagerly and curiously as a young boy separates the parts of a clock; he speculates about
them as seriously as a Ph.D. candidate examining his thesis. Over endless cups of coffee, Lennie listens and thinks and talks. Padding about
his apartment in slippers, his stocky, muscular frame clothed in
pajamas—unless he is expecting to go out and has reluctantly donned
street clothes—he carries his conversations from his living-room-
practice-room through his bedroom into his kitchen and dining room.
They usually begin at one or two in the afternoon and often carry
on into the hours he has found most fertile for his activities—
those from midnight until six, seven, eight, or even later in the morning.

At eight o'clock on Friday evening, May 13, 1949, after two hours
of fairly orthodox recording, Lennie and four other men—Billy
Bauer, Arnold Fishkin, Lee Konitz, and Warne Marsh—grouped
themselves around two microphones and began to make permanent
the most audacious experiment yet attempted in jazz. The experiment
was to create out of skill and intuition a spontaneous music that
would be at once atonal, contrapuntal, and improvised on a jazz base.
The microphones were provided by Capitol Records. Logically
enough, "Intuition" was the name Lennie gave the first side of the
four recorded between eight and nine that night. Not logically, but
perhaps understandably, Capitol was bewildered by and uncertain
about what it heard. As a result, two of the sides were erased from
the recording tape, and, of the remaining two, those chosen as the
best of the four, only one was released—and that two years after it
was recorded. And yet these adventures in musical intuition are among
the high points of jazz.

"Intuition," both the record and the procedure it names, is the
inevitable development of Lennie Tristano's years of laboratory,
living-room, and lounging-pajama experiment. You can hear his

growth, from the codas of the six sides made for Keynote—later gathered together in a Mercury album—through the two sides Disc issued ("Speculation" and "Through These Portals") and the many it didn't, through "Subconscious Lee" and "Judy" (on New Jazz), to the six Capitol sides. You can hear the individual melodic lines lengthen—first Lennie's and Billy's in the trio performances on Keynote, then Lee's, then Warne's, with Arnold's bass part taking on more and more individual life. You can almost see the long lines pair off, side by side, the improvised counterpoint taking shape, crackling with suggestions of atonality, all strung together with a toe-snapping beat. You can't miss the evolution from other men's chords, from established chorus lengths, from familiar sounds, to the individual freedom and group interdependence of "Intuition," all accomplished without relying on other men's devices.

Lennie and his group have labored at their music under many difficulties. The insistence of recording companies and some critics and disk jockeys on linking it with bop has hidden its own qualities and cloaked it in a ridiculous disguise. The envy of other musicians and the tin ears of night-club owners have kept the group from working under the right conditions or from working at all. The infrequency of work has kept Lennie and his men busy teaching, playing gigs—anything to stay alive—and, as a result, has kept them apart often. Hence, there have been too few opportunities for them to fashion new numbers, to expand in as direct and unimpeded a line as the music has demanded. The scarcity of engagements for music so frighteningly fresh and free has often reduced the playing edge of Lennie's musicians, who have rarely produced less than a good performance but who have often missed the peaks patently within them.

This new jazz is deeply moving to hear; it is, of course, even more satisfying to play. For it rests upon the pillars of all music, the great supports that buoyed the polyphony of Bach and gave depth to the elegance of Mozart. It marks a strong parallel to the development of the twelve-tone structure in classical music in the twentieth century —a parallel, but not an imitation. Whatever the limitations within the three-minute form on records and the only slightly longer elaboration off them, the performances of the Tristano group represent at least a partial unfolding of the resources of the participating men. Here are improvising musicians who are sufficiently disciplined on their instruments to give expression to almost any idea that they may think or feel, sufficiently free to vent those ideas together, with a beat, without preliminary map or plan.

A large number of jazzmen have paid lip service to Lennie and the music for which he stands, none more enthusiastically than another blind pianist, the recently Americanized Englishman, George Shearing. In interview after interview, in conversation after conversation, George has celebrated the advances for which Lennie and his associates are responsible. He has adopted some of the block-chord elaborations Lennie developed and introduced a single-line variation or two of Lennie's, as he has integrated many facets of Bud Powell's style in his playing. But George's major concern is a large audience, and he ingeniously united minor and major concerns to make his amalgam of styles the most pronounced jazz success of 1949 and 1950. George's music is cool, calm, and collected. The melodic line is carried alternatively or together by piano, vibes, and guitar; the beat by bass and drums, creating a texture as sweet and simple as possible within a modern jazz frame. George's arrangements change the accents of the famous standard tunes his quintet plays (e.g., "September in the Rain," "East of the Sun," "Summertime"); they never, however, stray far from the melody, the most ignorant and the more sensitive booker's measure of musical quality. Denzil Best, a better-equipped musician than most drummers, keeps a very light beat going with his brushes (you'd never know he was one of the first—and best—bop drummers). First Margie Hyams, then Don Elliott, caressed the vibraphone bars. John Levy plucks a mildly resolute bass. Of the group, only Chuck Wayne on guitar seems altogether mindful of his jazz responsibilities; without any large variation in volume, Chuck manages a sizable variety of idea, chiefly single-string, not necessarily on the melody. His predilection for the pseudo-Oriental he exercises in compositions such as "In a Chinese Garden," a whole-tone adventure in tea-room atmospheres which is best forgotten.

The success in clubs and hotels and on records of the Shearing Quintet let loose several imitative groups, most of which bettered the musical quality of George's product. Paul Smith, a magnificently fluent pianist with Les Paul's small band and Tommy Dorsey's big outfit, lost none of the fleetness of finger or facility of idea that characterized his work with Les and Tommy when he made Shearing-like records with rhythm section and Novachord and with rhythm alone for Discovery, George's first label. Red Norvo, recording for the same firm with his new trio, had so much to offer in himself, bassist Charlie Mingus, and, above all, guitarist Tal Farlow, that one could forget the more obvious machinations of imitation with which most performances began. And Marion Page McPartland, Jimmy's English wife, added sufficient wit and charm to match her skillful modern piano with harp, cello, and rhythm so that the connection with Shearing was, for all musical purposes, forgotten.

Stan Freeman, an indefatigable studio pianist and harpsichordist, stepped outside these mimetic precincts in 1950 into others more fertile. He began a series of recordings that year in which his command of the classical keyboard gave form and substance to show tunes and jazz standards. Though pianists such as Calvin Jackson and Johnny Guarnieri and composers such as Alec Wilder had made this attempt before, none succeeded half so well as Stan in maintaining a jazz beat and an improvising texture in a classical frame. Stan has style as well as technique, and a sense of form which sometimes takes his performances beyond jazz, but never so far that one forgets where he came from.

Not nearly as successful in the United States as George Shearing, in Europe the most warmly appreciated and avidly imitated of cool jazzmen is Miles Davis, both as a trumpeter and as leader of a recording band. The band sprang from a series of afternoon and early evening talking and playing sessions at the apartment of Gil Evans, chief arranger for Claude Thornhill. In those sessions Gerry Mulligan, a young baritone saxophonist from Philadelphia and Queens, and Gil worked out a voicing—trumpet, trombone, alto sax, baritone sax, French horn, tuba, and rhythm. When rehearsals of the new music were called at Nola's, New York's prime rehearsal studio for jazz and dance bands, Miles was called too. When Capitol decided, for a brief while at least, to go along with bop and the even more recherché elements of modern jazz, Miles was signed. He made a few dates with "the new sound," as musicians referred to it, and the sound was sent round the world. In England, Johnny Dankworth, a gifted alto man, perhaps the best jazz musician in his country, led his band through Miles' paces—and he himself sounded not a little like Lee Konitz, who played alto for Miles on Capitol dates. All over the continent of Europe youngsters playing jazz tried to achieve the sound of the Davis recording band, with the same instrumentation if possible—if not, with a different voicing of saxes and brass to get the same effect.

Miles' fragile quality, producing slight but coherent fragments, became the one to capture on trumpet, J. J. Johnson's swiftly moving slide the one to imitate on trombone. Bill Barber's facility on his instrument, the tuba—classically disciplined, articulate in jazz—was unique, recognized as such, and not imitated. Gerry Mulligan's soft baritone sound did make its way into saxophone sections, as his mode of lower register discourse was followed rather than his means.

The most eagerly imitated of them all, when imitation was possible, was Lee Konitz. As Stan Getz and Herbie Steward defined the cool sound for the tenor, Lee did for the alto. He also accomplished something more: along with his clean, clear, evenly inflected tone was a high level of musicianship; in one way or another, consciously or not, it was his level that one used as a criterion with which to judge the work of Stan, Herbie, Zoot Sims, Sonny Stitt, Art Pepper, and others. One could hear at moments, perhaps, that Zoot, a freebooting member of Woody's 1947–1949 cool band, was adding some thinking to perhaps the best beat among the Young tenors, or that Sonny, a similarly accomplished rhythmic tenorman, was adding Lee's furtive asides to Bird's vigorous line and growing in stature as a result. Certainly Art Pepper changed from an ordinary alto saxist to a meaningful musician—with Stan Kenton—as he came closer and closer to Lee. The same was true of Stan's tenor soloist, Bobby Cooper, who, like Art, took some lessons with Lennie Tristano. It was especially true of Warne Marsh, a brilliant youngster, whose tenor imagination grew as he got to sound more like Lee's conception—though not like Lee's tone—as he learned to play alongside Lee and still retain a personality of his own. As Warne matured, he began to think about what he was doing in a fresh way, to see, as few people did, that jazz—especially the new jazz—consisted of many things, attitudes, working procedures, disciplines, and combinations thereof.

To some people jazz is just a state of the glands. To others it is a series of beats, preferably banged or shrieked. To a few, jazz is a state of mind—a very low one, corrupt and questionable, but at least a state of mind and not just the rhythmic noise that awakens the elemental passions. Actually jazz is all of these things in part, but it is also something more, several things more—to be precise, the several things that lift the playing of Lee Konitz above the average, however pleasant and progressive it may be, of the other talented youngsters we have been listening to in recent years. For in Lee's playing, as in his talking and thinking, a degree of consciousness emerges which colors every solo line he essays on alto saxophone, which determines the precise valuation he gives the dot that extends each eighth note before each sixteenth, which moves his music from fragment to whole, from sound to statement.

It all started in 1938 at the Boston Store in Chicago—a department store dating from the last century, when the name of the chief city of the Commonwealth of Massachusetts carried such cultural cachet for settlers in the West. Lee was eleven and he wanted to play an instrument. For no reason that he can remember, he decided on the clarinet and went to the Boston Store to buy it because they threw in a coupon book giving him two hundred free lessons. And then the next year he bought a tenor saxophone—at the Boston, of course—and picked up another two hundred lessons. He had more lessons than he knew what to do with, but fortunately for him his teacher, Lou Honig, was resourceful, and the lessons made eventual sense, even if Lee's first job beyond the neighborhood circuit was with Gay Claridge at the Chez Paree. Then he went to work with Teddy Powell and Jerry Wald—just a sixteen-year-old alto man who could play clarinet and tenor. After three months with Wald, Lee decided to give his aching head a break and returned to Chicago to put in two years at the newly opened Roosevelt College, and, rested a little, left town again with Claude Thornhill's band in August 1947. A year's sojourn with the sweet nothings of that polished organization left him in New York, where he joined forces with Lennie Tristano.

"What I owe to Lennie," says Lee, "I can't put it in so many words, I'm afraid. I can only say it inadequately. If nothing else, he's given me such a tremendous insight into music, into jazz and all its counterparts. I'm not saying I have that insight, just that it's there, if I can only reach it. Knowing Lennie has made it available." Thus Lee sums up, cautiously, warmly, uncertainly, what he feels and would like to say better about a decisive influence in his life; talking slowly, worrying the words, because he is always careful about what he says, because he stops to consider, because he is a conscious musician, a conscientious human being.

"You know how I met Lennie? I was working with a society band and went over after the job across the street to some joint to see a friend who was supposed to be working there in a rhumba outfit. My friend's back was visible, that's all, but some remarkable music was audible. Lennie was playing—I can just about remember what he was playing. It was crazy! What he was doing to a rhumba! I sat in and blew a little. Lennie could detect nothing from what I played except my enthusiasm."

That meeting across the maracas was shortly before Lee left Chicago for his brief tours with Powell and Wald. He returned and soon afterward began to study with Lennie; Lee worked with Lennie until he joined Thornhill. After about a year with Lennie, Lee began to evolve his own style. "I actually hadn't ever fallen into any kind of idiom; there were touches of everything in my playing but nothing really definite. Lennie had a rough time with me. I knew I was playing something different, but I was insecure. I didn't think I got a beat. I didn't think I was playing anything—until I suddenly snapped out of it. Consciously. Suddenly I realized I was playing music."

Now Lee can sit down and analyze his playing, most of which he will describe as moving toward a goal rather than as achievement, though more of his goal is apparent in his music than he will permit himself to say. "The first thing," he says, "is sound. Actually there hasn't been a sound put down on alto as there has been on tenor—and I don't think I'm going to do it, but it's a thought anyway. I first became aware of sound with Santy Runyon, who was my teacher between Lou Honig and Lennie. Santy stressed a brilliant, piercing sound, and I was gassed with it at the time. Then there was the sound of Lester Young on the old Basie records—real beautiful tenor saxophone sound, pure sound. That's it. For alto too. Pure sound. How many people Lester influenced, how many lives! Because he is definitely the basis of everything that's happened since. And his rhythmic approach—complex in its simplicity. How can you analyze it? Shall we tag some words on it? Call it polyrhythmic?"

Lee describes the process of assimilating new rhythmic feeling, a process duplicated on all the levels of comprehension and expression in jazz improvisation. "First you write it out. Then you can improvise something." What do you improvise? That takes us to the melodic line.

"Superimposition, the superimposition of the individual line upon the basic chord structure. In addition to the changes in this line, the substitutions, there is the building on the fundamental chords. And then there is the use of intervals, different intervals, avoiding the banal and the obvious. I tell you what I mean. When the altering of the major construction of a melody is confined to an occasional flatted fifth, used as a stopping point, and no more, what you have is a very cute approach to melody—and no more. With us, the flatted fifth would be in the line, as would the other variations, thought of as regular intervals; the flatted fifth becomes the regular fifth of the tonic. This approach integrates the new intervals." And that brings Lee to the crux of the matter, the construction of new melodic lines. "It means getting away from the mass of popular music, doing as much as possible with the chord structure of pop tunes, and then doing away with the chord structure of pop tunes. Look what you're doing most of the time. In a thirty-two-bar chorus you get one eight-bar phrase three times and a second eight bars in the bridge; and so in three choruses of blowing you play the same eight bars nine times, and another eight bars three times."

Reflecting on the strictures of chorus construction, Lee offers an explanation of his conception of phrasing, an explanation notable for its clarity and cogency. "Let's say we change the punctuation of the thirty-two-bar structure, like carrying the second eight bars over into the bridge, making our breaks sometime within the second eight and in the middle of the bridge instead of at the conventional points. We reparagraph the chorus. Or better, since we have already altered the construction of the line, we reparagraph a paraphrase. And that leads to the next logical point, to continuity and development. Because you've got to think in terms of both, so that everything holds together, so that you get not four choruses but a four-chorus statement."

Thus a sensitive youngster sketches the outline of his own style, suggests the way music looks and sounds and feels to him and to the men with whom he plays. He leaves unsaid his contrapuntal convictions, assuming that anybody who listens to the Tristano group will perceive, by head or heart, the linear structure of their performances. But that perception alone is not enough; it is vital, if one is to apprehend the rich invention and feel the lovely texture of this music, that such sketches of style and suggestions of underlying conception inform one's every listening moment. For, as Lee will work his way back from the Museum of Modern Art to the Metropolitan, pacing the endless galleries with his sympathetic and encouraging wife, Ruth, in search of sources and understanding and insight—to correct an early antipathy toward the visual arts—so must his listeners dig beneath the rich sound and the tight organization. The fine facets of his music hide something even finer beneath, the conscious exploration of all that is or can be in jazz. It is almost as if Lee Konitz had made of his alto saxophone a thinking reed—almost, but not quite, for Lee, the best of Lennie Tristano's students, is to some degree afflicted, as the least of Lennie's pupils are, by a doctrinaire limitation of style and idea. It is from that limitation that John LaPorta broke away.

John LaPorta is a clarinetist of parts—fresh, new, and authoritatively original. He has been hidden for years in the saxophone sections of Buddy Williams (a local band in John's native Philadelphia), Bob Chester, Woody Herman, and a music school in Brooklyn. He was a kid with Williams, took some of his first professional breaths along with Buddy DeFranco and Bill Harris. With Chester he became a seasoned lead alto man and achieved dubious if anonymous notoriety in a stage-show review in *Metronome* magazine, in which he ("the alto sax soloist") was censured for his copying of a Johnny Hodges solo he had never heard and reproved "because his coat and pants looked as if he had just taken them out of a duffel bag" (it was hot at Harlem's Apollo Theatre that July, with no air cooling and the doors closed, and neatness went with the wind). On third alto with Woody, John won the considerable respect of his distinguished associates for his knowing musicianship, his proficiency as a sight-reader, and his modest demeanor. And then, on December 21, 1946, he was cast adrift along with the rest of that edition of the Herman band. It was the best thing that ever happened to him. He picked up his clarinet, played some with Lennie Tristano, composed some and taught more, to make a living.

John is a well-schooled musician; he had a couple of years at a Philadelphia school and several months with Ernst Toch on the West Coast, with Alexis Haieff, Igor Stravinsky's aide, behind him. He can teach almost anything in the clarinet tradition, from counterpoint to atonalist formulations. He's a far cry from the balling jazzman whose musical happiness lies in his ability to capture tonally last night's alcoholic and other excesses. To John jazz is an art and a science; it must be studied; it can be significant only if it is the end result of an intensive preparation. That preparation entails hours of work, of unrelenting attention to the interior detail of the creative process, and the very conscious avoidance of the clichés and banalities of most hot improvisation.

"Jazz," says John, "requires a virtuoso technique today. But, unlike the virtuoso of classical music, who doesn't have to be any more than a finished performer, the jazz virtuoso has continually to make harmonic and melodic progress; he has to be a first-rate performer and composer as well." John thinks he knows some of the progress which the jazz virtuoso can make. "The old idea of playing in major triads is trite today. Now we can alter chords and use all forms of inversion. But not by trial and error—a musician must know."

Meeting John LaPorta, one wonders where in his reticent person he holds the brilliant array of new ideas he has displayed in his few gigging appearances, his several broadcasts, and his two record sides with the 1951 Metronome All-Star Band. His myopic eyes behind heavy glasses, his mousy voice, his retiring disposition seem to betoken a student of one of the dead languages, perhaps, or a librarian in an institution devoted to research on extinct Australian birds. But challenge one of his musical ideas, carry the argument beyond words and put a clarinet in his mouth, and watch the mouse become man, an inspired man with a compelling message. If one probes enough, one may also stimulate words, and then the most alert musical mind in jazz may begin the constructive but relentless analysis of his own music and anybody and everybody else's—from Bach, whose harpsichord and organ music he has transcribed for jazz instruments, through Mozart, Schoenberg, Berg, and other contemporaries, to his jazz colleagues. He can also listen and learn, as he has in his participation, at rehearsal and performance, in the music of the Sandole Brothers.

Dennis and Adolph Sandole are Philadelphia jazz contemporaries of John's. They have both played with bands big and little, nationally famous and locally infamous; they play guitar and baritone sax respectively. After the war, teaching at Philadelphia music schools, they developed a brand of orchestral writing that is all by itself in jazz. Recognizing the inevitability of atonalism in jazz, they also understood the restrictions under which such a violent change of focus must be made. The necessary intermediate stage, as they saw it, was one in which polytonality—playing in two, three, or more keys at once—would dominate the jazz musician's consciousness. That in itself was enough for the Sandoles; it represented a challenging revolution that could, if properly directed, evolve in turn toward the expansionary goals of the atonalists. They themselves provided the direction, with supervisory assistance from a teaching colleague of great sensitivity and equipment in the modern classical idioms, Frank Caruso. In late 1949 they whipped together a concert in Philadelphia in which their ideas were put on full public display, with the sympathetic aid of some sixteen Philadelphia jazzmen, who sweated through many rehearsals and the concert itself for very little money because of their belief in the Sandoles' talents and convictions. The concert was a considerable musical success. It demonstrated the feasibility of the brothers' jazz conception; it revealed a handling of orchestral masses without precedent in jazz, in which soloists, sections, and the ensemble were bundled together to make a moving whole, sometimes the sum of its parts, sometimes setting them in parallel to each other, always integrating them.

The music of the Sandoles does not stand alone in modern jazz; it has an opposite number in the compositions, arrangements, and performances of Dave Brubeck, a fine pianist, who almost singlehandedly is responsible for a renaissance of jazz in San Francisco—before his coming a city singularly devoted to the raucous, if enthusiastic, revivals of pre-World-War-I Dixieland by such bands as Lu Watters' Yerba Buena group and Kid Ory's crew. Dave, a student of Darius Milhaud at Mills College, where he received his M.A. degree, and a teacher at the University of California, is another polytonalist. With a brilliant bass player, Ronald Crotty, and a doubly able drummer and vibraphonist, Callen Tjader, he recorded the most engaging and provocative jazz trio sides of 1950 and 1951. With the addition of horns and the filling out of his rhythm section, he did as much for the larger jazz chamber group—in his case an octet. Of the works for the latter outfit, a "Fugue on Bop Themes" is the most immediately arresting, but all of the trio and octet scorings and performances partake equally of Dave's active imagination, of the cool sound of the Miles Davis band, and of the controlled but not stifling disciplines of a music which is polytonal, polyrhythmic at times, and spontaneous too. This is the balance of cool jazz at its best, whether played by a big band like the Sandoles', a small one like Dave's, or a soloist such as Billy Bauer.

"He's the end! Have you ever heard anything like it? There's nobody like Billy Bauer!" That was Shelley Manne, running over with enthusiasm for the guitarist at a Metronome All-Star Band recording date.

"I don't like it. It doesn't sound right to me. Gee, I never seem to get what I want. That's pretty bad guitar." That was Billy Bauer, at the same date, and at all other record sessions, public and private performances in which he has been involved.

There is a marked difference of opinion over Billy's playing. Just about every musician who has ever worked with him thinks he's "the end!" or something very close to it; Billy himself isn't sure he has begun yet. When Arnold Fishkin brought his bass three thousand miles across the United States to rejoin the Lennie Tristano trio in 1947, one of the first questions he asked Lennie was about Billy. "Has he changed?" "He sure has," Lennie assured Arnold. Lennie was referring to Billy's playing. Arnold was referring to the guitarist's personality, specifically his incessant self-deprecating talk. He had and he hadn't changed.

For many years Billy was a first-rate rhythm guitarist, satisfying to jazzmen of several schools because of his superlative time, his superlative steadiness, drive, relaxation, and unrelaxed musicianship. Ever since joining Lennie, Billy has offered something new, a new conception of his instrument's place in jazz. He credits his initial interest in this new way of playing to Zeb Julian, a fellow guitarist. "He used to come back when I was with Woody and show me. He's a creative guy who first had the idea of playing that way. Maybe he didn't do it on the job, playing with other musicians, but he did it when he played alone."

The way? The guitar picks up and goes. It is no longer restricted to rhythm chords, with occasional sorties provided by note-for-note reiterations of piano arpeggios. Under the administration of Billy's fingers and the busy head that directs them, the guitar plays fill-ins wherever they fit, not where they fit by this man's jazz convention or that one's, but where they belong according to the mind and heart of Billy Bauer. The guitar, in this system, has all the autonomy of a trumpet, a trombone, a saxophone; it has the additional rhythmic duties it has always had, made broader, and more subtle too, by its departure from the one-two, or one-two-three, rhythmic straitjacket. The way has become the power.

It all started in the Bronx in 1916. Billy ambled along, not especially aware of music, until he was eleven or twelve years old, when, if the ukelele counts, he became aware of sound as something more than shouts on a New York City street. At fourteen he made a tentative beginning on the banjo, supported by a few lessons on its noisy strings. He did well enough at it to transfer his activities indoors and to play club dates with pick-up bands around town, including a quartet of his own. The summer of his fifteenth year he went up to play the Borscht Circuit with a small band, and, like the first long pants and the first drink, this changed Billy's life.

Back in school after this exciting musical adventure in the Catskills, Billy could talk about nothing else. He had learned about life, and he proceeded to tell his classmates in junior high all about it, his voice rising in coloratura accents from the lyric boy soprano which was and is its normal register. It was all right between classes; but his teachers didn't like having regular class procedure interrupted by these tales of derring-do on the American steppes. One of them rapped Billy's hands with a ruler in the midst of one of his heartfelt narrations.

"That's it," Billy said as he rose from his seat. "I'm through!" And he was. He rode out another year of part-time classes in continuation school and then scrapped formal education as an unnecessarily dangerous experiment.

When all the jazz world was shifting from banjo to guitar, Billy made a quick switch with the aid of Allan Reuss. He asked the eminent Benny Goodman guitarist for help. Allan got him started on the guitar, then sent him out on his own, suggesting that he add his own ideas and technique as he went. Billy has been following that advice ever since.

Before joining Woody Herman in mid-1944, Billy played with Jerry Wald's first band at an uptown Manhattan Child's restaurant, shifted from that Kemp-styled music to the bands of Carl Hoff and Abe Lyman, and played short terms around New York radio studios. In the early forties he jobbed with Flip Phillips—then a clarinetist—and ran a sextet with him. When Flip joined Woody and heard that a guitarist was needed, he recommended Billy. Woody called Billy.

"Would you like to sit in?" Woody asked Billy on the phone.

"When?"

"Tonight."

"I can't, Woody," Billy said. "It's my kid's birthday."

"Well then, come in tomorrow. Come to work."

Billy hadn't been playing hard to get. His family was, and is, important to him—so important that after more than two years with Woody, in August 1946, he left the band.

"I wanna get through, Woody," Billy announced simply. It wasn't that he was sick of the endless ribbing he took from the guys in the band for his high-pitched voice, his shrubby blond hair framing a gleaming, very high forehead. "I was a little panicky," he explains. "I didn't know where the band was going. Everything seemed uncertain, and my family couldn't be supported with uncertainties."

Billy came back to New York and the waiting charms of Chubby Jackson's great enthusiasm, Lennie Tristano, who had just arrived from Chicago. They paired instruments, ideas, fill-ins, point and counterpoint; and the Tristano trio, which has since made what can most seriously be called jazz history, was inaugurated. Now Billy has moved to the musicians' staff at the National Broadcasting Company studios in New York. Cool Jazz—hot jazz—good jazz has a representative in one of the most powerful of mass-communications media. It is at least an entry. It may be the beginning of a new era, in which jazz will have a proper voice in the culture it best represents.

Chapter 24

EVALUATION

In all arts violent changes occur with frightening regularity. Not only do customs and movements and fashions change, but so do their makers and their imitators. Jazz, youngest of the arts, is even more in the grip of bewildering upheaval than literature and painting and traditional music. There are almost as many temptations in the way of personal integrity for a jazzman as there are for a motion-picture artist. Between the tumult of change of custom and fashion on the one hand and commercial allures on the other, most jazzmen find it hard to hold on to themselves; ill-equipped, undisciplined, most of them lose their early purity, their musical as well as their moral wholeness. A slackening of standards occurs as obscure jazzmen become celebrities. One can sympathize; one can understand their plight and explain their change; but one must also deplore and sometimes condemn.

Some big names in jazz—notably Charlie Barnet, Duke Ellington, Dizzy Gillespie, Woody Herman, Stan Kenton, Billie Holiday, Mildred Bailey, Billy Eckstine, and Herb Jeffries—have made far more than a passing effort to give music as much due as money, with varying success in both categories. But they, like their more insistently commercial colleagues, have had to toe the box-office line to keep the money coming in, so that they could continue making music. And toeing that line, which definitely forms to the right, means finding an identifiable and popular style and sticking to it, no matter how low the musical depths that must be plumbed. Jazz has spent so many of its formative years just seeking an appreciative audience that most of its practitioners are content to find a formula that attracts people who will listen to them and buy their records and pay to see them; and when they have found it, they cling to it against all odds, even if depreciation of artistic quality follows. The results are often an almost violent decline in the quality of jazz musicianship, and a kind of abject slavery to the mawkish marks of immediate identity and mass favor.

The problem of when an artist is good and when bad—and that most difficult of all the attendant queries, why—is a poignant one. Critics who take their work seriously look for quality in a jazz musician. They often find it, usually when the musician is just getting started, or shortly after. Then, if well-deserved success comes to the musician, with that success comes the fixative. To make success permanent, the orchestra leader holds on hard to the more popular elements of his band's style and searches far and wide for superficial novelty while avoiding from then on the genuine novelty of artistic experimentation. The virtuoso instrumentalist comes to idolize his own technique, and his ideas get lost in a sea of slimy syllables. The singer subverts genuine feeling to the demands of a mechanical anguish. The bulk of beboppers, following this pattern, after having made a large collective contribution to jazz, became lost in trite formulas in which they found inner and outer security—the certainty that they could make it instrumentally and that audiences would get what they had come to expect. All too often, at this point in the career of a jazz artist, loss of creative imagination occurs just when one has hoped to see development into mature art.

When a budding artist becomes a blooming entertainer, the only standard that remains is the gold. If this seemingly ineluctable process cannot be stopped, jazz will turn out finally to be what its most carping critics have called it, a decadent form of entertainment, an aphrodisiac designed only to rouse flagging glands and lagging hearts, to set bodies in motion and numb minds and souls. But if this change is not inexorable, if some one or two or perhaps a dozen musicians continue to believe in the serious prospects of their own work and that of others in jazz, and if audiences can be educated to respect the genuine in place of the synthetic, then the garden will thrive.

All of this brings us to the positing of criteria. How do we know what's good and what's bad in jazz? We may agree that the majority of jazz musicians do not fulfill their early promise, that they yield to the importunities of hungry stomachs and ill-clad backs and the opportunities of success, financial and otherwise. One can't blame them entirely, but neither can one make a virtue of their needs and praise musicians for having given way to them. One can only look for standards, formulate a working set of values, and give due praise to those precious few who make similar values the canon of their professional life.

Actually, something close to a viable aesthetic standard has been arrived at in' jazz, if it is only the measure of the quality of outstanding performers; and maybe even broader criteria can be perceived hiding beneath the good of these musicians and the bad of the others who have sacrificed everything, consciously or not, for box-office survival.

Of all the arts there is none so perplexing as music, none so difficult to write about, none so productive of argument and disagreement. And of all the branches of music there is none about which people get so exercised as jazz, none about which they get so distraught, so determinedly disorganized, none in which they resist disciplined thinking and logical procedure so violently. And yet of all the arts and all their branches there is none in which discipline and logic, clarity and orderliness should be easier than in jazz. The art of creating spontaneous notes and chords and extemporaneous rhythms— the art of improvisation—is still small enough and young enough to be surveyed and assayed. It is worth while, therefore, to organize working criteria for jazz and to take a long, reflective, retrospective view of the achievements of jazz from its beginnings to the present.

Actually there are very few general standards with which most of us approach any of the arts. Basically, there seem to be three: freshness, profundity, and skill.

Freshness means, of course, freshness of idea. Another way of putting it offers an even more ambiguous debating term in the arts— inspiration. How do you ascertain a musician's freshness or inspiration? It seems to me that we can do no more than compute mathematically in this branch of musical activity—but that is not so little. It is altogether possible to name the figures a man plays, to compare his phrases with all those that have gone before, and to make a firm quantitative judgment and the beginning of a qualitative one as a result. In poetry or painting so much has gone before that just naming the stock phrases and figures, tropes and images and textures and color combinations, is an impossibility; but in jazz the process is not so difficult. The thirty, forty, fifty, or sixty years of jazz, depending upon how you date its history, can be totted up, listened to for the most part on records, and at least outlined on paper. It is possible to follow the blues tradition, the common variations on the even commoner themes, the rows of familiar riffs, and the mountains of only slightly different solos. And from this it is further possible to come up with common sounds, with basic ideas, to note one long curve on a graph, reaching to bop and then changing shape and direction abruptly, whether for good or bad. The very least, then, that we can do with freshness of idea or inspiration is to name the changes wrought by musicians, to discover exactly what they are doing with notes and chords and rhythms, and to make public that discovery. In the next category of standards we may find some way of deciding the value of those changes.

Profundity is one of those grimly determined words that cover a multitude of meanings and can be carried over from one field to another, from activity to activity, from level to level. In jazz, in its early years, the word was almost entirely missing from verbal discussion—and properly, because until some of the later Ellington, until Charlie Parker and Lennie Tristano, there was little if anything in jazz that could be called really profound. Nonetheless, profundity must be the end and purpose of jazz as it is of traditional music, of painting and poetry and the novel. And if jazz is a bona fide form of music it has a supreme opportunity to achieve profundity of expression; for a distinguishing mark of music is its ability to portray states of being rather than *things* with the qualities of those states— sorrow rather than a sorrowful girl, joy rather than a joyful boy, tragedy rather than a tragic event, pathos rather than a pathetic situation. While traditional music, however, must confine itself to the static, to the written mood, caught once forever, jazz can make an infinite number of grasps at profundity—profundity in its permanent forms and profundity at its most fleeting and elusive, its most transient—because jazz is by its very nature spontaneous, an improvised art.

If profundity is—or should be—the goal of jazz, how does a jazz musician achieve that end, and how does a listener recognize it when it has been attained? The answers to these two questions are not easy to find. Of course part of the procedure is to convince jazz musicians that every profound urge and effort they may feel and make should be expressed in their music, that their music comes closer to offering them an adequate expression for the intangible integers of sorrow and joy and tragedy and pathos than any other creative outlet they have. Then, the vital purpose of their work having been named and recognized, they will be well on their way toward achieving it, seeking always to perfect their skills, to find the means toward the end of profundity; even as Bach and Mozart did, as Stravinsky and Hindemith do; perhaps reaching the important conclusion that virtuosity with no other purpose than self-display is as pointless as words addressed to a mirror, and that exaltation and ecstasy are greater than "kicks" and "having a ball," and that they lie within the reach of musical talent and equipment. Exaltation and ecstasy can be achieved in music, even though they cannot be equated with any given set of notes. Thus must one consider the second standard, for no clearer description of it can be found outside of the great works of art themselves.

Skill is the easiest of the three standards to describe, to understand, and to recognize. The abundant technical skill of such men as Roy Eldridge, Johnny Hodges, Charlie Parker, Art Tatum, Charlie Shavers, Coleman Hawkins, and Benny Goodman is beyond argument. But what of that corollary skill, the ability to express fresh and profound ideas? This must come from practice and from conviction, from the desire to express such ideas, a desire which is really a need and as such molds the means necessary to its vital end. Because jazz musicians have almost always been interested more in achieving great control of their instruments than in controlling greatness, they have usually become mechanical virtuosos and little else. On rare occasions something more has appeared, and that brings us right back to the previous categories. For the something else that was added was spontaneity, and the spontaneity was compounded equally of freshness and profundity, since the truly spontaneous, the completely unrepetitious, is by definition fresh; and the fresh is by definition inspired; and the inspired more often than not contains elements of profundity. Spontaneity was recognized as the greatest of all the jazz skills when it was first heard; it remains the hallmark of a jazz musician who is also an artist.

Throughout this discussion, one working principle has been clear, I think: that these three criteria are interdependent, that each of the standards rests upon the others. Without skill, there can be no freshness or profundity. Without freshness, the skill is hardly noticeable and certainly of little worth. Without profundity, an artist is incomplete, having achieved his skill and freshness to no purpose. And yet, to reach that elusive profundity, a jazzman must have freshness and skill. Any two of the three are means to the end of the other standard. The most vital of the three, and the really important end of the other two means, is profundity; but it cannot be separated from the other two. Ultimately the relationship becomes triangular—an isosceles triangle of arrows, with profundity as its apex and the arrows flowing in both directions.

Having attempted to establish critical standards for jazz, it might be well to discuss for a moment the value of criticism in the arts. I know no statement of the function of the music critic, and the frequent abuses of that function, closer to what I regard as the truth than this paragraph from Igor Stravinsky's series of Harvard lectures on the *Poetics of Music:*

To explain—or, in French, to explicate, from the Latin *explicare*, to unfold, to develop—is to describe something, to discover its genesis, to note the relationship of things to each other, to seek to throw light upon them. To explain myself to you is also to explain myself to myself and to be obliged to clear up matters that are distorted or betrayed by the ignorance and malevolence that one always finds united by some mysterious bond in most of the judgments that are passed upon the arts. Ignorance and malevolence are united in a single root; the latter benefits surreptitiously from the advantages it draws from the former. I do not know which is the more hateful. In itself ignorance is, of course, no crime. It begins to be suspect when it pleads sincerity; for sincerity, as Remy de Gourmont said, is hardly an explanation and is never an excuse. And malevolence never fails to plead ignorance as an attenuating circumstance.

". . . to describe something, to discover its genesis, to note the relationship of things to each other, to seek to throw light upon them"—that, I think, sums up the critic's prime obligations to his readers. And ". . . the ignorance and malevolence that one always finds united by some mysterious bond in most of the judgments that are passed upon the arts"—that I think adumbrates the major offenses of which the critical gentry are sometimes guilty. The world of jazz has been subject to harrowing attacks—not always malevolent, but often ignorant, and just about never well-informed, rarely noting "the relationship of things to each other." Uncertainties continue to prevail in the average man's approach to jazz and jazz criticism. We have reached a point in the speedy maturation of jazz where it is necessary, therefore, to declare working critical principles. Not only must standards be named, but they must be referred to clearly and relentlessly.

In our time it has become fashionable to assert the eternal truth of the proposition that there is no eternal truth. The concomitant of that antidogmatic dogma is that there is no verifiable good or bad. And the inevitable conclusion of that pair of premises is that there is no way of ascertaining the value of a work of art. There are no guides, really, no standards, no criteria; there is only "taste," according to this view. And taste varies directly with the number of people in the world, all of whom, of course, though they have no standards by which to like or dislike anything, know what they like. By the simplest sort of deduction it becomes apparent that judgment is impossible, that criticism is unnecessary, and that critics are intolerable.

I start the other way round. Perhaps as a self-apologia, perhaps as a result of a naïve faith, but also because I cannot accept the chaos of such a ruthless relativism, I believe that music critics have the obligation to justify the ways of musicians to men. Many jazz musicians believe—they have more than an opinion about their music; they have a fierce faith in what they are doing. For those who are conscious of the direction they have taken, it is always possible to name and to define proper and improper procedure in jazz. I use these moral terms advisedly, for musicians have set standards for themselves with all the zeal of churchmen, and they have attempted to convert others to their position with all the superhuman strength of reformers. Such a setting of standards and such a drive for followers characterized the rise of bebop. Such a plotting of problems and suggestion of solutions identify the working method of the Lennie Tristano school of jazz. For jazzmen, as for painters and poets and architects, there must be a declarable end, and there must be a definable means of arriving there. It is my conviction that all the significant sounds of jazz have been produced as a result of some conscious merger of the three principles suggested above—profundity, freshness, and skill. The exact extent to which the vital men and women of jazz have been aware of this triangular relationship is certainly beyond proof. But a serious discussion with any of them at any important point in their careers would have yielded and will yield a clear demonstration of such concerns.

Now profundity, freshness, and skill, no matter how irrefutably discernible in the work of a jazzman, do not all by themselves produce finished masterpieces. The three elements must be joined together by some reactive force which assures a tight reciprocal relationship among them. In jazz, again as in most of the arts, there is, I think, no trouble in naming that reactive force. As it operates in each musician as an individual it can be called *intuition;* as it operates among a group of musicians playing together it can be called *tension.* In one of his most lucid passages Aristotle explains that intuition occurs when the mind is in direct contact with itself, when the subject of thought and the thinking process are identical, without any external object as a middle term. This seems to me an excellent description of intuition as its enormous constructive force is felt by the jazz musician. Carrying this description along to the realm of collective improvisation, one may say that tension, in the particular sense in which I am using the word, occurs when one musician's mind is in direct contact with another's—and perhaps another's, and still another's.

When skilled jazzmen can summon up fresh and profound ideas by using their intuitive resources, and can, beyond their individual contributions, contact the intuitive resources of their colleagues, you get that highly agreeable tension, that motion of minds expressed through instruments or human voices, which is first-rate jazz. The means are many: they may be melodic, rhythmic, or harmonic; they are always at least two of the three and often all three. Whatever the means, however many musicians are playing, their end is nothing unless it is produced with an unmistakable tension, the product, in turn, of individual intuition.

Enter now the music critic. This worthy (if such he be) has a function which parallels the jazz musician's, down the melodic line and up the harmonic chord. The minor aspects of that function come first, the clerical labors of naming the materials at hand, the tunes or chords with which the musicians are working, the accuracy with which they play, alone and together. An intelligent, trained, objective critic should be able to spot the familiarity or novelty of a musician's work, judging it by the standard of all the jazz that has gone before, with which the critic's acquaintance must be broad. For these duties, his faculties must be alert, disciplined; he must be able to hear all that he has ever heard at all times—or at least as much as is necessary to hear borrowings and describe them—and to know when what he hears is a new contribution; and when what he hears is new he must be able to sense its quality—if not to appraise it—and to decide whether or not a degree of profundity lurks within it.

A critic of jazz, be he a constructive guide to musicians, a professional interpreter of the musicians' music to its audience, or merely an enthusiastic and intelligent member of that audience, needs to acquire skill and intuition, like the musician he is criticizing. All the training available will not make it possible for you to recognize and appreciate freshness and profundity in music if you cannot to some large extent duplicate the performer's intuitive power. Days and nights bent over phonographs, huddled around bandstands, may permit you to hear how much of Roy or Dizzy, Bird or Lester or Hawk or Louie, Billie or Ella or Sarah has been borrowed by a trumpeter, saxophonist, or singer; but this equipment has a limited value. With it, you will be able to do your accounting; but you will not be able to do any more if you cannot yourself intuit as the jazzman does, when the jazzman does. Without intuition you will be merely an accountant adding up figures, making necessary but negligible arithmetical computations, deciding percentages of Eldridge, Parker, and Young, Holiday, Fitzgerald, and Vaughan. Freshness and profundity, the vital elements which cannot be assigned to direct influence or found in precise quotation, will remain blobs of uncertainty. For the informed and intuitive critic, however, accounting measurable elements only inaugurates activity; the freshness and profundity which mean so little to a comptometer mean everything to him. He looks for individual intuition and collective tension with the eagerness of a baseball scout on the trail of a new DiMaggio or Feller, and with the prospect of a far greater reward. And in his search he grows as his intuitions expand. He makes thrilling discoveries as he delves further into the work of musicians. If he is successful, he becomes genuinely, joyously creative. Creative criticism means really "digging," in both the conventional and the jazz sense of that word; you must penetrate deeply in order to learn, and, having delved deep, you may understand. The man who really "digs" can more often than not describe the next development in jazz before the musicians have reached it. His intuition is such that he always understands what is fresh, what may be profound, and welcomes it and fights for it, joining to the music in which he finds creative strength his own vigorous voice, in which musicians can find inspiration and untrained audiences can find a trustworthy guide.

The jazz audience is like no other in the world. It becomes a part of its music, falling in with foot, head, hand; bouncing in or out of time; surrendering to the jazzman's mood with an eagerness that often borders on hysteria, that sometimes produces rewarding reflection. As no other group of listeners or viewers, the jazz audience rises and falls with its stimulus, reaching manic heights at one moment, the depths of depression at another. Not the maddest balletomane, not the most stagestruck theatergoer, not the most starry-eyed movie fan, neither dog fancier, bird lover, nor baseball fanatic projects so completely into the working and playing frame of another living being. For the duration of a three-minute record, a half-hour radio program, a couple of hours in a night club, the jazz fan, according to his lights and loves, becomes Charlie Parker, Coleman Hawkins, Billie Holiday, Dizzy Gillespie, or Billy Eckstine. However unreal this transmigration of musical souls may actually be, to the jazz lover this foolish fancy is right and proper—and, furthermore, undeniable.

One of the salutary results of the remarkable identification the jazz audience makes with its heroes and heroines is an academic knowledge of its subject without precedent or comparison. The true jazz fan's ability to recognize dozens of trumpeters, trombonists, saxophonists, and pianists has long been properly celebrated. There are even some with so keen a sense of rhythm and sound that they can identify drummers with as little trouble as most people distinguish Vaughn Monroe from Dinah Shore. What is even more remarkable, many jazz fans listen with the kind of attention and intelligence which permits them to hear every technical facet of a performance, though they are sometimes without musical training. Again and again they can recognize the well-known chords on which an obscure melody is based; they hear subtle key changes and subtler variations based on passing tones; they follow the development of a solo, the spread of a section voicing, the break or continuity of an arrangement, with an accuracy that would do a brilliant musician or a trained critic credit—and all without knowing the right name of anything musical, without the vestige of a musical education. Such untrained understanding can proceed only from love. Such affection must be deserved.

One must respect the undying devotion of the jazz audience to the jazz musician, recognize its fruits, and even pay homage to it. One must also, I think, demand something more, in return for the pleasure and stimulation, the emotional and intellectual satisfaction, provided

346   A HISTORY OF JAZZ IN AMERICA

by the jazzman. One must insist on a double responsibility on the part of the audience—a responsibility to itself and to jazz musicians. The responsibility to itself takes one fundamental form—education. The responsibility to musicians is just as simply categorized—support.

To make its identification with the jazz musician complete and meaningful, the jazz audience should study music. It must learn the difference between a chord and a piece of string, learn the simple facts of musical life, the technique of the art, and set these in a more complicated context, the history of all the arts. When jazz audiences become better equipped, they can help to break the stranglehold of the great booking corporations and the alternate death-grip and whimsical relaxation of press-agent-promoted fads which now handicap jazz so seriously.

And what must the musician himself do on behalf of his art? His function is, of course, to play. But to play what, and how, and where, and when? It is easy to answer these questions if you are a musician or critic in the classical tradition. However much disagreement there may be over the merits of Tchaikovsky, Brahms, Beethoven, Berlioz, Debussy, or Ravel, there is general agreement that all of these men are part of the standard repertory, ranking somewhere under Bach and Mozart, and leaving much room for many others. However much contention there may be about the quality of contemporary music, it is clear by now that Stravinsky and Hindemith, Schoenberg, Berg, Bloch, Bartok, and a few lesser lights have earned a substantial place for themselves in the concert and recording activities of pianists, violinists, chamber groups, and symphony orchestras. But the jazz musician, who has to depend so much on his own resources, has no such simple solution to these several problems of what and how and where and when.

The jazzman in New Orleans before the closing of the red-light district in 1917 led an uncomplicated musical life. With only the blues and a few related tunes to rely upon harmonically and melodically, with rhythmic strictures to confine any desire to wander with the beat, he was not only able, he was commanded to know all the answers before he picked up his horn to blow. The result was a very narrow avenue for creative imagination—the exploitation of instrumental technique. A further result was the evolution of jazz sounds away from the crinoline and old lace of nineteenth-century Louisiana to the denim and pongee of the riverboats.

The jazzman in Chicago, Kansas City, or New York in the twenties followed somewhat more complex patterns, but his aim, like his sounds and sights, was trained on the same basic objectives. Men like Louis Armstrong and Fletcher Henderson, women like Bessie Smith, broadened the emotional and intellectual range of New Orleans jazz and brought dignity to their profession. It remained, however, for Duke Ellington, something more than a greatly skilled primitive, to suggest the profound potential of jazz. And it fell first to Benny Goodman and his generation, then to Coleman Hawkins, Roy Eldridge, Lester Young, Charlie Christian, Charlie Parker, and Lennie Tristano, in quick order, to translate the potential into the actual.

No longer, then, does the jazzman stand alone, uncluttered technically, emotionally constricted. Behind him is a history and a tradition. Before him is an art. But again: what, how, where, when?

In analyzing the functions of the jazz critic and the jazz audience, in attempting to set up working criteria for everybody seriously concerned with jazz, I have announced with considerable brazenness that a balance of inspiration, skill, and profundity, molded by the individual intuition and collective tension developed among jazz musicians, should produce first-rate jazz. These words shield a formidable brace of ideas, of sometimes impenetrable abstractions; the words and the ideas are too often loosely used, too little understood, too rarely invoked with consciousness by musician, critic, or audience. I have made some attempt to pin the words and the ideas to notes and chords and working procedure in jazz, because I think that such a stocktaking, such a review of principle and process, is fundamental to the healthy growth of this medium of expression. And of all those who may have the capability and/or concern to take this stock, to make this review, it seems to me that the most critical effort must be made by the jazz musician himself.

The man who plays jazz is faced with several cruel alternatives. He cannot in the future, unless he is intellectually slothful and emotionally spent, return to the kindergarten constructions of his New Orleans forebears, though he must pay his respects to them for yeoman service in building a craft with the crude implements at their disposal. If he is at all sensitive, he knows that the bop school, which at first surged so brilliantly through the jungle of jazz weed, later began to grow its own brand of weed—heavy, clumsy, too often aromatic of the worst of weeds, and rotten at the roots. Rejecting these choices, the creative jazzman is left at the mercy of his own inspiration, his own groping after profundity, his solo intuition, and the rich tension he may feel when playing in a group—all tempered, if meaning is to be achieved, by the skill in exercise of these faculties which can come only from hard, directed work. And there, I think, lies the answer to the perplexities suggested by the one-syllable queries.

What? The jazzman must give up the stagnating security to be found in playing in and around familiar chords, where he loses all his inspiration and any hope for profundity in the false comfort of hackneyed phrases, repetitious ideas, and fixed choruses. He must recognize that he as an improvising musician has for his basic materials the note and chord unburdened by other men's manipulation of them. Sooner or later he must learn the limitations of most of present-day jazz and the free field that lies ahead of him if his background permits him to explore the lines of polytonal and atonal music played in contrapuntal frames.

How? By accepting the existence of principle, by searching for and finding it, and then by practicing precept, the jazzman can, I am convinced, find his way to articulate communication of ideas at the art level which music that is at once polytonal or atonal, contrapuntal, and improvised must reach. What this means above all is a dedication to purpose, a governing humility, a refusal to accept adolescent success as any real indication of ability.

Where and when? The kind of jazz that seems to be growing up around us, less and less fitfully, more and more artfully, demands a hearing. It will out, but not necessarily before large audiences, almost certainly not within large ballrooms and theaters, and definitely not for great reward. This music will be played wherever and whenever a musician finds a friend—in his own home, in little studios, in big back rooms. It will be played with such conviction that its progress will become unmistakable and its difficulties desirable; it will make its way, as all enrichments of human culture have in the past propelled themselves, from obscurity to public acceptance.

Clearly I am demanding an assayable maturity of the jazz musician; I am insisting on the essential dignity of his calling; I am trying to demonstrate that out of the half-century or so of jazz an art has taken shape. The resources of jazz are huge. It is the function of the musician in jazz to cull and command those resources, to make of his work a vocation in all the beautiful meaning of that word.

GLOSSARY OF JAZZ WORDS AND PHRASES

The vocabulary of the jazz musician is spiced by a variety of terms of his own coinage. At any one time these may be vast or small in number, depending on the quantity of transient materials—such words as "mop!" an exclamation of wide currency in the early forties which accurately described a musical device (the final beat in a cadence of triplets, usually bringing the release of a jazz composition to an end). The "mops" of jazz are swept clean in the following list; only the durable terms have been given and explained. Thus you will not find the language which was carefully attached to jazz in the first spate of general magazine articles about swing—no "doghouse" for bass, no "licorice stick" for clarinet. The color of this glossary is musical; this is the way jazzmen speak when the English and American languages are inadequate for their needs. Here are the jazz terms used in this book and a few others that may prove valuable if you ever find yourself across a table from a musician and at a loss for words, or bewildered by the language of a blues or related jazz lyric.

air-check: a recording of a radio or television performance, usually made for purposes of demonstration.
apple: New York City (see Chapter 13).
ballad: a romantic popular song, usually slow or middle tempo and with a thirty-two-bar chorus (see Chapter 4).
barrelhouse: after the New Orleans cabarets in which liquor was dispensed from barrels; music that is rough and ready, chiefly applied to Dixieland, but not exclusively.
beat: jazz time; more meaningful to jazz musicians as an honorific description of rhythmic skill ("he gets a fine beat") than as a description of an underlying 2/4 or 4/4 or 6/8 or any other time (see Chapter 1). Also weary, exhausted ("I'm beat to my socks").
bebop: generic term for that modern jazz of which Dizzy Gillespie and

349

Charlie Parker are the most distinguished representatives; also known as "bop" (see Chapter 22).

bending: the process of altering pitch between notes, up or down, sometimes called "scooping pitch."

blow: verb used to describe playing of the brass and reeds; in modern jazz parlance, used of all the jazz instruments ("he blows fine piano").

blow one's top: phrase expressing exasperation, enthusiasm, or insanity; synonymous with "flip one's lid," "snap one's cap" or "wig," each of which describes the process of losing the hair or skin of the head.

blue notes: the flattened third and seventh in the blues scale (see Chapter 4); in classical music, synonymous with "clinker."

boogie woogie: a piano blues form (see Chapter 4).

bounce: used by some musicians, especially Duke Ellington, to describe a particularly buoyant beat; used by jazzmen in the phrase "businessman's bounce" to describe a monotonous two-beat played fast, usually by society bands, for the delectation of tired businessmen and their dance partners.

break: much used in the pre-swing and early swing days for inserted solos of two to sixteen bars; not without later currency.

break it up: to "stop the show," "kill 'em," "fracture 'em," to achieve the major success in a sequence of performances.

bridge: conventionally the third eight bars in a popular song chorus, the B section in the A-A-B-A pattern or any other which uses an A-B alternation; also called the "release" (see Chapter 4).

bring down: to depress (verb) or (as one word, "bringdown") one who depresses.

bug: to bewilder or irritate.

cat: jazz musician.

chick: girl.

clambake: earlier used synonymously (and honorifically) with "jam session," later descriptive of an improvised or arranged session which doesn't come off.

clinker: bad note.

combo: short for "combination" of musicians, usually a small band.

commercial: music or musicianship designed solely to garner money and/or fame; usually inflected with great scorn; also, a sponsored radio program.

cool: superlative, usually reserved for sizable achievement within a frame of restraint; for some, synonymous with modern jazz (see Chapter 23).

corny: stale, insipid, trite, usually the worse for age; and so too "corn" (noun), "cornfed," "cornball," and "off the cob."

crazy: superlative of the late forties, synonymous with "gone," "the end."

cut or *cut out:* to leave, to depart. "Cut" also means to best a soloist or band in competition.

dig: to understand; often to penetrate a hidden meaning, hence used of the process of intellection of the jazz initiate ("he digs!").

disk jockey: record announcer or commentator in radio or television.

Dixieland or *Dixie:* early jazz (see Chapter 8).

dog tune: a song of questionable musical quality.

drag: see p. 74.

drive: to play with concentrated momentum.

fake: to improvise (widely current through the swing era, not much thereafter, though still used).

four-beat: an even four beats to the bar.

fracture: see "break it up."

fly: smooth; to describe looks or manner or performance, usually the first two ("he's a fly cat").

gate: once (and occasionally used after the swing era) synonymous with jazz musician; also Louis Armstrong (see Chapter 7) and Jack ("Big Gate") and Charlie ("Little Gate") Teagarden.

gig: a one-night job.

give or *give out:* swing parlance for "let yourself go."

gone: superlative, may be further qualified, such as "real gone."

goof or *goof off:* to wander in attention, to fail to discharge one's responsibility (as for example, not to show up for an appointment and not to be provided with a clear excuse); in musical performance, to play without much attention, to miss coming in on time, etc.

groovy: applied to a good swinging beat (earlier, "in the groove").

gutbucket: music of the kind played in barrelhouses; synonymous with "barrelhouse."

have a ball: to enjoy oneself inordinately.

head arrangement: see p. 170.

hip: adjective to describe a jazz initiate, somebody who really "digs" the music and its performers (earlier, but never since swing, "hep").

horn: originally a generic term for the brass and reed instruments; in modern jazz used of all the instruments (see "blow").

hot: as distinguished from "sweet" (but not from "cool"), describes an improvising jazzman as against a studio musician who may be called upon to play music with a jazz feeling; not much used for music or musician after the swing era.

icky: a "cornball," one who doesn't "dig," who isn't "hip" (in the argot of jazz just before and through the first years of swing; afterward rare).

Jack: equivalent of "Mac" or "Bud" in American slang; means of address to the male; in later years sometimes replaced by "Jim."

jam: to improvise; hence, as a noun, a group of improvisers at work, a "jam session."

jazz: see Chapter 1.

jazzy: sometimes used as synonym for "corny."

jitterbug: a frantic dancer to jazz, generally adolescent, and after the early forties a rapidly disappearing species.

jive: comic speech, usually larded with ambiguous jazz terms; sometimes synonymous with "kid" ("don't jive me"); *never* a kind of jazz, as it has sometimes been thought to signify.

jukebox: electrical coin machine which plays records, usually at a nickel a spin.

jump: synonymous with "leap" and with "swing," although often used with overtones of quantity to describe the swinging of a large and powerful jazz band ("a jump band," or "he really jumps").

kicks: synonymous with "jumps"; also, as noun, meaning pleasure ("I get my kicks on Route 66").

kill: see "break it up," "fracture."

lead man: trumpeter, trombonist, or alto saxophonist who plays the top or melodic line in the brass or reed section, who shapes the sound of the section, usually a skilled technician, not necessarily a jazzman in a large band.

lick: see "break"; also used in early days of swing to designate any solo; sometimes called, in early days, "hot lick."

longhair: a classical musician or partisan of traditional music (not much used by musicians).

Mickey Mouse band: an orchestra that plays "corn," usually identifiable by some non-musical noise, such as agonizing trombone glissandos or out-of-tune saxes.

moldy fig: a modernist's name for an ardent admirer of Dixieland jazz.

novelty song: a song that depends upon some obvious contrivance for its appeal, such as a reorganized nursery rhyme ("A-Tisket, A-Tasket," "Mairzy Doats"), a sound ("Woody Woodpecker"), or an infectious sort of gibberish ("Come on-a My House").

off-beat: the weak or unaccented beats in a four-beat measure (see "two-beat").

out of this world: outmoded superlative, still occasionally used in modern jazz, to describe something so wonderful it's "gone."

pad: apartment or bed.

pop: abbreviation of "popular song."

release: see "bridge."

remote: late evening band broadcast from club, ballroom, or hotel.

ride: to swing, especially in last chorus or section, sometimes called "ride-out"; especially used of Dixieland and swing.

riff: two- or four-bar phrase; sometimes used for longer phrase in bop.

rock: synonymous with "jump" and "swing," except for tempo; "rock" is usually not fast.

scat: to improvise with nonsense singing syllables; earlier identified with Cab Calloway; brought to high art by the late Leo Watson with the Spirits of Rhythm; later further developed by Babs Gonzales and Ella Fitzgerald.

send: to stimulate, move; not much used after the swing era, and then usually in passive past tense ("I was sent" rather than "he sends me").

sharp: "hip"; used chiefly of clothing or verbal manner.

society band: orchestra that plays for latter-day equivalent of the cotillions, its tempos almost all "businessman's bounce," tenor saxophones replacing altos and baritone to give a plush reed sound to the band; tenors usually doubling on violin or vice versa; total personnel small, rarely with more than one or two brass.

solid: contemporary and synonymous with "groovy."

square: "cornball," one who is not "hip," who doesn't "dig."

standard: a tune such as "Stardust" or "Back Home in Indiana" or "How High the Moon," that has become a jazz classic and an inevitable part of the jazz musician's repertory, as opposed to a "novelty" or a "pop" that will be widely played for a while and then forgotten.

sweet: applied to music that is played straight, without improvisation, at slow and middle tempos, in which the melody can always be recognized and a conventional sound tending to lushness prevails; much used as a term in swing to distinguish strictly dance outfits from, for example, Goodman, Basie, or Lunceford.

swing: see Chapter 16.

tag: final ending to a composition, scored or improvised; "coda" in traditional musical terminology.

take five: (said to musicians, usually at rehearsal) you are entitled to a five-minute intermission.

the end: see "crazy," "gone."

ticky: synonymous with "corny," though more specifically addressed to a mechanical beat than anything else ("tick-tock, tick-tock").

torch: only occasionally used after the twenties and early thirties as a description of a ballad of unrequited love.

two-beat: four-four time in which two of the beats are accented and two are not, causing an alternation of weak and strong beats.

zoot: exaggerated clothing, especially in the wideness of the shoulders (padded) and narrowness of the trouser cuffs (pegged).

INDEX

355

INDEX

370

INDEX

"Lover," 248
"Lover Man," 271
Loyocano, Arnold, 82, 120
Lucie, Lawrence, 78
Ludwig, Ray, 134
Lunceford, Jimmie, 23, 85, 166, 190–93, 206, 232, 278, 311, 353
Lunceford Trio, 191
"Lush Life," 243
Lyman, Abe, 299, 334
Lynn, Ray, 295
Lyon, James, 15
lyrics, 16–19, 21, 26–27, 30–31, 33–34, 95, 105, 165, 272–73; "jive," 165; bebop, 272–73; blues, 19, 26–27, 30–31, 33–34, 95, 105; folk songs, 17; hollers, 18–19; minstrel songs, 21
Lytell, Jimmy, 151

Metro-Goldwyn-Mayer, 256
McCall, Mary Ann, 257–59, 295
McComber, Ken, 221
McConnell, Shorty, 217
McCoy, Clyde, 88
McDonough, Dick, 152, 210, 246
MacDowell, Edward, 111
McEachern, Murray, 204
McGhee, Howard, 282, 284–85, 297
MacIntyre and Heath, 22
McIntyre, Hal, 197, 248, 317
McKay, Claude, 104
McKenzie, Red, 118, 124–26, 160, 189, 210, 296
McKibbon, Al, 287
McKinley, Ray, 188, 207, 298, 302
McKinney, William, 162, 164
McKinney's Cotton Pickers, 147, 162–164, 238
McKusick, Hal, 309–10
McPartland, Dick, 118
McPartland, Jimmy, 118–20, 125–26, 131, 139–40, 160–62, 228, 298, 325
McPartland, Marion Page, 325
McRae, Ted, 170
McShann, Jay, 192–93, 269, 276
Madison, Kid Shots, 68
Madranga's (New Orleans), 72
Magenta Moods (record album), 265
Magnolia band, 67
Mahogany Hall (New Orleans), 42, 44
"Mahogany Hall Stomp," 42
"Mairzy Doats," 352

"Malbrouk s'en va-t-en guerre," 16
Malneck, Mattie, 249
"Man I Love, The," 33, 225
"Man on the Flying Trapeze," 165
Mandell, Johnny, 309
"Mandy Make Up Your Mind," 61
Manet, Edouard, 133
Manhattan School of Music, 226
Manne, Sheldon (Shelly), 271, 312–13, 332
Manone, Wingy (Joseph), 5, 121, 127, 155, 161, 210
Maple Leaf Club (Sedalia), 81
"Maple Leaf Rag," 47, 61, 80–81, 119
Marable, Fate, 67–68, 72, 91–93, 120, 241
marching bands, 46, 49, 50, 58, 63, 67, 71, 81
marching songs, 79
Mardi Gras, 38–39
Mares, Paul, 86, 160
"Margie," 84, 191
Margulies, Charlie, 136
"Marie," 210
marijuana, 272; *see also* drugs
Marinetti, F. T., 99
Markowitz, Irving (Marky), 303
Marmarosa, Dodo (Michael), 194, 213, 229
Marowitz, Sam, 301, 303
Marsala, Joe, 63
Marsh, Warne, 321–23, 326
Marshall, Kaiser, 147
Martin, Tony, 293
"Maryland, My Maryland," 24
"Mary's Idea," 232
Mascot (New Orleans), 39
"Maternity," 283
Matthew, Cliff, 93
Matthews, Dave, 63, 197, 295
Matlock, Matty, 162, 188, 206, 209
"Meatball Blues," 81, 84
"Melancholy," 59
"Mellow Bit of Rhythm, A," 232
melody, 4, 12, 27–30, 51, 65, 85–86, 244, 274, 288, 328–29; definition of, 4; in bebop, 244, 274, 288; in blues, 27–29; in Dixieland jazz, 85–86; in jazz, 12, 30; in modern jazz, 328–29; in New Orleans jazz, 51; in popular songs, 329; in ragtime, 65
"Melody in F," 210

INDEX

371

INDEX

373

INDEX

380

382

INDEX